United States 1917–2008
and Civil Rights 1865–1992

Derrick Murphy ■ Kathryn Cooper

Collins

Published by Collins
An imprint of HarperCollinsPublishers
The News Building
1 London Bridge Street
London
SE1 9GF

Browse the complete Collins catalogue
at www.collins.co.uk

11

ISBN-13 978 0 00 726870 2

British Library Cataloguing in
Publication Data
A Catalogue record for this publication is
available from the British Library

Edited by Graham Bradbury
Commissioned by Michael Upchurch
Design and typesetting by Derek Lee
Cover design by Joerg Hartmannsgruber,
White-card
Map Artwork by Tony Richardson
Picture research by Celia Dearing and
Michael Upchurch
Production by Simon Moore
Indexed by Christine Bernstein
Printed and bound by CPI Group (UK)
Ltd, Croydon, CR0 4YY

ACKNOWLEDGEMENTS
Every effort had been made to contact
the holders of copyright material, but if
any have been inadvertently overlooked
the publishers will be pleased to make
the necessary arrangements at the first
opportunity.

BAAS for the extract from *Vietnam:
American Involvement at Home and Abroad*
by John Dumbrell (1992). The Balkin
Agency for extracts from *A People's
History of the United States* by Howard
Zinn (1980). Blackwell Publishers for the
extract from *Franklin D. Roosevelt* by
Michael Simpson (1989). Fontana for the
extract from *American Presidents and the
Presidency* by Marcus Cunliffe (1970).

Harcourt for the extract from *America in
the Twentieth Century* by James T.
Patterson (1989). HarperCollins for the
extract from *Lyndon Johnson & the
American Dream* by Doris Kearns
Goodwin (1976). Henry Holt &
Company Inc. for the extract from *The
Vantage Point: Perspectives of the
Presidency, 1963–1969* by Lyndon
Johnson (1971). Houghton Mifflin
Company for the extracts from *The
Enduring Vision* by P. Boyer et al (1993);
*American Foreign Relations: a history since
1895* by Thomas G Paterson et al (2000)
and *Promises to Keep* by Paul Boyer
(1999). Indiana University Press for the
extract from *Decade of Disillusionment:
The Kennedy-Johnson Years* by Jim F.
Heath (1975). Alfred A. Knopf for the
extract from *Wars of Watergate: The Last
Crisis of Richard Nixon* by Stanley Kutler
(1990). Macmillan Press for the extracts
from *The New Deal, The Depression Years
1933–1940* by Tony Badger
(1989);*Mastering Modern World History*
by Norman Lowe (1982); *Reaganomics
and Economic Policy* by Joseph J. Hogan
(1990); *The Civil Rights Movement:
Struggle and Resistance* by William T.
Martin Riches (Palgrave Macmillan,
1997) and *Domestic Policy in the Era of
'Negative' Government* by Dilys Hill
(1990). The New American Library for
the extract from *Lyndon Johnson and the
Exercise of Power* by Rowland Evans and
Robert Novak (1966). W.W. Norton &
Co. for the extracts from *The Anxious
Decades* by Michael Parrish (1992);
*Richard Nixon: The Shaping of His
Character* by Fawn Brodie (1991) and
America by George Tindall and David Shi
(1984). Oxford University Press for the
extracts from *The Unfinished Journey:
America Since World War II* by William H.
Chafe (1999); *Franklin D. Roosevelt and
American Foreign Policy, 1932–1945* by
Robert Dallek (1995); *From Promises
Kept: John F. Kennedy's New Frontier* by
Irving Bernstein (1991) and *The Limits of
Liberty* by Maldwyn Jones (1995).
Pantheon for the extracts from *Who Built
America?* by Joshua Freeman (1992).
Pearson Education for the extracts from
*The Longman History of the United States
of America* by Hugh Brogan (1999);
Kennedy by Hugh Brogan (Longman,
1996); *Sweet Land of Liberty?: The
African-American Struggle for Civil Rights
in the Twentieth Century* by Robert Cook
(Longman, 1998); *State and Society in
Twentieth-Century America* by R. Harrison
(Longman, 1997) and *The Cold War: A
Study in US Foreign Policy Since 1945* by
Walter Lippmann (1973). Penguin for
extracts from *Coming of Age* by Donald
McCoy (1973). Regnery Publishing Inc
for the extract from *Witness* by Whittaker
Chambers (1952). Routledge for the
extracts from *Franklin D. Roosevelt* by
M.J. Heale (1999) and *Black Civil Rights

in America* by Kevern Verney (2000).
Thomson Learning for the extract from
America in the Twentieth Century by J.T.
Patterson (1994). Times Books for the
extract from *It's a Hell of a Life But Not a
Bad Living* by Edward Dmytryk (1987).
Transworld Publishers for the extract
from *Cold War* by Jeremy Isaacs and
Taylor Downing (Bantam, 1998) and *The
Glory and the Dream* by William
Manchester (Bantam, 1974). Twayne
Publishers Inc.,U.S. for the extract from
*The Roosevelt Presence: The Life and
Legacy of FDR* by Patrick J. Maney
(1992) *and Big Daddy from the Pedernales*
by Paul K. Conkin (1986). University of
Georgia Press for the extract from *To
Redeem the Soul of America: The Southern
Christian Leadership Conference and
Martin Luther King, Jr.* by Adam
Fairclough (1987). University Press of
Kansas for the extract from *The
Presidency of Herbert C. Hoover* by Martin
L. Fausold (1985); 'The War in Vietnam'
by G.C. Herring in *The Johnson Years:
Foreign Policy, the Great Society, and the
White House* edited by Robert A. Divine
(1987); *The Presidency of Lyndon B.
Johnson* by Vaughn Davis Bornet (1983)
and *The Presidency of John F. Kennedy* by
James N. Giglio (1991). WileyBlackwell
for the extract from *The New Deal:
America's Response to the Great Depression*
by Ronald Edsforth (2000).

The publishers would like to thank the
following for permission to reproduce
pictures on these pages.
T=Top, B=Bottom, L=Left, R=Right,
C=Centre

© Steve Bell 2004 341(T), 341(B);
Private Collection, Peter Newark
American Pictures / The Bridgeman
Art Library 66, 236, 279; © CORBIS 31,
49, 59, 67(L), 67(R), 103, 113, 156, 196,
277; © Bettmann/CORBIS 29, 32, 33, 38,
86, 183, 197, 207, 219(L), 219(R), 231,
238, 253, 255, 259, 276, 290, 305; ©
Underwood & Underwood/CORBIS 36;
© Morton Beebe/CORBIS 91; © Robert
Maass/CORBIS; © Brooks Kraft/Corbis
345; © Baldwin H. Ward & Kathryn C.
Ward/CORBIS 170; © Hulton-Deutsch
Collection/CORBIS 137; © Wally
McNamee/CORBIS 313;
© Reuters/CORBIS 335, 339; Getty
Images 125; ©2000 Topham / AP 229;
©2001 Topham / AP 199; ©
popperfoto.com 201; Unknown 60,
75(L), 75(R), 99, 138, 145, 153, 202,
206, 207, 285, 315, 316, 322(T), 322(L),
322(R), 329.

Contents

Study and examination skills

This section of the book is designed to aid Sixth Form students in their preparation for public examinations in History.

- Differences between GCSE and Sixth Form History
- Extended writing: the structured question and the essay
- How to handle sources in Sixth Form History
- Historical interpretation
- Progression in Sixth Form History
- Examination technique

Differences between GCSE and Sixth Form History

- The amount of factual knowledge required for answers to Sixth Form History questions is more detailed than at GCSE. Factual knowledge in the Sixth Form is used as supporting evidence to help answer historical questions. Knowing the facts is important, but not as important as knowing that factual knowledge supports historical analysis.

- Extended writing is more important in Sixth Form History. Students will be expected to answer either structured questions or essays.

Structured questions require students to answer more than one question on a given topic. For example:

> (a) What problems faced F.D. Roosevelt when he become president in 1933?
>
> (b) How successful was F.D. Roosevelt in dealing with these problems by 1941?

Each part of the structured question demands a different approach.

Essay questions require students to produce one answer to a given question. For example:

> To what extent was the improvement in Black Civil Rights due to action by the US Supreme Court in the period 1954 to 1968?

Similarities with GCSE

- **Source analysis and evaluation**

The skills in handling historical sources, which were acquired at GCSE, are developed in Sixth Form History. In the Sixth Form, sources have to be analysed in their historical context, so a good factual knowledge of the subject is important.

- **Historical interpretations**

Skills in historical interpretation at GCSE are also developed in Sixth Form

History. The ability to put forward different historical interpretations is important. Students will also be expected to explain why different historical interpretations have occurred.

Extended writing: the structured question and the essay

When faced with extended writing in Sixth Form History students can improve their performance by following a simple routine that attempts to ensure they achieve their best performance.

Answering the question

What are the command instructions?
Different questions require different types of response. For instance, 'In what ways' requires students to point out the various ways something took place in History; 'Why' questions expect students to deal with the causes or consequences of an historical event.

'How far' or 'To what extent' questions require students to produce a balanced, analytical answer. Usually, this will take the form of the case for and the case against an historical question.

Are there key words or phrases that require definition or explanation?
It is important for students to show that they understand the meaning of the question. To do this, certain historical terms or words require explanation. For instance, if a question asked 'how far' a politician was an 'innovator', an explanation of the word 'innovator' would be required.

Does the question have specific dates or issues that require coverage?
If the question mentions specific dates, these must be adhered to. For instance, if you are asked to answer a question on US foreign policy, 1917–1941, you must keep to those dates.

Planning your answer

Once you have decided on what the question requires, write a brief plan. For structured questions this may be brief. This is a useful procedure to make sure that you have ordered the information you require for your answer in the most effective way. For instance, in a balanced, analytical answer this may take the form of jotting down the main points for and against an historical issue raised in the question.

Writing the answer

Communication skills
The quality of written English is important in Sixth Form History. The way you present your ideas on paper can affect the quality of your answer. Therefore, punctuation, spelling and grammar, which were awarded marks at GCSE, require close attention. Use a dictionary if you are unsure of a word's meaning or spelling. Use the glossary of terms you will find in this book to help you.

The quality of your written English will not determine the Level of Response you receive for answer. It may well determine what mark you receive within a level.

To help you understand this point ask your teacher to see a mark scheme published by your examination board. For instance, you may be awarded Level 2 (10–15 marks) by an examiner. The quality of written English may be a factor in deciding which mark you receive within that level. Will it be 10 or 15 or a mark in between?

The introduction

For structured questions you may wish to dispense with an introduction altogether and begin writing reasons to support an answer straight away. However, essay answers should begin with an introduction. These should be both concise and precise. Introductions help 'concentrate the mind' on the question you are about to answer. Remember, do not try to write a conclusion as your opening sentence. Instead, outline briefly the areas you intend to discuss in your answer.

Balancing analysis with factual evidence

It is important to remember that factual knowledge should be used to support analysis. Merely 'telling the story' of an historical event is not enough. A structured question or essay should contain separate paragraphs, each addressing an analytical point that helps to answer the question. If, for example, the question asks for reasons why national prohibition failed, each paragraph should provide a reason which explains why the 'noble experiment' was not successful. In order to support and sustain the analysis, evidence is required. Therefore, your factual knowledge should be used to substantiate analysis. Good structured question and essay answers integrate analysis and factual knowledge.

Seeing connections between reasons

In dealing with 'why'-type questions it is important to remember that the reasons for an historical event might be interconnected. Therefore, it is important to mention the connections between reasons. Also, it might be important to identify a hierarchy of reasons – that is, are some reasons more important than others in explaining an historical event?

Using quotations and statistical data

One aspect of supporting evidence that sustains analysis is the use of quotations. These can be from either a historian or a contemporary. However, unless these quotations are linked with analysis and supporting evidence, they tend to be of little value.

It can also be useful to support analysis with statistical data. In questions that deal with social and economic change, precise statistics that support your argument can be very persuasive.

The conclusion

All structured questions and essays require conclusions. If, for example, a question requires a discussion of 'how far' you agree with a question, you should offer a judgement in your conclusion. Don't be afraid of this – say what you think. If you write an analytical answer, ably supported by factual evidence, you may under-perform because you have not provided a conclusion that deals directly with the question.

Source analysis

Source analysis forms an integral part of the study of History.

In dealing with sources you should be aware that historical sources must be used 'in historical context' in Sixth Form History. This means you must understand the historical topic to which the source refers. Therefore, in this book sources are used with the factual information in each chapter. Also, specific source analysis questions are included at the end of most chapters.

How to handle sources in Sixth Form History

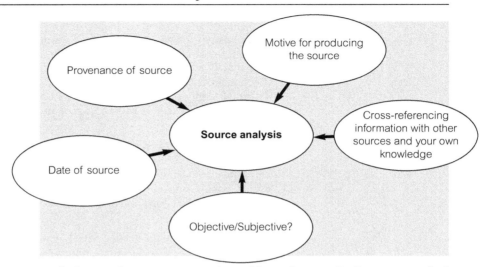

In dealing with sources, a number of basic hints will allow you to deal effectively with source-based questions and to build on your knowledge and skill in using sources at GCSE.

Written sources

Attribution or Provenance and date

It is important to identify who has written the source and when it was written. This information can be very important. If, for instance, a source was written by President Nixon in 1972, this information will be of considerable importance if you are asked about the usefulness (utility) or reliability of the source as evidence of Nixon's actions or policies in that year.

It is important to note that just because a source is a primary source does not mean it is more useful or less reliable than a secondary source. Both primary and secondary sources need to be analysed to decide how useful and reliable they are. This can be determined by studying other issues.

Is the content factual or opinionated?

Once you have identified the author and date of the source, it is important to study its content. The content may be factual, stating what has happened or what may happen. On the other hand, it may contain opinions that should be handled with caution. These may contain bias. Even if a source is mainly factual, there might be important and deliberate gaps in factual evidence that can make a source biased and unreliable. Usually, written sources contain elements of both opinion and factual evidence. It is important to judge the balance between these two parts.

Has the source been written for a particular audience?

To determine the reliability of a source it is important to know to whom it is directed. For instance, a public speech may be made to achieve a particular purpose and may not contain the author's true beliefs or feelings. In contrast, a private diary entry may be much more reliable in this respect.

Corroborative evidence

To test whether or not a source is reliable, the use of other evidence to support or corroborate the information it contains is important. Cross-referencing with other sources is a way of achieving this; so is cross-referencing with historical information contained within a chapter.

Visual sources

Cartoons

Cartoons are a popular form of source used at both GCSE and in Sixth Form History. However, analysing cartoons can be a demanding exercise. Not only will you be expected to understand the content of the cartoon, you may also have to explain a written caption – which appears usually at the bottom of the cartoon. In addition, cartoons will need placing in historical context. Therefore, a good knowledge of the subject matter of the topic of the cartoon will be important.

Photographs

'The camera never lies'! This phrase is not always true. When analysing photographs, study the attribution/provenance and date. Photographs can be changed so they are not always an accurate visual representation of events. Also, to test whether or not a photograph is a good representation of events you will need corroborative evidence.

Maps

Maps which appear in Sixth Form History are predominantly secondary sources. These are used to support factual coverage in the text by providing information in a different medium. Therefore, to assess whether or not information contained in maps is accurate or useful, reference should be made to other information. It is also important with written sources to check the attribution and date. These could be significant.

Statistical data and graphs

It is important when dealing with this type of source to check carefully the nature of the information contained in data or in a graph. It might state that the information is in tons (tonnes) or another measurement. Be careful to check if the information is in index numbers. These are a statistical device where a base year is chosen and given the figure 100. All other figures are based on a percentage difference from that base year. For instance, if 1932 is taken as a base year for unemployment in the USA it is given the figure of 100. If the index number for unemployment in 1939 is 62 it means that unemployment has fallen by 38 per cent below the 1932 figure.

An important point to remember when dealing with data and graphs over a period of time is to identify trends and patterns in the information. Merely describing the information in written form is not enough.

Historical interpretation

An important feature of both GCSE and Sixth Form History is the issue of historical interpretation. In Sixth Form History it is important for students to be able to explain why historians differ, or have differed, in their interpretation of the past.

Availability of evidence

An important reason is the availability of evidence on which to base historical judgements. As new evidence comes to light, an historian today may have more information on which to base judgements than historians in the past.

'A philosophy of history?'

Many historians have a specific view of history that will affect the way they make their historical judgements. For instance, Marxist historians – who take the view from the writings of Karl Marx the founder of modern socialism – believe that society has been made up of competing economic and social classes. They also place considerable importance on economic reasons in human decision making. Therefore, a Marxist historian of fascism may take a completely different viewpoint to a non-Marxist historian.

The role of the individual

Some historians have seen past history as being moulded by the acts of specific individuals who have changed history. F.D. Roosevelt, John F. Kennedy and Ronald Reagan are seen as individuals whose personality and beliefs changed the course of American history. Other historians have tended to 'downplay' the role of individuals; instead, they highlight the importance of more general social, economic and political change.

Placing different emphasis on the same historical evidence

Even if historians do not possess different philosophies of history or place different emphasis on the role of the individual, it is still possible for them to disagree because they place different emphases on aspects of the same factual evidence. As a result, Sixth Form History should be seen as a subject that encourages debate about the past based on historical evidence.

Progression in Sixth Form History

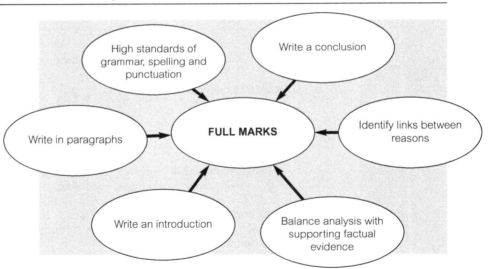

The ability to achieve high standards in Sixth Form History involves the acquisition of a number of skills:

- Good written communication skills
- Acquiring a sound factual knowledge
- Evaluating factual evidence and making historical conclusions based on that evidence
- Source analysis
- Understanding the nature of historical interpretation
- Understanding the causes and consequences of historical events

- Understanding themes in history which will involve a study of a specific topic over a long period of time

- Understanding the ideas of change and continuity associated with themes.

Students should be aware that the acquisition of these skills will take place gradually over the time spent in the Sixth Form. At the beginning of the course, the main emphasis may be on the acquisition of factual knowledge, particularly when the body of knowledge studied at GCSE was different.

When dealing with causation, students will have to build on their skills from GCSE. They will not only be expected to identify reasons for an historical event but also to provide a hierarchy of causes. They should identify the main causes and less important causes. They may also identify that causes may be interconnected and linked. Progression in Sixth Form History will come with answering the questions at the end of each sub-section in this book and practising the skills outlined through the use of the factual knowledge contained in the book.

Examination technique

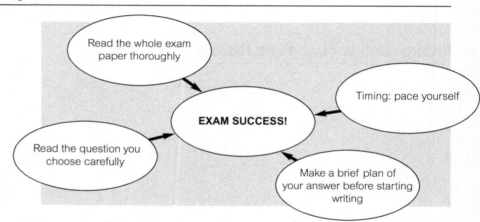

The ultimate challenge for any Sixth Form historian is the ability to produce quality work under examination conditions. Examinations will take the form of either modular examinations taken in January and June or an 'end of course' set of examinations.

Here is some advice on how to improve your performance in an examination.

- Read the whole examination paper thoroughly
  Make sure that the questions you choose are those for which you can produce a good answer. Don't rush – allow time to decide which questions to choose. It is probably too late to change your mind half way through answering a question.

- Read the question very carefully
  Once you have made the decision to answer a specific question, read it very carefully. Make sure you understand the precise demands of the question. Think about what is required in your answer. It is much better to think about this before you start writing, rather than trying to steer your essay in a different direction half way through.

- Make a brief plan
  Sketch out what you intend to include in your answer. Order the points you want to make. Examiners are not impressed with additional information included at the end of the essay, with indicators such as arrows or asterisks.

- Pace yourself as you write
  Success in examinations has a lot to do with successful time management. If, for instance, you have to answer an essay question in approximately 45 minutes, then you should be one-third of the way through after 15 minutes. With 30 minutes gone, you should start writing the last third of your answer.

Where a question is divided into sub-questions, make sure you look at the mark tariff for each question. If in a 20-mark question a sub-question is worth a maximum of 5 marks, then you should spend approximately one-quarter of the time allocated for the whole question on this sub-question.

Revision tips

Even before the examination begins make sure that you have revised thoroughly. Revision tips on the main topics in this book appear on the Collins website:

www.collinseducation.com

1 The United States 1917–2008: A synoptic overview

Key Issues

- How did the power of the President change from 1917 to 2008?

- How has the USA developed into a major world power?

- To what extent did US society change?

1.1 The rise to global power

The 20th century has been described as America's century, because during that period the USA became the world's most important power. By the time of the US entry into the First World War, in 1917, the USA was the world's biggest economic power. By the end of the Second World War, in 1945, the USA was the world's greatest military power. Since 1991 the USA has been the world's only global power. It possesses a vast arsenal of nuclear weapons and its military forces are stationed throughout the globe. Nowhere on earth is beyond the reach of US military power.

Not only is the USA the dominant world military and economic power, it also has the world's highest standard of living. The USA was the world's first consumer society. It developed the world's first supermarkets (Piggly Wiggly) and became the world leader in fast food. Companies such as McDonald's and KFC are now found throughout the globe. The USA also became the world's base for mass production. The Ford 'Model T' car and Coca Cola became worldwide examples of this development. In addition, American culture has been the dominant force in the world since 1917. From the beginning of the 20th century the USA dominated the new medium of cinema. Since the 1950s it has also dominated world TV – and popular music too, with Elvis Presley and Madonna becoming household names across the world.

To study US history from 1917 to 2008, therefore, is to study the country which has had the greatest influence on the development of the world over the last hundred years.

1.2 The power of the President

According to the historian Marcus Cunliffe, in *American Presidents and the Presidency* (published in 1970):

'The American presidency is the most important and, perhaps, most peculiar office on earth. The President is a monarch who must abdicate, a politician without a firm constituency, a man of formidable authority who is often derided and thwarted.'

Since the appointment of the first President, George Washington, in 1789,

Separation of powers: The principle in the US Constitution that prevents any one institution exercising complete power. Within the federal (national) government, for instance, the power to make laws was divided between the President, Congress and Supreme Court. Political powers were also divided between the federal government and state governments.

Federal state: A state where political power is divided between a federal government and state governments. In the USA, the federal government has responsibility for foreign relations, national defence and inter-state commerce; the states have responsibility for education, law and order and welfare.

Habeus corpus: A civil right where anyone arrested for a crime must either be formally charged within 24 hours or released.

the power of the President has been an issue of debate. Part of the problem lies in the position of the President as laid down in the Constitution (see page 17). With the operation of the principle of the **separation of powers**, the President has to work with Congress. Because the USA is a **federal state**, the federal government has to work with the states. As a result, presidential power is limited.

A theme of US history has been how individual presidents have used this power. Rexford Tugwell, a close adviser to President F.D. Roosevelt in the 1930s, stated that when the Constitution was drawn up in 1787 at Philadelphia:

> 'none could have had any definite picture of the official they had created – except that he would be very much like [George] Washington.'

Since George Washington, individual presidents have used their authority to increase their power. The clearest example of this trend was Abraham Lincoln. During the American Civil War, Lincoln used his powers to suspend *habeus corpus*, to imprison opponents and to call up troops. Lincoln's defence was that to save the Constitution he had to ignore it occasionally. His extension of presidential power was limited to the emergency of civil war. The presidents who followed him did not possess increased power as a result. In 1885, Woodrow Wilson wrote a study of the US political system, which he entitled 'Congressional Government'. This title reflected the authority of Presidents in the late 19th century. Nevertheless, the Civil War had decided one very important issue in US politics: the states' rights were reduced considerably with the triumph of the Union cause over the Confederacy.

The rise of presidential power mirrors the rise of the USA as a major industrial and military power. As an industrial power, the US government grew in size to reflect the complexity of society. As Chief Executive (Head of Government), the President began to be responsible for a larger and larger federal government. Extra departments were added: Agriculture in 1889 and Commerce and Labor in 1903 (see insert). In 1921, the Bureau of the Budget was created to aid the President in producing the annual

Cabinet: The heads of government departments, such as State, Treasury, Labor, who help the President run the Administration.

Evolution of the government departments in US Cabinet

Original members:
Secretary of State, 1789
Secretary of Treasury, 1789
Secretary of War, 1789 (loses **Cabinet** status, 1947)
Attorney General, 1789 (not head of Justice Department until 1870)

Added, 1798–1813
Secretary of Navy, 1798 (loses Cabinet status, 1947)
Postmaster General, 1829 (loses Cabinet status, 1970)
Secretary of Interior, 1849
Secretary of Agriculture, 1889
Secretary of Commerce and Labor, 1903 (office divided by 1913)
Secretary of Commerce, 1913
Secretary of Labor, 1913

Added, 1947–1977
Secretary of Defense, 1947 (subordinate to him, without Cabinet rank, are secretaries of army, navy and air force)
Secretary of Health, Education and Welfare, 1953
Secretary of Housing and Urban Development, 1965
Secretary of Transportation, 1966
Secretary of Energy, 1977

budget. By 1939, a separate Executive Office of the Presidency was formed to incorporate all the advisory agencies to the presidency which had developed during the early 20th century.

The development of US military power was even more significant for the role of the President. As Commander-in-Chief, he had the power to send US troops abroad, without Congressional approval, if he felt US lives or property were in danger. Theodore Roosevelt used this power to send US troops to the Caribbean and Central America during his presidency (1901–09). Woodrow Wilson (1913–21) sent US troops into Mexico in 1916.

As the USA entered the First World War, the President's role in foreign relations increased the prestige of the office greatly. As one of the 'Big Four' at the Paris Peace Conference in 1919, President Wilson personified US military and industrial power. He became the first US President to have a major input in European affairs.

The crisis of the 1930s increased US presidential authority at home. At his **inauguration**, in March 1933, President F.D. Roosevelt asked for powers to deal with the economic depression, which would be the same as if the country were facing the crisis of war. As a result, during the New Deal, the federal government greatly increased its role in American life. Alphabet agencies were involved in industry, agriculture and regional development. The President's position changed so much that commentators at the time were accusing Roosevelt of being a dictator.

The turning point in the rise of presidential power came with the Second World War. From 1941, the USA emerged as a world power, with its head of state as a world leader. From 1945, the USA entered the nuclear weapons age. From that day forward, the US President has had the awesome responsibility and power to authorise the use of nuclear weapons.

It is significant that the last time Congress was authorised to declare war was on 8 December 1941. Since that date, successive US Presidents have used their power as Commander-in-Chief to send large numbers of US armed forces abroad. In 1950, President Truman sent US troops to Korea. He used the defence that he was acting on behalf of the United Nations. Most significantly, Presidents Kennedy, Johnson and Nixon sent large numbers of troops to South East Asia during the Vietnam conflict.

Such a major growth of presidential power was reflected in Arthur Schlesinger's study *The Imperial Presidency* published in 1972. By that date, the office of President had become so powerful that it no longer reflected the original constitutional role of the office. As world statesman and head of the armed forces, the President of the USA became the world's most powerful politician.

However, in domestic affairs, the President's power remained limited. Without the support of Congress, it was very difficult for a president to implement a viable domestic programme. President Kennedy suffered from this problem between 1961 and 1963. Furthermore, the Supreme Court could declare government or Congressional Acts unconstitutional. President F.D. Roosevelt faced this problem in the First New Deal (1933–35).

In the year Schlesinger produced his book, the Watergate Scandal was developing – causing great damage to the office of President. Nixon's obstruction of investigations into White House activities during the 1972 presidential campaign and party financing led to calls for his **impeachment**. On 9 August 1974, when impeachment was almost certain, Nixon became the only US President to resign from office.

Since 1974, presidential power has not diminished in foreign and military affairs. In 1991, George Bush Senior sent US troops to fight in the Gulf

Inauguration: The official ceremony for the swearing in of a new President.

Impeachment: The trial of a public official, especially in the USA, for a serious crime committed while in office.

War. During the Clinton presidency, US forces were involved in conflict overseas in the Balkans and in Somalia. In 2003, George W. Bush led a coalition, including Britain, in the invasion and occupation of Iraq. In addition, the President still has authority over launching a retaliatory nuclear strike. Rather than seeing the power of the office changing through time, it is better to look at how individual presidents have been able to use their power. Political scientist Richard Neustadt, stated that presidential power is the 'power to persuade'. Certain presidents, because of their personality, political skill and circumstance, have used the full potential of the office. Strong presidents include Wilson, F. D. Roosevelt and, in the period 1963–66, Lyndon Johnson. Weak presidents include Gerald Ford and Jimmy Carter.

US Presidents 1917–2008

1913–21	Woodrow Wilson (Democrat)
1921–23	Warren Harding (Republican)
1923–29	Calvin Coolidge (Republican)
1929–33	Herbert Hoover (Republican)
1933–45	Franklin Roosevelt (Democrat)
1945–53	Harry Truman (Democrat)
1953–61	Dwight Eisenhower (Republican)
1961–63	John Kennedy (Democrat)
1963–69	Lyndon Johnson (Democrat)
1969–74	Richard Nixon (Republican)
1974–77	Gerald Ford (Republican)
1977–81	Jimmy Carter (Democrat)
1981–89	Ronald Reagan (Republican)
1989–93	George H. Bush (Republican)
1993–2001	Bill Clinton (Democrat)
2001–09	George W. Bush (Republican)

The separation of powers between the federal and state governments

The United States is a federal state. This means that political powers and responsibilities are divided between the central (federal) government, based in Washington DC, and the 50 state governments.

Powers reserved for the federal government alone
- Regulation of foreign trade
- Regulation of inter-state commerce
- Minting money
- Running the post office
- Regulating immigration
- Granting copyrights and patents
- Declaring war and peace
- Admitting new states
- Fixing weights and measures
- Organising the armed forces
- Governing the federal capital, Washington DC
- Conducting foreign relations.

Powers reserved for state governments only
- Conducting elections
- Establishing voter qualifications
- Providing local government
- Regulating contracts
- Regulating trade within the state
- Providing education
- Maintaining a police force and internal law and order.

Powers shared by federal and state governments
- Taxation
- Controlling the state militia, later known as the National Guard.

The three parts of the federal government

The Executive – the Government – comprises the President and the Departments of State.

The Legislature – the law-making branch of government – is the United States Congress, which is divided into two houses:

The Senate contains representatives of the 50 states. Each state – no matter how big or small – has two senators, so there are 100 senators.

The House of Representatives contains congressmen, who are elected from electoral districts with roughly equal populations. Two of the smallest states, Delaware and Rhode Island, have only one congressman each. But California, the most populous state in the Union, has 53 congressmen! There are 435 congressmen in all.

The Judiciary is the branch of government that interprets the laws passed by the Congress and state governments and actions by the President and state governments. The most important part of the judiciary is the US Supreme Court. It contains nine judges, nominated by the President and supported by the US Senate. It also has acquired the power to interpret the US Constitution. Under the Supreme Court are federal courts which deal with cases concerning federal or national law.

US elections: A brief guide

In the USA, people vote for the President and Vice President, the US Congress, State governments and legislatures, and city and county governments. Even the local sheriff is elected!

The President and Vice President are elected every four years by all US citizens over 18 (up to 1969 voters had to be 21).

Because it is a federal state, votes for the President are added up within each of the 50 states. Each state has votes to the 'Electoral College' based on its combined number of senators and congressmen.

The popular vote for the President takes place on the first Tuesday of November. The Electoral College then cast their votes for the President in December. The President then takes office on 20 January of the following year (up to 1933 it was not until March).

Senators are elected for six years. Congressmen are elected for two years.

Outline of the United States Constitution

Preamble

'We the people of the United States in order to form a more perfect union, establish justice, ensure domestic tranquillity, provide for the common defence, promote the general welfare, and secure the blessings of liberty to ourselves and our posterity, do ordain and confirm the Constitution for the United States of America.'

Article I: The Legislature (Congress)

Congress is divided into two parts:

1. The House of Representatives: 435 members determined by population.

2. The Senate: 100 members since 1959 – two from each state.

The House of Representatives:

● may start impeachment against a President or other high government officials.

● All bills that deal with money must begin in the House.

● Speaker of the House presides over proceedings.

● Members, known as Congressmen, are elected every two years (minimum age: 25).

The Senate:

● was originally elected by state legislatures, but since Seventeenth Amendment in 1913 they are directly elected.

● approves or rejects nominations from President for senior government officials and Supreme Court justices (Advice and Consent Power).

● approves or rejects treaties with other countries (Advice and Consent Power).

● Debate is unlimited.

● The Vice-President presides over proceedings and can only vote in the event of a tie.

● Senators are elected for six years (citizens over 30 years). A third are elected every two years.

Article II: The Executive (President and Government)

President is elected every four years. Originally elected without limit. Since the Twenty-Second Amendment, can only serve two terms. Must be native born and at least 35 years of age.

President is:

● Commander-in-Chief of the armed forces

● Chief Executive (Head of Government)

● Head of State

● Chief lawmaker.

Article III: The Judiciary

US Supreme Court created as highest court of appeal for federal and state cases. Precise composition of Courts defined by Judiciary Act of 1789.

Article IV: Inter-state relations

● All states are guaranteed a republican form of government.

● Any new state is equal to the original 13 states.

● Each state shall respect the laws of the other states.

Article V: Amending the Constitution

Amendments must receive two-thirds support from both Houses of Congress and three-quarters of the states before they become law.

Article VI: Ratification of the Constitution

Nine of the original 13 states had to accept the Constitution before it could become law.

Amendments to the Constitution

Amendments 1–10, made in 1791, are known as the Bill of Rights.

1. Freedom of religion; freedom of speech; freedom of the press.
2. Right to keep arms.
3. Troops cannot be housed in private citizens' homes.
4. Protects against unreasonable searches and seizures of property.
5. Protects rights of accused in trials; no citizens can be imprisoned without 'due process of law'.
6. Guarantees a speedy trial.
7. Guarantees a trial by jury.
8. Protects against cruel and unusual punishment.
9. Rights not mentioned above are still kept by the people.
10. States have power not expressly given to federal government by the Constitution.
11. States may not be sued by individuals (1798).
12. President and Vice-President must be elected separately (1800).
13. Abolished slavery (1865).
14. Guaranteed equal protection of the law to all citizens (1868).
15. Extended voting rights to African-Americans (1870).
16. Legalised federal income tax (1913).
17. Allowed senators to be directly elected (1913).
18. Outlawed the manufacture and consumption of alcohol (Prohibition) (1919).
19. Extended voting rights to women (1920).
20. Changed inauguration day from 4 March to 20 January (1933).
21. Repealed the Eighteenth Amendment (1933).
22. Limited President to two terms (1951).
23. Gave presidential voting rights to District of Columbia (1961).
24. Prohibited poll taxes (1964).
25. Outlined order of succession to the presidency (1967).
26. Extended voting rights to 18 year olds (1971).
27. Congressional pay increases could only take effect following next Congressional election (1992).

1.3 The role of the US in world affairs

Today the USA is the only truly global power. With the collapse of the USSR in 1991, the Cold War – which had dominated US foreign policy from 1945 to 1991 – came to an end.

Before 1917, however, the USA had played only a minor role in world affairs. The turning point in US relations with the outside world was the Spanish–American War of 1898. For the first time, the USA acquired colonies outside the North American continent. Also, during the presidency of Theodore Roosevelt, the USA began to play a more active role in international affairs. Roosevelt sent the US 'Great White Fleet' on a world tour to show off US naval might and, in 1905, he acted as peacemaker between Russia and Japan to end the Russo-Japanese War. Roosevelt was awarded the Nobel Peace Prize for his efforts.

Entry into the First World War in 1917 brought the USA, albeit temporarily, into the centre stage of world affairs. Woodrow Wilson's '14 Points' of January 1918 became the unofficial war aims of the Allies. At Paris in 1919, Wilson put forward his plan for a League of Nations as a guarantor of world peace (see Chapter 4). The high point of Wilson's presidency was quickly followed by its nadir (lowest point). In 1919, the Senate rejected the Treaty of Versailles. It later signed a separate peace with Germany. During the 1920s and 1930s, the USA entered a new period of isolation.

The involvement of the USA in the Second World War transformed it from a major power into one of two superpowers. The defeat of Germany and Japan and the weakening of the British Empire left the USA and USSR to dominate the post-war world. The end of the Second World War also brought the beginning of the nuclear age and the Cold War (see Chapters 5 and 6). The writer Gore Vidal regards 1947 as the beginning of the 'national security' state in the USA. The National Security Act of 1947 created the Central Intelligence Agency and the National Security Agency (see page 318). It also produced a new decision-making body in foreign and military affairs – the National Security Council. With the introduction of selective service (compulsory military service, or the 'draft'), the USA was on a war footing in peacetime.

In 1950, the issuing of the National Security Council paper NSC-68 and the outbreak of the Korean War led to a massive arms build-up by the USA. By that date, the USA was engaged in a global military and ideological conflict with communist states. The USA developed a worldwide network of military bases and alliances in an attempt to contain **communism**.

The demand for military equipment led to the development of the 'military-industrial complex' in the USA. This term describes those groups within the USA who benefited from massive **armaments** expenditure. It included **corporations** such as McDonnell Douglas, Lockheed and Boeing. It also included politicians whose states and districts benefited from armaments contracts. Union leaders saw the armaments industry as a lucrative source of work for their union members. The rise of these mutually-interested groups even worried President Eisenhower who, in his farewell speech of 1961, warned his successor of the influence of the military-industrial complex on foreign policy. Eisenhower clearly identified the group with an aggressive, anti-communist policy which would require considerable military expenditure.

The international tension created by the Cold War resulted in periodic crises. The most serious of these crises came in 1961 and 1962, over Berlin and Cuba respectively. On both occasions, the USA came close to all-out nuclear war with the USSR.

However, the most serious Cold War conflict was a conventional war in Vietnam. From March 1965, US combat forces were dispatched to 'save' South Vietnam from communism. By 1969, the numbers had risen to 600,000. The failure to 'win in Vietnam' created a major domestic crisis, which led to Lyndon Johnson withdrawing from the presidential race in 1968. The Vietnam War also caused Nixon considerable domestic problems during his first term, when he invaded Cambodia and engaged in a massive aerial bombing offensive against North Vietnam.

By the early 1980s, the presidency of Ronald Reagan led to another massive arms build-up by the USA. A 'New Cold War' developed when the USA sited Cruise and Pershing II missiles in Europe. However, the arms race between the USA and USSR did have a beneficial effect on America's world position. The USSR was economically incapable of producing the armaments necessary to compete with the USA. By 1986, the new Soviet leader, Mikhail Gorbachev, offered the USA an agreement to cut nuclear forces.

By the time President Bush entered office in 1989, the Cold War seemed to be coming to an end. By the end of 1989, virtually all the countries of Eastern Europe had overthrown their communist governments. In 1991, communist rule came to an end with the collapse of the USSR and its division into 15 separate states.

The USA emerged in1991, therefore, as the unchallenged world power. Not only had the USSR collapsed and the Cold War come to an end, but the USA led a coalition of countries which expelled Iraq from its occupation of Kuwait.

Throughout the 1990s the USA seemed to remain unchallenged. The former Soviet Union had disintegrated, and China had yet to emerge as a major world economic power. At the end of the Clinton presidency, in 2001, the USA remained the world's dominant military and economic power.

But everything began to change in that year. On 11 September 2001, the USA suffered attacks from an Islamic terrorist organisation called al-Qaeda. The World Trade Centre in New York was destroyed and the Pentagon, the

Communism: The political belief that the state should own and control the means of producing everything, so that all levels of society can be equal. Then everyone will do as much as they can and get as much as they need.

Armaments: Weapons and military equipment belonging to an army or a country.

Corporations: Large businesses or groups of companies that are all controlled and run together as single organisations.

Department of Defense building in Washington DC was attacked. From 2001 the USA has been involved in GWAT (the global war against terror). Under US leadership, the Taliban regime was deposed in Afghanistan. Afghanistan was seen as a training ground and major supporter of al-Qaeda. Al-Qaeda suspects were arrested and detained in a military prison at Guantanamo Bay, a US military base on the island of Cuba.

George W. Bush seemed to complete the work his father, George Bush Senior, had begun in 1991, when he decided in 2003 to topple the Iraqi dictator, Saddam Hussein. The USA led the invasion of Iraq in the spring of 2003. The conventional war was swift, Saddam was overthrown, and the USA and its allies quickly occupied Iraq. But from 2003 to 2008 the USA and its allies faced an insurgency, with guerrilla fighters constantly attacking coalition forces. In addition, the two dominant Muslim groups in Iraq – the Sunnis and the Shi'ites – launched terrorist attacks against each other.

By 2008 the USA was involved in a guerrilla war that it seemed it could not win, and its international prestige had declined considerably since 2001. Not only was the USA faced with protracted wars in Afghanistan and Iraq, it was also involved in a confrontation with Iran, which was accused of secretly developing the ability to produce nuclear weapons.

1.4 Changes in US society

In the 1920 Census, the USA, for the first time, contained more than 100 million inhabitants. The vast majority of the population had emigrated from Europe. First the Dutch and British arrived in the 17th and 18th centuries, followed by the Irish and Germans. In the late 19th century new immigrant groups appeared from Eastern Europe and Italy. The original Native American population had been decimated by disease and defeated in war. The vast majority now lived on reservations in the west. Approximately 10 per cent of the population were African-American, living primarily in the 'Old South'. Before 1865 nearly all African-Americans had been slaves. Even though they were free from 1865 onwards, the vast majority still lived in poverty and suffered discrimination by the White population. Segregation of African-Americans and Whites occurred in transportation, housing and education across the Old South.

In 1917 the USA was a land of contrasts. About half of the population lived in large sprawling cities, such as New York and Chicago, which contained large numbers of immigrants from Europe. These cities developed distinct ethnic neighbourhoods inhabited almost exclusively by Irish, Italians, Germans, Jews or Eastern Europeans. The other half of the population lived in small towns, villages and farms. In these areas, White, Anglo-Saxon Protestants (WASPs) predominated.

WASP America felt threatened by the influx of non-WASP immigration from Europe. Their resistance to immigration took many forms. The rise of the prohibition movement was in part due to opposition to the drinking excesses of the new immigrants. By the outbreak of the First World War the WASP opposition seemed to be triumphant. Prohibition had been introduced into many states by 1917. In 1918 the 18th Amendment to the Constitution was passed, introducing national prohibition from 1920 – a 'noble experiment' which lasted until 1933. WASP opposition also led to the recreation of the Ku Klux Klan, in 1915. This secret organisation against African-Americans had been created at the end of the Civil War. From 1915 it added Jews and Catholics as potential 'enemies' of WASP America. Finally, in 1924 immigration was severely restricted.

By 2008 the USA was a completely different land. Over 75 per cent of Americans now lived in urban areas. A major change during the 20th century was the development of suburbs around large cities. The African-American population was no longer confined to the Old South. The 'Great Migration' of the 1920s, 1930s and 1940s had seen large numbers of African-Americans move to the large cities. By 2008, Washington DC had an African-American majority. Other cities, such as New York, Chicago, Cleveland, Philadelphia and Los Angeles had large African-American neighbourhoods.

The late 20th century saw the development of the Civil Rights Movement, which had begun in the Old South in the 1950s. Through a variety of methods – mainly non-violent – African-Americans fought for and won civil and political equality with Whites. Using the court system and protesting against discrimination, African-Americans forced state governments to abandon **legal segregation** by 1965. But full civil and political equality did not bring social equality. Although many African-Americans joined the middle class in 2008 large numbers of African-Americans still lived below 'the poverty line' in either the rural South or the inner-city North.

Legal segregation: The deliberate creation by law of separate facilities for whites and African-Americans, mainly in the former Confederate states

Although African-American rights have been the dominant theme in civil rights, other groups within US society have also seen an improvement in their civil rights. In 1917, women campaigned for the vote and national prohibition, achieving their ends the following year when the vote was extended to women and national prohibition became federal law. From the 1960s onwards women have achieved full civil and political equality with men. The Civil Rights Act, 1964, was a major landmark in this process.

By the 1970s militant groups advocated greater civil rights for minority groups. Black Power, Gay Power and the feminist movement all demanded greater rights for their respective groups. There was even 'Red Power', when in 1970 Native Americans occupied the former federal prison of Alcatraz Island in San Francisco Bay as a protest about their treatment.

An important minority which grew rapidly from the mid-1960s were Hispanic Americans. Hispanic Americans had always formed an important minority in border states, such as California, Arizona, New Mexico and Texas. From 1965 a new immigration act allowed more Hispanic people to emigrate to the USA. But, along with legal immigration came illegal immigration. Thousands fled the poverty of Central and South America for a new life in the USA. By 2008 Hispanic Americans lived in large number across the USA. The question of illegal immigration became an important issue among Republican voters in the 2008 Presidential Election.

By 2008 in many respects the USA had turned into reality an important part of the Declaration of Independence of 1776 which stated:

> We hold these truths to be self-evident, that all men are created equal, and that they are endowed with certain inalienable rights.

The 20th century had also seen the USA become the first consumer society. The development of mass-production techniques and hire purchase allowed ordinary Americans to acquire goods previously owned only by the wealthy. The most obvious example was the motor car. By the late 1920s the motor car was seen as an essential item for most families, and by 2008 the USA was truly a car-owners' society. A vast network of roads criss-crossed the USA, and drive-in movie theatres and drive-thru' fast-food outlets became commonplace.

The other major change in society was the development of the mass media. In 1917 the USA was experiencing the rapid growth of cinema, with towns across the country acquiring movie theatres. The 20th century saw the USA dominate world cinema, with Hollywood, a suburb of Los

1. What do you regard as the most important development in the USA in the period 1917 to 2008? Explain your answer.

2. To what extent has there been a continual rise in presidential power in the period 1917 to 2008?

3. Why did the USA become the world's greatest power by 2008?

4. How far is the USA a freer and fairer society in 2008, compared to 1917?

Angeles, becoming the movie capital of the world. The USA was also the pioneer in the development of radio and television. In the 1920s local radio stations were established across the country, and in 1933 the newly elected president F. D. Roosevelt used the radio to communicate directly with the American people. His 'fireside chats' became an important part of his presidency. In the late 1940s and 1950s television developed rapidly, and by 1960 most American homes possessed a TV. In that year a televised debate between presidential candidates took place for the first time. Now most political campaigns use the TV as the main way of influencing potential voters. In the 1990s another media revolution began – the internet revolution.

By 2008 the USA was a more equal and affluent society than it had been in 1917. However, more wealth and new lifestyles brought new problems. In 2008, 66 per cent of adult Americans were 'overweight' and 33 per cent of these were 'obese'. This has major health implications for US society. The US population is also ageing. Large numbers of senior citizens have migrated from the old North to retirement communities in states such as Arizona and Florida. Also the USA is no longer predominantly populated by White people with their origins in Europe. Approximately 12 per cent of the population is African-American, but the biggest change has been the rapid growth of the Hispanic population. George W. Bush was the first president who learnt Spanish to help in his campaigning. It is predicted that by 2030 the non-White population will be in the majority in the USA.

2 Boom and Bust: the United States, 1917–1933

Key Issues

- Why did the United States' economy change between 1917 and 1933?

- What impact did national prohibition have on the USA?

- How far were the 1920s a period of intolerance?

2.1 Why was immigration restricted in the USA between 1917 and 1924?

2.2 What impact did national prohibition have on the USA between 1920 and 1933?

2.3 Why did the Ku Klux Klan at first revive and then decline rapidly in the 1920s?

2.4 In what ways were the 1920s a period of cultural change?

2.5 How far did the United States experience an economic boom in the 1920s?

2.6 Why and how did economic depression affect the United States from 1929?

2.7 Historical interpretation: Herbert Hoover

Framework of Events

1917	April: USA enters the First World War
1918	November: First World War ends
1919	January: Eighteenth Amendment ratified by states
	May: Attacks on socialists and communists across USA
	June: Congress agrees to Nineteenth Amendment of Constitution – giving women the right to vote (ratified by states in August 1920)
	July: Race riots across USA
	October: Volstead Act passed, over President Wilson's veto, enforcing Eighteenth Amendment introducing national prohibition
1920	January: Palmer Raids against communists
	May: Sacco and Vanzetti case
	Beginning of economic recession (which lasts until 1922)
	5 million become unemployed by 1921
	November: Republican Harding defeats Democrat Cox for the Presidency. Republicans also dominate Senate and House of Representatives in Congress.
1921	May: President Harding approves limitations on immigration
	Budget and Accounting Act establishes Office of Director of Budget
	November: Revenue Act cuts taxes
1922	July: Ku Klux Klan begin winning elective office across the USA
	September: Fordney–McCumber Tariff Act raises taxes on imports
1923	August: President Harding dies; succeeded by Vice-President Coolidge
	October: Senate investigations begin into corruption during Harding Administration
1924	January: First attempt to introduce McNary–Haugen bill to aid farmers
	February: Corruption scandals of Harding Administration begin to emerge as result of Congressional investigation
	May: Immigration Quota (National Origins) Act becomes law
	November: Republican Coolidge defeats Democrat Davis for Presidency
1925	July: The Scopes (Monkey) Trial in Tennessee
1926	February: Revenue Act cuts taxes
	Florida land deals collapse

1927	February: President Coolidge vetoes attempt to introduce McNary–Haugen Bill (vetoes it again in May 1928)
	August: Sacco and Vanzetti are executed
1928	November: Republican Hoover defeats Democrat Smith for Presidency
1929	April: Hoover calls a special session of Congress to deal with farm price crisis
	October: Wall Street Crash: collapse of prices on New York Stock Exchange
1930	June: Hawley–Smoot Tariff raises taxes on imports
	November: Mid-term elections: Democrats gain control of House
1931	Economic crisis spreads to Europe; economic crisis in USA deepens
1932	January: Reconstruction Finance Corporation is created: first direct attempt by federal government to offer economic aid in Depression
	July: Relief and Reconstruction Act provides $1.5 billion extra for public works
	Federal Home Loan Bank Act creates home loans with $125 million to prevent homeowners losing their homes
	November: Democrat Roosevelt defeats Republican President Hoover in Presidential election; Democrats control Congress
1933	March: Roosevelt becomes President. Beginning of New Deal.

Overview

Economic recession: A temporary decline or setback in economic activity or prosperity. A modern term for slump, or 'depression'.

THE period 1917 to 1933 was one of rapid change within the USA. After a short **economic recession** following the First World War, the decade was associated with lively economic growth. The United States became the world's first consumer society. The product most closely associated with the 1920s is the motor car. In the second decade of the century, Henry Ford, based in Detroit, Michigan, began producing cars through the assembly-line method of production. This greatly increased production and lowered the cost of motor cars. His 'Model T' Ford became the 'people's car' of the 1920s.

The growth of the car industry stimulated other industries, such as electrics, rubber and engineering. It also led to the development of the US road system.

The 1920s were also associated with other consumer goods such as refrigerators, washing machines, sewing machines and the radio. The radio became a major addition to the media. By the early 1930s, almost every US family possessed a radio. It was a major source of entertainment and news.

The economic boom of the 1920s created thousands of new jobs in industrial and commercial centres in the North, such as Chicago, Detroit and New York. Women took many of these new jobs, such as secretaries and telephonists. In 1920 women had also received the right to vote. Female fashion reflected the change in women's political and economic status.

Although the 1920s are associated with economic prosperity, many social groups and areas missed out. African-Americans were treated as second-class citizens across the USA. They received the lowest-paid jobs.

Farmers also suffered. The war period (1914–1918) had been a period of high farm prices. With the coming of peace and the mechanisation of farming, over-production led to lower farm prices. In the South, the boll weevil devastated the cotton crop forcing many farmers out of business.

Even though industry boomed, trade unionists faced a hard time. The Supreme Court and governments, both **federal** and state, tended to support employers in

Federal: A system of government consisting of a group of states controlled by a central government. The central government deals with things concerning the whole country, such as foreign policy, but each state has its own local powers and laws.

strikes and over working conditions. Several major strikes occurred in the period, such as the New Jersey textile strike of January 1926.

The 1920s was also a period when White, Anglo-Saxon Protestant (WASP), small-town America attempted to reassert itself. This process took many forms. One aspect was the introduction of immigration controls. The end of mass immigration was an attempt to prevent the USA being 'overrun' with people from eastern and central Europe. These immigrants were associated with 'un-American' ideas such as socialism and communism.

WASP America also asserted itself through the introduction of national prohibition. The Eighteenth Amendment to the Constitution was the culmination of a generation of campaigning by groups such as the women's Christian Temperance Union and the Anti-Saloon League. It was a religious, social and political campaign to enforce the views of WASP America on the whole nation. National prohibition – 'The Noble Experiment' – was a complete failure. Not only was it widely ignored, even in the White House, it also led to the rise in influence of organised crime. The 1920s was not only an era of prosperity, it was also the era of the gangster.

Ku Klux Klan: The original group was set up in the South in 1866 under the leadership of former Confederate general Nathan Bedford Forest. It aimed to terrorise black Americans freed from slavery. With their white outfits, covered faces and burning crosses, their appearance was intended to frighten. Their lynching of 'uppity niggers' was all too successful. The Ku Klux Klan (KKK) carried out 70 lynchings in 1919; the number declined to 11 by 1928. In the 1920s, a revived KKK's updated list of hate-figures included not only blacks but also Catholics, Jews and divorcees. They defended the values of rural WASPs.

WASP intolerance of other groups reached its height with the re-emergence of the **Ku Klux Klan**. From 1915, the new KKK was not only anti-African-American but also anti-Semitic and anti-Catholic. Its former heartland of the Old South was expanded to cover the entire nation. However, just as it rose rapidly, it also declined spectacularly from 1925. This followed several well-publicised scandals involving Klan members in Indiana.

Intolerance towards religious and racial groups was matched by opposition to new ideas. The Scopes Trial in Tennessee, in 1925, received national attention when a schoolteacher challenged state law which banned discussion of Darwin's theory of evolution in schools.

This opposition to modern trends stood in marked contrast to the development of the cinema industry. The USA led the world in the 1920s in the production of films. Hollywood became the centre of national and world attention as the home of film stars. Douglas Fairbanks Snr, Charlie Chaplin and Rudolf Valentino were stars of the 'silent screen'. Even here, by the end of the decade, the 'Hay's Code' laid down strict guidelines on what was allowed in films in terms of male–female relations.

How a federal bill becomes an act

1   A proposal for a change in federal law is called a Bill. It is usually introduced simultaneously into the Senate and the House of Representatives. The two sponsors of the Bill (a Senator and a Congressman) usually give their names to the proposal. Hence, Johnson–Reed Immigration Act, Glass–Steagall Banking Act.

2   The Bill is then discussed by a Senate Committee and a House Committee. The Chair of the Ways and Means Committee in the House has considerable influence over which Bills will become law. He/she has the power to assign a bill to a particular committee. For instance, bills on agriculture go to the Senate and House Agriculture Committees.

3   Committee membership reflects the proportion of seats held by Republicans and Democrats in Congress. The chairman of a committee is always from the majority party in that house.

4   Once both committees have discussed and amended the Bill, it goes to a joint committee of both houses where a compromise agreement is made.

5   The Bill is then presented to the President for signature before it can become an act. The President can veto the Bill by refusing to sign it. The President's veto can be overridden if two-thirds of both houses of Congress agree.

6   Even after the Bill has been signed by the President it can be declared unconstitutional by the US Supreme Court. An example is the decision in 1935 to declare unconstitutional the National Recovery Administration set up by the National Industrial Recovery Act of 1934.

Wall Street Crash: On 24 October 1929 nearly 13 million shares changed hands on the New York Stock Exchange. Shock waves from the 'Crash' were felt all around the world. Many people lost a lot of money.

Stock Market: A place where stocks (shares) in companies are bought and sold.

Hobos: American word for the tramps or 'bums' who travelled round looking for work, especially during the Depression.

Hoovervilles: Developments in the USA made up of up to 100 or so small dwellings, often made out of wooden boxes, metal cans, cardboard etc.

The turning point in the period was the onset of Depression from October 1929. Even before the **Wall Street Crash**, signs of an economic downturn were apparent. Share prices stopped rising, overproduction was taking place and workers were being 'laid off'. The **Stock Market** crash merely speeded up what was already happening. By 1930, the USA and the western world had entered the most serious economic depression the world had seen. The period 1929 to 1933 was characterised by widespread social and economic misery. **Hobos** and **Hoovervilles** spread across the country. By 1932, 25 per cent of the workforce were unemployed.

Faced with this national emergency, President Hoover seemed to be doing nothing. However, Hoover faced an economic crisis never before seen in the USA. In retrospect, it is easy to regard his efforts at dealing with the depression as too little too late.

By 1933 the USA was, in many ways, very different from what it had been in 1919. It had witnessed major social and economic change. This was most apparent in the changing role of women. It saw the USA brought closer together with the development of the motor car, radio and cinema. However, when President Roosevelt took the oath of office, in March 1933, the USA faced a crisis it had not seen since the Civil War.

---

1. In what ways did American society and the economy change between 1919 and 1933?

2. To what extent was the USA 'a land of intolerance' during the 1920s?

The system of federal government, 1919–1959

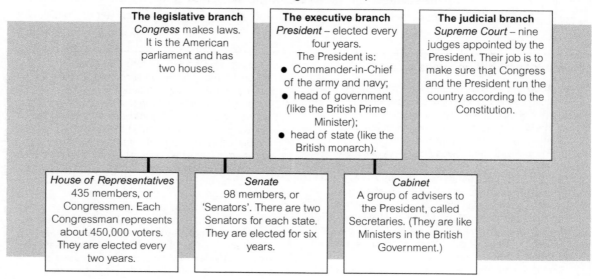

The legislative branch
Congress makes laws. It is the American parliament and has two houses.

The executive branch
President – elected every four years.
The President is:
- Commander-in-Chief of the army and navy;
- head of government (like the British Prime Minister);
- head of state (like the British monarch).

The judicial branch
Supreme Court – nine judges appointed by the President. Their job is to make sure that Congress and the President run the country according to the Constitution.

House of Representatives
435 members, or Congressmen. Each Congressman represents about 450,000 voters. They are elected every two years.

Senate
98 members, or 'Senators'. There are two Senators for each state. They are elected for six years.

Cabinet
A group of advisers to the President, called Secretaries. (They are like Ministers in the British Government.)

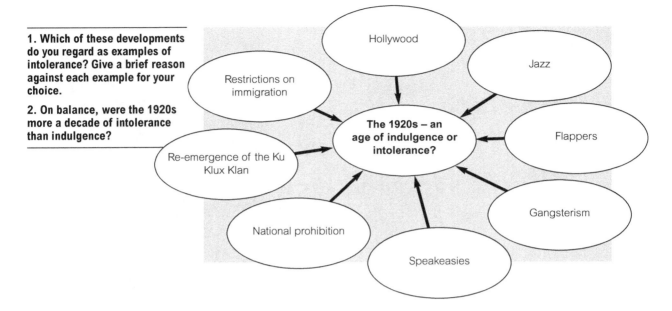

1. Which of these developments do you regard as examples of intolerance? Give a brief reason against each example for your choice.

2. On balance, were the 1920s more a decade of intolerance than indulgence?

2.1 Why was immigration restricted in the USA between 1919 and 1924?

The United States of America had long followed the policy of 'the Open Door' on immigration. Throughout the 19th and early 20th centuries, millions had emigrated from Europe. On the Statue of Liberty, in New York harbour, Emma Lazarus's words proclaimed:

'Give me your tired, your poor
Your huddled masses yearning to breath free.'

Even at the height of immigration, in the late 19th century, the 'foreign born' only constituted 15 per cent of the US population.

Although the USA had welcomed immigrants from across Europe, there had always been native opposition to the 'foreign born'. In the 1850s, the 'Know Nothing' Party opposed Irish Catholic immigration. In 1882, four years before the Statue of Liberty was unveiled, the Chinese Exclusion Act was passed. In 1907, Congress set up the Dillingham Commission into immigration. It recommended literacy tests for non-English-speaking immigrants.

However, it was the First World War that resulted in the calls for a restriction on immigration reaching national prominence. There were fears over the loyalty of new immigrants, particularly those from the Central Powers (Germany and Austria-Hungary). As part of the officer selection process, the US Army introduced Stanford–Binet tests. These discriminated against non-English speakers. But they reinforced growing hostility to central and eastern Europeans. In 1917, Congress overrode President Wilson's veto to pass the Immigration Act. This Act excluded immigrants who could not read or write English.

By the end of the First World War, opposition to immigrants was reinforced by the creation of a communist state in Russia. Many Americans feared the spread of socialist and communists ideas to the USA. This was seen by the outbreak of bitter industrial disputes during the economic recession of 1920–1922. The Red Scare of 1919 and the Palmer Raids of January 1920 confirmed the belief that the USA was under threat from new immigrants, bringing with them dangerous and un-American political ideas.

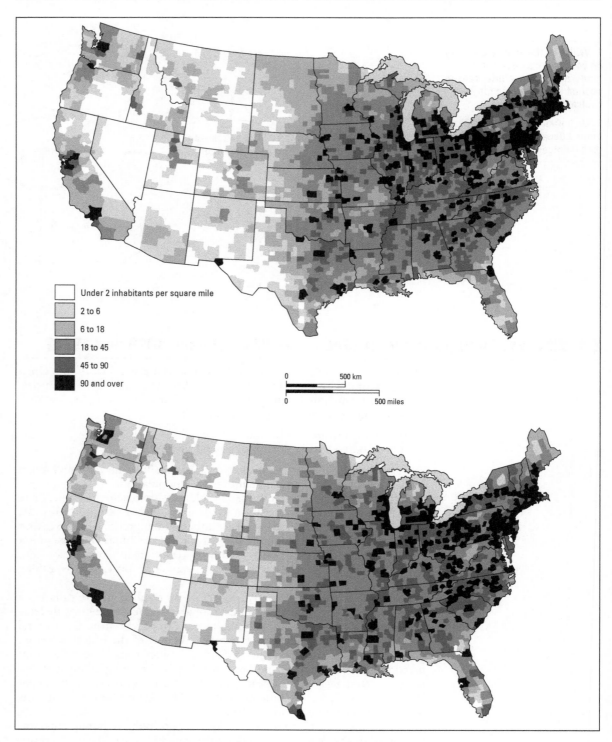

Population density of USA in 1920 (top) and 1930.

Sacco and Vanzetti arriving at court on 19 April 1927.

Anarchists: People who do not believe in any ruling power; they set out to upset settled power.

From 1920 to 1927, fears of new immigrants and left-wing ideas centred on the Sacco and Vanzetti trial in Massachusetts. These two Italian-Americans were **anarchists**. They had also avoided conscription into the armed forces. Nicola Sacco and Bartolomeo Vanzetti were accused of the murder of a postmaster. The trial divided the American nation because the judge showed considerable prejudice against the two defendants. Supporters of Sacco and Vanzetti believed they were scapegoats. However, evidence now suggests that Nicola Sacco was guilty. Opponents believed Sacco and Vanzetti epitomised all that was wrong with the new immigrants.

In 1921, Congress passed the Emergency Immigration Act. For the first time, a limit was placed on immigration. This restricted new European immigration to 3 per cent of the total number of that particular origin already living in the USA, as shown in the 1910 census. This greatly favoured emigrants from the British Isles and western Europe.

Quotas: Limitations on numbers of immigrants officially allowed entry into a country during a given period. It can also refer to quantities of goods or services imported into a country.

Restrictions on immigration were made permanent in 1924 with the Johnson–Reed Immigration Act. This set new **quotas** of 2 per cent, based on the 1890 census. The effect was to close the USA to emigration from eastern Europe because there had been little immigration from those parts in 1890. However, it did not apply to Hispanic Americans from Mexico who were an important labour source for Californian farmers. By 1929, Congress laid down that only 120,000 immigrants could enter per year based on 'the national origins of the American people of 1920'.

In signing the 1929 law President Coolidge claimed that, 'America must be kept American'. By this he meant WASP America. The restrictions on immigration confirmed White Protestants as the top social and political group. The defeat of Catholic Alfred Smith in the 1928 presidential election confirmed this position.

The impact of the loss of immigration was varied. It removed competition for jobs from would-be immigrants, in particular during the economic recession of 1920–1922, but more importantly during the great economic depression from 1929. On the other hand, it had a limiting effect. In 1972 the Nobel Prize Winner for Literature, Saul Bellow, gave a lecture in Chicago Public Library on 'The City in Historic and Philosophical Context'. He noted:

'Diversity made immigrant Chicago vivid 50 years ago. The immigration laws of the 1920s stopped the flow of labourers, shopkeepers, confectioners, upholsters, cabinet makers, cooks and waffle wagon

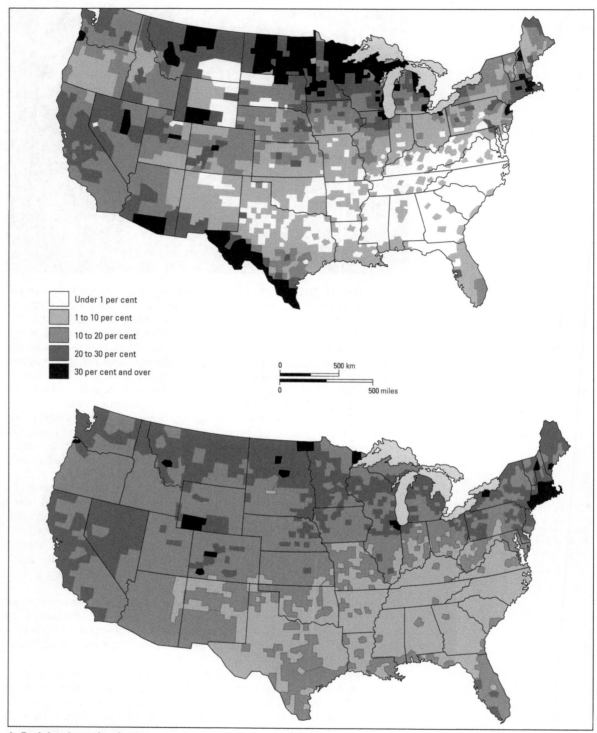

Under 1 per cent

1 to 10 per cent

10 to 20 per cent

20 to 30 per cent

30 per cent and over

0   500 km

0   500 miles

1. Explain why so few foreign-born numbers of white population lived in the South East USA.

2. Explain why the foreign-born population declined between 1900 and 1930.

Percentage of foreign-born people in the USA, 1900 (top) and 1930.

drivers who once filled the streets of Chicago. As time has deprived the city of its culture, so has it stolen its individuality.'

It was only with the relaxation of immigration laws, in the 1960s, that this racial and ethnic diversity began to return to the big cities of the USA.

1. What do you regard as the most important reason for the introduction of restrictions on immigration? Explain your answer.

2. To what extent had the United States been a land open to immigration from around the world?

The Harding Administration, 1921–1923: leading posts	
President:	Warren Harding
Vice President:	Calvin Coolidge
Secretary of Treasury:	Andrew Mellon
Secretary of Interior:	Albert Fall until 1923, then Hubert Work
Secretary of Agriculture:	Henry C. Wallace
Secretary of Commerce:	Herbert Hoover
Secretary of Labor:	James Davis

2.2 What impact did national prohibition have on the USA between 1920 and 1933?

Prohibition poster

The Eighteenth Amendment of the Constitution declared illegal the manufacture, sale and consumption of intoxicating liquor. The definition of what constituted 'intoxicating liquor' was made by the Volstead Act of 1920. This defined 'intoxicating drinks' as those containing at least 0.5 per cent alcohol. This prohibited beers, wines and spirits.

Known as 'The Noble Experiment', national prohibition proved to be a failure. In 1933, Franklin D. Roosevelt proposed a new amendment of the Constitution, the Twenty-First, which reversed the Eighteenth Amendment. Since then, prohibition has been a state, not a federal, matter.

The campaign for national prohibition was long, and involved a variety of pressure groups. The Women's Christian Temperance Union (WCTU) supported prohibition because intoxicating drink was seen as a threat to family life. Men would waste money on drink and/or engage in wife or child abuse as a result of drunkenness. Drink was seen as responsible for many crimes and acts of violence. In the 1870s, the WCTU was able, through their agitation, to force Kansas to become the first state to introduce prohibition.

The WCTU campaign was later supported by the Anti-Saloon League in the 1890s. Under the effective leadership of Wayne Wheeler, this pressure group supported pro-prohibition political candidates. By the outbreak of the First World War, many mid-western and western states had become 'dry'.

The First World War provided the basis for the proposal of the Eighteenth Amendment. How could the war effort be effective if people were allowed to drink? Why should valuable grain be used for alcohol at a time of war? These economic arguments were added to the moral and religious arguments which had been put forward since the 1870s.

Inside a speakeasy (illegal drinking establishment).

Warren G. Harding (1865–1923)
29th President of the USA (1921–23), a Republican. According to historian Patrick Renshaw, 'Every ten years American historians place past presidents in rank order. Harding always fills last place.' During his Presidency, the Administration was involved in a number of major corruption scandals. The most notorious was the sale of federal oil reserves at Elk Hills and Teapot Dome. However, during Harding's Administration the federal government was reorganised with the creation of the Office of the Budget. This enabled the President to produce the annual budget more effectively. This was an important development in increasing the power of the President.

'**Booze**': A slang word for alcoholic drink.

Prohibition was patriotic in another way. Most of the big brewers were of German origin: Budweiser, Pabst, Schlitz. Also, drink was closely associated with immigrant groups which WASP, small-town America disliked: Catholic Irish, Germans and East Europeans. In 1918, it took only three days' debate to pass the Eighteenth Amendment through Congress. Like restrictions on immigration, it represented another triumph for 'nativist' Americans against new immigrants.

Of all the laws passed in the USA, national prohibition was the most widely ignored. President Harding had alcoholic drinks delivered to the White House. Across the country, thousands of illegal drinking places (speakeasies) appeared. By the late 1920s, women who had been so prominent in supporting prohibition now began to campaign for its repeal. The Association against the Prohibition Amendment claimed that national prohibition encouraged crime and undermined the morals of America. It was supported by the Dupont family, who were prominent chemicals manufacturers.

National prohibition also had the effect of splitting the Democratic Party between 'wets' and 'drys': the 'dry' Democrats came from the rural areas of the South and West; the 'wets' represented the immigrant communities of the urban North and East. Divisive debates on prohibition affected the Democratic National Conventions of 1924 and 1928. In the latter, a north-eastern urban 'wet', Alfred Smith, was chosen as presidential candidate.

Prohibition failed on a national scale for a wide variety of reasons. One was the continued availability of alcoholic drink. '**Booze**' was still available in Canada and Mexico. With thousands of miles of land borders, it would have taken a considerable number of men to enforce compliance. At its height, the Treasury Department had about 3,000 prohibition agents to

Distilleries: Places where whisky and similar strong alcoholic drink is made by a process of distilling.

enforce prohibition nationwide. These agents were paid, on average, $2,500 a year. They could be easily bribed by those involved in the billion-dollar 'bootlegging' industry.

In addition to limited enforcement, the availability of industrial alcohol and the existence of illegal **distilleries** all over the country meant that the USA was still able to produce its own supplies without imports. Chicago proved the ideal centre for the distribution of 'booze'. It was near Canada and at the centre of a nationwide network of roads and railroads (railways).

What made national prohibition virtually unworkable was the involvement of organised crime. Such criminals had existed in the USA before national prohibition. They were heavily involved in prostitution and gambling. However, the manufacture and sale of 'booze' proved to be highly profitable. To ensure lack of interference of federal and state authorities, gangsters bribed and intimidated officials. The most celebrated gangsters were based in Chicago. The most effective were Italian-Americans, notably Al Capone. In the St Valentine's Day (14 February) Massacre of 1929, Capone removed his main rivals in Chicago. These were Irish and Jewish Americans associated with the gangster Dion O'Banion. Even when Capone was finally arrested and imprisoned in Alcatraz Jail, in San Francisco Bay, he was convicted for tax evasion, not murder or **bootlegging**. The Treasury Agent mainly responsible for Capone's capture, Elliott Ness, was an alcoholic!

Bootlegging: Engaging in the illegal manufacture and sale of alcoholic drink.

President Hoover established the Wickersham Commission to investigate prohibition. Although it favoured the continuation of prohibition, it also claimed it was impossible to enforce.

When Franklin Roosevelt became President, in March 1933, one of his first acts was to get Congress to pass the Beer Act. This amended the definition of intoxicating liquor made in the Volstead Act. It allowed the production of beer, which created jobs. To many Americans, FDR's campaign song, 'Happy days are here again', welcomed the return of 'booze.'

National prohibition had failed partly because the federal government had underestimated the money and personnel required for its effective enforcement. It also failed because it attempted to force one moral view of society on all Americans. To many immigrant groups, such as the Irish, Germans and Italians, drink was an essential part of their culture – which they were reluctant to give up.

1. Explain why national prohibition was introduced.

2. How far was the involvement of organised crime responsible for the failure of national prohibition?

On the negative side, the failure of the 'Noble Experiment' reduced respect for law and encouraged the involvement of organised crime in politics. On the positive side, it did alter American drinking habits. While it was in force, national prohibition proved a boon for the sales of firearms, motorboats and fast cars – and produced a lot of work for undertakers!

Alphonse Capone (1899–1947)

Most celebrated gangster of the 1920s, known as 'Scarface'. Rose to prominence as assistant to Johnny Torrio's Chicago gang in the early 1920s. In November 1924, Capone eliminated a major rival Dion O'Banion. This began a gang war in Chicago, which lasted until the St Valentine's Day Massacre of 1929 when Capone had seven of O'Banion's men gunned down in a garage. In 1927, Capone's 'business empire' was worth an estimated $27 million – coming from bootlegging, prostitution and gambling. Based in Cicero Park, Chicago, Capone controlled local politicians including the Mayor of Chicago, Big Bill Thompson. He was finally arrested and imprisoned in 1931 for tax evasion. During the trial he tried to bribe the jury but was eventually found guilty and served 11 years in jail. After his release in 1939, Capone suffered a long period of ill health, allegedly brought on by syphilis (a sexually transmitted disease).

2.3 Why did the Ku Klux Klan at first revive and then decline rapidly in the 1920s?

The strongest example of WASP intolerance in their attempts to maintain their dominance in US society was the reappearance of the Ku Klux Klan (KKK). Originally, the organisation aimed to protect white Southerners during the years of Reconstruction after the Civil War. Along with other white supremacist groups, such as the Knights of the White Camelia, the KKK terrorised the African-American community in the former Confederate states. However, following the establishment of white supremacist state governments in the Old South, the KKK had declined.

It reappeared, in 1915, as a result of the work of William J. Simmons, a former Methodist preacher. Two important influences resulted in the reformation of the KKK: the book *The Clansman* by Thomas Dixon and the film 'Birth of a Nation' directed by D.W. Griffith. Both of these works portrayed the KKK as an heroic organisation defending WASP America against forces which were trying to destroy it. In the 1860s and 1870s, these forces were African-Americans, carpetbaggers and scallywags who were exploiting the Old South. From 1915, Simmons and the new KKK added Catholics, Jews, bootleggers and atheists.

Apart from the example offered by *The Clansman* and 'Birth of a Nation', the KKK grew rapidly for a variety of reasons. Firstly, the First World War led to a rise in patriotism and opposition to 'alien influences' associated with non-Anglo-Saxon immigrants. It was also aided by the fear in many southern communities of the return of African-American servicemen who had fought in France. The 'Red Summer' of 1919 saw major race riots across America. In East St Louis, returning African-American servicemen were singled out for **lynching**.

Lynching: What happens when an angry crowd of people kills someone by hanging them without a trial, because they believe that the person has committed a crime.

Fundamentalism: The belief of religious groups that events described in the Bible or other sacred texts are literally true and should not be questioned.

Attorney General: The chief law officer who advises the government.

Impeach: To charge someone with committing a serious crime. Used especially in the USA when a senior official or politician is charged with a crime in connection with their job.

Although it was William J. Simmons who refounded the KKK, the two individuals most responsible for its rapid rise were Edgar Young Clark and Elizabeth Tyler. Using public relations techniques learned in raising funds for Liberty Bonds and the Red Cross during the War, Clark and Tyler appealed to Protestant **fundamentalism** and traditional moral values to 'sell' the Klan across America. With a $10 joining fee and an emphasis on robe wearing, cross burning and elaborate ceremonial, the Klan rose to a national membership of four million by the time of Elizabeth Tyler's death in 1924.

The Klan's rise also involved increased political influence. When the **Attorney General** of Maine, W. Pattangall, denounced the KKK at the 1924 Democratic National Convention he was defeated in the November elections of that year because of Klan opposition. The Klan also claimed it controlled the Governor of Colorado. It was able to **impeach** an anti-Klan Governor in Oklahoma. Klan members also became state assemblymen, sheriffs and judges. They even included a future US Supreme Court justice, Hugo Black of Alabama. By 1925 'Klaverns' of Klan members stretched across America to Oregon, Maine and Vermont, as well as to the Old South and the 'Bible Belt' of the Mid-West and West.

The rapid rise of the Klan was mirrored by its rapid decline. A major cause for decline was the actions of 'Indiana Grand Dragon', David Curtis Stephenson. In 1925, Stephenson was convicted of the rape and murder of a 28-year-old secretary. This severely damaged the claim that the Klan defended traditional moral values. The Klan was also affected by corruption and intimidation scandals in Pennsylvania.

The Klan's decline was also the result of the efforts of Imperial Wizard, Hiram Wesley Evans, to turn the organisation into a sort of social club. He even attempted to ban the wearing of masks in public.

1. Explain why the Ku Klux Klan grew rapidly between 1915 and 1924?

2. To what extent was the rapid rise and decline of the Ku Klux Klan due to the actions of individuals?

The combined effect of scandal and the efforts of Evans had reduced Klan numbers to 200,000 by 1929. However, its decline could also be attributed to the impact of the immigration restrictions imposed by Congress in 1919, 1924 and 1929. The Klan represented the sinister side of white supremacist views. The onset of economic depression also tended to lessen, rather than increase, tensions between different social and racial groups.

2.4 In what ways were the 1920s a period of cultural change?

Popular culture: Cultural pursuits followed by the majority of the population. Different from 'high culture', which is followed by a small number of intellectuals. Popular culture in the 1920s included reading comic books and newspapers, listening to radio and jazz, dancing the Charleston, and going to the cinema.

The 1920s were a decade of remarkable cultural change and creativity. In **popular culture** the decade was associated with the rapid growth of radio entertainment and, above all, the cinema. Hollywood became the world centre for film production. It was also the decade of mass spectator sport. Baseball and college football became national pastimes.

The changes in popular culture in America in the 1920s have been given various names. It is sometimes known as 'The Jazz Age'. This term reflects changes not only in popular music, but also in fashion and dance. The decade could also be known as the 'Age of the Flapper' to reflect the new social and cultural position of women. According to Gertrude Stein, a major literary figure of the decade, the artists and writers of the 1920s were 'The Lost Generation'. They had been disillusioned by the First World War and the 'botched' peace that ended it.

The leading literary figures of the decade included poet Ezra Pound and novelists Sinclair Lewis, F. Scott Fitzgerald and Ernest Hemingway. A leading critic of US society of the time was Baltimore journalist, H.L. Mencken.

Did the 1920s witness a 'sexual revolution' in the USA?

According to the authors of *The Enduring Vision* (1993): 'The most enduring twenties' stereotype is that of the flapper – the sophisticated, fashionable, pleasure-mad, young women.' The 'flapper' reflected important changes in the life of American women in the 1920s. New fashion and dance suggested a more carefree, pleasure-seeking lifestyle. No longer was the role of woman one of home making and child rearing. Many young women in the 1920s had the opportunity to follow an independent lifestyle, which was not dominated by the need to find a husband. Thousands of women were able to find employment as telephonists, typists, secretaries and clerks in the rapidly expanding American economy.

Quintessence: Most perfect version or example.

The individual who, at the time, symbolised these changes was the Hollywood film star Clara Bow, known as the 'It Girl'. The novelist Scott Fitzgerald called her 'the **quintessence** of what a "flapper" signifies: pretty, impudent, superbly assured, worldly-wise [and] briefly clad'. Amory Blaine, the hero of Fitzgerald's 1920 novel *The Other Side of Paradise*, 'saw girls doing things that even in his memory would have been impossible'. The decade did see the rise in the use of birth control to avoid unwanted pregnancies. It also saw the rapid growth of smoking among women.

Perhaps the most revealing development was the growth of women's cosmetics. Beauty salons appeared across America. The cosmetics industry increased its earnings during the decade from $17 million to $200 million per year. It helped to make Chanel, Helena Rubenstein and Elizabeth Arden household names in the USA. Previously, make-up had been associated with prostitutes. Now, women in America were taking control of their sexuality (i.e. using cosmetics, wearing shorter skirts and removing corsetry).

Two flappers dancing the Charleston on the roof of the Sherman Hotel, Chicago, 1926.

How useful is this illustration to a historian writing about US popular culture in the 1920s?

Like all stereotypes, the flapper reflected only one aspect of the life and role of women in American society in the 1920s. The prestigious women's college, Vassar, offered courses in 'Wife, Motherhood and the Family as an Economic Unit'. In many ways the decade was a period of unfulfilled expectation for many women. It had begun promisingly with the passage of the Nineteenth Amendment, giving women the vote. However, a distinctive 'women's' movement never really materialised. It is true that, in 1928, the League of Women Voters was able to proclaim that 145 women had won seats in 35 state legislatures and two had become governors, but these were the exceptions in the male-dominated world of politics.

Beginning in 1923 the National Woman's Party, led by Alice Paul and Rose Winslow, failed to get an Equal Rights Amendment accepted. They had wanted the Constitution to include an amendment stating that 'men and women shall have equal rights throughout the United States'. This campaign led to conflict with groups who had fought long and hard to protect women during the Progressive Era. If the Equal Rights Amendment (ERA) became law, labour laws restricting the number of hours and type of work open to women would be lost. The campaign from the political feminist movement did not reappear again until the late 1960s.

In what ways did popular music and dance change in the 1920s?

'The Jazz Age' of the 1920s saw the rise to national prominence, for the first time, of a type of music that came directly from African-American culture. It reflected one of the most important movements of population in the inter-war period, that of African-Americans from the Old South to the North. Chicago and the Cotton Club in Harlem, New York City, became centres for the development of jazz. It may have had its origins in the Deep South but jazz was an urban-based, northern brand of music.

New forms of popular music were accompanied by new forms of dance. Out went the waltz of the pre-war concert or dance hall. In came the 'Charleston', the 'Black Bottom' and the 'Turkey Trot'. These dances were associated with improvised steps and daring women's fashion, including dresses that only went down to the knee!

However, not all America flocked to these new music and dance crazes. Small-town and white working-class America in the South, Mid-West and West still clung to the 'hoe down' dance and country music, the forerunner of Country and Western music. The religious revival of the 1920s saw preachers, such as Billy Sunday and Aimee Semple McPherson, condemn the loose morals and sexual excesses of the decade, which were epitomised by these new musical and dance developments.

How important was mass spectator sport in American popular culture in the 1920s?

America in the 1920s is regarded as the world's first consumer society. With rising pay cheques and the development of radio and cinema, mass spectator sports benefited. The national game was baseball. However, in 1919, the national game was affected by scandal. The Chicago White Sox were accused of 'throwing' the World Series for money. Judge Kenesaw Mountain (he was named after the civil war battle in Georgia) Landis led an enquiry which banned most of the White Sox team. Professional base-ball in the 1920s was dominated by the New York Yankees and, in particular, Babe Ruth – the so-called 'Sultan of Swat'. Ruth held the professional baseball 'home run' record until overtaken, in the 1970s, by Hank Aaron.

Not all spectator sports were professional. College football was very popular. The 1920s saw the emergence of the Mid-Western Catholic team Notre Dame. Under coach Knut Rockne, 'the Fighting Irish' as they were called were unbeaten in 1924. Rockne revolutionised the game by inventing the forward pass.

Mass spectator sport and the radio came together most effectively in professional boxing. KDKA, the Pittsburgh, Pennsylvania radio station went on air to broadcast Jack Dempsey winning the world heavyweight boxing title in 1919. Throughout the decade, it continued to bring live commentary of matches to a wide American audience.

What impact did radio and cinema have on American society in the 1920s?

KDKA of Pittsburgh was America's first radio station. By the end of the decade, hundreds of radio stations had spread across the country. For the first time, small towns and remote rural areas were able to hear up-to-date news broadcasts, music, radio plays and comedy shows. These broadcasts were sponsored by private companies. This meant that the growth of radio was matched by the spread of advertising.

Of even greater significance was the development of cinema. By 1919 Hollywood, a suburb of Los Angeles, had become the major production centre for the world film industry. With silent films, the issue of language was unimportant. American stars dominated the 'silent screen'. Harold Lloyd, Buster Keaton and Charlie Chaplin provided comedy. The main 'action hero' was Douglas Fairbanks Snr. He married the leading female star of the period, Mary Pickford. Together they acted like cinema royalty such was their fame.

Every small town across America had its 'picture house'. Cinema became the main form of entertainment. Film gave even the remotest part of America glimpses of life in Ancient Rome, the Wild West, the First World War and of how the rich lived. Fashions that appeared in films were copied by film fans.

Perhaps the most influential film to come out of Hollywood in the silent era was D.W. Griffith's 'Birth of a Nation', in 1915. It dealt with the Civil War and Reconstruction period. Its heroic depiction of the Ku Klux Klan helped to increase racism in America and was an important factor in the re-emergence of the KKK.

In 1927, Hollywood faced major technological change with the development of 'talking pictures'. 'The Jazz Singer,' starring Al Jolson, was the first film that contained sound. This development made films even more popular. The establishment of the Academy Awards (Oscars), in 1928, gave Hollywood an annual showcase to prove its importance in American society and world cinema, which it has not lost since.

A huge billboard on the side of Warners' Theatre in New York advertises *The Jazz Singer* in 1927.

How important were the 1920s for the development of American literature?

The 'lost generation' of writers of the 1920s laid the foundation of modern American literature and provided an important insight into life in America. Sinclair Lewis from Minnesota wrote effectively about small-town, Mid-West America. In *Main Street* (1920), he wrote about the fictional small town 'Gopher Prairie', which he described as smug and culturally barren. He added to his view of America in 1922 with *Babbit* which took a critical look at middle-class life. In Oxford, Mississippi, William Faulkner wrote about life in a fictitious Mississippi County Yoknapatowpa from the Civil War to 1902.

The two most significant writers, however, were F. Scott Fitzgerald and Ernest Hemingway. Their writing epitomised the feeling of disillusionment with 1920s society. Fitzgerald's greatest novel, *The Great Gatsby* (1925), dealt with the material excesses associated with the economic boom. Hemingway, who was an exile for much of the period, wrote about those who had been affected by their experience of world war. *The Sun Also Rises* (1926) and *A Farewell to Arms* (1929) both deal with people damaged physically and mentally by war.

An important feature of literary development was the African-American cultural renaissance, centred on Harlem, New York City. This took many art forms. In 1921, an all African-American Broadway musical was produced, 'Shuffle Along'. In literature, Langston Hughes produced *The Weary Blues* in 1926, which explained the black experience. Finally, the National Association for the Advancement of Colored People used its periodical 'The Crisis' to publicise the works of young African-American poets and writers.

In spite of these cultural developments, African-Americans still faced discrimination across America in jobs, housing and education. The Harlem cultural renaissance must be placed against the re-emergence of the Ku Klux Klan to provide a broader perspective of society in the 1920s.

1. How important were the 1920s for the development of music, dance, sport and literature?

2. With what success did women improve their position within American society in the 1920s?

3. Why was the development of radio and the cinema so important to most Americans?

4. What do you regard as the most important cultural development in the 1920s? Give reasons for your answer.

2.5 How far did the United States experience an economic boom in the 1920s?

The Declaration of Independence, in 1776, had declared that the new state should aim to enable 'life, liberty and the pursuit of happiness'. The 1920s seemed to be the decade when this aim had been achieved, at least in an economic sense.

The 1920s were seen as a decade of unrivalled prosperity. However, the period did begin with an economic recession, from 1920 to 1922. The economic boom the USA had experienced during the First World War came to an abrupt end. The Government cancelled contracts once the war had ended. Bankruptcies and unemployment rose.

For the rest of the decade, the performance of the US economy was impressive. The **gross national product (GNP)** rose from $73.3 billion in 1920, to $104.4 billion in 1929 (in 1929 prices). This reflected an average growth rate of around 2 per cent per year. Unemployment never rose above 3.7 per cent. Compare this with the average of 6.1 per cent between 1911 and 1917. Inflation never rose above 1 per cent. The average working week in industry fell from 47.4 hours in 1920 to 44.2 hours in 1929. Real wages rose by approximately 13 per cent between 1922 and 1929.

These economic statistics meant that the purchasing power of Americans rose steadily. For instance, in 1922, some 100,000 radios were produced. In 1929, this had increased to 350,000 per year. The major US

Gross national product (GNP): This is a way of measuring the wealth of a country and is the total amount of production by US firms and businesses whether in America or abroad.

corporations saw profits increase by 62 per cent between 1923 and 1929. The industry that epitomised the 1920s boom was the motor car industry. General Motors saw its earnings rise from $173 million at the start of the decade to $1.5 billion by 1929. The 1920 census highlighted the social changes that fuelled the economic boom. For the first time in American history more people lived in towns than in the countryside.

What were the reasons for the economic boom of the 1920s?

(a) Size and economic wealth of the USA

In the 1920 census the population of the USA had reached 106.4 million. This compares with 42 million in Britain in 1921. Not only was the population large, it also had considerable purchasing power. Unlike in Britain, US manufacturers had a large domestic market in which to sell their goods.

The United States also had a very effective internal transportation system. Since 1869, transcontinental railroads united the country. These were supplemented by the development of a road system in the early 20th century. Roads allowed the newly invented car to provide communication in areas between the railroads.

To fuel economic growth, the USA possessed an abundance of raw materials. These provided the basis for the industrial revolution that the USA experienced from the 1850s. There were extensive coalfields in Kentucky, West Virginia and Pennsylvania. The country had large reserves of oil in Texas, Oklahoma and Pennsylvania. Iron ore, lead, tin, copper and other important metals were found across the West. **Lumber** came from the large coniferous forests of the Pacific North-West. The South provided cotton and the Mid-West and West an abundance of farm produce.

Lumber: North American term for timber sawn into rough planks or otherwise roughly prepared for the market.

(b) The entrepreneurial spirit and the American Dream

Thomas Edison, the American inventor, once said that genius is 1 per cent inspiration and 99 per cent perspiration. America had a gift for both of these. 'Yankee ingenuity' had resulted in the invention of the electric light bulb, the sewing machine, phonograph and telephone. Coupled with this was the 'work ethic' of the USA – 'rugged individualism', which encouraged hard work and thrift. Long before the 1920s, the USA had developed a strong business class and a powerful industrial **infrastructure**. Self-made millionaires such as Andrew Carnegie and John D. Rockefeller epitomised the 'American Dream'. If you worked hard enough, you could be prosperous. This idea led millions to cross the Atlantic in search of wealth. The immigrant population provided hard-working and cheap labour which made industrialisation such a success.

Infrastructure: The basic structure on which a country, society or organisation is built, such as the facilities, services and equipment which are needed for it to function properly.

(c) The impact of the First World War

In 1914, the USA had become one of the world's major industrial powers. It rivalled Britain and Germany. Fortunately for the USA, its major economic rivals virtually bankrupted themselves fighting the First World War. By 1918, Britain had lost almost one million dead and over two million wounded. It owed the USA millions in inter-allied war loans. Germany had fared even worse. It lost over two and half million dead. After the war, it faced a bill of £6.6 billion in **reparations** to the Allies. These problems led to the virtual collapse of the German economy by 1924.

Reparations: Payments made by a defeated state to compensate the victorious state(s) for damage or expenses caused by the war.

The USA benefited from the war in other ways. The demand for armaments stimulated the growth of American industry. By 1918, the United States emerged from the First World War as the world's major industrial power.

(d) Technological progress and 'Fordism'

According to Joshua Freeman in *Who Built America?* (published in 1992):

'Taken together, a series of new methods in manufacturing, labor relations, and consumer sales perfected during and after World War One constituted a virtual second industrial revolution.'

The centre for this 'second industrial revolution' was Detroit, Michigan. It was here that Henry Ford revolutionised car manufacture. Although cars had been produced in America since the 1890s, Ford introduced new industrial methods which led to their mass production. Firstly, he took the work to the man rather than taking the man to the work. An assembly line meant that unskilled and semi-skilled workers could learn how to assemble a specific part of a car quickly and easily. The assembly line, always working at the same pace, meant that the rate of production could be set.

Secondly, Ford concentrated production, until the mid-1920s, on one car type – the Model T. He stated that: 'The way to make automobiles is to make one automobile just like another, to make them come through the factory alike – just like one pin is like another pin.' As a result, Ford boasted that customers could have a Model T in any colour they liked as long as it was black!

Finally, Henry Ford introduced the $5-a-day rate for car workers. This was substantially above rates offered elsewhere. In return, workers were not expected to join trade unions and were expected to follow the company's strict policies on assembly line working. By 1926, Ford was producing a Model T car every 10 seconds.

The scale of car production at Fords was awesome. By the end of the First World War, Henry Ford had constructed the River Rouge plant in Detroit. This employed 75,000 workers. Ford benefited enormously from economies of scale. By 1927, 15 million Model T Fords had been produced.

By 1929, the motor manufacturing industry directly employed 7 per cent of all industrial workers and paid almost 9 per cent of industrial wages. Indirectly, motor car manufacture created thousands of jobs in the steel, rubber, paint, lumber and electrical industries.

As historian Donald McCoy noted in *Coming of Age* (1973):

'The rise of motor vehicle manufacturing contributed to the expansion of the petroleum industry, for the use of [petrol] shot up from less than 3 billion gallons in 1919 to 15 billion in 1929. Add to all this the development of tourism, roadside advertising and merchandising, garages, automobile dealerships and various other enterprises catering to motor traffic, and it is plain that within a decade the automobile industry and related businesses had become the most important and attractive element in the American economy.'

The federal government aided the development of the industry with the Federal Highways Act of 1921. This gave the Government responsibility for building roads. During the 1920s it built, on average, 10,000 miles of road per year (up to the Wall Street Crash). In the decade, surfaced roads grew from 350,000 miles in 1919 to 662,000 in 1929.

While motor manufacture and its related industries epitomised the decade, these new manufacturing techniques affected virtually all industries.

(e) New management and selling techniques

Alongside 'Fordism' came the development of business management. Frederick W. Taylor spread the idea of 'scientific management'. Taylor's idea was that all aspects of the manufacturing process should be analysed scientifically and that an efficient system should be adopted which would get the greatest level of productivity out of workers. These 'time and motion studies' became a feature of management as the decade progressed.

Economies of scale: The economic benefits of lower cost per unit of production that are made when large manufacturing companies are formed.

However, the most important development in manufacturing management was the growth and development of the large corporation. Large corporations were able to benefit from **economies of scale** and integration. Perhaps the clearest example of this development was the electricity supply industry. A key figure in this was Samuel Insull of Middle West Utilities, a holding company. Insull's corporation owned 111 subsidiary companies by the end of the decade, with an estimated value of $3 billion. Through his control of the market, Insull was able to provide cheap electricity to middle-class Americans.

By 1929, 16 holding companies controlled over 90 per cent of US electricity production. In that same year, the largest 200 corporations controlled 20 per cent of the nation's wealth and almost 40 per cent of its business wealth. These corporations were able to benefit from discount purchasing, and they engaged in research and development, which helped to produce cheaper and more efficient products. They could also staff their organisations with specialists.

The government encouraged corporate control of individual industries. Herbert Hoover, at the Department of Commerce, encouraged the growth of trade associations within an industry. The aim of a trade association was to allow firms to benefit from exchange of information, which would allow them to standardise manufacturing methods and take advantage of the latest technology. Although 2,000 trade associations already existed by 1920, hundreds more were created by 1929. Many criticised this development because trade associations acted like trusts.

Large corporations could also borrow money easily for the purposes of investment.

The 1920s was also the decade that saw the rapid growth of advertising and marketing. These were aided by the technological developments of the radio, the motor car and the cinema. New methods of high-pressure selling were pioneered by individuals such as Bruce Barton who claimed, in books such as *The Man Nobody Knew* (1926), that selling and Christianity were compatible. Barton claimed that Jesus 'would have been a national advertiser today'.

(f) Government policies

President Calvin Coolidge (1923–1929) once remarked that 'the business of the American people is business'. Throughout the 1920s the federal government, supported by Congress, helped to create the conditions for a business boom. The Republican Party, by the 1920s, was associated with **laissez-faire** economics.

Laissez-faire **economics**: The belief in free trade and that government interference should be kept to a minimum.

In fact, the Republican administrations of Harding and Coolidge, on occasion, went out of their way to aid business. In 1922, Congress passed the Fordney–McCumber Tariff Act. This placed import duties on a wide variety of goods including farm products, chemicals, textiles, chinaware and other industrial products. The Federal Trade Commission was given the power to advise the President on tariff increases up to 50 per cent. This had the effect of protecting American manufacturers against foreign competition.

Of more importance were the tax-cutting policies of Republican administrations. Secretary to the Treasury from 1921 to 1932 was Andrew Mellon who came from a rich banking family in Pittsburgh, Pennsylvania. In a series of revenue acts 1921–1926, he cut the tax on the rich (known as surtax) from above 50 per cent to 20 per cent. Mellon's favourable tax policy towards the rich and large corporations encouraged the development of business. In spite of tax cuts, the rapid growth in business meant that the Treasury had a surplus in the Budget for the 1920s.

Businesses also benefited from less regulation by the Federal Trade

Commission, and from State and Congressional support against trade unions. 'Yellow dog' contracts (no-strike agreements) were supported by the courts, which allowed greater management control over their work forces.

(g) Easy credit and hire purchase

New technological and management techniques allowed American manufacturers to produce more goods at a lower unit cost per item. However, an economic boom would not have taken place if there had been a lack of domestic demand to buy these goods.

Part of the answer was an increase in the average wage of Americans during the decade. Average wages rose from $1,308 to $1,716 per year in the USA in the 1920s. This was at a time of low inflation. There was also the development of hire purchase. This allowed consumers to buy goods at a small proportion of the price. They could then pay off the rest of the price, and a small rate of interest, in either weekly or monthly instalments. Encouraged by new methods of advertising, consumers bought a wide range of goods by this method – from cars to refrigerators. Between 1919 and 1929, the amount of consumer credit, outside agriculture, grew from $32 billion to $60 billion.

> **1. In what ways did new industrial and manufacturing methods help to create an economic boom in the 1920s?**
>
> **2. What do you regard as the most important reason for the economic boom of the 1920s?**
>
> **Give reasons for your answer.**

Americans plunged into debt in the 1920s in order to play the Stock Market and to buy new cars and other consumer products.

> **Do these figures suggest the US economy was facing an economic boom in the 1920s? Explain your answer.**

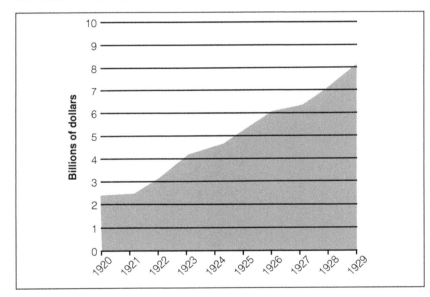

Which groups missed out on the prosperity of the 1920s?

Farmers

While the 1920s were a boom time for US industry, they were a period of decline for farmers. During the First World War, farmers had experienced a period of rising agricultural prices and increasing demand for their produce. Prices for farm goods rose 82 per cent between 1913 and 1917. In the same period, the number of farmers earning $2,000 per year rose from 140,000 to 1.8 million. However, by 1920, the fall in demand caused farm prices to drop. Those countries that had imported large amounts of US farm produce, such as Britain, had now begun to recover from war.

Also, the Fordney–McCumber Tariff Act of 1922 resulted in many foreign markets being closed off for US farm produce as countries began to raise duties from their own import duties on US imports. Even the introduction of national prohibition had an adverse effect on agriculture. Demand for grain from distillers and brewers simply disappeared from 1920.

President and Congress: the separation of powers

The United States Constitution created a series of 'checks and balances' between the Government (President) and the law-making institution (Congress).

When a President nominates someone to the Cabinet, he has to get approval from two-thirds of the Senate. This is part of the Senate's 'advice and consent' powers. This also includes appointments to the US Supreme Court and heads of agencies such as the Federal Trade Commission and Federal Bureau of Investigation (FBI).

The President also needs Congressional support if he is to implement laws. Congress can either delay proposals for laws, or amend them radically. The House of Representatives has considerable power over the granting of money and the raising of taxes for the federal government.

Therefore, it is possible for the President to face either a Senate or House, or both, who are opposed to his policies. As both Senate and House are elected separately from the President they may be from the opposing party. For the Republican presidents of the 1920s, both houses of Congress had Republican majorities. President Nixon (1969–1974) and President Clinton (1993–2001) faced a Congress controlled by the opposing party.

Finally, US agriculture faced overproduction because of the onset of mechanisation. The use of tractors, combine harvesters and other modern farming machinery greatly increased output, further depressing prices.

In the 1920 census, for the first time, more Americans lived in towns than in the countryside. By 1929, a further 5 per cent drop occurred in those who earned their living from agriculture. Also, between 1920 and 1930, the number of farms in the USA declined. Around 13 million **acres** (5 million hectares) of cultivated land were abandoned.

Acres: An acre is a measure of the area of land 4,047 square metres (or 4,840 square yards). One hectare equals 2.47 acres.

The 1920s were not the first decade in which farmers faced a crisis. In the 1880s and 1890s, farmers organised into the Granger and Populist parties to make a strong defence of farming interests. In 1915, many farmers formed the Non-Partisan League to defend farming interests. However, this had very limited impact. Instead, the dominant farmer group during that decade was the moderate Farm Bureau.

Nevertheless, farmers did gain some assistance from the Department of Agriculture under Secretary Wallace. The Agricultural Credits Act of 1923 gave low-interest loans to farmers. The Capper–Volstead Act, also of 1923, encouraged the creation of farm cooperatives. However, the main attempt in the 1920s to aid farmers, failed. This was the McNary–Haugen Bill. Initially introduced into Congress in 1924, it was vetoed twice by President Coolidge, in 1925 and 1927, and never became law. The aim of the Bill had been to cut supply to domestic consumers but to maintain farm incomes. The government would buy excess farm produce and sell it abroad. Historical research by Gary Koerselman of Northern Illinois University in 1971 showed that these proposals would have benefited large-scale farmers. Indeed large-scale farmers, such as the fruit growers in Southern California, fared well in the 1920s. They used cheap Hispanic-American labour.

Trade unionists

While 'big business' prospered in the 1920s, trade unionism declined. Union membership had grown during the First World War, from 2.27 million in 1916 to 5.03 million in 1920. It then declined to 3.6 million during the 1920s.

The Red Scare of 1919 and the Palmer Raids of the 1920s led many workers to avoid joining unions. Another factor was 'the American Plan', whereby non-union members would receive the same benefits as union members if made redundant.

A more important reason was the action of 'big business', which was usually anti-union. Union membership was either discouraged or employees were forced to sign 'yellow dog' contracts in which employees agreed not to strike.

The Coolidge Administration, 1923–1929: leading posts

President:	Calvin Coolidge
Vice President:	Charles Dawes
Secretary of Treasury:	Andrew Mellon
Secretary of Interior:	Hubert Work until 1929, then Roy West
Secretary of Agriculture:	Henry C. Wallace until 1924, then Howard Gore to 1925, then W. Jardine
Secretary of Commerce:	Herbert Hoover until 1928, then William Whiting
Secretary of Labor:	James Davis

Sharecroppers: Farmworkers who work for a share of the crops they grow, instead of a wage.

Segregation: The practice of keeping apart people of different racial or religious groups, or of different sexes.

1. For what reasons did different social and economic groups miss out on the economic prosperity of the 1920s?

2. 'The 1920s were a decade of economic prosperity for the mass of the American people.'

Explain why you agree or disagree with this statement.

Big business was supported by both the government and the judiciary. Attorney General Daugherty broke the 1922 railroad strike by getting a federal judge to declare union action illegal. Also, between 1922 and 1925, the US Supreme Court passed several anti-union judgements making it difficult both for unions to strike and for the creation of a minimum wage.

Trade unions did not help themselves. The American Federation of Labor (AFL) was interested only in skilled labour. It made no attempt to unionise the semi-skilled and unskilled workers.

African-Americans

During the decade, most African-Americans continued to live in the Old South. There they led a poverty-stricken existence, mainly as **sharecroppers**. They occupied the lowest economic position in a relatively poor region of the USA. The existence of **segregation** and, as a result, poor education reinforced the poor social and economic position of African-Americans.

However, during the decade approximately 850,000 African-Americans migrated North to cities such as Chicago and New York. By 1930, African-Americans were beginning to occupy industrial and manufacturing jobs. Even in the North they tended to get the worst-paid jobs. This was due to a mixture of racism and the poor education received by the majority of African-Americans, which was an aspect of the former.

2.6 Why, and how, did economic depression affect the United States from 1929?

Did the Wall Street Crash of October 1929 cause the Depression?

The economic depression, which first hit the United States and then the world, began with the collapse of share prices on the New York Stock Exchange in October 1929. The Bank of England raised British interest rates to 6.5 per cent in order to attract capital from the United States. As a result, many European investments were up for sale on the New York Stock Exchange. This resulted in a fall in the value of shares, which created an atmosphere of uncertainty among shareholders who began to sell their stocks. On Thursday 24 October 1929 (known as Black Thursday), 12.8 million shares changed hands. By the end of that day, overall share values had fallen by $4 billion.

On the following Tuesday, 29 October (Black Tuesday), a record 16 million shares changed hands at very low prices. By the end of November 1929, $30 billion had been wiped off the value of shares.

	3 March 1928	3 September 1929	13 November 1929
American Can	77 ¢	182 ¢	86 ¢
Anaconda Copper	54 ¢	162 ¢	70 ¢
Electric Bond and Share	90 ¢	204 ¢	50 ¢
General Electric	129 ¢	396 ¢	168 ¢
General Motors	140 ¢	182 ¢	36 ¢
New York Central	160 ¢	256 ¢	160 ¢
Radio	94 ¢	505 ¢	28 ¢
United States Steel	138 ¢	279 ¢	150 ¢
Westinghouse E & M	92 ¢	313 ¢	102 ¢
Woolworth	181 ¢	251 ¢	52 ¢

The prices of shares in ten US companies

Speculation: The purchase of land or shares in order to make a quick profit. A person who engages in share speculation is a stag.

Bull Market: A bull market occurs when share prices in a stock market are rising. A bear market occurs when share prices are falling.

The share collapse caused panic. On the trading floor of the Stock Exchange, fist fights broke out. Prices were so low that a messenger boy bid $1 for a share in the White Sewing Machine Company and, as a result, became a major shareholder! The President of the Union Cigar Company committed suicide by leaping to his death off the Beverly Hotel in Manhattan, New York.

According to the historian Michael E. Parrish, in *The Anxious Decades* (1994), 'The collapse of the stock market did not "cause" the terrible economic depression that followed.' Nevertheless, **speculation** in shares and land did contribute to US economic instability in the 1920s.

In 1925–26, a preview of the problems associated with share speculation had been apparent in land dealings in Florida. With promises of large financial returns on investment, thousands bought land and property in the 'Sunshine State'. One woman who bought Florida land for $25 in 1900 sold it for $150,000 in 1925. Areas such as Coral Cables and Biscayne Bay, near Miami, became some of the most sought after properties in the USA. The most notorious example of spurious land advertising was for plots of land near the prosperous town of Nettie, which had never existed.

The Florida Land Boom collapsed by 1926 for several reasons. Swindlers, such as Charles Ponzi, conned potential purchasers out of their money. Builders failed to meet construction deadlines. The lack of railroads impeded development. In 1925, the Internal Revenue Service began taxing profits made on property speculation. Finally, a severe hurricane on 18 September 1926 caused devastation in south Florida.

Speculation in land was replicated in share speculation. The 'Great **Bull Market**' on the New York Stock Exchange saw the number of shares listed rise from 500,000 in 1925 to 1,127,000 by October 1929. Using easy credit facilities offered by banks, thousands bought shares 'at the margin'. They offered to pay 10 per cent of the share value as a down payment. These would be paid off when profits were made from the sale of these shares at a later date. This system worked well when share prices continued to rise, but it collapsed dramatically when share prices fell. By October 1929, share prices had leaped ahead of the real business values. Sooner or later, an adjustment was bound to take place. On 5 September 1929, business analyst Roger Babson stated:

'Sooner or later a crash is coming, and it may be terrific. Factories will shut down, men will be thrown out of work, the vicious circle will get in full swing and the result will be a serious business depression.'

However, as historian Donald McCoy notes in *Coming of Age* (1973):

'The stock-market crash did play an important role, but its larger significance was as a trigger and as a dramatic symptom of deeper and more complicated national and international causes of the depression.'

Stock markets are inherently unstable. Even during the 1920s, the price of shares occasionally dropped, although there was an upward trend across the decade. In both the late 1980s and late 1990s, the New York Stock Exchange witnessed large falls in the value of shares. But, on both occasions, no economic depression followed.

The causes of depression must therefore be found elsewhere.

Underconsumption and overproduction

According to the historian Joshua Freeman, in *Who Built America?* (1992), underconsumption was the major cause of the depression. Throughout the 1920s, businesses had benefited from Treasury Secretary Andrew Mellon's low tax policies. Part of the result of this was that the bottom 40 per cent of the population received only 12.5 per cent of the nation's wealth. In contrast, the top 5 per cent owned 33 per cent of the nation's wealth.

This maldistribution of wealth had unfortunate consequences. Domestic demand for goods never kept pace with production. The problem of underconsumption was masked by the growth of easy credit and hire purchase. By 1929, it was becoming clear that mass consumption in the USA had reached a point where consumers were reluctant to take on more credit to sustain demand. Overseas demand was affected by the high tariff policies operated by many states in response to the Fordney–McCumber Tariff Act of 1922.

International economic problems

According to President Herbert Hoover (1929–1933), America's economic problems after 1929 could be traced to international, rather than domestic, causes. The world economy of the 1920s faced severe economic problems as a result of the First World War and the peace treaties which followed it. Allied powers, such as Britain, France and Belgium, owed the USA millions of dollars in inter-allied war loans. Germany, as a result of the Treaty of Versailles, had to pay the Allies £66 billion in war reparations. These financial burdens created economic instability. To raise money all European states, except Britain, placed tariffs on imported goods. They also raised taxes. These had the effect of cutting demand, especially demand for US goods. Therefore, the US economy could not expand its foreign markets as rapidly as it could increase its production. Manufacturing output increased 50 per cent in the USA, between 1920 and 1929, but exports rose only 38 per cent in the same period.

In addition, political unrest helped to destabilise other parts of the world. Political unrest was **endemic** in China. The establishment of communism in Russia excluded a large overseas market. In South America, Paraguay and Bolivia fought the Chaco War.

Government policy

The economist J.K. Galbraith is critical of the economic policies of Republican Administrations in contributing to the Depression. In the 1920s, there had been too little regulation of business by the Government. Wartime controls had ended as soon as the Wilson Administration had left office. Low taxes made the maldistribution of wealth greater. Also, failure to aid farming helped to perpetrate the depression in agriculture, which lasted the whole decade. Low capital gains tax encouraged share speculation, which resulted in the Stock Market crash.

To encourage business, stock exchanges such as Wall Street requested little investigation into firms who had placed their shares for sale. In hindsight, it is easy to criticise Republican governments for their *laissez-faire* economic philosophy. However, it was an economic policy followed by most western, capitalist economies when not faced by war.

Collapse of stock market prices on New York Stock Exchange and other stock exchanges across the USA.

Loss of savings, the collapse of banks and loss of business confidence results in closure of factories leading to sharp rise in unemployment.

Fall in domestic demand. Exports hit by high foreign tariffs and the spread of economic depression world wide as fall in US stock markets leads to fall in stock markets across the world. The withdrawal of US investment from Germany causes very severe economic depression.

More factories closing. Banks close because of loss of loans as companies become bankrupt.

Endemic: Peculiar to a people or to a district.

The weakness of the US banking system

If the Government can be criticised it is over the regulation of banks. Only one-third of US banks were under the jurisdiction of the Federal Reserve Board, the USA's central bank. Even here the Federal Reserve's powers were limited to dealing with short-term loans. Instead, the USA had a banking system made up of hundreds of small, state-based banks. If a crop failure in one state led to the collapse of a bank, it could lead to a 'run' on other banks resulting in a banking collapse. Between 1921 and 1928, 5,000

How far do these statistics and graphs suggest that the Wall Street crash caused the Depression?

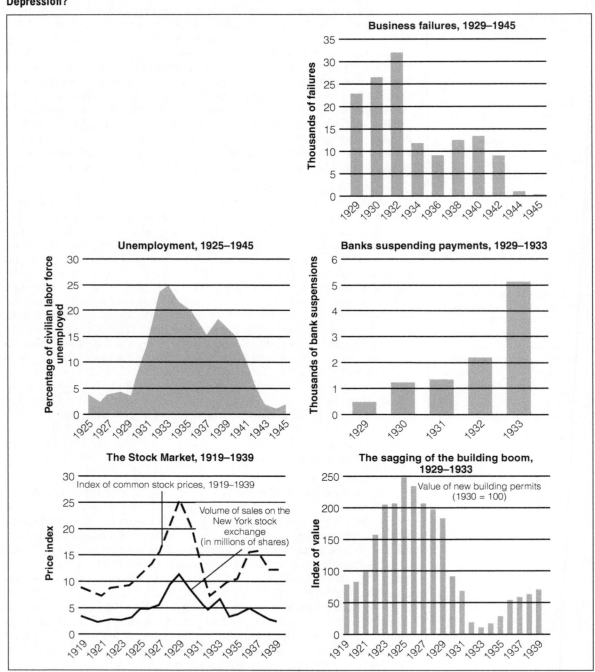

Graphs showing the statistics of hard times in the USA.

1. Explain the ways in which historians, economists and people at the time have disagreed over the main cause of the economic depression.

2. How important was the Wall Street Crash in causing economic depression from 1929?

How useful is this picture as evidence of economic conditions in the USA in the 1929–1933 period?

banks went out of business. In 1929 alone, 659 banks suspended operations.

The collapse of share prices had a devastating effect on banking. The resulting banking collapse led to the closure of thousands of businesses and farms. As historian Michael Parrish has noted:

'The stock market debacle [mess] dealt Americans both a financial and an emotional body blow … Within one year, GNP declined from $87.8 billion to $75.7 billion. The slide into economic chaos had begun, and the Great Crash had played something more than a minor role.'

How was the United States affected by economic depression from 1929 to 1933?

The most obvious effect on the lives of Americans was the sharp rise in unemployment. Before the Crash, unemployment had been rising in the coal and textile industries. On the eve of the Crash, unemployment had been 1.5 million. By March 1930, it rose to 3.25 million. By the time Franklin D. Roosevelt became President, in March 1933, the figure had risen to 13 million (24.9 per cent of the work force).

Unemployed men walking the road in search of jobs, mocked by the poster for train travel – California, 1938.

As economic activity collapsed, the gross national product fell from $103 billion in 1929 to $55 billion in 1933. Average weekly earnings fell, over the same period, from $25 to $17. Income from agriculture, forestry and fishing fell from $8.3 billion in 1929 to $3.3 billion in 1933. The number of banks operating fell from 25,500 in 1929 to 14,700 in 1933.

Taken together, the effects of these economic statistics were to plunge the United States into the biggest domestic crisis since the Civil War. As millions lost their jobs, thousands of men left home in search of work. Using railroads to travel, these hobos became a feature of American life in the depression. Farms were repossessed by banks. Soup kitchens, run by churches and charities, were to be found in every major town and city. Society was transformed from one based on confidence in the economic future into one based on disillusionment and despair.

The strain on society began to show. The suicide rate rose 14 per cent between 1929 and 1932. The number of marriages fell 10 per cent between 1929 and 1932, and with it the birth rate. Those who were affected particularly badly were children who suffered poor diet, clothing and education as the economic crisis worsened. Small-scale farmers, African-Americans and Hispanic-Americans suffered more than any other socio-economic group.

Faced with such a crisis, many Americans began to look for someone to blame.

Using the information above, draw a spidergram to illustrate how the USA was affected by economic depression between 1929 and 1933.

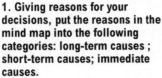

1. Giving reasons for your decisions, put the reasons in the mind map into the following categories: long-term causes ; short-term causes; immediate causes.

2. What do you regard as the most important long-term, short-term and immediate cause of the Depression? Give reasons for your answer.

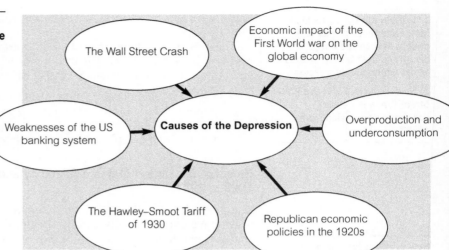

2.7 Herbert Hoover

A CASE STUDY IN HISTORICAL INTERPRETATION

The case against Herbert Hoover

Shanty towns: Areas where poor people live. The dwellings are small, rough huts built from tin, cardboard and other flimsy materials.

President Hoover has been a figure of ridicule for both people at the time and for historians since. The **shanty towns** of the homeless were called Hoovervilles. A newspaper covering a homeless person was referred to as a 'Hoover blanket'. The Broadway musical, and subsequent Hollywood film of the 1980s, 'Annie' was set in 1932. One of its more notable songs was 'We'd like to thank you, Herbert Hoover'. It is sung by homeless people in New York City. It ends with the verse:

> We'd like to thank you, Herbert Hoover
> For really showing us the way,
> You dirty rat, you bureaucrat,
> You made us what we are today.

To critics of Hoover, he always did too little too late. Historian Donald McCoy stated, in *Coming of Age*:

> 'What he [Hoover] and his administration did either was insufficient to combat the deep and long-extended economic crisis or came too late, and Congress did little to help. It is plain in retrospect that Hoover was too cautious.'

In dealing with the Depression, Hoover thought the main role of the federal government should be to coordinate private, state and local issues, rather than take direct action himself. Under the US Constitution, states, rather

Herbert Hoover (1874–1964) 31st President of the USA (1829–33), a Republican. Before the First World War he travelled widely as a mining engineer. After the War, he organised relief work in occupied Europe. Food Administrator for the	USA (1917–19), before becoming Secretary of Commerce (1921–28). Defeated Democrat Al Smith in 1929 presidential election. However, Hoover lost public confidence when he opposed direct government aid for the unemployed in the	Depression. Shanty towns, or Hoovervilles (see page 26), sprang up around large cities – evidence of Hoover's failure to cope with the effects of the Depression and to prevent the decline of the economy. F.D. Roosevelt succeeded him in 1933. Hoover was	later called upon to administer the European Food Programme (1947) and in the 1950s he headed two commissions into reforms in government structure and operations.

The Hoover Administration, 1929–1933: leading posts

President:	Herbert Hoover
Vice President:	Charles Curtis
Secretary of Treasury:	Andrew Mellon 1929–32, then Ogden Mills
Secretary of Interior:	Ray Wilbur
Secretary of Agriculture:	Arthur Hyle
Secretary of Commerce:	Robert Lamont until 1932, then Roy Chapin
Secretary of Labor:	James Davis until 1930, then William Doak

than the federal government, had responsibility for welfare. By the time of the Depression, only eight states had any kind of unemployment compensation. Instead the poor had to rely on the help of private charities. Support for 'voluntaryism' was a major feature of Hoover's early attempts at dealing with the depression. It coincided with his belief in 'rugged individualism' and the American tradition of independent action. Hoover argued that relief was a local responsibility; federal involvement would strike at the 'roots of self-government' and would destroy 'character'. Hoover did have some initial success in persuading business to help. Some companies froze wages to prevent further hardship, but this had limited success. By 1931, a major corporation, US Steel, introduced a 10 per cent wage cut.

In his reluctance to use the federal government directly in aiding the poor, Hoover was supported by important members of his Administration. Treasury Secretary, Andrew Mellon, declared that as a result of the depression 'people would work harder, live a more moral life' and, therefore was 'not altogether a bad thing'. It was up to individual, local politicians to take action. Elected in 1930, Mayor Frank Murphy of Detroit created food stations for 14,000 unemployed. In New York State, Governor Franklin Roosevelt successfully organised relief for the unemployed and poor, which gained him a national reputation.

Instead of looking for the causes of the depression within the United States, Hoover argued that international economic conditions were the root cause of problems. The breakdown in international trade and the economic crisis in Europe were more important than a lack of federal government involvement.

Hoover was president, though, when Congress passed the Hawley–Smoot tariff in June 1930, which raised import duties on the Fordney–McCumber tariffs on average by 30 per cent. Historian Michael Parrish claims that:

> 'as the stock market crash helped dry up the springs of international credit, the Hawley–Smoot tariff choked off international trade and compounded economic misery from Boise [Idaho] to Berlin, from San Diego [California] to Singapore.'

An episode which seemed to display the heartlessness of the Hoover Administration was the Bonus Army march of 1932. In May and June, First World War veterans marched on Washington DC demanding full payment of their veterans' bonus immediately, instead of having to wait until 1945 when it was due to be paid.

Following the Senate rejection of this demand, the Administration used the army, under General Douglas MacArthur, to remove the 21,000 remaining veterans and their families from a shanty town on Anacostia

Flats. Millions of Americans were horrified by the sight of tanks and cavalry, and by the use of tear gas, as troops destroyed the shanty town.

By November 1932, Hoover had become the most hated man in America. Hitch-hikers carried signs stating that if they did not receive a lift, they would vote for Hoover. Having won a landslide victory in 1928, Hoover was defeated by another landslide in November 1932. The American electorate of that year had given their verdict on Hoover's efforts.

The case for Herbert Hoover

According to British historian Hugh Brogan, in the second edition of *The Longman History of the United States of America* (1999):

> 'Hoover saw the peril [of the depression] and acted to avert it. During the rest of his Presidential term he was to act incessantly, doing more than any previous President had done in any previous economic crisis.'

Hoover's problem was that he faced an unprecedented economic situation. Depressions had occurred before, most notably in the 1890s and 1920–22. It was seen as a normal part of the business and trade cycle. Although we now know how deep this depression was to become, Hoover did not know this in 1929 and 1930.

Nevertheless, he did take action. In agriculture, even before the Wall Street Crash, he called a special session of Congress, in April 1929, to help farmers. The Agricultural Marketing Act established a nine-man Federal Farm Board with funds of $500 million to create farming cooperatives. In 1930, Hoover created the Grain Stabilisation Corporation, which bought surplus wheat from cooperatives as a way of stabilising grain prices. However, these attempts were destroyed by the world collapse in grain prices. By 1932, the Federal Farm Board had failed.

Moratorium: A legally authorised delay in the performance of a legal duty or obligation. From the Latin *mora* – delay.

To try to boost international trade, Hoover introduced a **moratorium** on inter-Allied war debts, in June 1931. This meant the USA would delay collecting debts for 18 months. Unfortunately, it came too late to save Europe from severe depression.

Hoover placed great hope in an international economic conference to be held in London in early 1933. However, F.D. Roosevelt (FDR) refused to cooperate with other countries, claiming that America's economic ills were caused by domestic rather than international problems.

Although an initial opponent of direct federal aid, Hoover did change his policy once he became aware that voluntaryism and cooperation were failing. The first significant departure in this direction was the creation of the Reconstruction Finance Corporation (RFC). This was approved by Congress, in January 1932. It had the power to lend up to $2 billion to rescue failing banks and insurance companies. Ninety per cent of loans went to small- and medium-sized banks. When he became president, FDR continued to use the RFC as part of his economic policy towards the depression.

Direct federal help for the unemployed came with the passage of the Emergency Relief and Construction Act on 21 July 1932. To receive aid, state governments had to declare that they had run out of money to help the unemployed. The corporation that was set up by the Act had the authority to lend up to $1.5 billion to states to fund public works for the unemployed.

In July 1932, Congress also passed the Federal Home Loans Act. Federal home loan banks were created to provide up to 50 per cent assistance for those persons who could not pay off their mortgages.

Taken together, these measures were as far as Hoover was willing to go to involve the federal government directly. They were introduced only after voluntaryism and state action had failed. They were also the result of consistent Congressional pressure from Senators such as Robert Wagner of

New York, Robert La Follette Jr from Wisconsin and Edward Costigan of Colorado.

Verdict?

Historian Martin L. Fausold, in *The Presidency of Herbert C. Hoover* (1985), claims:

> 'It has been said that the jury on the Hoover presidency is still out – that scholars who seek to assess American presidents react differently depending upon their sources of information, their times and their values.
> The jury consists of three important constituencies:
>
> ● Hoover's close associates at the close of his presidency
> ● the majority of Americans throughout the half century following his presidency
> ● historians at the half-century mark after his presidency.
>
> [They all] agree that the Hoover presidency was a failed one.'

Increasing numbers of historians, including this author, see Hoover's many qualities. It is regrettable that, as the 21st century begins, many of the nation's citizens continue to see in Herbert Hoover what he himself saw in his presidency: 'the dark side first'. Given the emphasis that is placed on the presidency in public affairs, it is improbable that this assessment will ever change.

1. Why do historians and people at the time have such varied views of the role of Herbert Hoover in the depression from 1929–1933?

2. How far do you agree with Martin L. Fausold's verdict of Hoover's presidency in dealing with the Depression?

Study the figures in the table.

(a) What trends in voting behaviour can be made from studying these figures?

(b) Why do you think some counties of Georgia voted against Democrat candidate Alfred Smith in the 1928 election?

Presidential elections, 1920–1932

		Popular vote	Electoral College vote
1920:	Warren Harding, Republican	16.1 million	404
	James Cox, Democrat	9.1 million	127
1924:	Calvin Coolidge, Republican	15.7 million	382
	John Davis, Democrat	8.3 million	136
1928:	Herbert Hoover, Republican	21.4 million	444
	Alfred Smith, Democrat	15.0 million	87
1932:	Franklin Roosevelt, Democrat	22.8 million	472
	Herbert Hoover, Republican	15.7 million	59

Source-based questions: The US economy in the 1920s

SOURCE A

Economic growth in the USA 1919–1929

	Gross national product (in billions of dollars)	Income per head (in dollars)
1919	78.9	755
1920	88.9	835
1921	74.0	682
1922	74.0	672
1923	86.1	769
1924	87.6	768
1925	91.3	788
1926	97.7	832
1927	96.3	809
1928	98.2	815
1929	104.4	857

SOURCE B

We in America today are nearer to the financial triumph over poverty than ever before in the history of our land. The poor man is vanishing from among us. Our workers with their average weekly wages, can today buy two or even three times more bread and butter than any wage earner in Europe. Today we demand a larger comfort and greater participation in life and leisure.

From Herbert Hoover's acceptance speech as Republican Party Presidential candidate, June 1928

SOURCE C

Depression? Most Americans had come to assume during the 1920s that there would never be another depression. This misguided optimism proved to be an important factor in generating an economic freefall after 1929. Throughout the 1920s the idea grew that American business had entered a new era of permanent growth. Such naïve talk helped promote an array of foolhardy get-rich-quick schemes. Speculative mania fuelled the Florida real-estate boom.

From *America* by George Tindall and David Shi, 1984

SOURCE D

During the 1920s the gap between the well-off and the not-so-well-off widened greatly. Between 1922 and 1929 wages rose an average of about 40 per cent, but in the latter year the 36,000 wealthiest families received as much as the 12 million poorest.

From *Who Built America?* by Joshua Freeman, 1992

---

1. Study Sources A and C and use information from this chapter.

Explain the meaning of:

(i) 'Gross national product' (Source A)

(ii) 'speculative mania' (Source C).

2. Study Sources A and B and use information from this chapter.

Of what value are these two sources to a historian writing about the US economy of the 1920s?

3. Study Sources C and D and use information from this chapter.

What do these sources suggest were problems facing the US economy in the 1920s?

4. Study Sources A–D and use information from this chapter.

'The growth of the US economy during the 1920s benefited the few rather than the many.'

Explain why you agree or disagree with this view.

Further Reading

Texts designed for AS Level students

Prosperity, Depression and the New Deal by Peter Clements (Hodder & Stoughton, Access to History series, 1997) – an accessible text but the sections on the Wall Street Crash are difficult to understand.

The USA 1917–1929 by Doug and Susan Willoughby (Heinemann, 2000) – a simple, lightweight text covering the main issues.

The Enduring Vision by P. Boyer and others (D.C. Heath & Co., 1993) – a US-produced text which is easy to read. Contains good illustrations.

Texts for A2 and advanced study

The Anxious Decades by Michael Parrish (Norton, 1992) – a US-produced text which contains effective analysis of the main issues.

The Longman History of the United States of America by Hugh Brogan (Longman, Second edition 1999) – highly readable, scholarly text by leading British historian of the USA.

The Twenties in America by Paul Carter (Harlan Davidson, Second edition 1975) – a short, US-produced text which offers a good overview of the decade.

The Great Crash by J.K. Galbraith (Hamish Hamilton, 1955) – still an authoritative account of the causes of the Depression by a leading neo-Keynesian American economist.

3 FDR and the New Deal, 1933–1945

Key Issues

- How successful was FDR as president in domestic affairs between 1933 and 1945?

- How important was opposition to the New Deal?

- Did the New Deal bring fundamental change to the United States?

3.1 Why did Franklin D. Roosevelt win the 1932 Presidential election?

3.2 How successful was the First New Deal in dealing with the effects of the Depression?

3.3 How significant were the reforms of the Second New Deal of 1935–1937?

3.4 How serious was opposition to the New Deal?

3.5 What impact did the Second World War have on the domestic history of the USA, 1941–1945?

3.6 Historical interpretation: Did the New Deal bring fundamental change to the USA?

3.7 An in-depth study: Was the New Deal a success or a failure?

Framework of Events

1932	November: FDR wins presidential election: receives 22.8 million votes and wins 472 electoral college votes against Hoover's 15 million votes and 59 electoral college votes
1933	February: Twentieth Amendment of Constitution
	March: FDR is inaugurated as president
	March–June: First 100 Days of New Deal
	November: Civil Works Administration established under Harry Hopkins
1934	January: Gold Reserve Act
	June: Securities and Exchange Commission is created
	Silver Purchase Act
	November: Coughlin forms National Union of Social Justice
	Mid-term elections give Democrats majority of 45 in Senate and 219 in House of Representatives
1935	April: Emergency Relief Appropriations Act creates Works Progress Administration
	May: Resettlement Administration is created
	Rural Electrification Administration is created
	27 May: Black Monday, when Supreme Court invalidates Farm Mortgage Act and NIRA
	June: National Youth Administration is formed
	July: National Labor Relations or Wagner Act is passed
	August: Banking Act; Revenue Act; Social Security Act; Public Utility Holding Company Act
	September: Huey P. Long assassinated
1936	January: Supreme Court invalidates AAA
	June: FDR nominated as Democrat candidate for presidency
	November: Landslide victory for FDR over Landon (wins 46 out of 48 states)
1937	February: FDR submits 'Court Packing' bill to Congress
	March: In 'West Coast Hotel v Parrish', Supreme Court upholds Washington state minimum wage act
	April: Supreme Court upholds Wagner Act and Social Security Act
	June: Roosevelt Recession begins

1938	February: Second Agricultural Adjustment Act
	June: Fair Labor Standards Act
1939	April: Executive Office of President is created by Executive Order 8248
1940	November: FDR re-elected for unprecedented third term as president
1941	December: USA enters Second World War
1942	January: Emergency Price Control Act sets maximum prices
	Creation of War Labor Board and War Production Board
	February: Japanese Americans removed from west coast
	April: Creation of War Manpower Commission and Office of Price Administration
	October: James Byrnes is placed in control of Office of Economic Stabilisation
	November: Mid-term elections bring big gains for Republicans
1944	November: FDR wins fourth term as President
1945	12 April: FDR dies at Warm Springs, Georgia.

Overview

'Welfare state': Provision by the state of a basic level of income and services for all citizens: health services, housing, education and, ideally, maintenance of full employment.

Socialism: The extension of the role of the state in the economy, with the intention of creating a more equal society.

Socialists: People who believe in the principles of socialism.

Communists: People who believe in communism – the political belief that the state should own and control the means of producing everything, so that all levels of society can be made equal. In this way, everyone should do as much as they can and get as much as they need.

THE period when Franklin D. Roosevelt (FDR) was president was one of the most monumental in the history of the United States. When he became president, in March 1933, the USA faced the worst economic crisis in its history. Twenty-five per cent of the workforce was unemployed and the banking system was on the verge of collapse. When FDR died in office, in April 1945, the United States had recovered from economic disaster to become the world's greatest economic power.

The period began with FDR's attempts to get America out of economic depression. His first 100 days in office (March–June 1933) was a period of frantic law-making activity in the US Congress. No less than 14 major Acts were passed, establishing government agencies that dealt with different aspects of economic activity. The First New Deal of 1933–35 brought the economic decline to an end. However, it took the Second New Deal of 1935–37 to bring major change to the social and economic structure of the USA. Legislation – such as the Wagner Act, the Revenue Act and the Social Security Act, all in 1935 – helped to lay the foundations of the American 'welfare state'.

For all its achievements, the New Deal received criticism. At the time, criticism came from both the right and left of US politics. The Liberty League accused FDR of trying to introduce socialism. Huey Long of Louisiana, as well as socialists and communists, believed FDR had not gone far enough in bringing about social and economic change.

The most serious challenge to the New Deal came from the US Supreme Court. In a series of judgements in 1935 it declared large parts of the New Deal unconstitutional. Fortunately for FDR, the Supreme Court changed its views towards New Deal legislation from 1937, following the resignation of the more conservative justices.

FDR stated that 'Dr New Deal' had saved the US economy from collapse. It took 'Dr Win the War' to bring about complete economic recovery. Even in 1941, on the eve of US entry into the Second World War, the country was affected by serious labour disputes. However, the drive to aid the Allies, from 1939, and then to win the War, made the USA the 'arsenal of democracy' (see page 78).

The end of economic depression was the result of unprecedented federal intervention in social and economic affairs. FDR's Administrations exploited the phrase in the US Constitution which gave the federal government the right 'to promote the general welfare'.

Once the USA had become involved in the war, in 1941, the federal government took over large sections of US industry. By 1945, the federal government had intervened in the lives of ordinary Americans, which would have been unthinkable in 1933.

The New Deal era also brought about important changes in politics. In 1932, FDR had won the election by bringing together a range of different groups in a 'New Deal' **coalition**. This helped the Democratic Party dominate Congress and the presidency until the late 1960s. The coalition was made up of southern whites, **blue-collar workers** in trade unions, northern liberals, African-Americans, Catholics and Jews.

Coalition: A government containing representatives of more than one party or group. In the USA in 1932, the 'coalition' was made up of representatives of southern whites, blue-collar workers in trade unions, northern liberals, African-Americans, Catholics and Jews.

The year 1932 can be seen as a 'turning point', or 'watershed', in US history, or for many reasons. One of the most important was that it marked the end of 'WASP'-dominated America. From 1933, large numbers of Irish, Italian and Jewish Americans entered national government for the first time.

Blue-collar workers: People who do manual jobs – as opposed to white-collar workers in offices.

FDR's period in office also saw the rise of the 'Imperial Presidency'. Under FDR, the power of the president increased considerably. This was due, in part, to the growth of the federal government. It was also due to FDR's style of presidential politics. His 'fireside chats' on the radio brought the US President in direct verbal communication with the US public for the first time. FDR's personal charm and 'patrician' style made him widely popular. By 1939, presidential government had grown so much that the Executive Office of the Presidency was created to include all the presidential advisers. The US involvement in the Second World War merely accelerated a trend which was already apparent in the 1930s.

'WASP': Stands for 'White Anglo-Saxon Protestant'.

Certain social groups within the USA clearly benefited from the 'New Deal' years. The Agricultural Adjustment Acts of 1933 and 1938 laid the foundations of modern US farm policy. Together with other New Deal initiatives – such as rural electrification – farmers faced a more stable, prosperous future. In industrial America, some of the beneficiaries of the New Deal were the trade unions. Legal recognition and the right to strike were firmly established by the end of the 1930s. Also, the rapid growth of the Congress of Industrial Organisations gave FDR and the Democrats an important **voting bloc**.

Voting bloc: The supporters of a particular political party who come from different regions and different social and ethnic groups.

Less certain was the impact of the New Deal on African-Americans. They clearly benefited from agencies such as the Works Progress Administration (WPA), which provided much-needed jobs. However, very little progress was made in civil rights. Attempts to make lynching a federal offence came to nothing. FDR was too sensitive to southern white opinion within the Democratic Party to make any radical changes, especially in tackling segregation in the South. Nevertheless, FDR's wife, Eleanor Roosevelt, took a personal interest in assisting the social, political and military advancement of African-Americans.

Similarly, women's rights did not develop significantly in the New Deal years. In 1933 Frances Perkins, the Secretary of Labor, became the first woman Cabinet member. However, the traditional role of women as the 'home minder' remained. It took the major manpower shortage caused by the Second World War for women to enter blue-collar jobs in large numbers for the first time. Even here, the

New Left historians: This term is used for historians from the 1960s who have studied the 1930s from the perspective of socialists. They contend that FDR should be criticised for defending socialism, rather than for being more radical.

---

1. In what ways did the New Deal change the economy in the USA?

2. What do you regard as the most important area of change brought about by the New Deal:

(a) the economy

(b) the lives of women and African-Americans

(c) politics?

Give reasons for your answer.

---

increased female involvement in the workforce was seen as temporary due to the wartime emergency.

Historians are divided about the impact of the New Deal years on US politics and society. To **New Left historians** the New Deal was conservative, helping to preserve capitalism. Others, such as William Leuchtenburg, believed the New Deal brought fundamental change. It greatly increased the power of the presidency and federal government. It also laid the foundations of a national system of social welfare. To other historians, such as Peter Clements and Tony Badger, many New Deal agencies overlapped and worked inefficiently with contradictory aims. The National Recovery Administration – one of the central agencies of the First New Deal – had achieved little by the time it was declared unconstitutional by the Supreme Court. Other agencies, such as the Civil Works Administration (1933–34) and the Works Progress Administration (1935–42), brought genuine relief to millions.

3.1 Why did Franklin D. Roosevelt win the 1932 Presidential election?

The 1932 elections were a turning point in US political history. They brought Republican control of the federal government and of the Congress to an end. They also saw Democrats replace Republicans across America in state governorships and state legislatures.

The central triumph was the election of Franklin D. Roosevelt (often referred to as 'FDR') as president in a landslide victory against Herbert Hoover. Roosevelt had been Assistant Secretary for the Navy under Woodrow Wilson during the First World War. In 1920, he was Democrat Vice-Presidential candidate when James Cox lost heavily to Warren Harding. However, his political career seemed to come to an abrupt end, in 1921, when he contracted polio.

For the rest of his life FDR lost the use of his legs. What was remarkable

Franklin D. Roosevelt (1882–1945)

32nd President of the USA (1933–45), a Democrat and a lawyer. Educated in Europe and at Harvard and Columbia universities. Elected to the New York State Senate in 1910. F.D. Roosevelt (FDR) was Assistant Secretary for the Navy (1913–21). He suffered from polio in 1921 but returned to politics, winning the governorship of New York State in 1929. Became President in 1932. With a group of experts around him, he launched his reform programme. The 1936 presidential election was won by FDR entirely on the record of his New Deal policy. In 1938 he introduced measures for farm relief and for the improvement of working conditions in the USA. Soon after the outbreak of the Second World War, FDR launched a vast rearmament programme, introduced conscription and provided arms to the Allies on a 'cash-and-carry' basis. FDR was re-elected for a third term as President in 1940. From the point at which the USA entered the War on 7 December 1941, Roosevelt concerned himself solely with the conduct of the war. He was re-elected President for a fourth term in 1944, but died the next year.

An American cartoon of the 1936 Presidential election. Only two states, Vermont and Maine, did not vote for Roosevelt in the election.

was the fact that FDR did not appear in public in a wheelchair or using crutches. He kept up the pretence of being able to walk by using steel leg braces and by using his son and other helpers to lean on so that he appeared to walk.

FDR's political comeback came in 1928 when he won the governorship of his home state of New York by a small margin. During the early depression, his state administration received a reputation for acting decisively to aid the poor and the unemployed. When he was chosen as Democrat candidate for the presidency in the summer of 1932, FDR was a popular political figure. This popularity was enhanced by his campaign call for bold government experimentation to end the economic crisis. This stood in marked contrast to Hoover's Administration, which was perceived as incapable of dealing with the crisis.

Although FDR had many fine attributes, it was Hoover and the Republicans who lost the election. Faced with the worst economic crisis in US history, the Republicans were slow to act. Believing that it was the 'business cycle' and economic system which had brought prosperity in the 1920s, they hoped that the economic downturn would be short. By late 1931, the Hoover Administration began to act more decisively – but this was seen as too little too late.

By November 1932, the presidential election result had become a foregone conclusion. It was only the scale of Democratic victory that was in question. The Democrat Vice-Presidential candidate, John Nance Garner, stated that FDR was successful because he was able to put together a coalition of different groups that would allow the Democrats to dominate national politics for a generation. The coalition included traditional Democrat groups, such as southern whites. The 'Solid South' remained loyal to the Democrats until the 1960s. They were also supported by immigrant groups such as Irish, Italian and Jewish Americans. These groups were not attracted by the Republicans' 'WASP' leadership and

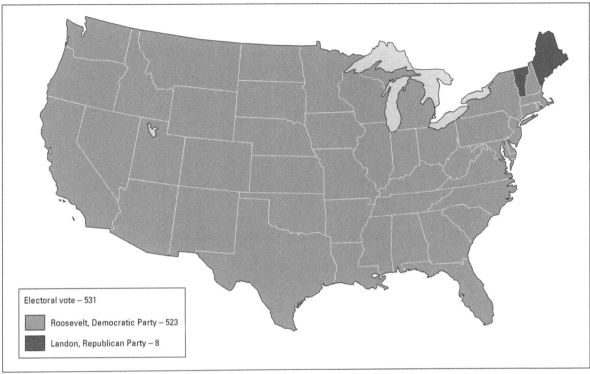

Electoral vote – 531

Roosevelt, Democratic Party – 523

Landon, Republican Party – 8

Presidential election results, USA, 1936

1. What do you regard as the most important reasons for FDR's win in the 1932 Presidential election?

Give reasons for your answer.

2. To what extent did Herbert Hoover lose the election, rather than FDR winning it?

support for racial and religious reasons. In addition, trade unionists and blue-collar workers formed an important source of support. These had suffered under the pro-business policies of the Republicans. They were also unimpressed by Hoover's limited attempts to deal with the economic crisis.

For the first time, the majority of African-Americans voted for the Democrats. During the 1920s, tens of thousands of African-Americans had migrated north to industrial cities such as Detroit and Chicago. Freed from the oppression of segregation, they no longer feared the WASP-dominated Democratic Party.

3.2 How successful was the First New Deal in dealing with the effects of the Depression?

FDR was inaugurated as President on 4 March 1933. His acceptance speech has rightly been regarded as one of the most important in US history. On that date, most of the banks across America were closed. One in four of the workforce was unemployed. Faced with such a crisis, FDR's speech was a rallying cry to the American people. He called for a 'New Deal' to rebuild the US economy. He also called for wide, sweeping powers to meet the economic crisis and he stressed that the only thing Americans needed to fear was fear itself. Followed shortly afterwards by his first radio 'fireside chat', FDR gave the American people hope.

However, between his election in November 1932 and his inauguration in March 1933 – known as the 'lame duck' period – FDR did nothing to stop the economic collapse. He gave no real indication of what he planned to do once he became president. Also, he refused to take up President Hoover's offer to work together during this period. As a result, the economic crisis became worse over the winter of 1932–33. Hoover was already discredited, FDR had yet to offer leadership.

When it came, FDR's leadership was decisive. Calling a special session of Congress, FDR launched the '100 Days' of frantic legislative activity. The 100 Days brought an end to prohibition, reformed the banking and financial system, and began the first steps on the road to 'Relief, recovery and reform'. This meant:

- relief from the effects of the economic depression

- recovery from economic depression

- reform of the economic system to prevent further depressions in the future.

Reforming the banking and financial system

Emergency Banking Act, March 1933
FDR acted quickly to end the crisis in banking and finance. He used the Trading with the Enemy Act, which had been introduced by President Woodrow Wilson during the First World War. This allowed him to proclaim a national bank holiday from Monday 6 March to Thursday 9 March. In this period, he persuaded Congress to pass an Emergency Banking Act. It did so in just seven hours. The aim of the Act was to restore confidence in the banking system. It gave the Treasury power to investigate all banks threatened with collapse. This was supported by the Reconstruction Finance Corporation, which took over bank debts. To gain public support, FDR made his first 'fireside chat' on national radio on 12 March.

The effect of the bank holiday and the Act was to save US banking. FDR had relied on advice from the banking community. He had no other choice, given the crisis he faced. The banks did not encourage the development of branch banking. This had prevented major bank closures in Canada. Nevertheless, one of FDR's 'brains trust' advisers, Raymond Moley, claimed that FDR had saved American capitalism in just eight days.

Glass–Steagall Act, June 1933
In order to bring reform to the banking system, the Glass–Steagall Act prevented commercial 'high street' banks from taking part in investment banking. This had been a major cause of bank collapse following the Wall Street Crash of 1929. The Act also created the Federal Deposit Insurance Corporation (FDIC). This federal agency guaranteed all bank deposits up to $5,000.

Between them, the Emergency Banking Act and the Glass–Steagall Act stabilised US banking. Although the division between state and federal banking remained, FDR's first two terms as president (1933–41) saw less bank closures than any previous Administration. For the first time in almost 60 years, no national banks collapsed in 1936.

Farm Credit Administration, March 1933
Even though a banking collapse was averted, FDR still had to deal with the debt problem faced by farmers. By Executive decree on 27 March, he created the Farm Credit Administration (FCA). This helped farmers to meet their mortgage repayment by offering lower **interest rates**.

Home Owners' Loan Act, 13 June 1933
This Act created the Home Owners' Loan Corporation (HOLC), which

Interest rates: The price of borrowing money to purchase things.

gave urban householders similar financial aid to that offered to farmers under the FCA.

The Federal Securities (Truth in Securities) Act, May 1933
To limit share speculation, this Act stated that all new share purchases had to be registered with the Federal Trade Commission. However, it took until June 1934 for the creation of the Securities and Exchange Commission (SEC) to regulate the share and stock market. Between 1934 and 1941, the SEC's budget rose from $1.5 million to $5.3 million and it had control over 20 stock exchanges across America.

The London Economic Conference, July 1933
On 19 April 1933, the USA left the Gold Standard. This standard had been the basis of international trade for over a century. It also meant that the values of separate currencies were kept stable. The USA was not alone in leaving the Gold Standard. Britain had left at the height of the economic crisis in 1932.

President Hoover had always claimed that the causes of economic depression were worldwide and not unique to the USA. He had placed great faith in the major industrial countries working together to solve the world economic depression. As a result, a world economic conference was held in London on 6 July 1933. FDR, in contrast, believed that the solutions to the USA's economic problems were domestic. He supported the idea of lowering the value of the US dollar against other currencies. Other countries wanted currencies stabilised. As a result, FDR brought about the collapse of the London Conference by announcing the devaluation of the US dollar. According to Paul Conkin, in *The New Deal* (1967):

> 'Roosevelt completely bungled the affair by reversing himself, betraying his own delegates, misleading other countries, and revealing his ignorance of the principal issues involved.'

The Gold Reserve Act, January 1934
This Act accepted the new devaluated value of the US dollar. The dollar was set at $35 per ounce (28.35g) of gold. This would make imports dearer and exports cheaper. FDR hoped that it would raise prices, aiding economic recovery

---

The 100 Days of the First New Deal (March–June 1933): major developments

9 March	Emergency Banking Act
20 March	Economy Act
22 March	Beer and Wine Revenue Act
31 March	Unemployment Relief Act creates Civilian Conservation Corps (CCC)
19 April	USA leaves the gold standard
12 May	Federal Emergency Relief Administration (FERA) is created
	Agricultural Adjustment Administration (AAA) also created
18 May	Creation of Tennessee Valley Authority (TVA)
27 May	Federal Securities Act
13 June	Home Owners' Refinancing Act
16 June	Glass–Steagall Banking Act
	Farm Credit Act
	National Industrial Recovery Act created:
	• Public Works Administration (PWA)
	• National Recovery Administration (NRA)

The Silver Purchase Act, June 1934

FDR also hoped to raise prices by increasing the amount of silver in the coinage. He increased federal silver stock until it reached an equivalent of 30 per cent of the gold reserves.

However, the attempt to use monetary policy and changes in the money supply to bring about economic recovery had little impact. If economic recovery was to take place, it had to be brought about by increases in output and not changes in the currency.

Overall, FDR's attempts to reform the banking and financial systems of America were essentially conservative. He wanted to preserve the economic system, not to transform it.

Getting America back to work

In his inauguration address of 4 March 1933, FDR had stated that the 'greatest primary task is to put people to work'. In the 100 Days and the First New Deal, the Roosevelt Administration tried a number of different initiatives to reduce unemployment. These initiatives became known as the 'alphabet agencies'. You will see why in the following section.

The Civilian Conservation Corps (CCC), March 1933

This 'alphabet agency' aimed to give work to young men aged 18 to 25 years. Under the direction of the army, three million young men were given the opportunity to work in developing the national and state park systems, building roads, felling trees and engaging in conservation. They earned $30 a month, of which $25 was sent back to their families. Initially for two years, the CCC lasted until 1942. It helped in developing literacy and in ending, at least temporarily, the problem of unemployment. However, once young men left the CCC there was no guarantee that they would get a job.

The Federal Emergency Relief Administration (FERA), May 1933

Harry L. Hopkins (1890–1946)
Close confidant of FDR who began his career as a social worker. Head of Federal Emergency Relief Administration (1933–35). Then became head of Works Progress Administration (1935–38). Helped the unemployed with ambitious programmes of public work. He was FDR's leading advisor during World War II and was put in charge of lend-lease.

This 'alphabet agency' was placed under the control of Harry Hopkins, a social worker by profession. It aimed to give relief to the unemployed. However, aid was given through states. A 'FERA' office was created in each state. With a budget of $500 million, FERA organised relief programmes. It supported state construction of over 5,000 public buildings, 7,000 bridges and various schemes to aid the poor and disadvantaged, such as literacy schemes.

According to historian Tony Badger, in *The New Deal, The Depression Years 1933–1940* (1989):

'By the end of 1933 [Hopkins] was a key figure in the development of New Deal strategy. His relief programmes were the key to the success of Roosevelt's short-term efforts to alleviate mass distress.'

Hopkins spent much of his time trying to force reluctant state governments to implement relief programmes. Governor Talmadge of Georgia and Governor Martin of Oregon prided themselves on not offering direct aid to the poor. To force states to comply, Hopkins threatened to cut off federal funding. In six states, Hopkins had to take over relief programmes directly because of local resistance.

The Civil Works Administration (CWA), November 1933

Even with the FERA, relief for the poor and unemployed failed to deal with the huge problems of the economy as winter approached in 1933. As a result, Hopkins was able to gain support for direct federal involvement in relieving economic hardship. The CWA was given a budget of $400 million. Within weeks of its launch, the CWA was providing work for nearly one million. By Christmas, three million were employed on its projects, rising to 4.2 million by 18 January 1934. Although most jobs were for manual labour, almost 10 per cent of jobs created were in the white-collar, clerical sector.

For all its success, FDR was concerned at the vast expense of the agency. It was costing around $200 million a month, compared with $60 million for FERA. Under the advice of the conservative Budget Director, Lewis Douglas, the CWA came to an end on 31 March 1934.

The Public Works Administration (PWA), June 1933

This agency was created by the National Industrial Recovery Act and was placed under the control of Secretary of the Interior, Harold Ickes. It was given a budget of $3.3 billion to help stimulate economic growth. However, Ickes took a completely different view from Hopkins in helping America to get back to work. Hopkins wanted to give hope back to the unemployed by giving them any type of job. He was accused of creating 'boondoggle' jobs. These had no real purpose other than providing some form of employment. Ickes was determined to use his agency's monies wisely. While Hopkins spent $5 million of FERA's budget within two hours of taking office, Ickes had spent only $110 million of the PWA's budget in the first six months.

Demanding that all money be spent on worthwhile projects, the PWA was eventually responsible for building some 13,000 schools and 50,000 miles of roads. However, it failed to offer sufficient support to reduce unemployment to any significant extent. In this respect, it stood in marked contrast to the work of the CWA under Hopkins.

Reforming business

The National Recovery Administration (NRA), June 1933

The most well-known alphabet agency of the First New Deal was the NRA. Its 'Blue Eagle' sign was seen across America. It was led by General Hugh Johnson, whose energetic leadership added to the NRA's high profile.

The NRA made many changes. As stated by one of FDR's advisers, Raymond Moley, the NRA represented a major step away from the economic philosophy of laissez faire which had been followed by the Republicans before 1933. It aimed to provide codes of practice for industry. These aimed to ensure fair competition, and to lay down wage rates and hours of work. Child labour under the age of 16 was made illegal. It also aimed to help workers. Under Section 7(a) of the National Industrial Recovery Act, it gave employees the right to bargain 'collectively' for wages. This had been the call from American trade unions for generations. The NRA also had $3.3 billion to spend on public works projects over two years.

During its lifespan – 1933–1935 – the NRA drew up 557 different codes of practice for different industries. Once these codes were accepted, firms could display the Blue Eagle sign of the NRA. Unfortunately, many of these codes proved to be unworkable. This was mainly due to the speed with which they were adopted. The NRA also excluded agricultural workers and domestic servants. These were areas which contained large numbers of African-Americans. According to historian Tony Badger, in The New Deal:

> 'to radical critics the National Recovery Administration epitomised the capture of a regulatory agency by the special interests who were supposed to be regulated. The effect of business control of the NRA was to dash the hopes of all the groups whose ideas had influenced the Recovery Act.'

Businessmen played a key role in drafting the Act and in its implementation. The NRA did not deal, either, with trusts that controlled whole industries. This led to price fixing, which disadvantaged small firms. By

---

Harold L. Ickes (1874–1952)
Progressive Republican who backed Theodore Roosevelt in 1912 presidential election. Made Secretary of Interior in 1933. Given control of Public Works Administration (PWA) budget of $3.3 billion in 1935. Criticised for using PWA too slowly and too cautiously. Served in FDR Cabinet (1933–45).

the time the NRA was declared unconstitutional by the US Supreme Court in 1935, it was becoming unworkable.

Nevertheless, the NRA had helped with economic recovery. Hugh Johnson proved to be an effective head of the agency – a skill he transferred to leading the Works Progress Administration (WPA) from 1935. Also, while Harold Ickes at the PWA was reluctant to spend money, the NRA helped with relief in 1933–34.

Helping farmers

The Agricultural Adjustment Administration (AAA), May 1933

Under the leadership of Secretary for Agriculture, Henry A. Wallace (son of former Secretary for Agriculture Henry C. Wallace), the AAA laid the foundations for modern farming policy. Throughout the 1920s, farming had been in crisis. Overproduction had resulted in low farm prices. The Act that created the AAA gave Wallace the power to deal with farm problems. As a result, the AAA helped to reduce supply and to stabilise farm prices. The AAA was based on a 'domestic allotment' plan. Farmers agreed either to reduce the area they cultivated or to reduce production. The plan affected major commodities such as wheat, cotton, pigs, corn and milk. Thousands of piglets were slaughtered, milk was poured away and crops were ploughed up. Reduction in crop yields was also aided by the drought of 1933.

By 1935, over 75 million acres (30 million hectares) had been removed from cultivation. Farm incomes rose from $4.5 billion in 1933 to $6.9 billion by 1935. The historian Arthur Schlesinger, in Coming of the New Deal, stated that this policy 'assigned the federal government the decisive role in protecting farm income'. These federal payments greatly aided farmers. However, with a reduction in production less farm labourers, such as sharecroppers and migrant workers, were needed. It took the Resettlement Administration of 1935 to deal with this problem.

For all its benefits, the US Supreme Court declared the AAA unconstitutional, in January 1936, in the case of 'United States versus Butler'. It took another Agricultural Adjustment Act of 1938 to restore many of the features of the first act. However, the benefits which farmers received during the New Deal were not solely the result of the AAA.

According to historian M.J. Heale, in *Franklin D. Roosevelt* (1999):

'Farm prices rose although it is unclear how far production controls themselves were responsible. More helpful to farmers was the credit made available by New Deal programmes. Late in 1933 the Commodity

Does this poster suggest the New Deal was not successful in dealing with the effects of the Depression? Explain your answer.

Poor blacks line up for government relief alongside a billboard in 1937 – part of a national advertising campaign to encourage business in America.

1. What do these two images show about the plight of agricultural workers in the 1930s?

2. How successful was the New Deal in tackling problems in American agriculture?

Two images of the USA in 1936 (the year of the dust bowl): (left) a government poster for the Resettlement Administration by Ben Shahn; (right) a photograph by Dorothea Lange for the Farm Security Administration entitled 'Migrant Mother, Nipomo, California', which appeared in newspapers throughout the country in March.

Credit Corporation was established to provide loans on stored crops like cotton and corn.'

Also important was the creation of the Farm Credit Administration, mentioned above.

Regional development

The Tennessee Valley Authority (TVA), May 1933
The Tennessee Valley Authority provided a model for regional planning in a traditionally poor part of the Upper South, which contained two million people and covered around 40,000 square miles in seven states. It was also a major area of support for the Democratic Party. Its aims were flood control, agricultural regeneration and cheap electric power. Under the chairmanship of Arthur Morgan, the TVA faced opposition from private business. However, by 1945 it had established a network of dams, which regulated the flow of the Tennessee river. This prevented flooding and soil erosion. It also had a major impact on the provision of electricity. In 1933, only 2 per cent of the Tennessee Valley farms had electricity; by 1945, the number had risen to 75 per cent.

According to historian James T. Patterson, in *America in the Twentieth Century* (1989):

The area administered by the
Tennessee Valley Authority (TVA)

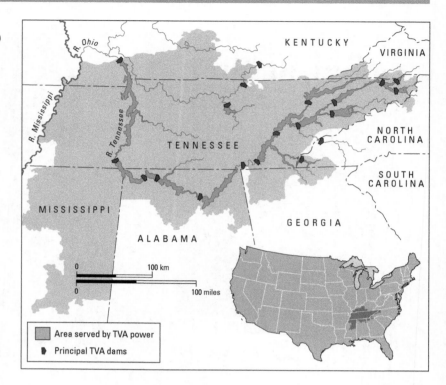

Area served by TVA power

Principal TVA dams

Fascism: The beliefs of nationalists, which started in Italy in 1919 in opposition to Communism. As part of the *partito nazionale fascista*, under the leadership of Benito Mussolini (1883–1945), the fascists controlled Italy from 1922 to 1943.

---

1. In what ways did the First New Deal bring 'relief, recovery and reform' to the USA?

2. How successful was the First New Deal in:

(a) aiding the unemployed

(b) reforming the banking and financial system

(c) helping farmers?

Give reasons for your answers.

'Critics complained that the TVA was state socialism. But Roosevelt thought not. The TVA he said was "neither fish nor fowl but it will taste awfully good to the people of the Tennessee Valley".'

Historian Paul Conkin, in The New Deal, believes that: 'the TVA proved the efficiency, flexibility and social concern possible in government-owned, non-profit corporations. Of all the New Deal programs, the TVA had the most impact on foreign countries.'

The First New Deal faced many critics. On the left, many thought it had not gone far enough. Instead of changing the economic system it had merely prevented it from collapsing. However, by February 1934, the FERA, PWA and CWA had offered work to 20 per cent of the workforce. Yet millions were denied relief by reluctant state governments.

To others, the New Deal had gone too far. It had introduced either a form of **fascism** or a form of socialism to the United States of America.

The historian Peter Clements, in Prosperity, Depression and the New Deal (1997), questioned the coherence of the First New Deal. Some New Deal agencies overlapped in their areas of operation; some had contradictory aims. However, as FDR stated before he took office, he would engage in bold experimentation. If one plan failed, he would try another. The First New Deal is evidence of this approach. Its plan was to get America back to work by whatever means.

Whatever the verdict of some critics at the time and historians since, the First New Deal was popular with the US electorate. In the mid-term elections of 1934, the Democrats increased their majority in both the Senate and the House of Representatives. As FDR stated: 'Everyone is against except the voters!'

3.3 How significant were the reforms of the Second New Deal of 1935–1937?

The American political commentator Walter Lippmann called the Second New Deal 'the most comprehensive program of reform ever achieved in this country in any administration'.

The Second New Deal went much further than the First. This was due, in part, to a reaction by FDR to his critics on the left of American politics. Individuals such as Louisiana Senator Huey P. Long, Catholic priest Charles Coughlin and Francis Townsend had called for more radical reform. Following the mid-term elections of 1934, the 75th Congress contained more radical elements who wanted to bring permanent change to US society.

The result of all these pressures was the Second 100 Days of 1935. The combined effect of these reforms was to lay the foundations of an American welfare state in which the federal government played a central part.

The Works Progress Administration (WPA): help for the unemployed

Created by the Emergency Relief Appropriation Act on 8 April 1935, the WPA became the most significant relief agency in the New Deal. Under the direction of Harry Hopkins, it received $4.8 billion from Congress.

As historian Michael Parrish notes, in The Anxious Decades (1992):

'from its creation until its official demise in 1943, the WPA spent over $11 billion on work relief and ultimately employed eight million Americans, about one-fifth of the nation's entire workforce. In seven years they built 2,500 hospitals, 5,900 schools, 350 airports, 570,000 miles of rural roads and 8,000 parks.'

The WPA was particularly significant in helping white-collar professionals, women, artists, young people and African-Americans. For instance, in 1936 the WPA ran camps along CCC lines for 5,000 women. Although they were paid, they also received education.

● Federal Project One aided musicians and actors.

● The Federal Writers' Project aided writers, especially African-Americans.

The Second New Deal (April–August 1935): major legislation

April 1935	Emergency Relief Appropriation Act created the Works Progress Administration (WPA)
May 1935	Resettlement Administration
	Rural Electrification Administration
June 1935	National Youth Administration
July 1935	Wagner National Labor Relations Act
August 1935	Public Utility Holding Company Act
	Social Security Act
	Banking Act
	Revenue Act
	Guffey–Snyder Coal Act

- The Theatre Project employed 11,000 performers and workers in 22 production centres. Film stars such as Orson Welles and John Huston benefited from WPA money to fund their productions.

- The Music Project funded 38 symphony orchestras.

- The Public Work Art Project employed artists to decorate federal buildings.

In four years, the WPA spent $46 million aiding unemployed artists.

Of particular significance was the creation of the National Youth Administration (NYA), which encouraged education and provided part-time jobs for students. The NYA Division for Negro Affairs was headed by African-American Mary McLeod Bethune, who ensured that African-Americans benefit from NYA and WPA initiatives.

As a result, the WPA stands out as the most significant relief agency in the whole New Deal period.

The Wagner National Labor Relations Act, July 1935: a 'new deal' for labour

According to historian Tony Badger, 'The 1930s saw the largest ever growth in union membership in a single decade. Trade union membership trebled. The gains were decisive and permanent.'

Trade unionists were some of the most enthusiastic supporters of FDR's first two administrations. By 1932, some progress had been made in defending trade union rights. In that year the Norris–La Guardia Act outlawed court injunctions which upheld 'yellow dog' (no strike) contracts. However, it was not until the New Deal that substantial headway was made. Section 7(a) of the National Industrial Recovery Act gave unions the right to bargain with employers collectively. NRA codes helped to raise wages and to improve working conditions in many industries.

The centrepiece of trade union legislation was the Wagner Act of 1935. It helped to make up for the loss of the NRA (which was declared unconstitutional by the US Supreme Court in May 1935). However, the main drive for legislation did not come from FDR himself. He had always been reluctant to get involved in labour relations. Instead, it came from those Democrats in Congress who supported organised labour.

Collective bargaining: Talks that a trade union has with an employer, which are intended to settle what the workers' pay levels and/or conditions should be.

The Wagner Act confirmed the right to **collective bargaining**. It also allowed workers to join unions of their own choice through secret ballot. To ensure that both employers and unions acted correctly, a three-man National Labor Relations Board was created.

The Act did not bring labour disputes to an end. The January–February 1937 sit-down strike by United Auto Worker Union members at General Motors plant in Flint, Michigan was a success which further helped union growth; as was the creation of the Congress of Industrial Organisations (CIO), mainly through the efforts of Al Lewis of the coalminers in November 1935.

Other legislation was also important. The Guffey–Snyder Act of 1935 and the Guffey–Vinson Act of 1937 enabled a national coal commission to set minimum prices for coal and, more importantly, to ensure fair labour standards in the coal industry.

Finally, the Wagner Act benefited from the change in view of the US Supreme Court which took place in 1937–38. Unlike the NRA, it survived a challenge in the Court which upheld the act in the case of 'National Labor Relations Board versus McLaughlin Steel, 1937'. According to the historian M.J. Heale, 'the Act did represent a major step in the mutually supportive accord that was forged between the New Deal and organised labour'.

The Act may have aided organised labour, but trade unions still faced attack. Members of the House Committee on Un-American Activities (HUAC), set up in 1938, attacked the National Labor Relations Board as pro-communist. In 1943, the Smith–Connally War Labor Disputes Act gave the President power to seize strike-bound factories and made it a crime to encourage strikes.

The Social Security Act, August 1935: an American 'welfare state'?

While the Works Progress Administration dealt with the immediate problem of giving relief to the unemployed, the Social Security Act attempted to provide long-term permanent assistance.

The Act introduced federal-funded old age pensions and unemployment benefit (the dole). The Progressives had advocated pensions since 1912. In 1932, the state of Wisconsin introduced its own scheme of unemployment assistance. More recently, FDR had faced criticism on these issues from the left. Upton Sinclair, in his 'End Poverty in California' campaign, and Francis Townsend's 'Old Age Revolving Pension Plan' pressured the Administration for change. When this Act was introduced, it fell far short of their expectations.

The Social Security Act was financed by contributions from employers and workers. However, federal/state relations complicated it. The federal government provided the pension scheme, while the states administered the unemployment insurance programme. This development was due, in part, to FDR's fear that the US Supreme Court might declare the act unconstitutional if he did not include a role for the states.

Pensions were to be paid out at a rate between $10 and $85 per month, according to the degree of contribution. Unemployment benefit was to be paid at a maximum of $18 per week for 16 weeks only.

The Act provided the basis for welfare for decades to come. However, from the outset, it excluded millions of workers who pursued occupations not covered in the act. Also, pensions were not to begin until 1940.

The Revenue Act, August 1935: 'soaking the rich' or a 'raw deal'?

Franklin Roosevelt had always been a conservative in matters of tax and finance. He had found it difficult to accept a deficit budget to help get the economy working again during the First New Deal. Although he may have engaged in **Keynesian demand management of the economy**, he did not do it knowingly. Already, in 1934, a Revenue Act had been passed, mainly because of the pressure of radicals in Congress on those Americans who earned over $9,000 per year.

To help pay for the New Deal reforms, taxation had to be raised. This was achieved with the Revenue Act of 1935. It raised the top levels of income tax from 63 per cent to 79 per cent. It also increased **estate taxes**. An undistributed profits tax was introduced in order to force large companies (corporations) back into the Stock Market to raise money for investment.

These changes, as one might expect, were not popular with 'big business' and the wealthy. The newspaper magnate, William Randolph Hearst, termed it the 'soak the rich' act. Big business was particularly upset by the undistributed profits tax. Yet only 10 per cent of US families earned over $3,200 per year! Less than 5 per cent of Americans paid federal income taxes throughout the 1930s.

However, paying for the New Deal reform was only partly the reason for the Act. FDR also wanted to silence critics on the left of US politics. Louisiana's Huey P. Long ('The Kingfish') had launched the 'Share Our Wealth' campaign, which demanded a major redistribution of income. Long was planning to run for the Democratic Presidential ticket in 1936.

Keynesian demand management of the economy: Ideas associated with the British economist John Maynard Keynes (see page 90). He criticised the traditional views that government intervention in economic matters should be kept to a minimum. This was known as *laissez-faire* economics (see page 42). Instead, Keynes believed the government could, and should, intervene in economic matters to get an economy out of depression. He suggested that, through government spending, demand would be increased. This would have the 'knock on' effect of creating more employment, and then more demand. The use of government spending to get economies out of depression occurred in Germany and Britain, as well as the USA.

Estate taxes: Property taxes due when someone dies.

Also, FDR had to pay for the veterans' bonus in 1936 rather than waiting until 1945. This had been the demand of the 'Bonus Army' in 1932. Finally, the US Supreme Court had declared the agricultural processing tax unconstitutional.

The Resettlement Administration and The Rural Electrification Act, 1935: aiding poor farmers

The Agricultural Adjustment Administration during the First New Deal helped to regulate agricultural prices by reducing output. Part of the impact of this policy was to reduce demand for farm labourers. In addition, the mid-1930s saw the developments of the '**Dust Bowl**' in areas such as Oklahoma, the panhandle of Texas and southern Kansas. The combined result of these developments was increased poverty in rural areas.

'**Dust Bowl**': Flat grasslands that were ploughed in order to grow cereals were hit by prolonged drought followed by high winds. In many areas, the topsoil blew away. In the Tennessee valley, it was washed away – producing poor growing conditions.

The aim of the Resettlement Administration was to relocate over 450,000 poor farming families away from the worst affected areas. This would involve the federal government buying more suitable farming land, as well as educating people to move and to develop better farming skills.

In the end, under 5,000 families moved to 'green communities' in states such as Wisconsin and Ohio. This was due, in part, to the cost of the operation and the reluctance of families to move.

In 1930, only 10 per cent of farmers had electricity. Most power companies thought it too expensive to provide power lines to rural areas. Already, under the Tennessee Valley Authority, cheap electricity was provided for rural areas in the Upper South.

Cooperatives: Factories, shops or farms that are owned by the people who run them.

In 1935, the Rural Electrification Act created the Rural Electrification Administration (REA). The REA granted low-interest loans to rural **cooperatives** so that they could provide electricity. Partly as a result of the Act, 417 cooperatives were providing electricity for over 250,000 homes by 1939. By 1945, 40 per cent of American farms had electricity.

The Banking Act, 1935: a modern banking system?

Although the 1933 Banking Act had helped to save the US financial system from collapse, it still left the federal and state banking systems intact. By 1935, the head of the Federal Reserve Board (the American equivalent of a federal central bank) wanted to increase federal control over the system.

The 1935 Banking Act created the Federal Reserve Board, in which governors were chosen by the President, with Senatorial advice and consent. The new Federal Reserve Board had direct control over the 12 regional branches.

As historian M.J. Heale states, in *Franklin Roosevelt: The New Deal* (1999):

'The measure served to enhance the authority of the federal government and to centralise the power of the Federal Reserve System over monetary policy. Very belatedly in the western world, the United States had a central banking system.'

Public Utility Holding Company Act, 1935: a replacement for the NRA?

A holding company owns several other companies which are actually involved in trading and manufacturing. As a result, a small number of holding companies can control large parts of the industry. This was particularly true of the power generation industry in the USA in the 1930s. The practice led to the high cost of electricity for industry. According to historian Tony Badger, in *The New Deal*:

'The top holding company secured lucrative management fees and dividends from its subsidiaries, hindered improved service and effectively escaped state and federal regulation.'

The Public Utility Holding Company Act aimed to end these practices. Under the Act, all holding companies had to register with the Securities and Exchange Commission (SEC). The SEC was also given power to control the issue of shares of holding companies on the stock market. All holding companies more than two stages away from the production of goods or services were to be prohibited.

Although FDR wanted to end the practice of holding companies altogether, the Act was a compromise following extensive pressure on Congress from holding companies.

The Second New Deal: a verdict

According to P. Boyer et al, in *The Enduring Vision* (1993):

'By September 1935, the Second New Deal was complete. A set of laws had been enacted promoting the interests of the jobless, the elderly, the rural poor and the blue-collar workers; regulating major business enterprises more strictly; and somewhat increasing the taxes paid by the wealthy.'

The Second New Deal helped to divert some of the criticism FDR had faced from radicals in Congress and from the left of US politics around the country, such as Francis Townsend, Huey Long and the socialists. It could also be regarded as providing the basis for modern American trade unionism. Historian Michael Parrish describes the Wagner Act as labour's **Magna Carta**. The Social Security Act laid the foundations for a federal welfare state system which lasted until the 1980s.

Magna Carta: The document by King John granting English freemen basic rights in 1215.

However, FDR's aim was never to destroy the US economic system, but to strengthen it. This was to be done by distributing the benefits of the economic system more fairly. Many of the reforms passed were compromises between the views of radicals and pressure from business interest groups.

In drafting the Democratic Party manifesto for the 1936 elections, one of FDR's advisers, Samuel Rosenman, declared that the basis of the New Deal was 'that the government in a modern civilisation has certain inescapable obligations to its citizens among which are:

(1) protection of the family and the home.

(2) establishment of democracy of opportunity for all the people

(3) aid to those overtaken by disaster.'

The Second New Deal clearly went a long way towards achieving these ideals.

1. In what ways did the Second New Deal help workers and the unemployed?

2. What do you regard as the most important reform of the Second New Deal? Give reasons for your answer.

3. Compare the reforms of the Second New Deal in this section with the reforms of the First New Deal in the previous section. What do you regard as the most significant period of reform: the First New Deal or the Second New Deal? Explain your answer.

To prove the popularity of the Second New Deal one does not have to go beyond the 1936 elections. As historian Hugh Brogan points out, FDR's re-election was as certain as George Washington's. On election day, FDR received 27,750,000 votes. The Republican candidate, Alfred Landon of Kansas – known as the 'Kansas Coolidge' for his quiet, unassuming manner – polled a mere 16,600,000 votes. In the electoral college, FDR won 46 states (523 votes to 8). Only the small north-eastern states of Vermont and Maine voted for Landon.

In Congress, the Democrats won a landslide. In the House of Representatives they outnumbered the Republicans 331 to 89, and in the Senate 76 to 16. The 1936 elections proved to be the 'high tide' of the New Deal.

3.4 How serious was opposition to the New Deal?

The New Deal attracted critics from both left and right of the American political scene. To many socialists and communists the New Deal did not go far enough. It was seen as helping to preserve, rather than destroy, the capitalist economic system. This was FDR's plan all along. On the right, FDR was seen as a dangerous radical. His Administration had abandoned laissez-faire economics and had used the powers of the federal government in a way not seen in peacetime. Even FDR recognised, in a newsreel broadcast in 1935, that he had been accused of being either a fascist or a communist. Many of the critics of the New Deal from the left of American politics helped to push FDR in a more radical direction than he wished to go. Other critics from the right forced FDR and his Administration to compromise on many reforms.

How important was opposition from the US Supreme Court?

Advice and consent: Under the US Constitution, several Presidential appointments must receive two-thirds support in the US Senate if they are to be legal. These appointments include the Cabinet and all US Supreme Court justices.

Charles Evans Hughes (1862–1946)
Republican Presidential candidate against Woodrow Wilson in 1916. Made Chief Justice of the Supreme Court in 1930. Hughes was in favour of judicial restraint, which resulted in declaration of major New Deal legislation as unconstitutional in 1935. Resisted FDR's 'court packing' plan of 1937. Retired in 1941.

The US Supreme Court is held in high esteem by the vast majority of Americans. It is regarded as the 'watchdog' of the US Constitution. Under the Constitution, the Supreme Court is the highest court of appeal for all state law and federal law cases. It also has the power to declare unconstitutional: acts of state governments, the federal government or Congress. The President, with the **advice and consent** of the Senate, nominates Supreme Court judges. Once nominated, they are in office until they decide to resign or are impeached. So far in US history, no Supreme Court judge has been impeached. When FDR took office, judges appointed by Republican presidents dominated the US Supreme Court. Under the Chief Justiceship of Charles Evans Hughes, the Supreme Court proved to be the most formidable opponent of the New Deal.

In 1935, the Court virtually wrecked the main reforms of the New Deal. The Court declared the National Industrial Recovery Act to be unconstitutional in 'A.L.A. Schechter Poultry Corporation v United States' in May 1935. Known as the 'sick chicken case', a New York firm of Jewish poulterers were accused of selling diseased chickens, thereby breaking a NRA code. The Court declared that the federal government had exceeded its powers by interfering in intra-state commerce, which was a state matter. Part of the problem for FDR was the fact that the National Recovery Administration was introduced very quickly and had not been properly drafted. As historian Hugh Brogan points out, 'the NRA was a premature experiment in a fully planned economy conducted with inadequate tools'.

In fact, the Schechter Corporation received financial support for bringing the case to court by the owners of US Steel in order to challenge the NRA's right to regulate commerce.

In January 1936, the Court, in 'United States v Butler', also declared the Agricultural Adjustment Administration (AAA) unconstitutional for similar reasons to the Schechter case. In a private memorandum, FDR wrote: 'The decision virtually prohibits the President and Congress from the right, under modern conditions, to intervene reasonably in the regulation of nationwide commerce and nationwide agriculture.' In all, the Court declared 11 New Deal laws unconstitutional, including the Farm Mortgage Act. Up to 1933, the Court vetoed 60 federal acts. This places in perspective the amount of opposition from the Court to the New Deal.

Fortunately for FDR and his Administration, many of the features which had been in the NRA and Agricultural Adjustment Act were later incorporated into the Second New Deal and the Agricultural Adjustment Act of 1938. Nevertheless, FDR was determined to thwart any further attempts by the Court to damage the New Deal.

1. In what ways do these cartoons differ in their view of the New Deal?

2. Which do you regard as more reliable? Explain your answer.

Two cartoons on the quarrel between Roosevelt and the US Supreme Court: (left) an American cartoon by Clifford Berryman which appeared in 'Washington Star', 23 April 1937; (right) a British cartoon from 'Punch', June 1935.

Following his landslide victory in 1936, FDR began his second term as President with a direct attack on the Court. In spite of his enormous popularity, this attack proved to be FDR's major mistake in domestic affairs in his long tenure as president. It lost him valuable support in Congress and the nation.

In February 1937, FDR submitted a bill (The Judicial Procedures Reform Bill) to Congress which, if passed, would have forced all justices over the age of 70 to retire. Although this applied to the whole federal judiciary, it was clear where FDR was aiming his attack. In 1937, six of the nine US Supreme Court justices were over 70 years old. It would also give the President power to appoint up to six new justices, thus increasing the number of justices to 15. If passed, the Act would have given FDR enormous power as President. He would have had the right to 'pack' the court with his own nominees. It also brought to a head the criticism that FDR was amassing too much political power. Since 1933, federal government powers and, in particular, the powers of the President had grown considerably. FDR's plan was rejected in the Senate by 70 votes to 20.

What also undermined FDR's planned reform was a change in attitude in the Court. On 29 March 1937, the Supreme Court upheld a minimum wage act passed by the state of Washington. Six months earlier, it had invalidated an almost identical act from New York State. This 'switch in time that saved nine' took away many of FDR's criticisms of the Court. To the shock of most of the country, on 12 April, the Court upheld the Wagner Act of 1935.

Finally, the most conservative justice, Willis van Devanter, announced his retirement in 1937. This allowed FDR to nominate his own justice.

As a result of all these changes, the Second New Deal did not face the same fate as the First New Deal at the hands of the Court. However, FDR's reputation had suffered a major knock. Never again would he be able to command such support in the Congress for his domestic reforms. The 'Third' New Deal – of 1937–39 – was a pale shadow of the other two. A new Agricultural Adjustment Act and a Fair Labor Standards Act were the only two notable reforms. The period was also one of increased unemployment – known as 'The Roosevelt Recession'.

What impact did opponents from the left have on the New Deal?

Socialists and Communists

The most extreme opponents of the New Deal from the left of US politics were socialists and communists. Both wanted to see the destruction of the capitalist economic system, which they regarded as beyond reform. However, even in 1932, these groups had little impact on national politics. In the presidential election of that year, Norman Thomas, the socialist, received 883,990 votes, compared with FDR's 22.8 million. William Foster of the Workers' Party polled just 102,000 votes. In 1935, Thomas's vote dropped to 187,000, while Earl Browder, the Communist presidential candidate, received a derisory 79,000 votes.

Huey P. Long ('The Kingfish')

Of greater significance was opposition from the Louisiana Democrat Huey P. Long. He launched the 'Share Our Wealth' campaign in February 1934. He was a serious and voluble critic of FDR from within his own party. Long wanted to guarantee to every American family a 'homestead allowance' of $5,000 and a minimum annual income of $2,500. To finance such a grand scheme, Long planned to increase income and inheritance taxes to a point where no individual could earn over $1.8 million a year. Although personally opposed to 'big federal government', Long's own proposals would have led to an increase in government involvement in people's lives.

Long's plans were popular. By early 1935, there were 27,000 chapters of the 'Share Our Wealth' campaign across America with over eight million members. By the summer of 1935, Long was taken seriously as a possible presidential candidate for 1936. However, Long was gunned down in September 1935 by a disgruntled supporter. Nevertheless, support for schemes such as Long's helped to push the FDR Administration further to the left during the Second New Deal.

Charles E. Coughlin, the radio priest

By 1930, Father Coughlin had over 35 million regular listeners to his radio programme 'The Golden Hour of the Little Flower'. Coughlin regularly blamed American and British bankers for the depression. Initially, he supported the New Deal, stating that 'The New Deal is Christ's Deal'. Yet, in 1934, he formed the National Union of Social Justice, which was an alternative to the New Deal. Father Coughlin claimed that FDR had become influenced by the banking community. He advocated monetary reform, including the introduction of silver coinage and the encouragement of inflation. Those in debt welcomed his support for inflation. However, by 1935, his attacks on the New Deal were becoming more **anti-semitic**, with criticism levelled at Jews in the Administration – such as Henry Morgenthau and Felix Frankfurter.

Francis Townsend and the Old Age Revolving Pension Plan

A retired doctor from Long Beach, California, put forward a plan for old age pensions in 1933. Under the plan, all those over 60 years would receive a government pension of $200 a month, as long as they spent all the money within 30 days of receiving it. Townsend hoped that it would

---

Huey P. Long (1893–1935)
Democrat. Governor for Louisiana 1928–31; US Senator for that state from 1931 to his death. Under the slogans 'Every man a king' and 'Share our Wealth', he became a major critic of the First New Deal. Private polls conducted by FDR's adviser James Farley suggested Long could have won around 10 million votes if he had run as a third-party candidate in the 1936 presidential election. However, he was assassinated in September 1935 in Baton Rouge, state capital of Louisiana, by a deranged doctor.

Anti-semitic: Against Jews or the Jewish religion (Judaism).

Communism: The political belief that the state should own and control the means of producing everything, so that all levels of society can be made equal. Then everyone should do as much as they can and get as much as they need.

> ## A popular joke against the New Deal during the 1930s
>
> **Socialism**: If you own two cows you give one to your neighbour.
>
> **Communism**: You give both cows to the government and the government gives you back some milk.
>
> **Fascism**: You keep both cows but give the milk to the government who sells some of it back to you.
>
> **New Dealism**: You shoot both cows and milk the government.

prevent poverty in old age and would stimulate domestic demand at the same time. By 1935, over 500,000 old people had joined Townsend clubs across the country. In January of that year, a bill was submitted to the House of Representatives based on Townsend's plan and supported by a petition of 20 million signatures.

It seems clear that the pressure from these various groups helped to push the FDR Administration into more radical legislation during the Second New Deal. However, the political threat they posed was marginal. Following Long's assassination in September 1935, the supporters of Long, Coughlin and Townsend got together to support a presidential candidate for the 1936 election, William Lemke of the Union Party. Lemke polled 892,000 votes, compared with FDR's 27.7 million.

How important were opponents from the right to the New Deal?

The New Deal was opposed by a large number of groups on the right of US politics. Most notable was the Republican Party. However, for most of this period the Republican Party was largely ineffective against the New Deal. In the 1936 election, Alfred Landon of Kansas proved to be a poor opponent. In 1940, when FDR decided to run for an unprecedented third term as president he was faced with a more formidable opponent, Wendell Willkie. This time, the Republicans polled 22.3 million votes against FDR's 27.2 million. However, the Republicans won only 82 electoral college votes against FDR's 449, the Democrat carrying 38 of the 48 states.

Outside national politics, the New Deal found opponents in local state governments who were reluctant to introduce the new reforms. This was most notable in states such as Mississippi, even though the Democratic Party controlled the state.

Much New Deal legislation was opposed by 'big business'. They fought individual New Deal measures by putting pressure on Congress. This was true of the Public Holding Utility Act of 1935. They also took the FDR Administration to court, as in the 'sick chicken case' of 1935.

Mogul: An important, rich and powerful businessperson, especially one in the movie (film) or television industry.

---

1. In what ways did opponents influence New Deal legislation?

2. Why was the US Supreme Court such a formidable opponent of the New Deal between 1935 and 1936?

3. How significant was opposition to the success of the New Deal?

The most notable opponent on the right was the Liberty League. Formed in the summer of 1934, it drew support from various anti-FDR groups. These included Alfred E. Smith, the Democrat candidate for the presidency in 1928 and former Governor of New York State. The aim of the League was 'to defend and uphold the Constitution and to foster the right to work, earn, save and acquire property and to preserve ownership and the lawful use of property'.

However, to see the Liberty League as representing all American big business is wrong. The New Deal did have support from several big industrialists, such as movie **mogul** Jack Warner of Warner Bros. and Walter Teagle of the Standard Oil (Esso) corporation. Many businessmen were advisers to the Administration. This was particularly true during the First New Deal when FDR relied heavily on the banking community for his banking and financial legislation.

3.5 What impact did the Second World War have on the domestic history of the USA, 1941–1945?

What impact did the War have on the economy?

'Dr Win the War', as FDR termed it, did what 'Dr New Deal' had failed to do. It brought economic prosperity back to the USA. By 1942, the USA was enjoying full employment as the country developed a war economy. However, ever since the outbreak of European War, in September 1939, the USA had benefited from the demand for armaments by Britain and France. Even after France was defeated, the USA remained 'the arsenal of democracy' by providing weapons through the **Lend–Lease programme** of early 1941. Gross national product almost doubled between 1939 and 1942.

The Second World War had a significant impact on taxation and government spending in the United States. The Revenue Act of 1942 brought large numbers of Americans into the federal income tax system for the first time. In 1939, less than four million paid federal income taxes. This had risen to almost 43 million by 1945. In 1940, total federal revenue was $7 billion. By 1944, it had risen to $51 billion. The increased revenue was needed to pay for war expenditure. However, even the rise in taxes could not provide enough money. The rest was made through borrowing. Much money was raised through selling **war bonds**. Famous Hollywood film stars such as Bing Crosby and Bob Hope went on fundraising tours selling war bonds.

All this extra spending had a major impact on economic growth. In 1938, the GNP was $85.2 billion. This had risen to $100 billion by 1940. By 1945, it had reached $213.6 billion. Even allowing for inflation, the US economy grew a staggering 73 per cent during the War.

These changes had a huge impact on US industry. Corporate profits rose from $6 billion in 1939 to $10.5 billion in 1945 as companies benefited from government contracts. Usually, large firms received defence contracts and this led to mergers and the growth of larger firms. By 1943, 100 large firms were providing 70 per cent of manufacturing output. In achieving these changes, the US economy provided the backbone of Allied armaments against Germany, Italy and Japan. During the war, the USA produced over 300,000 aircraft, 100,000 tanks and 93,000 ships. Most of the Red Army was transported to Berlin in US trucks.

The War also saw a major increase in the powers of the federal government. From December 1941, the federal government took a major role in the direction of the economy. The Office of Price Administration (OPA) controlled prices. In October 1942, the Office of Economic Stabilisation replaced it. The War Production Board oversaw defence production. The War Manpower Commission allocated labour between industries. In May 1943, these were subordinated to a super ministry, the Office of War Mobilisation, which ran the US economy on a war footing.

The most awesome task of the federal government was to mobilise men for the armed forces. The USA had, traditionally, a small volunteer army numbering just over 250,000 in 1939. By 1945, over 12 million men (12 per cent of the population) were in uniform.

What impact did the War have on US society?

With 12 million men in uniform by 1945, and the economy growing at a rapid rate, the shortfall in workers had to be made up by women. In all, hundreds of thousands of women became involved in the war effort. Many served in the armed forces as telephonists, car drivers and secretaries. Many more worked in war industries doing blue-collar jobs. 'Rosie the

Lend–Lease programme: An American policy introduced during the Second World War by which military aid was given to Britain, and other allied countries, with the aim of acquiring payment for such aid after the war.

War bonds: A form of loan to the US government. These were government certificates sold during the Second World War to raise money for the war effort. Individuals were encouraged to buy them. Once the War was over, the government planned to repay the purchaser.

Propaganda: Information, often exaggerated or false, which is spread by political parties, governments or pressure groups in order to influence others.

Riveter' became a **propaganda** character to represent women in the aircraft manufacturing industry.

The War also presented new opportunities for African-Americans – serving in the forces and working in industry. If black people could fight for freedom from oppression for others, then why not for themselves? This period, 1941–43, saw a rise in racial tension across America. Major race riots occurred between whites and African-Americans in Detroit in 1943. Riots also occurred in many northern cities. The armed forces were not immune. The USA still segregated white and African-American troops. Fighting occurred in several locations overseas between these racial groups. Nevertheless, FDR issued presidential Executive Order 8802 in 1941, which banned discrimination against African-Americans in federal employment and the defence industries. It also established the Fair Employment Practices Commission to supervise the labour market. The number of African-Americans in federal employment rose from 3 per cent in 1942 to almost 10 per cent by the end of the war.

The most notorious example of racism during the War was made against Japanese Americans, most of whom lived on the west coast. In February 1942, FDR's Administration authorised the relocation of all Japanese Americans to camps away from the coast. It was believed they might cooperate with a possible Japanese invasion. In all, 112,000 Japanese Americans were forced to leave their homes and businesses despite the fact that none were arrested for espionage.

1. In what ways did the Second World War change the lives of ordinary American men and women?

2. What do you regard as the most significant development in US economy and society between 1941 and 1945? Give reasons for your answer.

---

1. How successful was the New Deal in bringing about economic recovery from 1933 to 1940?

2. What impact did the Second World War have on US economic prosperity?

Unemployment and manufacturing output in the USA, 1928–1944

Year	% Unemployed	Index of Industrial Output (1926 = 100)
1928	4.4	104
1930	8.7	96
1932	23.6	60
1934	21.7	78
1936	16.9	110
1938	19.0	92
1940	14.6	132
1942	4.7	220
1944	1.2	260

---

1. Explain why the National Debt rose during the period 1910–1920 and again between 1930–1940?

2. Do the figures suggest that the US economy was in difficulty between 1930–1950?

Explain your answer.

US National Debt, 1900–1950

Year	National Debt	Debt per person
1900	$1,263,417,000	$17
1910	$1,146,940,000	$12
1920	$24,299,231,000	$228
1930	$16,185,310,000	$132
1940	$42,967,352,000	$325
1950	$257,357,352,000	$1,697

3.6 Did the New Deal bring fundamental change to the USA?

A CASE STUDY IN HISTORICAL INTERPRETATION

Since the 1930s, the New Deal has received a wide variety of assessments. In 1992, in *The Anxious Decades*, Michael Parrish declared:

'Franklin Roosevelt and the New Deal failed the American people: in six years of effort, economic prosperity had not returned and the Depression lingered. Nearly 10 million citizens, over 17 per cent of the labor force, remained out of work in 1939. A much larger percentage remained in 1939 as in 1936 "ill housed, ill clothed, ill nourished".'

To many conservative critics of the New Deal, these development were easy to explain. Roosevelt had introduced too much reform and there was too much regulation of the US economy. As a result of government interference, the economy had not recovered. Far too many of the New Deal 'alphabet agencies' had unclear goals. Many of the agencies had overlapping areas of responsibility. Some were in competition with each other.

In a study of economic statistics, the New Deal failed in one of its main aims – 'to get America back to work'. As historian Paul Conkin stated in *The New Deal* (1967): 'From almost every perspective, the New Deal solved a few problems, ameliorated [solved] others, obscured many and created unanticipated new ones.'

From this perspective, FDR's achievements seem shallow. Although critics might accept that he was charismatic, eloquent and flexible in approach, he was nothing more than a con artist who hoodwinked the American people into believing 'Happy days are here again' – as his campaign song stated.

Compared with other western economies, the US economy took longer to get out of depression than any other. Yet to others, FDR did not go far enough. To left-wing critics, he failed to nationalise the banking system, refused to pass laws banning lynching and did little to provide affordable public housing. Even where reforms were made, such as the Social Security Act of 1935, it fell far short of similar measures in Britain, Australia and New Zealand.

To the left in America, FDR's greatest crime was in helping to preserve the capitalist economic system. Instead of being the enemy of 'big business', he helped to save it. Far from bringing fundamental economic change, FDR prevented it from taking place.

Even where advances were made for working people in the USA, FDR and his Administration did not get the credit. In 1992, the American Social History project published *Who Built America?* It stated that:

> 'In the last half of the 1930s, working people made America a more democratic nation. By organising, protesting, sitting-in, and voting as a **progressive bloc**, they forced the federal government to begin acting as a guarantor of workers' rights to organise, bargain collectively, and earn a decent wage.'

Progressive bloc: Those members of Congress who supported the involvement of federal government in social welfare.

Yet FDR and the New Deal did achieve much. Tony Badger, in *The New Deal*, contrasts FDR with Hoover's efforts of 1929–33. In industry, agriculture and banking, FDR made considerable strides. He helped to put the unemployed back to work, he aided farmers, he prevented a complete banking and economic collapse. FDR restored hope to people who had grown fatalistic.

When assessing FDR's performance, the obstacles he faced must be taken into consideration. He had to work within a federal system which had given state governments considerable authority in social and economic matters. He had to win the support of Congress for his reforms. He also had to battle against a US Supreme Court which almost destroyed the First New Deal in 1935–36. From a position of serious crisis, in March 1933, FDR had laid the foundations for economic recovery. As historian Hugh Brogan writes, in *The Longman History of the United States* (1999):

'Thanks to Franklin Roosevelt, in short, six years (1933–1938) transformed America from a country which had been laid low by troubles which in its own incompetence had brought on it, and which it was quite unable to cope with, to a country superbly equipped to meet the worst shocks that the modern world can hurl at it. It was enough.'

In addressing Congress, in 1938, FDR defended his own record:

'Government has a final responsibility for the well-being of its citizenship. If private cooperative endeavour fails to provide work for willing hands and relief for the unfortunate, those suffering hardship from no fault of their own have a right to call upon the Government for aid; and a government worthy of its name must make a fitting response.'

In FDR's own words, the New Deal did bring a fundamental change in American thinking about distress and in the government's role in dealing with it.

It is clear that the New Deal years left a profound mark on the USA. Nowhere more so than in the role of the federal government. By the outbreak of war, in 1941, the federal government's role had expanded out of all recognition. With it had grown the role of the President. The creation of the Executive Office of the Presidency, in 1939, underlined this change. What the New Deal had started, the war years finished. By 1945, the 'Imperial Presidency' had been created with the federal government playing a dominant role in the lives of virtually every American.

The New Deal years also brought about a political realignment, which lasted until the 1970s. The coalition of southern whites, African-Americans, blue-collar workers, Catholics and Jews meant that the Democrats dominated the presidency and Congress for over a generation. Democrat dominance was also reflected in the control of state governorships and state legislatures.

However, the New Deal brought little change in the plight of women or African-Americans. What the New Deal had failed to do was provided by the huge social changes brought about by the Second World War. Any assessment of the New Deal is complicated by the fact that it was immediately followed by a period of considerable social and economic change.

1. Why do historians have differing views on the success of FDR and the New Deal?

2. In what ways did the New Deal bring fundamental change to the USA?

3. Which was more significant in bringing about social, economic and political change:

(a) the New Deal years 1933–1940

(b) the Second World War years 1941–1945?

Explain your answer with reference to (i) social, (ii) economic and (iii) political change.

1. From information contained in this section find out what is the full title of the alphabet agencies in the mind map. Write a brief account of what role they had in the New Deal.

2. What do you regard as the most successful alphabet agency? Give reasons for your answer.

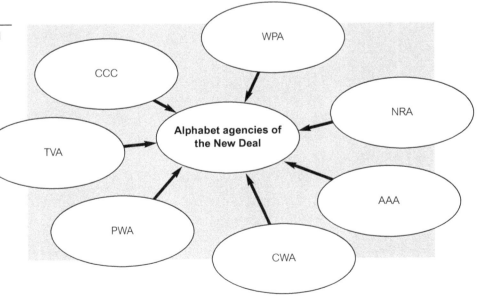

Source-based questions: FDR and the New Deal

SOURCE A

In this nation I see millions of families trying to live on incomes so meagre that the threat of family disaster hangs over them day by day.
I see millions whose daily lives in the city and on the farm continue under conditions labelled indecent by so-called polite society a half-century ago.

I see millions denied education, recreation and the opportunity to better their lot and the lot of their children.

I see millions lacking the means to buy the products of farm and factory and by their poverty denying work and productivity to many other millions.

It is not in despair that I paint you a picture but in hope – because the nation, seeing it and understanding the injustice in it, proposes to paint it out. The test of our progress is not whether we add more to the abundance of those who have much, it is whether we provide enough for those who have too little.

From a speech by President Roosevelt on his inauguration as
President, 20 January 1937

1. Study Source A.

What problems does Roosevelt identify as facing the United States in 1937 and what attitude does he reveal to the solving of these problems?

2. Use your own knowledge.

Why, and in what ways, did the Supreme Court oppose the New Deal in the years 1933–1936?

3. Use your own knowledge.

How successful was the New Deal in promoting the recovery of agriculture and industry in the United States in the years 1933–1941?

3.7 An in-depth study: Was the New Deal a success or a failure?

3.7.1 Did the New Deal bring about economic recovery?
3.7.2 Did the New Deal 'save' America?
3.7.3 How radical was the New Deal in protecting working people?

Framework of Events

1932	November: FDR elected thirty-second president of United States
1933	March: '100 days' begins with Emergency Banking Act
	Civilian Conservation Corps (CCC)
	May: Federal Emergency Relief Administration (FERA)
	Agricultural Adjustment Act (AAA)
	Tennessee Valley Authority (TVA)
	June: National Industrial Recovery Act (NIRA) establishes National Recovery Administration (NRA), including what becomes Public Works Administration (PWA)
	November: Civil Works Administration (CWA)
1934	June: Securities and Exchange Commission (SEC)
1935	January: Second New Deal begins
	April: Works Progress Administration (WPA)
	May: Supreme Court declares Title I of the NIRA unconstitutional (PWA unaffected)
	Rural Electrification Administration (REA)
	July: National Labor Relations Act
	August: Social Security Act
1936	January: Supreme Court declares AAA unconstitutional
	February: Soil Conservation and Domestic Allotment Act
	November: FDR elected for second term
1937	June: FDR cuts government spending and unemployment starts to rise
1938	April: Increase in spending to off-set 'Roosevelt recession'
	June: Fair Labor Standards Act
1939	September: Outbreak of World War II in Europe
1940	November: FDR elected for third term
1941	December: US enters World War II after attack on Pearl Harbor
1944	November: FDR elected for fourth term
1945	April: FDR dies in Warm Springs, Georgia

Overview

WHEN Franklin D. Roosevelt took office in March 1933, the United States was facing its worst crisis since the US Civil War of 1861–5. The new president promised a 'New Deal' for the American people. Consequently, expectations for the administration were high. FDR did not disappoint them. The next eight years saw America transformed, with programmes for the financial system, schemes for the unemployed, measures to help industry and agriculture, as well as policies that took the USA in a whole new direction, such as the introduction of social security. The impact of the New Deal was immense; every American government since has consciously tried to build on it or tried to dismantle it.

In the 1950s and 1960s, US presidents, Democrat and Republican alike, attempted to build on the legacy of the New Deal to a greater or lesser extent. Historians of the period such as William E. Leuchtenburg (*Franklin D. Roosevelt and the New Deal, 1932–1940*, (1963)) saw the New Deal as a success, albeit a qualified one. FDR had managed to balance the needs of business and employees, of farmers and industrialists and saved America from the kind of extremism that the Depression gave rise to in Europe. Despite this, the problems faced by the United States in the 1960s and 1970s over civil rights, poverty and Vietnam led many historians and writers to look more critically at American **capitalism** and how it operated. These 'new left' writers are much more critical of FDR and the New Deal. They argue that capitalism had brought about the crisis of 1929 and the American Government should have taken the opportunity to change the economic and political system in a much more radical way. They argue that FDR was far too cautious and gave in too much to the interests of big business and the big banks. Historians such as Paul K. Conkin, in *The New Deal* (1968), and Howard Zinn, in *New Deal Thought* (1966), see the New Deal as a wasted opportunity.

To an extent, the **historiography** of the New Deal has followed the economic trends of the periods in which the historians were writing. In the 1980s, with the growth of right-wing politics and **monetarist** economics, historians began to criticise the **Keynesian** nature of the New Deal. Historians like Milton Friedman, in *Free to Choose: A Personal Statement* (1980), argue that far from doing too little, the New Deal had done too much and stifled recovery by too much interference from the Federal Government. They also point out that this growth in federal power did not end with the New Deal but remained and set a trend that has seen the Federal Government continue to grow and continue to expand its power into more and more areas of life.

In the last two decades, historians have once again given FDR and the New Deal a better press. By looking beyond the White House, historians like Anthony J. Badger, in *The New Deal: The Depression Years, 1933–1940* (1989), have pointed out the constraints under which FDR operated. No American president can do just as he likes, and taking into account the pressure from Congress and the restrictions of the Supreme Court, not to mention the conflicting needs and desires of the various groups within American society, the New Deal in fact achieved a lot.

Capitalism: an economic system that is based on the private ownership of property and individual wealth.

Historiography: the differing views and explanations that historians have of events in the past.

Monetarist: economic view that argues for a free market with minimal government interference; control of the money supply and interest rates should be used to direct the economy, not government spending.

Keynesian: named after British economist John Maynard Keynes, who argued that governments should get out of depression and reduce unemployment by spending, even if it means going into debt.

3.7.1 Did the New Deal bring about economic recovery?

FDR's reaction to a financial crisis

When FDR took office, the American financial system was in crisis; businesses were losing money, farmers were losing their land and families were losing their homes. Above all, 25 per cent of the workforce (almost 14 million people) was unemployed. The New Deal attempted to tackle all of these problems and much more. Any visitor to the US can see the physical evidence of the New Deal, which produced 3,700 playgrounds, 1,050 airfields, 500 water treatment plants, 19,700 miles of water pipes, 822,000 miles of roads and streets, 122,000 bridges, 8,000 parks, 22,000 housing projects, electrification for 780,000 farms and much, much more. But did the New Deal bring recovery to the economy?

Did FDR achieve industrial recovery?

Anti-trust legislation: anti-trust laws prohibited companies from joining together to fix prices. The laws were put in place to ensure competition among businesses.

To stop the wasteful competition that was driving down prices and profits, FDR introduced the National Industrial Recovery Act of 1933 (NIRA), which suspended **anti-trust legislation** and set up the National Recovery Administration (NRA), which got groups of companies together to set 'codes of fair competition' – prices and production levels – for their particular industry. The Act also set a minimum wage and maximum working hours, and abolished child labour. It has been estimated that the NIRA created two million jobs and increased purchasing power by $3billion. However, few people would disagree with Anthony J. Badger's comment, in *The New Deal: The Depression Years, 1933–1940* (1989), that 'the success of New Deal efforts to secure industrial recovery was strictly limited' and, in spite of its stated aim, the New Deal did not solve the problem of overproduction. The traditional criticism is that the 'codes of fair competition' were set by big businesses in their own favour and that they then proceeded to ignore them. There is some truth in this. In 1933, there were 10,000 complaints of code violation. Yet, Badger disputes the amounts of influence big business are credited with having over the NRA. He points out that industries, such as car manufacturing, were already **oligopolies** that had little to gain from the NRA codes and that, when the Supreme Court struck it down in May 1935, the business community did not lament its passing.

Oligopolies: where just a few companies control a whole section of industry.

Did FDR achieve rural recovery?

FDR had much more interest in rural affairs than in industrial issues. He was deeply involved in the Civilian Conservation Corps (CCC), the Tennessee Valley Authority (TVA), the Public Works Administration (PWA) and the Civil Works Administration (CWA). All were considered great New Deal successes.

The CCC, set up in March 1933, gave young men, aged 17 to 25, nine months of work – planting trees, laying telephone lines, managing forests, and so on. They lived in camps and earned $30 per month, of which $25 had to be sent home. This was based on a project FDR had introduced when he was governor of New York State and was very much his own idea. He said:

> 'The idea is to put people to work in the national forests and on other government and state properties.'

It was very important to FDR and the US Government that these young men worked for their wages and were not given handouts. The 'rugged individualism' of the 1920s was still strong in the USA. The army built the camps and military discipline was enforced on the young men. There was a 10 per cent drop-out rate, which was largely due to the military discipline, but the agency remained popular. By August 1933, there were 275,000 men in 1,300 camps around the country, which rose to half a million in 2,500 camps at its peak at the end of the 1930s. In all, almost three million young men went through the CCC before it ended in 1942.

The TVA, created in May 1933, was based on a plan put forward by Republican Senator George Norris, and was as much about helping farmers as providing jobs and flood relief. Norris had a plan to build dams in the Muscle Shoals area of Alabama to provide power for farmers and jobs in nitrate plants. Twenty dams were built along the Tennessee River to control floods in seven of the poorest states. There was also soil conservation, welfare programmes, fertiliser factories, and so on. The dams provided cheap hydroelectric power in the Tennessee Valley and, along with the Rural Electrification Administration created in 1935, the number

Senator George Norris (third from right) and various members of Congress from the Tennessee Valley Authority (TVA) region look on as FDR signs the TVA into existence, 18 May 1933. The TVA was one of the largest and most successful of the New Deal agencies.

of rural homes with electrical power increased from one in 10 to nine in 10. According to Michael J. Heale, in *Franklin D. Roosevelt: The New Deal and War* (1999):

> Probably no other single measure of the New Deal was as responsible for transforming life in the American South.

The CWA, created in November 1933, was crucial in providing jobs during the winter of 1933/4 on various public works. Without this emergency programme many civilians would have starved. When it was clear that public work would be needed for longer, the PWA, which had been set up in June 1933, took over. These agencies built schools, airports, hospitals, bridges, roads and more, and provided jobs for thousands. A total of $3,300 million was spent on the PWA alone and, at its peak in the winter of 1933/4, the CWA employed 4.25 million men. Work on the PWA was slow because the projects, such as building airports, were capital intensive. However, the agency built a third of all US hospitals. Altogether, the PWA spent $6 billion on providing a massive boom to the construction industry.

How did farmers benefit from the New Deal?

Farmers got more from FDR and the New Deal than from any other group. FDR wanted to make agriculture more efficient. He wanted to *help* the rural poor, not just bail them out. In March 1933, various agencies were brought together to form the Farm Credit Administration (FCA), which gave relief on mortgages, saving as many as 300 farms a day; and the Commodity Credit Corporation, which gave farmers loans against their crops. According to Ronald Edsforth, in *The New Deal: America's Response to the Great Depression* (2000):

> [These measures] helped to diffuse the farm crisis in the rural regions hit hardest by the Great Depression [and ensured that] traditionally Republican farm states in the Midwest voted for Franklin Roosevelt in the presidential election of 1936.

The Agricultural Adjustment Act 1933 (AAA) was based on Montana's Domestic Allotment Plan, which was a voluntary scheme where farmers were paid to reduce their acreage. Under the AAA, farmers were to group together and set production quotas. In return for cutting production they received a subsidy, from the US Government, which was paid for by a tax on food processing. In 1933, for example, the AAA destroyed 4.5 million acres of cotton but the price rose from 10¢ a pound to 65¢.

By 1941, farm incomes had doubled from their 1932 levels and agricultural debt was reduced by $1 billion. Although agricultural **foreclosures** did not stop, Anthony J. Badger, in *The New Deal: The Depression Years, 1933–1940* (1989), asserts that far more farmers would have lost their land if it had not been for the New Deal.

Foreclosures: when the bank takes back land or property because the mortgage payments have not been met.

Yet, many historians are critical of FDR's agricultural policies. Left-wing writers in the 1960s and 1970s, who were concerned about world hunger, were very critical of a policy that destroyed crops when people were going hungry. Howard Zinn, in *A People's History of the United States* (1980), argues that neither the AAA nor the FCA helped the very poor, such as the **sharecroppers** who made up half of the agricultural population in the 1930s and were living on an average yearly income of $312. Badger, however, argues that FDR could not be too revolutionary because workable radical solutions were not there and what was needed was fast action to deal with the crises.

Sharecroppers: farmers who work on land owned by someone else. The owner provides the land, seed, and tools in exchange for part of the crops and goods produced on the farm. Many sharecroppers in the 1930s were African-Americans.

There is no doubt that farmers saw their standards of living rise in the second half of the decade. However, there is some dispute as to whether FDR should take the credit. It is unclear if the rise in agricultural incomes was due to AAA quotas or the effects of the dust bowl (see page 72) in cutting production. Michael Simpson, among others, points out, in *Franklin D. Roosevelt* (1989), that farmers were not spending the money that they received but were saving it in case of future difficulties. By doing this, they were not increasing the demand for industrial goods. At the same time, the taxes on food processing increased the price that urban dwellers had to pay for food. In other words, farmers were doing better at the expense of the urban population. The Supreme Court agreed, in United States versus Butler in 1936, that the AAA was taking money from one group to benefit another and declared the AAA unconstitutional. FDR had to present agricultural subsidies as soil conservation payments; instead of paying the farmers to cut production the Federal Government paid the farmers to conserve the soil by allowing it to lie fallow (unused) until another AAA could be passed in 1938.

Did the New Deal reduce poverty and unemployment?

According to Michael Simpson, in *Franklin D. Roosevelt* (1989), the New Deal cannot be judged a tremendous success in reducing poverty and unemployment. He points out that at any one time only one in three Americans was benefiting from a New Deal programme, and each of the programmes had severe limitations. He states:

> [As] thousands of blacks, senior citizens and sharecroppers could testify, the 'forgotten man' often remained forgotten.

However, both he and Ronald Edsforth, in *The New Deal: America's Response to the Great Depression* (2000), emphasise that when judging the New Deal one must take account of the scale of the problem that FDR faced. FDR had to balance the competing interests within the Democratic Party and society. He also believed in a balanced budget, and neither he nor the American public were prepared to spend the amounts of money that would be needed to get the US out of the Depression.

Although the standard view is that the New Deal did not bring about recovery, Edsforth's book, The *New Deal: America's Response to the Great Depression* (2000), gives FDR's performance much more approval. He points out that, although unemployment was still high, the economy was growing until the mid-1930s and would have continued to grow if FDR had not cut spending in 1937. The fact that spending was important in growth was shown in the war when spending ended the Depression. The 1937 budget cut led to a 33 per cent decline in industrial production, a 35 per cent fall in wages and a 13 per cent fall in national income, as well as a rise in unemployment of four million. Edsforth writes:

As most Americans now know, full employment and dramatic reductions in poverty were not achieved until 1942/3 when 13 million men and women were serving in the armed forces and the United States was supplying huge quantities of war materials and food to its wartime Allies. These facts alone force us to conclude that the New Deal failed to promote real economic recovery; and that it took massive government borrowing, investment and spending during World War II to end the Great Depression. [But] the economic record of the New Deal did not appear dismal to contemporaries.

Contemporaries saw a growth in GNP, a growth in earnings and a fall in unemployment, and for that they thanked FDR.

3.7.2 Did the New Deal 'save' America?

Did the people have faith in the President?

According to historian Ronald Edsforth, in *The New Deal: America's Response to the Great Depression* (2000), American capitalism was in crisis in the early 1930s. Not only was there mass unemployment and the collapse of industry and agriculture but, as Edsforth writes:

[There was also] daily theft and looting of stores for food, farm strikes, anti-eviction and anti-foreclosure riots, communist-led hunger marches, seizures of public buildings, police gassing and shooting of unemployed workers, attempted assassinations of public officials, lynch mobs and vigilante violence … .

During FDR's 1932 election campaign, a friend said to him that if the New Deal were a success he would be remembered as the greatest American president. Roosevelt replied that if it were to fail he would be remembered as the last.

In the months between the election and the inauguration, 5,000 banks closed, and 20,000 farmers lost their land. Unemployment had reached almost 14 million, and 9 million people had lost their savings. Historians disagree on whether the United States was actually on the verge of collapse but many people at the time felt that this was the case. If nothing else, FDR gave confidence back to the American people. He talked about 'bold persistent experimentation'. 'Try something', he said, 'and if it fails, admit it frankly and try something else.'

The first '100 days' of FDR's first administration saw Congress pass 15 major pieces of legislation to tackle the worst problems of the Depression. After the seeming inaction of the Hoover years, FDR's energy and confidence was crucial in raising morale. People wrote to the President in unheard of numbers: as many as 8,000 letters a day were sent to the White House. Millions tuned in to hear his radio broadcasts. He was re-elected in 1936 with a massive 61 per cent of the popular vote and, in spite of problems with the Supreme Court, a recession and a difficult Congress, he was also re-elected for an unprecedented third term in 1940, winning 55 per cent of the votes cast. He won again, for the fourth time, in 1944. It would be hard to dispute that the majority of American people had faith in their president and his leadership.

Was FDR's action on the banks successful?

Action on the banks was crucial to preserving capitalism in the US. Banks were going under at the rate of 40 a day by the time FDR took office. There were $41 billion deposits in US banks but only $6 billion in cash to cover them. In March 1933, the President obtained Congress's permission to close the nation's banks for four days. The so-called 'banking holiday' meant that no more withdrawals could be made and it gave the Federal Government time to act. Under the Emergency Banking Act 1933, FDR used the **Reconstruction Finance Corporation** to assess the viability of banks. It decided that it was necessary for the Federal Government to buy shares in the bank to give it stability. When the banks reopened after the 'banking holiday', the amount of money being put back into accounts was more than the amount being taken out for the first time since the Wall Street crash. FDR had restored people's faith in the banking system. In 1936, there were no bank failures for the first time in 59 years.

Reconstruction Finance Corporation: established by President Hoover, in February 1932, to give emergency loans to businesses in danger of going bankrupt. In July 1932, it was given the power to lend money to states for poverty relief. FDR took it over when he became president.

FDR also stabilised the New York stock exchange on Wall Street through the creation, in June 1934, of the Securities and Exchange Commission (SEC). Although businessmen at the time resented this interference from the Federal Government, '[they] reluctantly accepted that [it] had brought order to financial markets' (Anthony J. Badger, *The New Deal: The Depression Years, 1933–1940* (1989)). In fact, when President Reagan proposed abolishing the SEC in the 1980s, the New York stock exchange on Wall Street itself objected.

Some historians, notably those on the left, have criticised FDR for not taking the opportunity to **nationalise** the banks. But, as Anthony J. Badger and Michael Simpson point out, this would have led to a long-drawn-out argument with Congress at a time when quick action was essential and when there was no real call for nationalisation. In fact, Hoover had wanted to close the banks in February 1933 and had asked for FDR's cooperation, which was refused. Ronald Edsforth, in *The New Deal: America's Response to the Great Depression* (2000), points out that there were differences in their policies but the real reason was political – FDR did not want Hoover to get the credit if it worked.

Nationalise: to take under government control.

To what extent was America 'saved'?

William E. Leuchtenburg, in *Franklin D. Roosevelt and the New Deal, 1932–1940* (1963), disputes whether FDR 'saved' America. He maintains that, although there was unrest, the people did not want to overthrow the system. The people were angry and bitter but they still believed in American democracy, as shown by the lack of support for extremist parties such as the Communist Party. He argues that the overwhelming emotion in 1932 was apathy. Ronald Edsforth, in *The New Deal: America's Response to the Great Depression* (2000), paints a different picture. He argues that despair affected everyone from poor farmers to millionaires. People did not know which way to turn or how the Depression would end, and there were 'real fears of revolution, or anarchy, or race war, or some awful combination of these'. FDR played down these fears, famously saying that Americans only had to fear 'fear itself' and, by his rapid actions, he restored their confidence in the system and the government.

3.7.3 How radical was the New Deal in protecting working people?

How radical was the '100 days'?

Fiscal conservative: someone who believes in a balanced budget – not spending more than the government gets in taxation.

Deficit financing: government spending more money than it takes in taxation, with the hope that it will increase purchasing power and get the country out of depression.

John Maynard Keynes (1883–1946)
Keynes was an influential British economist. As an adviser at the Paris Peace Conference in 1919, he walked out over what he believed were the errors being made over reparation payments. In 1936, he published *The General Theory of Employment, Interest and Money*, which argued for government spending to promote economic stability and recovery from depression. His ideas became widely accepted after World War II until challenged in the 1970s.

Efficacy: positive effect.

Throughout the 1920s, economists and presidents believed firmly in the necessity of strong financial control and balanced budgets. When the Depression hit, Hoover, and leaders in other countries, believed that if they did not cut spending they would bankrupt their countries. Yet, the New Deal had an average annual deficit of $2.7 billion a year. Was this taking America in a new direction? FDR was, at heart, a **fiscal conservative** like Hoover and his own Treasury Secretary, Henry Morgenthau, but some economists, most notably John Maynard Keynes, were arguing that governments should spend their way out of the Depression. FDR was not convinced that **deficit spending** was the answer but he knew that something had to be done and he was prepared to take America into debt in the short term if that was what it took.

During the '100 days', FDR got the Federal Emergency Relief Act (FERA) passed to give money to states to help the poor and unemployed. While this measure was undoubtedly radical in that the Federal Government was stepping into an area that had previously been a state responsibility, the amount given out prevented it from being as successful as it might have been. FERA gave $500 million to feed the poor and unemployed. Half the amount was given as direct federal relief and the other half was made up by the Federal Government giving $1 to match every $3 that the state promised to raise. However, many states cut relief spending knowing that Harry Hopkins would have to give them FERA money anyway. Some states and cities were unable or unwilling to raise taxes to match the federal funds. And, as Michael Simpson points out, FERA was paid for with money raised from cutting the pay and pensions of federal employees under the Economy Act of March 1933. FDR wanted as much of the New Deal to be as self-financing as possible.

How radical was the Second New Deal?

It seemed that during the Second New Deal (1935–7), FDR had been persuaded of the **efficacy** of federal spending. The Works Progress Administration (WPA), set up in April 1935, was originally allocated just under $2 billion for relief and public works, yet ended up spending more than $5 billion, becoming the most important New Deal agency. Rather than conversion to a more radical Keynesian policy, FDR was acting in response to riots, in the winter of 1934, protesting at the slow progress of recovery, and he continued to believe in the desirability of a balanced budget. In 1937, he became concerned by the rising deficit and cut spending by over $1 billion. Unemployment shot up to 10.2 million and FDR had to ask Congress once again for money for public works.

The WPA was, at the time, one of the more controversial elements of the New Deal. Although public works money had been given to artists and writers in other programmes, there had been nothing to match the scale of the WPA. The WPA paid out $4.8 billion, funding artists to paint murals in public buildings, the Federal Theatre Project to take plays on tours of the USA and the Federal Writers' Project to produce a set of guides for each of the 48 states. It was also the New Deal agency that gave most help to groups previously ignored, including African-Americans and women. Although it only reached a third of those in need, the WPA showed how federal money could be used imaginatively. It moved Federal Government into the arts, which continued under President Johnson with the creation of the National Endowment for the Arts. Critics, at the time and since,

California by Maxine Albro. A mural as part of a WPA initiative. The WPA received much criticism for employing actors, writers and painters, but their work brought art to the masses and can still be seen in many American cities today.

have debated whether it is the government's job to subsidise the arts. However, the WPA made the arts accessible to the lower classes. The Federal Theatre Project, for example, allowed poor people to see theatrical productions for the first time in their lives.

Also, in 1935, the National Labor Relations Act (or Wagner Act) gave legal rights and protection to trade unions for the first time, allowing them to grow and to represent the ordinary worker. Historians Michael Simpson and Patrick Maney argue that the Act was entirely the work of Senator Robert Wagner and that FDR even considered vetoing it. On the other hand, Michael J. Heale, in *Franklin D. Roosevelt: The New Deal and War* (1999), argues that the Act only received such a speedy passage through Congress because FDR put his weight behind it. Whatever the case, the Act spurred a massive growth in union membership. In 1935, the Congress of Industrial Organisations was formed to represent semi-skilled and un-skilled workers, including women and black people. Trade union membership grew from just under three million in 1930 to almost nine million in 1940. It continued to grow throughout World War II when the labour shortage put ordinary workers in a much more powerful position. By 1950, there were 15 million members. Labour laws also strengthened the link between workers and the Democratic Party, and by 1940 the unions were the biggest contributors to Democratic Party funds.

The Social Security Act, according to Carl N. Degler, in *Out of Our Past* (1984), was a 'revolutionary' measure. This was not designed to deal with the immediate problems but designed to ensure that, in the future, no economic recession could have the same devastating effects on people's lives as the Depression, which had left millions with no income. Wisconsin State was the only state that had any form of unemployment insurance when the stock exchange crash hit in 1929. US states were totally unpre-pared to deal with mass unemployment, so FDR aimed to provide Americans with a basic welfare system. He introduced: pensions for the over-65s financed by a payroll tax; unemployment benefit paid for by a tax on employers (who during the New Deal got a rebate for not laying people off); and categorical assistance to those who could not work (for example disability benefit paid for by federal and state funds). The United States lagged well behind other developed countries in introducing a welfare system. Britain had had similar programmes since 1911, and Bismarck had introduced social security in Germany as early as the 1880s.

At the time, there were many criticisms of the Social Security Act. Knowing that pensions would not be due until 1940, **Progressives** argued that the people needed the money immediately. They also argued that increasing taxes on employers and employees would reduce spending at a time when spending needed to go up. Also, left-wing critics disapproved of the lack of health insurance in the Act. Above all, there were major discrepancies. In Arkansas, for example, families got $8.10 for each dependent child, whereas in Massachusetts it was $61.07.

However, in FDR's defence, he had to give the states a role within social security to get the Act through Congress. As Anthony J. Badger points out, in *The New Deal: The Depression Years, 1933–1940* (1989), the Federal Government had neither the manpower nor the structures for such a massive programme. FDR was dependent on the states for the implementation of the policy. His insistence on funding social security from taxation was so that people would feel that they had contributed to it and so would not allow future politicians to cut it. FDR would have had to fight Congress and the American Medical Association to get healthcare included in the Act. The New Dealers were fully aware of the weaknesses of the Social Security Act but they felt that additions and improvements could be added later. The important thing was to make a start.

Progressives: people who believe that the government should use its power for social reform.

Assessment

The social policies of the Second New Deal do seem to portray a government moving in a more radical and left-wing way. Arthur M. Schlesinger Jr. is one historian who, in *The Imperial Presidency* (1973), argues that there was a definite shift in policy, but William E. Leuchtenburg, in *Franklin D. Roosevelt and the New Deal, 1932–1940* (1963), maintains that it was a change of emphasis rather than a change of direction. He points out that many of the measures had been 'in the works' for a while and it was simply due to timing that they were passed in 1935.

Most historians agree that FDR had no coherent ideology, but Ronald Edsforth, in *The New Deal: America's Response to the Great Depression* (2000), says that the New Deal had an ideological commitment to economic security for every American citizen. In his 'fireside chat' on 11 January 1944, FDR talked about an Economic Bill of Rights that planned to provide every American citizen with access to a job, a decent home, food, clothing, education, and protection in old age, sickness and unemployment. However, Patrick J. Maney, in *The Roosevelt Presence: The Life and Legacy of FDR* (1992), argues that FDR believed that the capitalist system would put this in place and that the Federal Government would only need to step in to fill in the gaps. He writes:

> Yet in subsequent speeches, it became clear that Roosevelt envisaged no great expansion of government. He seemed confident that the free enterprise system would be able to make the Economic Bill of Rights a reality, with government limiting itself to a supporting role.

World War II and FDR's death, in 1945, prevented this from happening, but the ideas were to become dominant in the Democratic Party for the next 20 years.

Left-wing historian Howard Zinn, however, is much more critical of how much the New Deal changed things. In *A People's History of the United States* (1980), he states:

> Enough help had been given to enough people to make Roosevelt a hero to millions, but the same system that had brought depression and crisis – the system of waste, of inequality, of concern for profit over human need – remained.

New Deal: success or failure?

1. Read the following extract and answer the question.

This is truly legislation in the interests of national welfare. We must recognise that if we are to maintain a healthy economy and thriving production, we need to maintain the standard of living of the lower income groups of our population who constitute 90 per cent of our purchasing power.

From a speech, given in September 1935, by Frances Perkins on the Social Security Act. Frances Perkins was the first female Cabinet minister in US history. She was appointed by FDR, in 1933, as Secretary of Labor.

Using the information in the extract above, and from this section, explain the reasons for the passing of the Social Security Act.

2. To what extent did the New Deal improve 'the standard of living of the lower income groups'?

Further Reading

Texts designed for AS Level students

FDR by Kathryn Cooper (Collins Historymakers, 2005)

Prosperity, Depression and the New Deal by Peter Clements (Hodder & Stoughton, Access to History series, 1997) – a readable, accessible text.

Franklin Roosevelt: The New Deal and War by M.J. Heale (Routledge, Lancaster pamphlets, 1999) – a short and very useful pamphlet which covers 1933–1945.

America by G. Tindall and D. Shi (W.W. Norton & Co., Third edition 1993) – a large history of the USA which has a useful section on the New Deal and the War.

The Enduring Vision by P. Boyer (D.C. Heath & Co., 1993) – a large but highly accessible general history of the USA which has a good section on the New Deal.

The New Deal by John A. Salmond (Frederick Warne, 1970) – succinct and readable coverage of the New Deal.

Texts for A2 and advanced study

The Anxious Decades, USA 1920–1941 by Michael E. Parrish (W.W. Norton & Co., 1992) – a scholarly and detailed coverage.

The Longman History of the United States by Hugh Brogan (Longman, Second edition 1999) – extremely readable, scholarly work by Britain's leading historian of the USA.

The New Deal, the Depression Years 1933–1940 by Tony Badger (Macmillan, 1989) – detailed and readable text which is about the best individual text on the New Deal by a British historian.

The New Deal by Paul Conkin (Harlan Davidson, Third edition 1992) – a short but scholarly account of the New Deal.

Who Built America? Volume II by the American Social History Project (Pantheon, 1992) – an extremely good study of social history.

Franklin D. Roosevelt and the New Deal, 1932–1940 by William E. Leuchtenburg (HarperCollins, 1963) – dated but still excellent study of FDR and the New Deal.

FDR by Ted Morgan (Simon & Schuster, 1985) – a very readable but large biography.

Video

'FDR' – a video written and produced by David Grubin for 'The American Experience' series (1994); four one-hour episodes covering FDR's political life and his relationship with his wife Eleanor.

4 US foreign policy, 1917–1945

Key Issues

- How far did US foreign policy change between 1917 and 1945?

- How important were US presidents in the conduct of foreign affairs?

- Why did the USA emerge as a major world power in the period from 1917 to 1945?

4.1 Why did the USA become involved in the First World War?

4.2 How successful was Wilson's foreign policy 1917–1919?

4.3 How far was the USA 'isolationist' between the two world wars?

4.4 Why did the USA become involved in the Second World War?

4.5 What role did the USA play in achieving Allied victory in the Second World War?

4.6 Why had the USA become a superpower by 1945?

4.7 Historical interpretation: Was FDR's foreign policy isolationist or interventionist?

Framework of Events

1914	Outbreak of First World War in Europe
1915	Sinking of the *Lusitania*
1917	USA enters the First World War
1919	Paris Peace Conference
1920	US Senate refuses to ratify the Treaty of Versailles
1922	Washington Naval Conference
1924	Dawes Plan
1929	Young Plan
1931	Japan invades and occupies Manchuria, China
	1935–37 Neutrality Acts
1937	Outbreak of Sino-Japanese War
1938	Munich Agreement
1939	Second World War breaks out in Europe
	USA introduces 'Cash and Carry' programme
1941	USA introduces 'Lend-Lease' Programme
	Atlantic Charter between USA and Britain
	Japanese attack US base at Pearl Harbor in the Hawaiian Islands.
1942	Battle of Midway
	Operation Torch: US troops invade French North Africa
1943	US troops invade Sicily and mainland Italy
1944	D-Day: US involved in invasion of France
	Battle of the Philippine Sea
1945	May: VE Day in Europe
	August: Atomic bombs dropped on Hiroshima and Nagasaki

Overview

BETWEEN 1917 and 1945 the USA rose to the position of a superpower. Up to 1917 the USA was mainly involved in winning control over the west. In 1890 the Indian Wars came to an end and the US government controlled all the lands between the Atlantic and Pacific Oceans. In 1898 the USA became a colonial power. In the Spanish-American War the USA acquired Puerto Rico and the Philippine Islands.

Over the turn of the century, Presidents Roosevelt and Taft consciously expanded America's role in the world. Theodore Roosevelt believed that the USA had a duty and a right to take a more prominent role in international affairs. Under his administration, the so-called 'Roosevelt Corollary' stated explicitly that the USA had the right to interfere in the affairs of the states of Latin America. Roosevelt also increased American involvement in the Far East – a policy continued by Taft with his encouragement of American financial investment in China.

When war broke out in Europe in 1914, many felt it was an argument between the 'old powers' and was of no concern to the United States. However, once it affected American liberties – such as the freedom to travel and to trade – the President, Woodrow Wilson, became more concerned. German naval attacks eventually forced America into the War, where its role in providing extra equipment and a supply of fresh soldiers was instrumental in the final Allied victory. But the losses of the War and the disappointment of the peace conference made Americans cynical about playing a world role and they retreated into **isolationism**.

Isolationism: A policy by which a state (e.g. the USA in the early 1930s) pursues its own domestic interests, in isolation from the wider considerations of international politics.

Even though the 1920s and 1930s are seen as the great period of isolation, American financial connections with Europe made it impossible for the United States to remove itself from the affairs of the continent. Likewise, an internal desire for cuts in spending meant the USA took an important role in international arms control. It was only really in Latin America that the American governments of the period pulled back.

The Great Depression of the 1930s turned American attention firmly to domestic affairs. Even while trouble bubbled in Europe, Congress passed a series of Neutrality Acts in an attempt to ensure that the USA was not pulled into another European war. But even then, they gave support to the British cause, due to the destructive nature of the Nazi regime and a belief by Roosevelt that a German victory would be bad for American security. What finally brought America into the Second World War was the attack on Pearl Harbor – itself a culmination of rivalry in the Pacific going back half a decade. With American manpower and economic might, victory was assured in 1945 and the United States emerged from the War as the most powerful nation on earth. From then on, there could be no return to the isolationist policies of the past.

Throughout the period 1890–1945, the United States of America had both a desire to increase its role in world affairs, yet at the same time not to get too involved in them. In fact, this period saw a fairly steady growth in American involvement overseas.

Latin America continued to be seen as an area of legitimate American interest for both strategic and economic reasons. The level of direct interference simply varied depending on the particular policies of the Presidents or events in Latin

America itself. The US attitude to Europe was more mixed. As the majority of American citizens were descended from Europeans they were affected by events on the continent, but as refugees who had left Europe's problems behind they were reluctant to get involved. However, the ties of history and its economic power meant the United States found itself drawn into European affairs through two world wars. It was perhaps in the Pacific and the Far East that one can see most clearly a definite growth in American influence.

In 1945, the USA was a world power. The desire for focusing only on its own interests was still there, but the USA's economic and military might meant its role in the world had changed dramatically. In 1890 the USA was potentially very powerful: it had a large population, a strong economy and an important geographical position, but its political influence in the world was not as great. By 1945, the United States had become, quite simply, the world's most powerful nation.

4.1 Why did the USA become involved in the First World War?

In August 1914, war broke out in Europe between Britain, France and Russia on one side, and Germany and Austria-Hungary on the other. Over the next three years the war spread, dragging in many of the other European nations. Even the Japanese joined the war, on 23 August 1914. The war would last four years and cost the lives of 18 million people.

The eight million Americans of German descent were sympathetic to the so-called Central Powers. Irish-Americans were also sympathetic due to their resentment of British rule in Ireland, as were many Jews and Poles who had fled to America to escape Russian persecution. But support for the Allies was stronger. Ties of language, culture and history meant that the majority of Americans supported Britain. There was also a long friendship with France going back to the War of Independence. With the exception of autocratic Russia, the Allied Powers were seen as the decent and democratic nations defending Europe from the unprovoked aggression of the **militaristic** Germans. This attitude was encouraged by very effective British propaganda which emphasised German 'atrocities', particularly against the defenceless Belgians.

Militaristic: Aggressive, heavily relying on military force.

There were some in America who thought that the United States should take part in the War. Ex-president Theodore Roosevelt thought staying out was cowardly. Others, including some in the Administration, felt that America needed to be prepared to defend democracy. They formed groups such as the National Security League. President Wilson himself was appalled by the German attack on neutral Belgium. However, he felt, as the vast majority of Americans did, that the war was a European affair and they did not want to be dragged into it. Wilson urged the people to be neutral in thought and deed, to show by example that Americans were somehow 'better', that there were other ways to resolve issues. The American public might be sympathetic to the Allied cause, but it was not their fight and, above all, they wanted to keep out of it.

Being neutral, however, proved more difficult than the Americans had imagined. They had an economic involvement in the War long before their military involvement. The First World War created a boom in American industry and agriculture with sales of goods and supplies to both sides. Money was loaned to enable the Europeans to pay for the goods they bought. By 1917, the USA had loaned over $2 billion to the Allies and $27 million to the Germans. Understandably, the Germans complained that this was hardly neutrality, but even before the War the United States had done a great deal more trade with Britain than with Germany. This led some to believe that America got involved in the war for financial reasons. Clearly, an Allied victory was preferable in order to protect American investment and it was probably a contributory factor to the decision to enter the War in 1917. Public opinion and American security also favoured an Allied victory and may have affected the Senate's decision. But it was the war at sea that was the ultimate cause of US entry into the First World War.

Early on in the war, Britain had used its naval strength to blockade the German coast and to stop and search vessels believed to be taking goods to the Central Powers. Some shipping lanes were also mined. America protested when its own ships were stopped or goods seized, but for Britain the blockade was an effective weapon. By 1915, the blockade was already causing shortages in Germany.

The Germans responded with submarine warfare to try and sink British ships and starve Britain into surrender. In February 1915, they announced that Allied ships would be sunk without warning. Though this made sense militarily, it went against accepted 'rules' of warfare. In the USA, it was seen as barbaric and as an infringement of the freedom of the seas. The American government protested. Some proposed banning US citizens from travelling on Allied vessels, but Wilson felt that this limited American freedoms. Then, on 7 May, the Germans sank the British passenger liner the 'Lusitania'. Of the 1,200 who died on the ship, 128 were Americans. In fact, the ship had been carrying ammunition. The Germans knew that Britain used liners for that purpose and saw the ship as a fair target, but public opinion in America was incensed. When two more Americans were killed on the 'Arabic' in August, the Germans seemed to back off in the face of American anger. In 1916, more Americans were hurt when the 'Sussex' was sunk. Wilson made it clear to Germany that if they continued to endanger American lives there would be serious consequences. The Germans were anxious to keep the Americans out of the War and they abandoned the U-boat (German submarine) campaign.

The crisis seemed to have been averted and Wilson went to the polls in 1916 on the slogan of having kept America out of the war. He won by a narrow victory of 277 electoral college votes to 254. Throughout 1916, Wilson had worked to avoid war. He proposed a peace conference to Edward Grey, the British Foreign Secretary, indicating that, if the Allies accepted the conference and the Germans did not, the USA might join the war against Germany. It came to nothing, as neither side really believed America would join. It is doubtful if Wilson could have carried Congress with him had he proposed it seriously. He knew that the public still did not want war.

Wilson also realised that, should war come, America needed to be more prepared than it was. He asked Congress for an increased army and navy. The army was increased to over 200,000 men and the National Guard to 400,000. (Just how unprepared America was is illustrated by the fact that General Haig was able to field 200,000 British soldiers at the Battle of the Somme alone.) A massive naval building programme was also embarked on which would soon see the American navy as one of the two most powerful in the world. This build-up caused criticism, with accusations that Wilson was getting America ready to join the War. Wilson did not want war, but as President, and Commander-in-Chief, he knew that he had to be ready if it came.

By the 'turnip winter' of 1916–1917, Germans were suffering severe hardship and hunger due to the British blockade. In January, in an effort to end the war, they announced the resumption of unrestricted U-boat warfare. After the agreement over the 'Sussex', the Germans knew they were risking bringing the United States into the conflict, but they felt they had to take the risk. They gambled that the Americans might not fight, or that if they did it would take too long for them to mobilise, by which time the Germans would have won. In both of these, they were wrong.

Although the January announcement led to a break in diplomatic relations, Congress was not yet ready to declare war. They even refused Wilson's request to have American merchant ships armed. Two events strengthened Wilson's hand. Firstly, the February Revolution in Russia ended the **autocracy** and brought in a Provisional Government promising democratic reforms. This meant that the Allied cause could now be seen as thoroughly democratic. Secondly, the British presented the Americans with a copy of the 'Zimmerman Telegram'. The British had intercepted the telegram from the German Foreign Minister, Arthur Zimmerman, to the German ambassador in Mexico. It suggested to the Mexican government that if they joined the war against the USA, Germany would ensure that in the end they got back New Mexico, Texas and Arizona, which they had lost to America in the 1840s. This was a violation of the Monroe Doctrine and put America and Germany on a collision course. The further loss of American lives at sea, in February and March of 1917, finally turned public opinion. Although there were a few Mid-Western Congressmen and Senators who held out, when Wilson asked Congress for a declaration of war in April it was granted by 82–6 votes in the Senate and 373–50 in the House of Representatives. He promised to make the world 'safe for democracy', and on 6 April the United States declared war on Germany.

Autocracy: Political system in which the ruler has total power and is answerable to no one.

1. In what ways did the United States have an interest in the outcome of the First World War before 1917?

2. 'It was the U-boat campaign of 1917 which brought America into the First World War.' How far would you agree with this view?

4.2 How successful was Wilson's foreign policy 1917–1919?

America and the First World War

When America declared war, it was expected that its contribution would be primarily economic, but by 1917 the Allied forces were exhausted and their economies in collapse. In the first few months of the year, almost two million tons of shipping had been lost, 340,000 British soldiers had been killed or wounded in the mud of Passchendaele and the French Army was in mutiny. Americans had not been prepared by Wilson for the necessity of sending their young men to fight in Europe, but American troops were vital to the war effort.

The Selective Services Act introduced conscription in May 1917.

US soldiers leaving for France in August 1917.

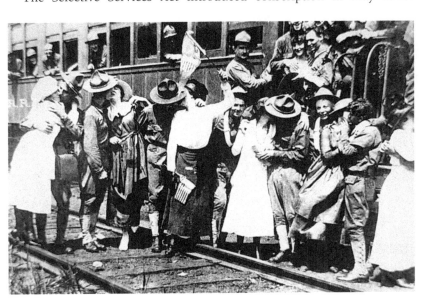

Does this picture tell us anything about attitudes to the War?

Vladimir Ilyich Ulyanov, 'Lenin' (1870–1924)
Russian revolutionary and leader of the Bolshevik or Communist Party. Along with Leon Trotsky, he organised the communist seizure of power in November 1917. He was leader of Russia until his death in 1924.

General John Joseph Pershing (1860–1948)
American army officer. Commanded soldiers in the Mexican War and led American Expeditionary Force in the First World War.

Ferdinand Foch (1851–1929)
French soldier and Chief of the General Staff in 1917. In 1918 he was put in overall command of the Allied armies on the Western Front.

Why was the victory at Château-Thierry important?

Initially, men aged 21–30 were called up, though this was later extended to men aged 18–45. During the course of the War, 3.5 million men were drafted, with an additional 1.5 million who volunteered, including 260,000 African-Americans. Over half of these men eventually served on the Western Front, and over 100,000 would give their lives to the War.

Training and equipping these men took time and, by March 1918, only 84,000 American soldiers had arrived in Europe. When they arrived in Europe the American soldiers wore British helmets, as America was not producing its own. A War Industries Board was set up to organise supplies and raw materials. Wilson put financier Bernard Baruch in charge, and although there continued to be many inefficiencies and mistakes it was soon supplying the needs of the military. It taught a useful lesson, for those involved in the Second World War, of the need for government control of the economy. However, it was late summer before there were significant numbers of US soldiers ready to fight, by which time they were needed to help defend Paris.

In October 1917, Lenin's Bolsheviks had carried out the second Russian Revolution. The world's first communist government was set up and it immediately condemned the War and announced its intention to back out, which it did in March 1918. This freed up a million German soldiers from the Eastern Front. General Ludendorff launched a spring offensive, hoping to take Paris before the Americans arrived in force. The gamble almost succeeded and the Germans got to within 40 miles of the French capital.

American forces were under the command of General John J. Pershing, a veteran of the Cuban and Mexican wars. As an 'Associate' power rather than an Allied power, American forces were not integrated into the Allied army under General Ferdinand Foch, but they formed an important part of

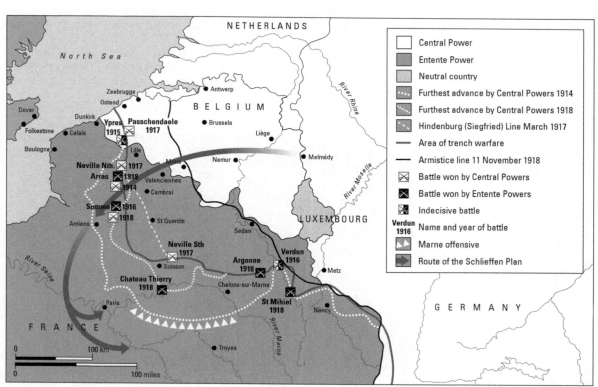

The Western Front

his counter-offensive launched in the summer. Pershing's men halted the German advance at Châateau-Thierry and at Bellau Wood. By September, American soldiers were arriving in large numbers. More important, was the psychological effect they were having on both sides. Their youth, enthusiasm and the resources on which they would eventually be able to call breathed new life into the Allied cause. As for the Germans, they knew that if Ludendorff's gamble failed they had lost the War. In September, Foch launched the Argonnes Offensive. The French and Americans defeated the German army at St Mihiel, and the Germans were pushed back. The Ludendorff Offensive had failed and Paris was saved. In October, a new German government was set up under Prince Max von Baden and they asked for an armistice. The War ended on 11 November.

The Americans also contributed to the victory in other ways. When they joined the War in April 1917, Allied shipping losses for that year were already two million tons. With the American navy joining the campaign against German U-boats, Allied losses fell by two-thirds by the end of the year. In addition, American shipyards embarked on a building programme which meant that they could replace any ship the Germans sank, and more. By the start of 1918, the war at sea had been won. The strength of the American economy was vital. Altogether, they had spent around $35 billion on the war, and their supplies and loans to the Europeans between 1914 and 1917 had been crucial in enabling the Allies to maintain the fight. The Americans may only have been in the First World War for 19 months and their losses may have been low, compared to those of the other powers, but their contribution to victory was as important as that of any of the Allies.

Peacemaking and the Treaty of Versailles

When the Germans asked for peace it was to the Americans that they went, not the British or French. They believed that the Americans would be more lenient. This belief was partly due to the fact that the Americans had not been fighting for so long nor on their own territory, as the French had. They also understood that Wilson's Fourteen Points (see overleaf) would form the basis of the peace treaty. In all, there were five treaties with each of the Central Powers which made up the Versailles Settlement of 1919, but by far the most important was the Treaty of Versailles itself with the Germans. The Treaty is generally considered to have been a failure, given that war broke out again between its signatories just 20 years later. Woodrow Wilson is given much of the blame for this failure.

President Wilson was an academic, a history professor who moved into politics in his 40s. He was very bright and, like many presidents, had a great interest in foreign policy, as it is one area of American Government over which the Administration had undoubted control. Wilson believed in America's role as an influence for good in the world. Its power would spread the ideals of liberalism, democracy and capitalism. He was a deeply religious man and is frequently referred to as an idealist. He was an idealist in that he believed in the good in people and had a desire to improve the world, but he was not a fool and he was not weak. His willingness to send troops into Mexico, as well as his support for the Allies in the first three years of the War, showed an understanding of the necessity of force in politics. Like Roosevelt, he used the power of his office to full effect.

Even before US entry into the War, Wilson had a desire to influence the peace. For example, his insistence that American citizens be allowed to travel freely in spite of the dangers from German submarines illustrates one of his foreign policy goals, freedom of the seas for all. As the War was coming to a close in 1918, he outlined his aims for the post-war peace, in common with other leaders. These aims were most clearly laid out in a speech to the Senate on 8 January and became known as the 'Fourteen Points'.

The causes of the First World War are complex and widely debated, but Wilson believed that if one identified the causes of the war and removed them, this would guarantee peace for the future. For example, he believed the network of secret treaties and the arms build-up in the years preceding 1914 had created an atmosphere of mistrust, which was sparked into war by the assassination in Sarajevo. Hence, points 1 and 2 would prevent a recurrence. Likewise, the clauses on **self-determination** would address the issue of Serbian nationalism. Self-determination also embodied Wilson's own belief in democracy and in the American anti-imperialist tradition. By giving as many people as possible a say in their own future, Wilson hoped the causes of conflict would be removed.

Self-determination: The right of people to decide their own future.

In this sense, Wilson was too idealistic. The clauses on Poland illustrate the difficulty of putting things into practice. The peacemakers had to balance the ideals of self-determination with the practical issues of security and economics. Without access to the sea, Poland would be severely weakened, but giving it access meant putting a large area of German territory under Polish rule. However, the practicalities of re-drawing the map of Europe were the least of Wilson's problems. It was the ambitions and desires of the other powers that drove him to distraction and even illness.

When Wilson arrived in Paris, he was greeted as a saviour. European people were grateful for the American contribution to ending the War and believed the ideals Wilson spoke of would, as he said, 'make the world safe for democracy'. But France had fought Germany twice in the previous 40 years, and the First World War had cost them 1.4 million lives. Britain had been bankrupted by the War and had lost 900,000 men. They wanted to make Germany pay. The arguments between the 'Big Four' – Wilson, Britain's Prime Minister Lloyd George, France's Premier Georges Clemenceau and Italy's Prime Minster Orlando – were fierce. The Europeans were determined to have their territorial and reparation demands met. Some were valid and

---

Summary of Wilson's 'Fourteen Points'

1 Open covenants openly arrived at
2 Freedom of the seas
3 Free trade
4 Disarmament
5 Impartial adjustments of all colonial claims
6 Evacuation of Russia by the Germans and self-determination for the Russian people
7 Evacuation and restoration of Belgium
8 Return of Alsace-Lorraine to France
9 Re-adjustment of Italian frontiers based on nationality
10 Self-determination for the people of Austria-Hungary
11 Evacuation and restoration of Romania, Serbia and Montenegro
12 Self-determination for the peoples of the Turkish Empire
13 Establishment of an independent Poland with access to the sea
14 Establishment of a League of Nations (see next page) with mutual guarantees of independence and security.

Points 1 and 4 were an attempt to address the European causes of the War, and for the Americans it was Point 2. Wilson's belief in free trade was emphasised in both Points 2 and 3. Points 5–13 show how important the idea of self-determination was to the President. He felt that if the principle could be applied as widely as possible, then the causes of much conflict would be reduced. Point 14 was an attempt to bring about peace through cooperation.

The 'Big Four' at Versailles –
Lloyd George, Orlando,
Clemenceau and Woodrow
Wilson

How far did these men share common goals?

easy to accomplish, such as the return to France of Alsace-Lorraine, which had been taken by the Germans in 1871. Others, such as Italy's claims in the Adriatic, were considered too extravagant. Arguments over the issue had Orlando in tears. Compromises had to be made. Wilson could never have hoped to gain all that he set out to achieve. Whether the claims of the other Allies were just or not, the fact remains that they did have claims. Having fought the War for four years, the Allies would not let Wilson and America dictate terms to them.

However, Wilson did make many mistakes in his handling of the negotiations. He was dead set against imposing reparations on Germany, believing that this would cause resentment and future conflict. But France and Belgium insisted on reparations in order to rebuild the devastated towns and villages of the Western Front. Wilson was forced to give in and accept these demands. Had the Americans not insisted on repayment of the money they had loaned to Europe, the European nations may have been more willing to listen to him. As it was, the Reparations Commission in 1921 saddled Germany with a debt of $33 billion, which they were to pay to the Allies who in turn would use part of it to repay the Americans. The economist John Maynard Keynes resigned from the Conference in protest at the reparations issue and called Wilson 'incompetent'. Given the economic costs of the First World War, it was unlikely the Europeans would ever have agreed to a peace without some form of financial settlement.

League of Nations: Association of self-governing states created as part of 1919 Peace Treaty 'to promote international cooperation and to achieve international peace and security'. The USA did not join, and the association's failure to deal effectively with outbreaks in Japan, Italy and Germany in the 1930s meant that it had lost its relevance by the outbreak of the Second World War. It was subsequently replaced by the United Nations (see overleaf).

Another mistake was Wilson's insistence on having the **League of Nations** as part of the Treaty. Building on an idea that had originated in Britain during the War, Wilson proposed an organisation of nations at which issues and problems could be talked through, instead of resorting to war. The members would also promise to protect each other in the event of an attack, thus making war less likely. This concept was known as 'collective security'. This was so important to Wilson that instead of having a separate agreement, he wanted it written into all five of the treaties. It was written into all five treaties, but it allowed the other powers to use it as a bargaining chip to have their demands met. It was also to cause problems at home.

It was in the domestic arena that Wilson made his most serious errors with regard to Versailles. Firstly, in the mid-term elections of November

'Round-robin': A letter signed by several people indicating agreement. No single person is seen as the author.

1918 he made the forthcoming peace conference a party issue, hoping to give himself a strong Democratic Congress. The plan completely backfired and the Republicans gained control of both Houses. Wilson also made no real attempt to work with the Republicans to gain their support.

When he returned from Paris to present the Treaty to Congress, 39 Senators signed a letter – a **'round-robin'** – refusing to accept the Treaty as it stood. There were some objections to the Treaty itself, but the main objection was to the League of Nations and Article Ten of the Covenant (the clause on collective security). For many Americans this would involve their being dragged into Europe's wars, which were really none of their concern. Wilson made some changes but Article Ten continued to be the sticking point. In an effort to raise support in the country for the Treaty and the League, Wilson went on a speaking tour. Already ill from the stress of the Conference itself, the tour proved too much and Wilson suffered a severe stroke, which was to leave him infirm for the rest of his life. The Treaty was amended in the Foreign Relations Committee, so when it went to the Senate to be voted on Wilson insisted that the Democrats vote against it. He would not accept the Treaty with the amendments. The Treaty failed to get the necessary two-thirds majority vote for **ratification**. A peace was signed with Germany, but for all Wilson's efforts and insistence that the League of Nations be written into the treaties, the United States never joined.

Ratification: Vote in the Senate giving legal recognition to a treaty. The vote must have a two-thirds majority to pass.

Had Wilson handled the Republicans better, or been more willing to compromise, he might have got the League of Nations accepted. Undoubtedly, the absence of the United States was fatal to the League, but America's presence would no more have been a guarantee against war than its presence in the **United Nations** has been. The Treaty of Versailles had many faults:

United Nations: Organisation formed after the Second World War. It tries to encourage international peace, cooperation and friendship.

- Self-determination set up the weak 'successor states' in Eastern Europe which would fall to the Nazis in the 1930s.

- The 'mandates' allowed powers like Britain to maintain imperialist control of areas like the Middle East, but under a different name.

- The treaty overall created a fierce resentment in Germany and a determination among all political parties to see it destroyed.

However, Wilson did achieve many of the Fourteen Points. The Treaty of Versailles was, of necessity, a compromise between the conflicting demands of the victorious powers. Most historians agree it was a bad treaty: harsh enough to create resentment but not harsh enough to prevent a resurgence of German power. Yet Wilson is not wholly to blame for this. He made mistakes, but so did Lloyd George, Clemenceau and Orlando. The collapse of the settlement was as much an outcome of the events of the 1920s as of the Treaty itself.

The Wars of Intervention

One result of the First World War had been two revolutions in Russia. November 1917 had seen the Bolsheviks take control and pull Russia out of the War. But rather than returning to peace, Russia was plunged into civil war between the Bolsheviks and their enemies. British and French troops were sent to Russia, partly to reclaim supplies they had sent to an ally who had now pulled out of the fight, but also because they supported the anti-Bolshevik cause. The Japanese also sent troops to Vladivostok. In March 1918, Wilson sent 7,000 American troops to Russia, from where they were not finally removed until 1920. They had little effect on the civil war, so why did Wilson send them?

One reason was to support his Allies. The British and French had felt betrayed by Russia's withdrawal and wanted to help defeat the Bolsheviks and possibly bring Russia back into the War. Wilson was showing his support for them by backing their efforts. There was also concern that the Japanese might use the 'Wars of Intervention' to gain territory in the East and Wilson wanted to prevent this. It may also have been, as Lenin had suggested, that the capitalist nations wished to crush Communism at birth. Whatever Wilson's motives, it led to many hundreds of American casualties for no perceptible gain to the USA. More damagingly, it left the Russians with a mistrust of the Americans that was to continue right through to the Cold War.

1. In what ways did the USA contribute to the Allied victory in the First World War?

2. How far did President Wilson achieve his aims at the Paris Peace Conference?

Source-based questions: President Wilson and the First World War

SOURCE A

The people of the United States are drawn from many nations, and chiefly from the nations now at war. It is natural and inevitable that there should be the utmost variety of sympathy and desire among them with regard to the issues and circumstances of the conflict. Some will wish one nation, others another, to succeed in the momentous struggle. It will be easy to excite passion and difficult to allay it. Those responsible for exciting it will assume a heavy responsibility, responsibility for no less a thing than that the people of the United States, whose love of their country and whose loyalty to its government should unite them as Americans all, bound in honour and affection to think first of her and her interests, may be divided in camps of hostile opinion, hot against each other, involved in the war itself in impulse and opinion if not in action. Such divisions amongst us would be fatal to our peace of mind and might seriously stand in the way of the proper performance of our duty as the one great nation at peace, the one people holding itself ready to play a part of impartial mediation and speak the counsels of peace and accommodation, not as a partisan, but as a friend.

President Wilson's Declaration of Neutrality, 19 August 1914

SOURCE B

Unless the Imperial Government should now immediately declare and effect an abandonment of its present methods of submarine warfare against passenger and freight-carrying vessels, the Government of the United States can have no choice but to sever diplomatic relations with the German Empire altogether.

President Woodrow Wilson to the German government, 19 April 1916

SOURCE C

On the first of February we intend to begin submarine warfare unrestricted. In spite of this, it is our intention to endeavour to keep neutral the United States of America.
If this attempt is not successful, we propose an alliance on the following basis with Mexico: That we shall make war together and together make peace. We shall give general financial support, and it is understood that Mexico is to re-conquer the lost territory in New Mexico, Texas and Arizona. The details are left to you for settlement.

Note from the German Foreign Minister, Zimmermann, to the German Minister to Mexico, 19 January 1917

SOURCE D

We have loaned many hundreds of millions of dollars to the Allies in this controversy. While such action was legal and countenanced by international law, there is no doubt in my mind but the enormous amount of money loaned to the Allies in this country has been instrumental in bringing about a public sentiment in favour of our country taking a course that would make every bond worth a hundred cents on the dollar and making the payment of every debt certain and sure. Through this instrumentality and also through the instrumentality of others who have not only made millions out of the war in the manufacture of munitions, etc., and who would expect to make millions more if our country can be drawn into the catastrophe, a large number of the great newspapers and news agencies of the country have been controlled and enlisted in the greatest propaganda that the world has ever known to manufacture sentiment in favour of war.

Speech by Senator George W. Norris in opposition to Wilson's War Message, 1917

Source-based questions: President Wilson and the First World War

SOURCE E

The committee finds, further, that the constant availability of munitions companies with competitive bribes ready in outstretched hands does not create a situation where the officials involved can, in the nature of things, be as much interested in peace and measures to secure peace as they are in increased armaments.

While the evidence before this committee does not show that wars have been started solely because of the activities of munitions makers and their agents, it is also true that wars rarely have one single cause, and the committee finds it to be against the peace of the world for selfishly interested organisations to be left free to goad* and frighten nations into military activity.

Report of the Special Committee on Investigation of the Munitions Industry (The Nye Report),24 February 1936

*goad = provoke

1. Read Source A. What reasons does President Wilson give for the need for Americans to remain neutral in the War?

2. Read Source B. What had led President Wilson to issue this warning to Germany?

3. Read Sources D and E. What support is there in Source D for the view of the Nye Commission on the role of the arms industry in the outbreak of war?

4. How valuable are Sources D and E to a historian studying the causes of the First World War?

5. Using all the sources and your own knowledge, assess the extent to which submarine warfare led to American entry into the First World War.

4.3 How far was the USA 'isolationist' between the two world wars?

By 1920, Wilson was ill and had failed to gain American approval for his aims to create a new world order. In the 1920 presidential election, the uninspiring James Cox represented the Democrats. The Republicans comfortably regained control of Congress and the White House, under Warren G. Harding. Both Harding and his successor, Calvin Coolidge, believed America's role in the world was primarily economic, not political. This led to the foreign policy of the inter-war years being called 'isolationist'. While it is certain that the American people and governments of the 1920s and 1930s desired to stay out of European affairs, America's economic influence and its interests in Latin America and the Far East meant that it continued to be a player on the world stage, albeit a reluctant one.

Isolation in the 1920s

America's turning in on itself can be seen in several of the policies it pursued in the 1920s. Immigration restrictions, such as the Quota Act 1921 and the Johnson–Reed Act 1924, reflected Coolidge's view that 'America must be kept American'. Although the legislation was primarily a response to domestic pressure, it was indicative of the mood of the times that the rest of the world was not really of concern to America. Likewise, tariff polices reflected this new mood. The Fordney–McCumber Act 1922 introduced the highest **import tariffs** in US history in order to protect American goods from foreign competition.

Import tariffs: Taxes on goods coming into a country.

While legislation of this kind was motivated by domestic considerations, it does indicate that in the inter-war period the United States was looking inwards rather than outwards. Also, these measures affected its foreign policy. The immigration laws, particularly the clauses cutting Asian immigration, were interpreted as racist. They worsened relations with Japan. The high tariffs made it difficult for European economies to grow by cutting off the American market to their goods. Both of these problems were to worsen significantly in the 1930s. (Even when Hitler came to power and began persecuting Jews, the American government refused to relax the immigration laws, letting in only 60,000 Jewish refugees between 1933 and 1938.)

Yet even in the Republican era of the 1920s, the United States could not be said to be totally isolationist. Although American observers refused to join the League of Nations, they attended more than 40 meetings of the assembly, and the USA supported much of the work done by the League in areas such as health. The USA was a member of the International Labour Organisation, which monitored labour conditions throughout the world and worked to improve them. However, proposals for full membership of the World Court were defeated in the Senate in 1935.

Economic considerations meant the USA could not fully retreat from world affairs. In some ways, they did not want to. All three Republican Presidents of the decade – Warren Harding, Calvin Coolidge and Herbert Hoover – believed that a strong world economy, governed by free trade, was the best guarantee of peace. Ironically, their own protectionist policies made this more difficult.

The United States emerged from the First World War with the strongest economy in the world and a larger share of world trade. The economies of Europe, on the other hand, were devastated by four years of fighting and they owed enormous sums, principally to the USA. The Senate estimated that America was owed $22 billion dollars. To pay this back, the European nations needed to expand their trade, but American tariffs made this difficult. There was a feeling among some European countries that, as an ally in the War, the Americans should have written off this money, but the feeling in America was very different. For one thing it was a vast amount. As Coolidge said, 'they hired the money didn't they'. There was also a fear that if the debt was written off the money would simply be used to buy arms. However, the need to pay back the loans meant the Allies had to press hard on Germany for reparations.

In 1922, the Germans had announced that they could not pay the next instalment of the $33 billion they owed. This led, the following year, to an invasion by the French and Belgian armies of the heavily industrialised Ruhr area of Germany in an attempt to get the coal and steel they felt they were owed. The German government responded with a policy of 'passive resistance', where they refused to cooperate with the invaders. Production shut down and **hyperinflation** resulted. The crisis was causing the collapse of the German economy and relations between the French and Belgians and the German people threatened to break into violence or all-out war the longer the occupation went on. No one wanted to see a resumption of the war, least of all America, so a conference was organised in 1924 to sort out the problem.

Hyperinflation: Extremely severe price rises.

The conference was presided over by Charles Dawes, a Chicago banker. The solution it came up with was to reschedule Germany's repayments. The USA was to grant $200 million in loans to Germany in order to help them rebuild their industry and enable them to pay the reparations. Secretary of State Charles Evans Hughes made a tour of European capitals to encourage support for the Plan. It was accepted and the crisis came to a peaceful end. (Four years later a further conference, again presided over by the Americans, came up with the Young Plan, which cut reparation payments to $9 billion to be paid over 59 years.) Even though the issue was primarily economic and the loans were made by private bankers not by the US government, these ties meant that though the Americans might like to believe they had removed themselves from European affairs it was not so simple.

Disarmament was another area in which the USA played a world role. After the War, disarmament was popular with the populations of most of the combatant countries as a way of avoiding another war. For the Republicans it also had the advantage of allowing them to cut military spending and, therefore, cut taxes. At the Washington Naval Conference 1921–1922, three agreements were signed. The first set limits on naval capacity regarding battleships. There was to be a ratio of $5 : 5 : 3: 1\frac{3}{4} : 1\frac{3}{4}$ for the navies of the United States, Britain, Japan, France and Italy respectively. In fact, the American navy was still considerably smaller than the British, so they were encouraging others to cut their capacity while not having to cut their own. A further conference, in London in 1930, made a similar agreement over cruisers and destroyers, with ratios of $10 : 10 : 7$ and $10 : 10 : 6\frac{1}{2}$ for America, Britain and Japan.

Also at Washington a Four-Power Treaty was signed between the USA, Britain, Japan and France agreeing to consult on matters in the Pacific. A further Nine-Power Treaty was signed, in which the signatories agreed to respect the territorial position of China.

These agreements were popular and allowed the Republicans to cut military spending. They also prevented a naval race of the kind that, it was believed, had led to the First World War. To some extent, they also eased tensions in the Pacific where Japanese expansion was a concern. But again Japan resented the way it had been put in an inferior position to the other powers. Also, none of the agreements had enforcement clauses. When the Nine-Power Treaty was broken in the 1930s, the Americans did nothing.

The problem of enforcement lay at the root of America's reluctance to get too involved in world affairs. In 1927, a conference in Geneva attempted to negotiate arms limitations for land armies, similar to those in the Washington Treaties. It was one thing for the French to agree to cuts in their navy, but quite another to agree to cuts in their army and without any guarantees of security against another German attack. Having rejected the League of Nations, the American Congress was hardly likely to give such a guarantee – and the conference broke up. But the desire for peace was real.

In 1928, the French Foreign Minister Aristide Briand and US Secretary of State Frank B. Kellogg signed an agreement renouncing war. The Kellogg–Briand Pact condemned 'recourse to war for the solution of international controversies and [renounced] it as an instrument of national policy'. Two million people signed petitions supporting the Pact and 62 countries signed it. Yet for all its popularity, it meant little. It had no mechanism for enforcement and, before the Senate gave it its 85–1 approval, they made it clear that signing the Pact would have no effect on the Monroe Doctrine or on America's self-defence. The principles behind the agreement were commendable, but it was no more than an expression of hope for a peaceful world. In practice, it had no effect whatever.

One area of the world where the Americans took a more active interest was Latin America. Yet the 1920s saw a change. Between 1922 and 1925, American troops were withdrawn from Cuba, the Dominican Republic and Nicaragua. In 1921, Colombia was paid $25 million compensation for America's role in the Panamanian revolution. Hoover made a goodwill tour of Latin America in 1930 and the Roosevelt Corollary was officially **repudiated** in the **Clark Memorandum**. When revolutions broke out or debts were defaulted on, Hoover took no action. Yet this was only part of the policy of 'isolation'. America's chief concern in 1930–31 was the worsening Depression, not Latin American revolts. In some areas those revolts produced governments more to America's liking, such as Trujillo's dictatorship in the Dominican Republic in 1924 and Somoza's in Nicaragua in 1925. Some historians argue that the United States could afford to interfere less politically in Latin America because they had established American

Repudiated: Disowned, saying something no longer applies.

Clark Memorandum: State Department document issued in 1930 laying out America's policy towards Latin America.

economic power in the area so effectively. For example, in the 1930s, two-thirds of Cuban sugar production was owned by American companies, as was half of all Venezuelan oil production. As shown by David Ryan, in *US Foreign Policy in World History* (2000), by 1929 American investments in Latin America were worth $3.52 billion.

America responded to the experience of the First World War with a determination to stay out of the entanglements of other countries. To an extent they succeeded, though their economic power and ties still gave them enormous influence. In the 1930s, the Great Depression encouraged them to be even more inward looking at a time when the deteriorating international situation meant they had to take more notice of the outside world.

Franklin D. Roosevelt's foreign policy

Understandably, FDR's first few years were focused on domestic issues. With 25 per cent of the workforce unemployed, the Great Depression was the worst domestic crisis faced by any American government. The Depression was a worldwide phenomenon and might have been tackled internationally. Instead the United States pursued its own interests. In 1930, Congress had passed the Smoot–Hawley Tariff Act, increasing tariffs even further than the 1922 Act. This discouraged international trade when it needed to be increased. Rather than help the USA, it meant Europeans could not buy up American agricultural surpluses. A world economic conference, in 1930, collapsed when Roosevelt announced that the United States would pursue its own tariff policy. To an extent, he was responding to the Ottawa Conference of the year before where Britain had made an agreement that gave preference to trade within its own Empire. This economic isolationism encouraged still further American political isolationism. In 1934, however, the Trade Agreements Act allowed the signing of tariff agreements with 18 countries, mainly in Latin America.

Roosevelt largely continued the Republican policy of reducing American involvement in Latin America. In 1933, at a conference in Montevideo, Roosevelt signed an agreement not to interfere in the internal and external affairs of other Latin and South American states. The following year, the Platt Amendment was finally removed, giving control of their own state back to the Cubans.

As before, this new mood had its limits. When the radical Cuban government of San Martín was replaced by the Batista regime, it was with the active support of the American ambassador and an American warship. Fulgencio Batista's government trampled on the rights and freedoms of the Cuban people, but it was supported because it encouraged American investment.

The new mood also had no effect on the Monroe Doctrine, which continued to be American policy. However, by the late 1930s, the Americans had reason to be worried by European intervention on the continent. The **fascist** governments of both Italy and Germany made no secret of their desire for influence in South America. To improve ties, therefore, a Pan-American Conference was held in Lima in 1938. It was agreed that all 21 republics of the continent would consult in the event of a threat to any of them. So, although many Nazi war criminals may have fled to South America after the War, at no point was American influence in the Western Hemisphere seriously threatened.

From 1933, the real danger spot as far as Roosevelt was concerned was Europe. There was support in the USA for the Nazi Party and its succession to power, notably from the **German-American Bund**. However, most Americans saw it as being none of their concern who ran Germany. The public mood continued to be strongly isolationist. As Nazi aggression increased tension in Europe throughout the 1930s, Americans became

Fascist: Nationalistic political ideology, which aims to overthrow democracy and replace it with a dictatorship. Central to such groups is the heroic leader and the extensive use of propaganda.

German-American Bund: A pro-Nazi organisation made up largely of Americans descended from German immigrants.

more determined than ever to ensure they were not dragged into conflict as they had been in 1917.

The publication, in 1934, of the report of the Nye Committee into the causes of the First World War increased this determination. The Committee blamed the War on the lobbying of arms manufacturers keen to increase their profits. In a poll, 70 per cent of Americans said that looking back they should never have joined the War. In 1936, half a million American students took part in a boycott of classes as part of a 'peace strike'. But the Americans were not the only ones hoping for peace. In a debate in the Oxford Union, British students voted to support a motion that 'this house will in no circumstance fight for its King and country'.

In the 1936 election, Roosevelt promised to keep the United States out of any war, but Wilson had made similar promises so Congress passed a series of neutrality acts in the 1930s in an attempt to prevent a repeat of the circumstances that led to American involvement. The 1935 Neutrality Act provided for an **arms embargo** on any warring nations and allowed the President to warn Americans against travelling on their ships. The 1936 Neutrality Act prohibited loans to **belligerents** and in 1937 Americans were banned from travelling on the ships of belligerent nations. The economic ties to the Allies in the First World War, as well as the role of the 'Lusitania', were clearly on the minds of the legislators.

In the meantime, the situation worsened in Europe. In 1935, the Nazis re-introduced conscription and announced a rearmament programme. The following year, the Rhineland was re-occupied. All of this was in breach of the Versailles Treaty. No one in Europe was inclined to take action any more than the Americans were. In 1936, the fascist nations of Germany, Italy and Japan came into alliance through the Anti-Comintern Pact. American economic interests in Europe and the Pacific could be threatened by the spread of fascism. When Roosevelt suggested, in 1937, the '**quarantining**' of warring nations, the reaction was very hostile and he backed down. The depth of isolationist feeling is illustrated by an attempt by Congressman Louis Ludlow to introduce a constitutional amendment requiring a **referendum** before the President could declare war. Roosevelt argued forcefully that such an amendment would completely tie a president's hands in the conduct of foreign policy, but it was only defeated by a narrow majority of 209–188 in the House.

Roosevelt realised the growing danger of war. In the spring of 1938, the Nazis were 'invited' into Austria and it was clear Czechoslovakia was next. The President asked Hitler for a guarantee not to attack certain countries, but Hitler responded by making a joke of the request in a speech in the German parliament. A proposal to Britain for a conference to discuss the international situation was rejected. Britain, too, was anxious to avoid war but believed **appeasement** was the answer. The British Prime Minster, Neville Chamberlain, went to Munich and an agreement was reached with Germany gaining a large area of Czech territory, the Sudetenland. But Chamberlain knew that the 'piece of paper' Hitler had signed would not prevent war: it had merely bought time. Early in 1939, the German army took the rest of Czechoslovakia.

War in Europe was now on the cards. Roosevelt wanted to prepare America for the worst. He believed that the security of Europe was crucial to the security of America. He was able to persuade Congress to approve the Naval Expansion Act allowing a 20 per cent increase in the US navy (although this would only take it up to the equivalent size of the German and Japanese navies). In 1939, he got an extra $525 million for air defence. At the start of the Second World War, however, the American army still only numbered 185,000.

Arms embargo: Political action in which pressure is placed upon other states to stop fighting by banning the sale of arms (weapons) to them.

Belligerents: Nations, states or groups waging war on others.

Quarantining: Cutting someone off from usual trade and relationships as if they were infected.

Referendum: A form of political consultation in which the electorate is asked for its response to a specific measure proposed by the government.

Appeasement: The policy of giving in to someone's demands in the hope that it will satisfy them and discourage further demands.

Why was isolationism popular with the American public in the 1920s and 1930s?

4.4 Why did the USA become involved in the Second World War?

When Britain declared war on Germany, in September 1939, American sympathy was strongly on its side. Unlike Wilson, FDR made no attempt to appear neutral in attitude. Like him, many Americans felt that what happened to Britain could affect American security, and they set up groups such as The Committee to Defend America by Aiding the Allies. As in the First World War, there was still no desire among the general public to join in – as shown by the America First Group. To give some help, a neutrality act was passed allowing the British to buy American goods. But these had to be carried on British ships – hence the nickname the 'cash and carry' act – and America would grant no loans. The supplies were important to the Allied war effort, but they could not prevent the fall of France in 1940.

The speed with which the German army overran Western Europe shocked the American public. By June 1940, the Nazis were in control of Norway, Denmark, Holland, Belgium and France. Through the summer and autumn, the Battle of Britain was fought, with Britain and its Empire standing alone against the Nazi threat. The broadcasts of journalist Ed Murrow from London during the Blitz did much to communicate to Americans the intensity of the struggle taking place.

A Europe controlled by Nazi Germany would not only be bad for American trade, it also represented a strategic threat. The USA now began to step up its defensive preparations. The army was expanded in September under the Selective Service and Training Act, which introduced America's first peacetime conscription. It required all men aged 21–36 to register. The air force was also increased and the National Defence Research Committee was set up to produce new weapons, beginning a process that would culminate in the development of the atom bomb. Although America was preparing itself, it was Britain who needed aid. Roosevelt wanted to help but the Neutrality Acts and the forthcoming election prevented him. He managed to get around the terms of the various Neutrality Acts in order to swap 50 old First World War destroyers for naval bases in British colonies. The move was criticised on many sides. To Americans, Roosevelt was evading Congressional legislation while, to the British, he had taken advantage of their plight. Nevertheless, Roosevelt had provided 50 more ships for Britain.

In the 1940 election, both Roosevelt and the Republican candidate Wendell Willkie supported the British in the War. Both were aware of public opinion. Willkie presented Roosevelt as a **warmonger** and Roosevelt responded by promising not to send American soldiers to fight in Europe. Willkie was a popular candidate and he did very well, but he was running against an even more popular man who, many believed, had rescued America from the Depression. Roosevelt was elected for an unprecedented third term.

In March 1941, Roosevelt was able to persuade Congress of the importance to America of helping Britain. The Lend–Lease Act allowed the United States to lend or lease arms, supplies, food etc. to any nation if it was felt that country's defence was necessary for the defence of America. Congress voted for the Act 317–71 in the House and 60–31 in the Senate. Even at this stage there was no desire among the American public to join the War, but there was a feeling that this was different from the First World War. The Nazi regime was clearly destructive, if not evil, while Britain could still call on the ties of history, language and friendship with America. When Hitler attacked the Soviet Union in June 1941, lend–lease was immediately extended to the Russians. There is no doubt that American aid was a crucial factor in Britain's survival.

Step by step, throughout 1941, Roosevelt increased support for Britain,

---

Ed Murrow (1908–1965)
Respected journalist in radio and later in television. Reported from Europe in the 1903s and during the Second World War. After the War, he was a critic of the anti-communist hysteria and of McCarthy (see Chapter 8).

Wendell Willkie (1892–1944)
Lawyer, businessman and politician. Willkie started out as a Democrat but later became a Republican. A popular man, he supported FDR's government during the War. He spoke out and wrote in favour of international cooperation.

Warmonger: Someone who encourages people to expect war, or someone who tries to get a war started.

especially at sea. His critics accused him of trying to take America into the war by stealth. While he may not have been guilty of this, there is no question he was giving as much help as he could short of entering the war. In April, the western half of the Atlantic was declared a neutral zone allowing American ships to patrol it and pass on information to the Royal Navy about German shipping. This was later extended to cover routes as far as Greenland and Iceland. When the Germans fired on the 'Greer' on 4 September, Roosevelt responded by ordering German U-boats to be sunk on sight. The stakes were raised, in October, by the sinking of the 'Kearney' and the 'Reuben James', killing 126 Americans. Congress voted 212–194 and 50–37 to repeal the Neutrality Acts and allow merchant ships to be armed. The closeness of the vote shows the unease among many congressmen and senators. It also showed the fear that, just as in 1917, the United States was being sucked into a war 2,000 miles away due to its naval policies.

Tyranny: Cruel and unjust rule by a person or small group of people who have absolute power over everyone else in their country or state.

The British Prime Minister, Winston Churchill, still hoped to persuade the Americans to join the fight. He and Roosevelt met on a ship off the Newfoundland coast in August. Roosevelt would not declare war, but he did promise to help the fight against **tyranny**. The two men also agreed on a set of war aims, which became known as the 'Atlantic Charter'. Like Wilson's Fourteen Points, the Charter talked of self-determination, free access to trade, freedom of the seas and disarmament. It included clauses on economic collaboration and freedom from want. They were, in fact, laying the foundations of the United Nations.

By the end of the year, America had joined the War. Hitler declared war on the USA in support of his allies, the Japanese. They were at war with the United States because of their attack on Pearl Harbor.

Pearl Harbor

Relations with Japan had been deteriorating since the 1920s; in the 1930s, they worsened. In 1931, the Japanese invaded Manchuria. In fact, they already had many links to this part of China through investments and control of the South Manchurian railway. Like America, Japan was suffering the effects of Depression, and the pressure from its rapidly growing population meant that it was looking for expansion in Asia. However, the invasion broke the nine-power agreement to respect the territory of China and the Covenant of the League of Nations. The League was found to be fatally weak, but the Americans took no action either other than refusing to recognise the **puppet-state** of Manchukuo (formerly Manchuria) which the Japanese had established.

Puppet-state: Control of one state by the government of another (i.e. someone else 'pulling the strings').

China was in no state to defend itself against Japanese expansion. They had their own internal conflicts and by 1937 had descended into civil war. The Japanese took advantage of the chaos to attack. The Americans were keen to support China but were no more anxious to go to war in the Far East than they had been in Europe. Likewise, the Japanese did not want to draw the United States into a war. When they sank the US gunboat 'Panay', they apologised immediately and paid an indemnity. Roosevelt protested about the invasion but took no action. As the Japanese made further inroads, the American government worried for its trade and the open door policy. In 1938, they loaned $25 million to the Chinese, and increased it to $250 million two years later.

Japanese ambitions went beyond China. They spoke of creating a Greater East Asia Co-Prosperity Sphere while expanding into the Dutch East Indies and French Indo-China. When they formed a military alliance with Germany in 1940, Roosevelt took action. He feared that if America found itself in the War it would not have a big enough navy to fight in both

Pearl Harbor, 7 December 1941

Does this picture tell you anything about America's ability to fight Japan after Pearl Harbor?

oceans. Trying to make the Japanese pull back, America banned a number of exports and only allowed the sale of oil with a licence. Rather than have the desired effect, however, it made relations worse.

In July, Roosevelt froze all Japanese assets in the USA and closed the Panama Canal to Japanese shipping. The turning point came in August, when they banned oil exports. Without access to foreign oil, Japan could fight for no more than 18 months. On both sides there were real attempts to negotiate a peace. Japan offered to withdraw from South East Asia if the Americans would unfreeze their assets, allow oil to flow and cease their aid to Chiang in China. Roosevelt refused. If he agreed it would leave China extremely vulnerable and he was not prepared to do this. In spite of this failure, many in the government in Tokyo wanted to continue the search for a peaceful settlement but, in October, Tojo became Prime Minister and the voice of the military was now the loudest. They believed that if Japan were going to have to fight America, then their only hope was a surprise attack.

If Japan was to fight the USA it would be a war at sea, in the Pacific. Pearl Harbor in Hawaii was America's most important Pacific base. The Japanese hoped that the surprise attack would destroy the power of the US navy and thereby weaken America's ability to fight.

On 7 December 1941 – which Roosevelt famously called 'a day that will live in infamy' – 350 planes launched from six carriers attacked the US naval base at Pearl Harbor. In fact, the American military had cracked the Japanese codes in November and knew an attack was imminent, but they

1. In what ways did Japanese–American relations worsen between 1937 and 1941?

2. Why did the United States enter the war in 1941 and not in 1939?

did not know where. They expected it to be in the Philippines. When the young radar operator on duty spotted the planes, they were believed to be American B-17s. As luck would have it several US Navy ships, including aircraft carriers, were out of port that Sunday morning on exercise. This saved hardware, which was to prove vital in the War. Even so, eight battleships, three cruisers and three destroyers were sunk. Hundreds of planes were bombed as they sat on the airfields and more than 2,000 Americans were killed. The following day, with only one dissenting voice, the US Congress gave Roosevelt the authority to declare war on Japan. Three days later, on 11 December 1941, Hitler declared war on the United States.

4.5 What role did the USA play in achieving Allied victory in the Second World War?

The United States had been supporting Britain in various ways for over a year, but they were not ready to take a full part in the War. The War Powers Act 1941 gave the President wide-ranging powers and he used them to mobilise the American population and economy for total warfare. Boards were set up to control labour, production and prices. In 1943 the Office of War Mobilisation was set up under James Byrnes, who did a similar job to that done by Baruch and the War Industries Board in the First World War. The Second World War saw a massive growth in federal government and federal power.

When America entered the War, this time as an ally, things were not going well. The Germans controlled most of Europe – from the Atlantic coast to the Balkans – and were occupying large areas of the Soviet Union and North Africa. In the East, the Japanese expansion was rapid. By May 1942, they had taken Guam, Wake Island, the Dutch East Indies, Singapore, Hong Kong and the Philippines. Roosevelt knew the American public wanted to focus on Japan and take revenge for Pearl Harbor, and it was in the Pacific theatre that the **Axis'** advance was stopped. However, Churchill was able to persuade the President that the military focus should be on defeating Hitler in Europe.

Axis: The name given to the alliance between Germany, Italy and Japan during the Second World War.

The War in Europe

There were many arguments between the Allied political and military leaders during the War. At the beginning, they focused on tactics. As well as arguing for the concentration on Europe, Churchill also argued for an attack in the Mediterranean and not in France. The Russian leader, Joseph Stalin, was keen for the Allies to open a 'second front' in the West to take pressure off the Red Army. But Churchill persuaded Roosevelt that any second front would take a long time to plan fully. In the meantime, an attack on Italy, the weakest Axis power, would be more effective. (This delay in organising the second front was to cause much suspicion between the Great Powers but, given how close the D-Day landings were to failure, an early attack might have delayed victory even longer.)

In October 1942, the first important Allied victory of the War occurred when Montgomery's troops defeated the Germans at El Alamein and began to push them out of Egypt. In November, General Dwight D. Eisenhower led Allied landings in North Africa at Oran, Algiers and Casablanca. The weakness of American preparation was clear, but they soon learned and they had talented leadership under General 'Blood and Guts' Patton. With American and British soldiers advancing from the West and the British Eighth Army advancing from the East, the Germans and Italians were trapped. In May 1943, around 250,000 Axis soldiers in Tunisia surrendered.

Controlling North Africa both allowed the Allies to maintain control of the Suez Canal and gave them a launching point for the attack on Italy. Sicily was attacked from the sea and the air in July, and fell quickly. From there they moved on to the Italian peninsula itself, taking Naples in October 1943. It seemed the victory would be quick and easy but, though the Italians surrendered in September, the German army moved in to take control. They proved to be a more effective adversary. The Americans had heavy fighting around Monte Cassino and it was not until 1944 that Rome finally fell and Italy was taken.

1943 was a crucial year in the War. Not only were there victories in North Africa and Italy, but the Battle of the Atlantic had turned. The 'wolf packs' of German U-boats had been very effective in sinking Allied shipping. However, superior technology such as radar (developed by Britain), sonar, depth charges etc., and above all the ability of American shipyards to replace ships as fast as they were being sunk, kept the supply lines of the Atlantic open. This kept Britain fed and allowed the build-up of men and equipment ready for D-Day.

Timeline of the USA and the Second World War

1941   (August) Meeting between Franklin Roosevelt and Churchill off Newfoundland, leading to signing of **Atlantic Charter**, which condemned aggression and proposed self-determination and collective security.

(December) Pearl Harbor and German declaration of war

1942   (January) UN Declaration putting forward proposals for new international organisation

(May) Battle of the Coral Sea

Surrender of the Philippines

(June) Battle of Midway Island

(November) Allied landings in North Africa

1943   (July) Allied invasion of Sicily

(November) **Tehran Meeting** between FDR, Churchill and Stalin, agreeing to post-war division of Germany and neutrality of Austria

1944   (June) D-Day landings

Fall of Rome

(July) **Bretton Woods conference** to discuss post-war economic settlements. Eventually leads to establishment of International Monetary Fund and World Bank.

(September) US soldiers land in Philippines

(December) Battle of the Bulge

1945   (February) Capture of Iwo Jima

Yalta conference – discussion of reparations from Germany, free elections in Poland and USSR agrees to join war against Japan

(April) Fall of Berlin

(May) German surrender

(July) **Potsdam conference** – meeting between Truman, Stalin and Attlee. Further discussion of German settlement.

(August) Dropping of atom bombs

(September) Japanese surrender.

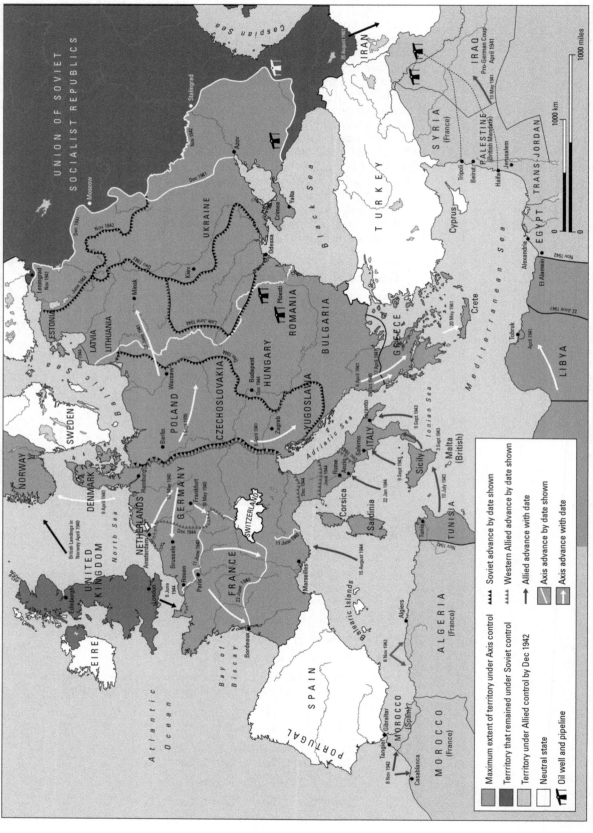

Military campaigns in Europe, 1939–1945

1943 was also the year of the victory at Stalingrad. This was easily one of the worst battles of the war: at its height, life expectancy of the soldiers involved was three days. The Soviet victory in February began the retreat of the German army from the East.

In the West, little could be done until the Allies were prepared for the invasion. The bulk of the fighting in Europe until 1944 had fallen on the Russians. Allied air forces, however, played their part with the continuous bombing campaigns of Germany. The actual effect of these campaigns is debatable. They probably had little effect on German morale while costing the loss of 10,000 planes. A question frequently asked is why none of these bombing raids was conducted against the death camps of the **Holocaust**. The Allied leaders argued that bombing places like Auschwitz would take effort away from the main targets in Germany and the extra distance to Poland was difficult to manage. These arguments may have some truth, but there is little doubt that bombing the camps might have saved thousands of lives in the long run.

By 1944, the invasion was ready. On D-Day, 6 June 1944, it was launched. Over the next two weeks, over one million men were landed on the beaches of Normandy, but it was July before General Bradley's men finally broke through the German lines at St Lô. From there they advanced quickly and, in August, American soldiers liberated Paris. Then the Germans rallied and the Ardennes Offensive pushed the Americans back, echoing Ludendorff's gamble a quarter of a century earlier. At the so-called Battle of the Bulge, the Americans lost 55,000 killed or wounded.

By 1945, the Allies were again on the advance and, in January, crossed into Germany. Tragedy came in April, but not on the battlefield. On 12 April, Franklin Roosevelt died. He had been elected for a fourth term just five months earlier, but his struggle against the Depression and the tyrannies of Japan and Germany had finally taken their toll. He was by no means a perfect leader in either peace or wartime and he made a lot of mistakes. In negotiations during the War he could be too idealistic and naïve, particularly regarding political and diplomatic issues. But any man who could work with, and stay on good terms with, such individuals as Churchill and Stalin, not to mention egos, was no fool. Roosevelt deserves much of the credit for keeping the Grand Alliance together during the Second World War. He managed to defend American interests, occasionally at the expense of the wider picture, but his support of Britain before 1941 was crucial to Britain's ability to continue the fight. He left many complex issues for his successor, Harry Truman, to deal with, but Roosevelt is without doubt one of the greatest and most important presidents in America's history.

Roosevelt did not live to see the victory he had done so much to bring about but, on 7 May, the Germans surrendered. Full attention could now be turned to defeating the Japanese.

War in the Pacific

Although Germany fell first, the US Navy brought initial American victories in the Pacific. In May 1942, the Battle of the Coral Sea stopped the rapid Japanese advance and secured Australian safety. The Battle of Midway Island, the following month, resulted in the sinking of four Japanese carriers and the destruction of more than 300 planes. From then on, the Japanese were on the retreat. Coral Sea was a battle fought entirely by aircraft carriers, and illustrates the importance of luck in war. Had the American carriers not been out at sea when Pearl Harbor was attacked, the whole Pacific War could have been different.

Although the British took a major role in the war in the East on land (e.g. in Burma), the Pacific War was largely an American affair. The

Holocaust: The mass murder of Jews by the Nazis (members of the Nationalist Socialist Workers' Party in Germany, led by Adolf Hitler) during the Second World War. The term was introduced by historians during the 1950s, as an equivalent to the Hebrew *hurban* and *shoah* meaning 'catastrophe'; but contemporary references to the Nazi atrocities as a 'holocaust' (meaning 'great slaughter') have overtaken the earlier meaning.

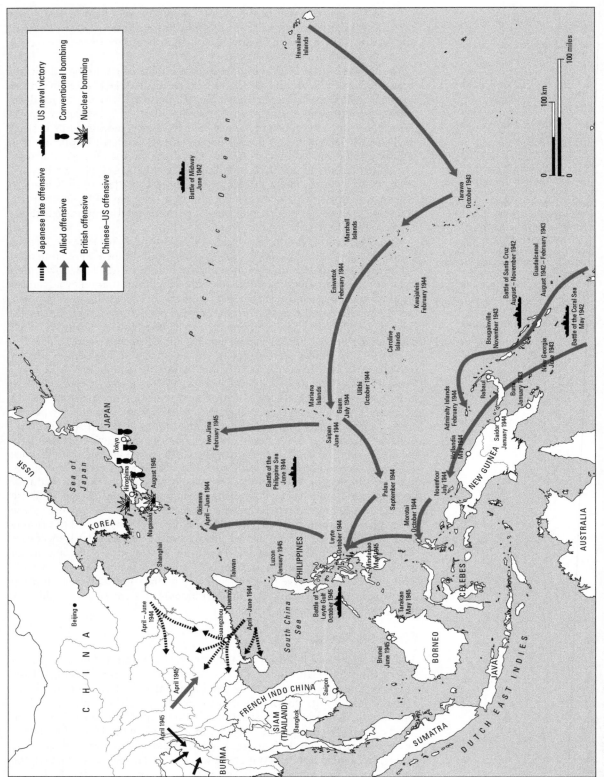

The War in the Pacific

Americans launched a two-pronged attack across the Ocean led by Admiral Chester Nimitz in the North and General Douglas MacArthur in the South. They 'island hopped' their way to Japan. In August, American marines landed at Guadalcanal. But it took six months for the island to fall into their hands. Throughout the next year they fought for and captured islands including Tarawa and Saipan, the latter putting them within 1,500 miles of Japan itself. From there, air force B-29s launched firebombing raids on the Japanese mainland. Further naval battles in 1944 effectively destroyed the Japanese navy. The Battle of Leyte Gulf, in October 1944, was the largest naval battle in American history. It seemed that the war in the Pacific was to be the story of hard, but steady, advance.

The brutality and difficulty of the battles worried the American military. Guadalcanal had taken six months to capture. When the marines took control of Iwo Jima, they had more than 25,000 casualties and 21,000 Japanese were killed. Taking Okinawa cost even more. Japanese '**kamikaze**' pilots had sunk more than 30 ships. It was believed the Japanese would fight equally hard to protect their homeland, meaning that their defeat would take at least another 18 months as well as cost an additional million lives. In July, Truman warned the Japanese that if they did not surrender unconditionally the Americans would unleash on them a new weapon. Atomic bombs were dropped on Hiroshima on 6 August and on Nagasaki three days later. Five days later Japan surrendered, the formal ceremony taking place on 'USS Missouri' on 14 September.

The decision to drop the bomb has been the subject of controversy ever since. The main argument has been that it was unnecessary and was done to stop Russian advances in the East. There is little doubt that Truman was influenced by a desire to contain Russia. It had been agreed at Yalta in February 1945 (see Chapter 5) that in return for its declaration of war on Japan the USSR would gain territory in Sakhalin and the Kurile Islands. It was feared that once war started it would advance quickly and capture not only Japanese territory, but also occupied areas such as Korea. If the Russians then held on to these areas it would upset the balance of power in the East. Russia declared war on 8 August and a second bomb, argued to be unnecessary by Truman's critics, was dropped the following day. Even Secretary of State James Byrnes admitted that the bomb would 'make Russia more manageable'. Though it was a factor, this had not been Truman's primary motive.

The Manhattan Project had spent $2 billion developing the bombs – among many new weapons developed during the Second World War to make victory more likely. It was hardly likely that given this investment they would not use the weapon once it had been tested successfully. The USA was in a race. Had the Germans developed the atomic bomb first there is little doubt that they would have used it.

It has sometimes been claimed that the United States had a racist motive for dropping the bombs on Japan. Even though their previous treatment of Asian peoples is hardly a record to be proud of, the atom bomb was initially developed for use against Germany. That it was ready for use only after the fall of Europe was simply a matter of timing.

The cost of taking the islands, and the perceived cost of taking Japan, was Truman's main motive. The War, as already stated, was expected to cost at least a million American lives and last another year. The use of the atom bomb was to end the War with the loss of as few American lives as possible. Even after the bombs had been dropped, it was five more days before the Japanese finally surrendered. Few soldiers in the Pacific at the time would have criticised Truman's decision.

'**Kamikaze**': Suicide pilots who flew bomb-laden aircraft at American ships.

1. With reference to the maps on pages 116 and 118, explain the contribution of the USA to the Allied victory.

2. Explain the reasons why Truman dropped the atom bombs on Japan in August 1945.

4.6 Why had the USA become a superpower by 1945?

Throughout the Second World War, the United States had been a full member of the Grand Alliance. They took part in the political and strategic discussions at Casablanca, Cairo and Tehran in 1943, at Yalta and at Potsdam. Unlike in the First World War, they were full Allies. But this time round, American involvement did not stop with the end of the war. The United States of America emerged from the Second World War as the world's leading nation, playing a full role in international affairs. Why was this so?

Firstly, the American contribution to the War had been crucial in the victory. It has been said that Britain provided the time, the Russians provided the blood and the Americans provided the money – there is some truth in this. The sheer size of the American economy and productive capacity was incredible. Fifteen million men and women served in the War; America produced 86,500 tanks, 300,000 aeroplanes and six million tons of bombs. The list goes on. Sixty per cent of the world's oil production and 50 per cent of the world's steel production was American. Its GNP had doubled and the value of its agricultural land had increased by $2 billion. Rather than fall back into Depression, as many feared, the ending of the War saw the American economy continue to grow. By the end of the Second World War the USA was the economic superpower of the world.

The economy was also technologically advanced thanks to the new developments of the War. There were new military technologies, such as radar, but also others such as the development of synthetic fuels and fabrics. And, of course, there was the atom bomb, which for the moment was an American monopoly.

This pre-eminence was added to by the destruction of Europe and Asia which the war had brought. Thirty million people had been killed (an incredible half of whom were Russian). There were more than 20 million refugees. Hundreds of cities and factories and acres of farmland throughout Europe and Asia had been destroyed. The economies of the European powers had been bankrupted by the cost of the War and their people were starving. The great European empires were also being lost.

Power vacuum: A term used to describe a region in which no state exercises effective control. Such areas are always liable to be occupied by expansionist powers.

The devastation left a **power vacuum** in the world, into which the Americans stepped. The crucial point was that this time round they were willing to do so. Even before the end of the War, the Atlantic Charter indicated a change of mood. When the United Nations was set up in 1945 at the San Francisco Conference, the Senate voted 89–2 to accept the Charter and American membership. Americans were worried by worldwide commitments and there continued to be an isolationist pull on their foreign policy, but their view of themselves and of their position in the world had changed. They had fought a war in which they were clearly the 'good guys' and now their power would enable them to shape the new order in their own image. Whether or not they would succeed, where Wilson had failed, remained to be seen. But there was no question that, in 1945, the United States was *the* superpower.

1. What do you understand by the term 'superpower'?

2. Why do you think the USA was regarded as a superpower by 1945?

4.7 Historical interpretation: Was FDR's foreign policy isolationist or interventionist?

4.7.1 What were FDR's foreign policy beliefs?
4.7.2 To what extent did FDR pursue an isolationist policy towards Europe and Japan?

Framework of Events

1932	FDR elected thirty-second president of United States
1933	Hitler comes to power in Germany
	FDR establishes diplomatic relations with USSR
1935	Neutrality Act prohibits export of US arms to belligerents
1936	Neutrality Act prohibits loans to belligerents
	FDR elected for second term
	Nye Committee Report
1937	Neutrality Act bans Americans from travelling on ships of belligerent nations
	Japanese attack on Nanking
	FDR makes Chicago speech
1938	Munich Agreement between Britain and Germany
1939	Outbreak of war in Europe; FDR declares 'limited national emergency'
1940	Selective Training and Service Act introduces conscription
	Destroyer Deal, trading 50 ships for British colonial territory
	FDR elected for third term
1941	Lend-Lease Act
	Attack on USS *Greer*
	Atlantic Charter agreed
	Japanese attack on Pearl Harbor
1943	FDR, Churchill and Stalin meet at Tehran to map out strategy
1944	FDR elected for fourth term
1945	Meeting at Yalta by 'Big Three' to discuss post-war world

Overview

THE United States in the 1920s followed a policy of isolationism, attempting to stay out of the affairs of European countries. The US did not want to get pulled into another war as it had been in 1917. Yet, under FDR's presidency, the United States did in fact find itself in another war; one much longer and more destructive than the first. Why did this happen? Was FDR an interventionist, who pursued an active foreign policy with the intention of supporting the Allies all along, or was he honestly attempting to keep the US free from entanglement in Europe and the Far East?

Some historians, such as William E. Leuchtenburg, in *Franklin D. Roosevelt and the New Deal, 1932–1940* (1963), argue that FDR hoped to keep the US out of the war but that he did not really know how to respond to events in Europe and the Far East. These historians believe that FDR intended to give material support to the Allies in the event of war but he did not intend for the US to send troops to fight in Europe. Others argue that, far from trying to maintain an isolationist stance, FDR went so far as to manipulate events to ensure America's entry into the war. Thomas Fleming, in *The War Within World War II* (2001), for example, argues that the Roosevelt administration purposefully leaked a secret report planning to send to Europe a five-million-man army. This leak prompted Hitler to fear American involvement, and he declared war on the USA. Others, such as Robert Dallek, in *Franklin D. Roosevelt and American Foreign Policy, 1932–1945* (1995), argue that FDR was an interventionist but in the sense that he felt he could influence events and *prevent* war by taking an active role in foreign policy.

In many ways it is difficult to say what FDR's beliefs were regarding isolationism and interventionism. He always played his cards close to his chest, and even men who worked closely with him throughout his career were never sure exactly what he believed in.

4.7.1 What were FDR's foreign policy beliefs?

FDR's upbringing and long-held interest in foreign affairs

It is clear that, although domestic economic pressures brought FDR to office, he had a long-held interest in foreign affairs. Robert Dallek, in *Franklin D. Roosevelt and American Foreign Policy, 1932–1945* (1995), points out:

> Aside from his [fifth] cousin Theodore, Franklin D. Roosevelt was the most **cosmopolitan** American to enter the White House since John Quincy Adams in 1825.

Cosmopolitan: having knowledge and understanding of foreign places and customs.

Throughout FDR's childhood, his family took regular holidays in Europe, and he was taught to speak both French and German. As a young man, he continued to travel, visiting the Caribbean and cycling through Holland and Germany. At Groton School, he joined the missionary society and took part in several debates on foreign affairs.

FDR as nationalist

FDR's political hero was his fifth cousin Theodore Roosevelt. Theodore Roosevelt was a skilful politician, who believed that the United States should play an active role in world affairs. FDR actively copied his cousin's career, becoming Assistant Secretary of the Navy in 1913. This was a position that Theodore Roosevelt had held in 1897/8. In this post, FDR argued that the US should have a 'big navy' to allow it to meet any threats to its security, and to allow it to pursue an active policy around the world for the benefit of the American people and of other countries. (These beliefs often led to conflict between FDR and his superior – Secretary of the Navy Josephus Daniels.)

While as Assistant Secretary of the Navy, FDR supported the Preparedness Movement, which argued for the need for the United States to prepare its military and economy more effectively should the country find itself having to join in the war that was looming in Europe. FDR argued, for example, that the navy, army and State Departments should form a Council of National Defense to coordinate military policy. When the US did join the war, FDR gained a reputation as an extremely capable administrator.

FDR as internationalist

As well as supporting Theodore Roosevelt's nationalist concept of America's role in the world, Patrick J. Maney, in *The Roosevelt Presence: The*

Life and Legacy of FDR (1992), argues that Franklin was also an internationalist like Woodrow Wilson.

FDR strongly supported US involvement in the League of Nations, believing that the League would make rearmament unnecessary and war less likely. Robert Dallek, in *Franklin D, Roosevelt and American Foreign Policy, 1932–1945* (1995), however, sees this support of the League as more opportunistic; Wilson was immensely popular immediately after World War I and allying himself with this policy would advance FDR's political career. However, even when the public turned against the League and the Senate refused to ratify American membership, FDR continued to believe that active engagement in the League was the best way to protect American interests. According to Michael Simpson, in *Franklin D. Roosevelt* (1989):

> By the time he left office, he was developing a more responsible attitude to war and peace and a positive conception of America's global role.

When FDR became president, the mood of the United States was distinctly against foreign adventures. But, according to Michael Simpson, FDR remained convinced that the US had a role to play in defending democracy and human rights, especially in the face of the growing threat from fascism. Unlike most New Dealers, FDR was not an isolationist; instead he believed that the best way to prevent war was to intervene in international affairs, not avoid them. When war did come, he felt that giving the British moral and material support would mean they could win without the need for American military action (what William E. Leuchtenburg calls being a 'grand neutral'), and even if military action were needed it would require no more than naval and air support. FDR did not foresee the US having to support the Allied cause with American troops.

Contradictory policies

Despite FDR's internationalist outlook, he also worked hard to ensure American neutrality throughout the 1930s. He seemed to agree with the findings of the Nye Committee, whose report in 1936 argued that **lobbying by arms manufacturers** had pushed the US into World War I. FDR also supported neutrality legislation and worked hard to ensure that the US did not become embroiled in the Spanish Civil War. With regard to Latin America, FDR announced as early as 1933 that the US would pursue a Good Neighbour Policy and would not intervene in the affairs of Latin American states. This promise was confirmed at the Pan-American Conference later in the year, and put into practice when US troops were removed from Haiti and the Dominican Republic. In 1936, when the New Mexican Government nationalised US owned oil companies, Roosevelt looked for a compensation deal instead of confrontation. Yet, at the same time, a visit by an American warship to Cuba, in 1934, was instrumental in helping rebels overthrow the democratic rule of Grau San Martín and replace it with the dictatorship of Fulgencio Batista. And, in both Nicaragua and the Dominican Republic, American-trained soldiers helped dictators like Somoza and Trujillo remain in power. To some, it seemed that the US was prepared to be a 'good neighbour' so long as governments remained pro-American.

FDR's policies, throughout the 1930s, seemed frequently to be contradictory. William E. Leuchtenburg, in *Franklin D. Roosevelt and the New Deal, 1932–1940* (1963), says that FDR was deeply troubled by the events in Europe but did not know what to do for the best. Robert Dallek, in *Franklin D. Roosevelt and American Foreign Policy, 1932–1945* (1995), places more emphasis on the domestic constraints under which FDR operated. He

Lobbying by arms manufacturers: pressure put on the government, by weapons manufacturers, to take a more active foreign policy and build up the country's military.

recognises that for FDR to achieve what he wanted at home, he needed the support of Congress and had to go along with a Congressional desire for a passive foreign policy.

4.7.2 To what extent did FDR pursue an isolationist policy towards Europe and Japan?

Isolationism and the public's needs

Two months before FDR took his oath of office, Adolf Hitler came to power in Germany in January 1933. Fascism was on the rise throughout Europe in Italy, Germany and Spain, yet foreign policy experts in the US were telling the President that there would be no war. If there were to be a war, FDR knew how inadequately prepared the United States was. The US had an army the size of Sweden, an industry in deep depression, and a military so poorly equipped that, when America did finally go to war, US troops were initially training with cardboard weapons. If nothing else, these considerations limited FDR's ability to pursue an interventionist foreign policy.

FDR was also highly aware of the mood of the American public. The events of World War I were still strong in people's memories. The losses and seeming futility of that conflict had led America, in the 1920s, to adopt a foreign policy of isolationism. As many historians have shown, this isolationism was only partial. In the 1920s, the USA had not supported the League of Nations and had taken no action when Japan invaded Manchuria. However, the USA had participated in world trade, developed the **Dawes Plan**, attended the League-sponsored disarmament conference and the Washington naval conference, and signed the **Kellogg-Briand Pact** outlawing war. However, isolationism was a belief strongly held and supported by the public and, therefore, a belief FDR could not ignore.

During the election, and in a speech in 1933, FDR asserted his belief that the USA should remain free from foreign entanglements. William E. Leuchtenburg, in *Franklin D. Roosevelt and the New Deal 1932–1940* (1963), puts FDR's protestations down to the need for support from the news media rather than a sincerely held belief. The publication of the Nye Committee Report in 1936, however, strengthened support for an isolationist stand. As late as 1937, Indiana Congressman Louis Ludlow put forward a constitutional amendment to require a referendum before the President could declare war. The measure was defeated in the House of Representatives but, in spite of FDR strenuously arguing that the amendment would tie the hands of any president, 209 members voted in favour. The narrowness of the vote convinced FDR that the nation still 'wanted peace' and, according to William Leuchtenburg, shows how tenuous FDR's control of foreign policy was.

The Neutrality Acts

The support for isolation, was translated into the Neutrality Acts of 1935, 1936 and 1937. These Acts respectively provided for an arms embargo against warring nations, the prohibition of loans to **belligerents**, and a ban on US citizens travelling on the ships of belligerent nations. Robert Dallek, in *Franklin D. Roosevelt and American Foreign Policy, 1932–1945* (1995), states that FDR pushed for a more flexible measure in 1935 that would give him the power to decide who was and who was not a belligerent. Congress rejected the idea and, because FDR needed their support for his

Dawes Plan: signed in 1924, this was the agreement, between the USA, France, Britain, Belgium and Germany, for the rescheduling of the reparations payments that Germany owed at the end of World War I. Germany's refusal to pay its instalment in 1922 had led to an invasion by the French and Belgians in 1923. The American Government came up with the Dawes Plan to try to resolve the situation and prevent the outbreak of another war.

Kellog-Briand Pact: the agreement made in 1928, signed by 65 nations, outlawing war as a method of policy.

Belligerents: those actively involved in war or conflict.

domestic programmes, he was unable to achieve a modification of the legislation.

Americans continued to fear that the European nations would drag them into a war. The invasion of Ethiopia by the Italian army, and the outbreak of civil war in Spain, confirmed the belief among many Americans of the necessity of the Neutrality Acts, which were even extended in January 1937 to cover civil wars. According to William E. Leuchtenburg, this was done with FDR's support. Michael Simpson, in *Franklin D. Roosevelt* (1989), feels that FDR failed to support those senators wanting to give help to the Spanish republicans, not because he wished to but because he did not feel the American public was ready to support the change. According to Michael J. Heale, in *Franklin D. Roosevelt: The New Deal and War* (1999):

> [FDR] blamed the neutrality laws for encouraging fascist aggression, but Congress was loath to amend them.

Did FDR's policy change with the build-up to war?

In 1936, the Nazi army moved into the Rhineland, breaking the terms of the Treaty of Versailles. In the Far East, Japan continued to expand its territory and, in 1937, attacked the Chinese city of Nanking, massacring thousands of its inhabitants.

On 5 October 1937, FDR made a speech in Chicago in which he spoke of the epidemic of lawlessness around the world. He said that America had to oppose this trend and 'quarantine' those nations responsible for the epidemic. The speech caused a stir at the time as to exactly what FDR meant. Robert Dallek, in *Franklin D. Roosevelt and American Foreign Policy, 1932–1945* (1995), maintains that FDR was doing nothing more than warning the American people that as the world became more 'lawless' they too could be in danger. Dallek believes that the President was not trying to institute a change of policy, such as the introduction of a policy of sanctions against Japan, or persuade the people of the need for such a change. Likewise, William Leuchtenburg, in *Franklin D. Roosevelt and the New Deal, 1932–1940* (1963), points out that FDR was at pains to say that he

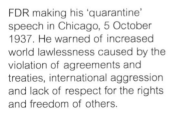

FDR making his 'quarantine' speech in Chicago, 5 October 1937. He warned of increased world lawlessness caused by the violation of agreements and treaties, international aggression and lack of respect for the rights and freedom of others.

Impeachment: to remove the president from office and put him on trial.

was not referring to some kind of trade embargo, and that the speech is not evidence that FDR was an internationalist. However, Patrick J. Maney, in *The Roosevelt Presence: The Life and Legacy of FDR* (1992), says it is still not clear what FDR meant when he talked about the 'quarantine' of aggressors and, certainly at the time, some saw the speech as heralding a change in US policy. If, as some historians suggest, FDR made the speech to test public support for a more interventionist foreign policy, he got his answer when he was threatened with **impeachment**.

It was not only Americans who wished to avoid war. In September 1938, British Prime Minister Neville Chamberlain travelled to Munich to talk to Hitler to try to avert a crisis over Czechoslovakia. Chamberlain returned to Britain claiming to have achieved peace, but it was at the expense of giving a large chunk of Czech territory – the Sudetenland – to the Nazis. FDR telegraphed Chamberlain, calling him a 'good man' for agreeing to meet Hitler. Patrick Maney and William Leuchtenburg both say that FDR supported the agreement and Chamberlain's policy of appeasement (see page 110). Michael Simpson, however, says that FDR was very angry at the outcome of the conference and believed it only delayed war. Eleanor Roosevelt said that FDR opposed the agreement in private but did not say so in public. FDR's actions after the conference indicate that he saw the emergence of German power as of great consequence to the US. He pushed Congress for an expanded air force and a naval build-up. He also wanted to sell planes to the French, but public hostility and the Neutrality Acts prevented this. He did, however, initiate secret military talks between Britain, France and the USA.

Did FDR remain 'neutral' with the onset of war?

When war did come, in September 1939, FDR immediately made it clear to the American people that he intended to remain neutral. However, in his 'fireside chat' on 3 September he famously said that 'even a neutral cannot be asked to close his mind or his conscience'. In *Franklin D. Roosevelt and American Foreign Policy, 1932–1945* (1995), Robert Dallek states:

> [To FDR] morality and self-interest … compelled America to aid Britain and France: the preservation of American values and national peace depended on the defeat of Berlin.

Like the American public, FDR wanted to stay out of Europe's war, but he believed the best way to do this was to support the Allied cause. Polls showed that the public supported Britain and that the majority of Americans wanted the US to supply arms but not get involved. Some, however, opposed FDR's view and argued, somewhat cynically, that if Germany won it would leave the US in control of the western hemisphere. In *The Roosevelt Presence: The Life and Legacy of FDR* (1992), Patrick J. Maney criticises FDR for attacking these people instead of educating them to his own view. He also points out that FDR treated those who opposed him like enemies. He even had their phones tapped.

In the election in November, FDR had to be wary of Republican attacks and so promised not to send 'our boys' to fight in Europe. The fall of France had made the American public more supportive of FDR's policies and more willing to give material aid to the Allies, but divisions remained strong. 1940 saw the creation of both the internationalist Committee to Defend America by Aiding the Allies (CDAAA) and the isolationist America First Committee (AFC). FDR strengthened his position by taking two Republicans into the Cabinet – Henry Stimson as Secretary of War and Frank Knox as Secretary of the Navy. With their support, and support from veteran groups, FDR was able to get Congress to pass the Selective Service

Conscripts: men called up by the government to serve in the military.

Act. This was America's first ever peacetime draft, making men aged 21 to 45 years old eligible for one year of military service and providing $500,000 million for defence. Veteran organisations supported the Act, but William E. Leuchtenburg, in *Franklin D. Roosevelt and the New Deal* (1963), says the measure was opposed by the military, who believed that **conscripts** would weaken the regular army.

FDR still saw this measure as a precaution. He believed that the best way for the US to avoid war was to provide support to the Allies to strengthen their ability to fight and defeat the Nazis. The Neutrality Acts, however, made this difficult. FDR proposed to amend them to allow Britain to buy arms, which they would have to carry in their own ships to avoid American ships becoming targets. He talked carefully to both Republican and Democrat representatives to ensure **bipartisan** support and, according to Dallek, FDR was able to persuade Congress to pass this 'cash and carry' measure by presenting it as a strategy to keep the United States out of the war.

Bipartisan: having the support of both the Republican and Democratic Parties.

Did FDR's actions tie the US more tightly to the Allied cause?

FDR's critics believed that the President's actions were tying the US more and more tightly to the Allied cause. Criticism increased with the Destroyer Deal of 1940 and the Lend-Lease Act of 1941.

In 1940, the US exchanged 50 old destroyers in return for British colonial territory where the US could develop bases. William E. Leuchtenburg, Michael Simpson and Michael J. Heale all emphasise how FDR **circumvented** Congress over the deal. Leuchtenburg asserts that FDR did this because he knew that if he did not he would fail to get their support. If the rise of Nazism was the threat to the US that FDR asserted it was, then why, congressmen asked, was the President giving away ships that might be needed to defend America? Once again FDR 'sold' the deal to the public by saying it was in America's interest to help Britain. He said the deal was the most important defence measure for the US since the **Louisiana Purchase**. Having bases around the world would enable the US to protect its interests more effectively, and the destroyers would allow Britain to continue its fight against fascism.

Circumvented: by-passed the power of Congress and used the Executive power of the President.

Louisiana Purchase: in 1803, the US bought, from the French, an area between the Rocky Mountains and the Mississippi River. It cost $15 million but added the whole of the Mississippi Valley to the United States.

In spite of the help given by the United States, by the spring of 1941 Churchill was warning FDR that Britain could no longer afford the arms it needed to continue the war. On 11 March 1941, Congress passed the Lend-Lease Act. This gave Britain arms and supplies that would be returned or paid for after the war. Over the next four years Britain received $50 billion worth of supplies. By claiming that the assets were being loaned or leased, FDR got around the terms of the Neutrality Acts. FDR again presented the measure as essential to US defence. He likened it to lending your neighbour a garden hose because their house is on fire – if you refused or made them buy their own hose your house could burn down too. In his 'fireside chat' at the end of December 1940, FDR had emphasised the danger to America if Britain lost the war. He said that the Americans would find themselves living at the point of a gun. He once again emphasised that the best way to avoid war was to become 'the great arsenal of democracy'. In *Franklin D. Roosevelt and American Foreign Policy, 1932–1945* (1995), Robert Dallek says it was one of the most successful speeches that FDR ever gave and, in spite of protests in New York and Washington against lend-lease, opinion polls showed an 80 per cent approval of the speech.

Although FDR presented lend-lease as a defence measure, Michael J. Heale says that it was the greatest commitment the President could make to the Allied cause short of war. In *Franklin D. Roosevelt* (1989), Michael Simpson asserts that FDR himself acknowledged this view. FDR seemed to be making good the promise he had made in Virginia during the election campaign to 'extend to the opponents of force the material resources of [the] nation'.

Did FDR fully intend to go to war?

FDR does appear to have gone beyond simply supplying material resources to the British. In the Atlantic, attacks by German U-boats were having a devastating effect on British shipping. In 1941, 1500 ships were sunk. FDR gave secret instructions to the US navy to escort British ships crossing the Atlantic. He also announced an extension of America's security zone as far north as Greenland, although he refused to provide the convoys Churchill asked for. The navy ships escorting the British vessels had been given permission by FDR to fire at German ships if necessary and, in September, an incident occurred that seemed it might lead to war.

On 4 September 1941, a British plane and the USS *Greer* spotted a U-boat and gave chase. The plane dropped depth charges and the U-boat fired a torpedo at the ship. The USS *Greer*, in turn, dropped depth charges, and more torpedoes were fired. Neither vessel was sunk in the chase, and the navy told the President that the Germans probably did not know the ship's nationality. FDR, however, told the public that the Germans knew it was an American ship and that the Germans fired first. Michael Simpson, in *Franklin D. Roosevelt* (1989), sees this as hypocrisy, saying that FDR talked about peace while he courted war. In *Franklin D. Roosevelt and American Foreign Policy, 1932–1945* (1995), Robert Dallek justifies FDR's deception and blames the American public who, at the time, wanted to defeat Hitler but did not want to go to war to do it. He says:

> In the light of the national unwillingness to face up fully to the international dangers confronting the country, it is difficult to fault Roosevelt for building a consensus by devious means.

Dallek believes that, by the spring of 1941, FDR had come to believe that the US would have to fight but that if he waited the Allies would be weaker. Although Dallek defends FDR's lies as being in the national interest, even he admits this did set a dangerous precedent for future leaders to mislead the public in time of war.

Some of FDR's opponents believed the USS *Greer* incident was manufactured to create the pretext for war. Certainly, Secretary of War Henry Stimson advised FDR to do more to help the British and argued that the summer and autumn of 1941 was a good time to act as the Germans were tied up with their invasion of the USSR.

Patrick J. Maney is not convinced that FDR's policies were a pretext for war. As he points out, in *The Roosevelt Presence: The Life and Legacy of FDR* (1992), polls showed that three out of five people believed it was more important to defeat Germany than to stay out of the war. If he had wanted to, FDR could have used the USS *Greer* incident as a way to persuade the public to go to war with Nazi Germany, but he did not. Yet, in the August, FDR had met with Churchill just off the coast of Newfoundland, and Churchill had come away from the meeting convinced that FDR would manufacture an incident to take America into the war. Also, at the meeting, the two men issued a set of principles that became known as the Atlantic Charter. These principles included arms reduction, self-determination, freedom of the seas, free trade, and so on. As Michael J. Heale, in *Franklin D Roosevelt: The New Deal and War* (1999), points out; the Atlantic Charter was a list of war aims issued by a country that was not at war.

After the incident with the USS *Greer*, FDR gave US navy ships permission to sink German ships on sight. The Americans were in the war in the

Atlantic in all but name. If FDR had indeed come around to the view that America would have to fight, it is possible that he would have joined the Allied cause. In the end, however, it was the Japanese not the Germans who made him make that decision.

Did FDR invite the attack on Pearl Harbor?

Moralistic: believing and acting as though you are in the right when it is not necessarily the case.

According to Michael Simpson, in *Franklin D. Roosevelt* (1989), American policy with regard to the Far East was muddled and **moralistic** in the 1930s. On the one hand, the American public and the administration saw the rise of fascism in Europe and in the Far East as intimately connected but, on the other hand, Japan was seen as different from Germany. While the public wanted to avoid war in the East, as they did in Europe, many felt war with Japan was inevitable. While isolationism was largely seen as a policy towards Europe, the public still did not want FDR taking US troops to fight in the East. To prevent war, FDR tried to work with moderate Japanese leaders. At the same time, he tried to send messages that would halt Japanese expansion. Unfortunately those messages were not always understood; by taking small measures against the Japanese, the hard-liners in Japan's Government believed that FDR did not have the will to act.

Great power: a state that, through a mix of economic, military and political power, has a lot of influence on other states.

According to Michael Simpson, in *Franklin D. Roosevelt* (1989), FDR was obsessed with China's **great power** status. He hoped that, with American support, China would develop into a democratic nation and be a beacon for the rest of Asia. A strong China would also act as a block on Japanese expansion. Patrick J. Maney, in *The Roosevelt Presence: The Life and Legacy of FDR* (1992), points out that, in fact, the US did more trade with Japan than it did with China. When Japan attacked China in 1937 and massacred the people of the city of Nanking, the US took little action. In fact, the US administration argued that no state of war existed between China and Japan, so the Neutrality Acts did not apply and the US could continue to send supplies to Chiang Kai-Shek. This double standard led some critics to argue that FDR was hoping to provoke Japan. According to Michael Parrish, in *Anxious Decades: America in Prosperity and Depression, 1920–1941* (1992), the policy encouraged Chiang Kai-Shek to believe he had US support and made him less willing to negotiate with Japan.

Chiang Kai-Shek (1887–1975)
Chiang Kai-Shek was a soldier, a politician and a revolutionary. In 1928, he became the leader of the Chinese Nationalist Movement and helped to defeat the Manchu dynasty and establish a new republican government in China. He fought against the Japanese during World War II but, after the war, his Nationalists fought and lost a civil war to Mao Zedong's Chinese Communist Party. In 1949, he and his followers fled to Taiwan, which became a strong ally of the US and, until 1971, held the Chinese seat on the United Nations Security Council. Chiang Kai-Shek became president of Taiwan in 1949 until his death.

It was shortly after the attack on China that FDR made his Chicago speech (5 October 1937) condemning lawless nations. To some it seemed that FDR was moving away from isolationism, but FDR still hoped to work with moderate Japanese leaders to avoid war. However, Howard Zinn, in *A People's History of the United States* (1980), criticises American inaction over Nanking, saying that America did nothing about the massacre and only acted when its economic interests were at stake. Michael Simpson, however, argues that the American public was not ready for war, and that when the Japanese sank USS *Panay* there was great relief when the Japanese apologised and offered compensation.

As Japan continued to expand aggressively into Dutch and French territory, the American Government was divided on how to act. According to Patrick Maney, in *The Roosevelt Presence: The Life and Legacy of FDR* (1992), FDR saw the issue in a European context – Britain's ability to fight the Nazis might be impeded by its need to defend its colonies in the East. FDR continued to negotiate, but he cut off supplies of scrap metal and sent the Pacific fleet to the base at Pearl Harbor. Some historians have seen these moves, and the subsequent oil embargo, as moves to invite an attack on the Pacific fleet, giving FDR the excuse for war. Michael Heale, Patrick Maney and Robert Dallek refute this. They believe that FDR's aim was to show the Japanese how serious he was and hopefully force them to back down. James T. Patterson, in *America in the Twentieth Century* (1994), also

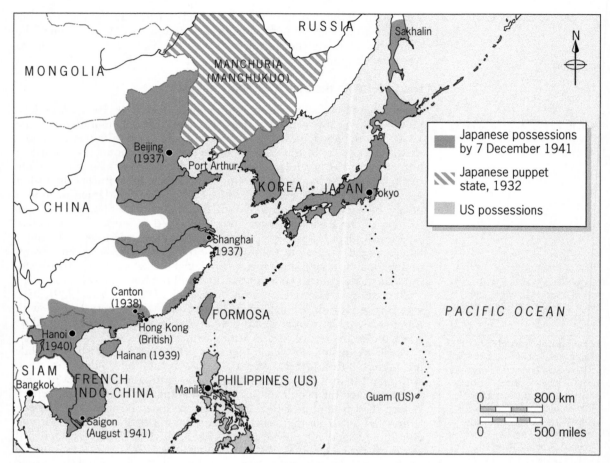

Japanese expansion until 1941.

argues in favour of FDR's policies, saying that their advantage was that they were restrained and incremental.

FDR was still keen to avert war with Japan as he seemed to be moving closer to war in Europe, and he did not want war on two fronts. However, the Japanese saw the oil embargo as a potentially fatal blow to their ability to fight. They believed they had to attack first and defeat the US before they were no longer able to do so. This is why they launched a surprise attack on Pearl Harbor. Patrick Maney, in *The Roosevelt Presence: The Life and Legacy of FDR* (1992), states:

> No persuasive evidence has ever surfaced to suggest that, as some people suspected, Roosevelt knew in advance of the attack on Pearl Harbor but allowed it to proceed in order to bring a reluctant nation into the war against Germany.

Nevertheless, both sides continued to negotiate into October and November 1941. They failed, however, to agree on the status of Manchuria, on withdrawal from China, and on sanctions. According to James Patterson, the Japanese had decided on war as early as August 1941 and nothing FDR did would have avoided it. Rather than invite war with Japan, FDR had done all he could to avoid it but, in the end, the most he could have hoped for was to postpone it.

Assessment

FDR's freedom to act was limited throughout the 1930s by both Congress and the American public. Like them, he wanted to avoid war and protect American lives but, unlike many, he did not believe the way to do it was through isolating the US from world affairs. FDR attempted to educate the public to the dangers facing them but, because that took time, he also took what steps he could to support Britain in its fight against fascism. With regard to Japan, he supported the moderate elements in government while trying to make clear his opposition to Japanese expansion in China.

FDR was not an isolationist in his foreign policy; he clearly intervened in European affairs and gave real support to Churchill. He did agree with the isolationists on one thing – he wanted to keep the peace. However, he knew that, with the growing strength of those he called 'the bandit nations', keeping the peace was increasingly unlikely.

Was FDR's foreign policy isolationist or interventionist?

1. Read the following extract about FDR's 'quarantine' speech, and answer the question.

In the fall of 1937 he appeared to edge cautiously away from non-involvement … At last, so it seemed, Roosevelt was moving toward a policy of resistance.

J.T. Patterson, *America in the Twentieth Century*, Harcourt Brace, 1994.

Using the information in the extract above, and from this section, explain to what extent you agree that FDR's speech in Chicago, 1937, marked a turning point in his foreign policy.

2. 'For the first five years of his presidency, FDR steered cautiously between isolationism and interventionalism.' How far do you agree with this view of FDR's foreign policy?

Further Reading

Texts designed for AS Level students

FDR by Kathryn Cooper (Collins Historymakers, 2005)
The Enduring Vision by Paul Boyer and others (D.C. Heath & Co., 1993) – easy to read and well-illustrated narrative.
The USA and the World, 1917–1945 by Peter Brett (Hodder & Stoughton, 1997) – clear narrative with practice exercises and note-making guide.
A History of the United States of America by Hugh Brogan (Longman, Second edition 1999) – good introductory text.
The Limits of Liberty by Maldwyn Jones (Oxford University Press, 1995) – clear narrative account.
Hell in the Pacific by Jonathon Lewis and Ben Steele (Boxtree, 2001) – a revisionist account, based on the Channel 4 series, giving the vivid story of the brutality of the Pacific war.

Texts for A2 and advanced study

The Unfinished Nation by Alan Brinkley (McGraw Hill, 1993) – easy to read and scholarly, with good maps.
The War of 1898 by Louis Perez (Chapel Hill, 1998) – a study which provides different historical interpretations.

US Foreign Policy in World History by David Ryan (Routledge, 2000) – analysis of motives behind US foreign policy.

Manifest Destiny by Anders Stephanson (Hill & Wang, 1995) – study of American expansion.

Television and video

'The World at War' – Thames TV programmes (1973) shown on BBC in 2001 in 'Second World War' series. Available from Pearson TV International Ltd on either WWW.WORLDATWAR.COM or WWW.PEARSONTV.COM.

'FDR': episode 4 – PBS/BBC

'Truman' – written and produced by David Grubin for 'The American Experience' series (1994). It is divided into three one-hour episodes: the first covers Truman's political rise and the dropping of the atom bomb on Japan in 1945; the second episode covers Truman's Administration in domestic and foreign affairs up to 1949; the third episode concentrates on the Korean War.

Useful websites

http://www.historyofcuba.com – useful information and lots of documents on the Spanish–American War.

HTTP://WWW.THEODOREROOSEVELT.ORG – contains documents, speeches etc. as well as biographical detail on Theodore Roosevelt.

HTTP://WWW.AMERICANPRESIDENT.ORG – based on PBS television series; covers the US Presidents and US foreign policy.

HTTP://TLC.AI.ORG – contains lots of links to other sites on US foreign policy.

5 The USA and the Cold War in Europe, 1945–1991

Key Issues

- Why did a Cold War develop between the United States and the Soviet Union?

- How did the USA attempt to contain the Soviet Union in Europe?

- How did US policy help bring about the end of the Cold War?

5.1 Why did the Grand Alliance break down?

5.2 Historical interpretation: How far was Truman responsible for the development of the Cold War?

5.3 Why was Germany central to the Cold War in Europe?

5.4 How far did American–Soviet relations in Europe improve under Eisenhower?

5.5 How effectively did Kennedy pursue the Cold War in Europe?

5.6 How successful was Nixon's policy of *détente*?

5.7 How far did *détente* continue under Carter?

5.8 Why did the Cold War in Europe come to an end?

Framework of Events

1945	February: Yalta Conference
	July: Potsdam Conference
1947	Truman Doctrine
	Marshall Plan
	National Security Act
1948–1949	Berlin Blockade and Airlift
1949	North Atlantic Treaty Organisation
1955	May: Warsaw Pact
	July: Geneva Summit – Eisenhower meets Khrushchev
	Austrian State Treaty
	German re-armament
1956	Hungarian Revolution
1957	Launch of 'Sputnik'
1958	Berlin Crisis
1960	Paris Summit
	U-2 crisis
1961	Vienna Summit – Kennedy meets Khrushchev
	Berlin Wall Crisis
1969	Strategic Arms Limitation Talks begin in Helsinki
1972	Moscow Summit
	SALT I
1975	Helsinki Agreements
1979	SALT II
	Soviet invasion of Afghanistan
1980	Solidarity Movement begins in Poland
1982	Strategic Arms Reduction Talks (START) in Geneva
1986	Reykjavik Summit
1987	Intermediate-range Nuclear Forces (INF) Treaty
1989	November: Fall of the Berlin Wall
	Velvet Revolution in Czechoslovakia
1990	Germany Re-unified
	Communists overthrown in Romania
1991	Collapse of Soviet Union.

Overview

Containment: American policy for much of the Cold War, aimed at limiting the spread of world communism (see page 77). It was put forward by President Truman in April 1947 as the Truman Doctrine.

Ideologies : These are sets of beliefs about the world and how it works (e.g. communism; nationalism).

A T the end of the Second World War, the alliance between East and West, which had been so successful against the Nazis, began to break down. Fears and suspicions surfaced, creating a climate of mistrust between the United States and the Soviet Union. The imposition of communist governments on to eastern European states made the Americans fear for the freedom and security of Western Europe. As this would affect their trade and security, a policy of **containment** was established. It was the aim of the United States to halt the spread of communism throughout the world. The Soviets saw this as unnecessarily aggressive. The Second World War had cost the Soviet Union as many as 27 million lives. They were determined that they would not be attacked again from the west. To ensure their protection they established friendly, communist governments on their borders. This fear and hostility was not simply a product of events at the end of the War: the two superpowers had conflicting **ideologies** and world views, and both came to the conclusion, in the late 1940s, that the two ideologies could not live side by side. The next 45 years would be a struggle to win this conflict. In an age of nuclear weapons, conflict could not be allowed to become a war – so the Cold War was fought through propaganda, through the exercise of economic power, particularly by the Americans, and through the build-up of military strength in an arms race. Occasionally, the Cold War would turn 'hot' in some part of the world, but the Soviets and Americans never faced one another over a battlefield.

In 1947, President Truman set the tone for the Cold War with the Truman Doctrine and the Marshall Plan, which established the policy of containment in Europe. The following year, when the Soviets blockaded Berlin in an attempt to get the Allies to withdraw from the city, Truman successfully enacted his policy forcing the Soviet Union to back down. Containment was tried and succeeded again, though somewhat less successfully, two years later and 5,000 miles away in Korea (see Chapter 6).

When Eisenhower entered the White House in 1953, there was something of a change of policy. Though containment continued, the Americans took on a more aggressive tone, talking about 'rolling back' the borders of communism and liberating people from its grasp. However, in a world that now had the hydrogen bomb as well as the atom bomb, the stakes in the Cold War, and its costs, had been raised. The Americans also tried to pursue a policy of 'peaceful co-existence'. If the opportunity arose, they would try to free people from communism but, at the same time, make an effort to get on better with the Soviet Union and avoid possible conflict which could lead to nuclear war. Meetings at Geneva and Camp David went a long way to improving relations, but the bloody crushing of the Hungarian uprising by the Red Army in 1956 and the shooting down of an American spy plane in 1960 soured relations once again. When Kennedy became President in 1961, the Cold War was very tense.

Kennedy was determined to stand up to the Soviet Union as Truman had done. He did so by embarking on a massive arms build-up, and by responding to the Russian space programme by promising to put an American on the moon. Yet he also wished to continue the work begun by Eisenhower. Kennedy, too, travelled to Europe to meet the Soviet leader, Nikita Khrushchev, face to face in Vienna. After the building of the Berlin Wall in 1961, conflict over Europe had lessened notably.

For Kennedy's successor, Lyndon Johnson, it was events in Vietnam, not in Europe, that took his attention.

By the time Nixon came to office in 1969, the danger of war in Europe seemed to be a thing of the past. The Cold War was by no means over, but the two sides had long had two alliance systems – NATO and the **Warsaw Pact** – protecting their interest and making war unlikely. Behind these two systems had been a massive build-up of arms. While in no way abandoning its hostility to communism, the American government launched a policy of **détente**. This looked back to Eisenhower's policy of peaceful co-existence, but this time was centred around talks to reduce nuclear weapons. It was a successful policy in that in the 1970s it produced SALT I and SALT II, the first agreements by the superpowers to limit nuclear weapons.

Many Americans, though, remained deeply suspicious of communism and believed that the Soviets were not abiding by their promises. Old fears of Soviet expansion were revived when they invaded Afghanistan in 1979. America's President Carter tried to take a firm stance, but there was little he could do beyond boycott trade and forbid American athletes from attending the Moscow Olympics. Ronald Reagan, the Republican President who took office in 1981, took a much firmer stance and embarked on the biggest arms build-up the world has ever seen. America's allies became very nervous that relations between East and West seemed worse than at any time since the 1940s. But things were different. Although he was determined to be strong, Reagan was also willing to talk to the Soviets and the 1987 Intermediate-range Nuclear Forces (INF) Treaty was the first arms agreement which actually dismantled some weapons rather than just limiting build-up. It was a very small change, but it was a start. The Soviet Union had a new leader, Mikhail Gorbachev, who knew that his country could not afford to compete against the Americans in another arms race. To do so would cause their economy to collapse. He also wanted to bring real change and openness to the Soviet Union, so improving relations with the United States was part of his policy. These policies led to demands for change throughout Eastern Europe, which were encouraged by the West. By 1989, these demands had become so strong that the Berlin Wall was torn down and communism throughout Eastern Europe collapsed. The Americans, it was claimed, had won the Cold War.

Warsaw Pact: The military alliance of Eastern bloc states created in 1955. It came into being one week after West Germany was allowed to join NATO.

Détente: Relaxation of tension between countries. Also characterised by increased cooperation and cultural exchanges, such as overseas tours by Soviet athletes and ballet companies, particularly to the USA.

Secretaries of State during the Cold War

Truman's Administration:	Edward R. Stettinus Jr (1945)
	James F. Byrnes (1945–47)
	George C. Marshall (1947–49)
	Dean Acheson (1949–53)
Eisenhower's Administration:	John Foster Dulles (1953–59)
	Christian A. Herter (1959–61)
Kennedy's Administration:	Dean Rusk (1961–63)
Johnson's Administration:	Dean Rusk (1963–69)
Nixon's Administration:	William P. Rogers (1969–73)
Ford's Administration:	Henry A. Kissinger (1973–77)
Carter's Administration:	Cyrus R. Vance (1977–80)
	Edmund Muskie (1980–81)
Reagan's Administration:	Alexander M. Haig Jr (1981–82)
	George P. Schulz (1982–89)
Bush Senior's Administration:	James A. Baker III (1989–92)

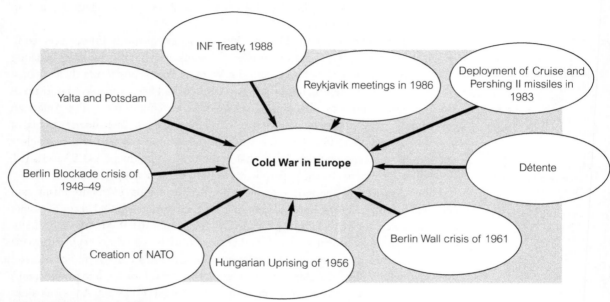

1. Which of the developments in the mind map were the result of actions by the USSR?

2. On balance, who was more responsible for the tension between East and West in Europe from 1945 to 1991, the USA or the USSR? Give reasons for your answer.

5.1 Why did the Grand Alliance break down?

What agreements were made at Yalta?

During the Second World War, the Americans, Soviets and British worked well together in their common fight against the Nazis. The friendship of the three greatest powers in the world was known as the 'Grand Alliance'. However, there were old suspicions and hostilities between the three and the leaders had to work hard to maintain cooperation. Roosevelt set great store by personal contact and throughout the War there were face-to-face meetings between the 'Big Three'. At their meeting in Yalta on 4–11 February 1945, Stalin, the Soviet leader, agreed to help the Americans in the East against Japan and to put pressure on the Chinese communists to end their civil war. Roosevelt also got Stalin's promise to support the setting up of the United Nations. In return, the Soviets demanded reparations for their losses in the war, a weakened Germany and land in Asia. Not

Josef Stalin, real name Josef Vissarionovich Dzhugashvili (1879–1953) Communist revolutionary; leader of the USSR (1928–53). He was responsible for modernising Russian industry and building up its military power so that it was able to fight when the war came. His continued build-up of military power and the control he established over Eastern Europe after the War meant Stalin turned the USSR into a superpower. He was also a ruthless dictator. To enforce his agricultural polices, thousands were sent to labour camps and he allowed no opposition: those who did criticise also went to the camps. In the 1930s and again after the war, Stalin launched a series of 'purges' where his enemies – real or imagined – were removed. Millions of people died in this terror, killed on the orders of their own leader.

Winston Churchill, Franklin Roosevelt and Josef Stalin at the Yalta Conference, February 1945

everything was agreed to, but it was accepted that Germany would be divided between the Grand Alliance and the French, until its fate was decided. It was also accepted that each of the 'Big Three' would have a **sphere of influence**: the Union of Soviet Socialist Republics (USSR) in Eastern Europe, the United States in Western Europe and Britain in Greece. Roosevelt and Churchill were criticised for this. However, the fact was that the Red Army already controlled much of Eastern Europe, and the 'Big Three' could not afford to fall out while Germany and Japan still remained to be defeated.

Despite the agreements reached at Yalta, cracks in the Alliance had begun to appear, particularly over Poland. In 1944, the Red Army was close to liberating Warsaw, the Polish capital, so the Poles rose up against the Germans expecting aid from the Red Army. Instead the Russian advance halted and tens of thousands of Poles were killed by the Nazis, including many supporters of the Polish government-in-exile in London. This allowed Stalin to establish a pro-Soviet government there instead. At Yalta, though, he promised to allow free elections for the Poles. Many in the West doubted he would keep that promise, and he did not.

How did policy change when Truman came to power?

In April 1945, Russian and American troops met on the banks of the River Elbe and, within weeks, the Germans surrendered unconditionally. However, it was not Roosevelt who celebrated the victory but the new president, Harry S. Truman. As Roosevelt's Vice-President, he took office when FDR died on 12 April. According to historian William Chafe, in *The Unfinished Journey* (1986), 'few people were less prepared for the challenge of becoming president'. Even Truman himself said he felt as though the moon, stars and planets had fallen on him. Under Truman, American

Sphere of influence: An area of the world considered to be under the protection and control of a more powerful nation. That nation does not rule or own that area but has an accepted influence there so other nations should keep out.

Northern liberal: Liberals tend to be in favour of change and reform. In the USA, the North-East is more closely identified with this kind of view than other parts of the country.

Southern conservative: Conservatives tend to favour things the way they are. In the USA, although the Democratic Party was strong in the South, many there disliked the Party's liberal tendencies over certain issues, notably civil rights. They were suspicious of anything that seemed too left wing or tending towards giving the federal government too much power. Southern Democrats were also against segregation.

| **Harry S. Truman (1884–1972)** From a Missouri farming family. He served in Europe during the First World War and entered local politics in the 1920s. Elected to the Senate in 1935, where he served for 11 years. | Appointed Vice-President to Roosevelt in 1944 as a compromise man, someone who would offend no one: he was neither a **northern liberal** nor a **southern conservative** and was considered a moderate on most issues. On | Roosevelt's death in 1945, Truman took office as President, serving for seven years. Truman was regarded by many in the Democratic Party as hard working but somewhat colourless. |

policy towards the Soviet Union became much tougher. When the 'Big Three' met in Potsdam in July and August 1945, little was agreed. It was determined that Japan had to surrender unconditionally, and more details about the division of Germany were discussed. Exactly what to do about Germany was a real problem (see section 5.4), but the changes in personnel made the discussion tense. (Churchill was also replaced when a general election in Britain put Clement Attlee in Downing Street.)

Truman was determined not be seen to be soft on communism. Anti-communism in the USA had subsided during the War but it quickly resurfaced, and Truman could not afford to ignore it. There had been criticism that FDR was too soft with Stalin. Truman did not want to suffer the same accusation. When Churchill made his famous speech in Fulton, Missouri, on 5 March 1946, saying that an iron curtain had descended across Europe, Truman was by his side nodding approvingly.

The desire to stand up to Stalin was encouraged by a 16-page memorandum written by George Kennan, a diplomat in Moscow. Kennan was a leading authority on the USSR so when Truman found himself having to deal with Stalin, he asked Kennan to give him some background and advice. Kennan said that conflict between the two powers was inevitable so there was no point in trying to get along. Instead, he advised a policy of containment (i.e. the United States should stand up to the USSR when they tried to expand aggressively). He also wrote an anonymous article in

George Kennan (1904–2005)
US diplomat who worked extensively in Eastern Europe and USSR in the 1920s and 1930s. In 1946, he wrote the memorandum for President Truman advising the policy of 'containment' with regard to Soviet Communism – a view which he later rejected. Though he served as US Ambassador to the USSR briefly (1951) and Yugoslavia (1961–63), after 1949 he was primarily a lecturer and historian.

A 'Punch' cartoon of 1947. 'Punch' is a British political magazine.

1. What message is the cartoon trying to make about Stalin's policy in Eastern Europe?

2. Is the USA portrayed in a positive way in the cartoon? Explain your answer.

'Foreign Affairs' magazine, in July 1947, in which he argued that 'the main element of any United States policy towards the Soviet Union must be that of a long-term patient but firm and vigilant containment of Russian expansive tendencies'. Many years later, Kennan said that he had been wrong and cooperation should have been tried, but at the time it was a popular view. Many Americans believed that given the chance the communists would try to take over Europe, so it was up to the USA to keep them to the areas they controlled already.

What other factors damaged the Grand Alliance?

Totalitarian: Not allowing criticism or opposition. There is usually one party in control and people are rarely allowed to vote. The press and media are usually controlled and censored. Nazi Germany was a totalitarian state.

Ideological thinking also affected the relationship between the USA and Russia. Truman saw communism as a **totalitarian** ideology. Communism was the opposite of what he believed in, which was American democracy and capitalism. The two were incompatible – a view which Stalin seemed to share. In a speech in 1946, he said that the two ideologies could not live side by side.

Economics were also a factor in the break-up of the Alliance. Truman believed that a communist-dominated world would be closed to American trade. American economic power at the end of the Second World War was as strong as its military power, but the United States feared slipping back into the Depression of the 1930s, so trade with Europe was essential. Although it had been involved in the War for four years, America had come nowhere near the extent of its industrial strength and had lost 405,400 men. The Soviet Union had lost 25 million people and more than 25 per cent of their property. At the end of the War, the Americans gave loans of $3.75 million to help the Poles re-build their land, but nothing to the Soviets. Exploiting the resources of Eastern Europe was equally essential to the USSR for rebuilding its shattered economy. Both nations feared that the other wished to squeeze them out of Europe economically.

A major factor in the continued tension between the Soviet Union and the United States after the War was atomic power. America had decided on the dropping of the atom bomb on Japan in August 1945 without any reference to its allies. Stalin now believed that with this power the Americans could do just as they liked and would not abide by any agreements they made. Truman knew the Soviets were working on their own atom bomb. He did not want to get into an arms race, so the Baruch Plan was proposed in 1946. The proposal was for an international authority to control atomic power, together with the agreed destruction of existing nuclear weapons in stages, with the USA being the last to give them up. Unsurprisingly, the Soviets rejected it.

What was the Truman Doctrine and how did it come about?

This was the situation in 1946. The Grand Alliance was already in trouble and the USA were worried by the spread of communism in Eastern Europe to Poland, Hungary, Romania, Bulgaria, Yugoslavia and Albania. The Soviets had also taken direct control of the Baltic States – Latvia, Estonia and Lithuania. They also appeared to have their eye on the Mediterranean and on oil lands in the Middle East. In Iran, it had been agreed that all the allied armies there would leave within six months of the end of the war. The British did, but the USSR held on because they knew Britain and the USA had negotiated rights from the Iranian government to drill oil and they wanted the same rights. In the end, the Red Army was forced to leave and the Soviets failed, but to Truman it seemed yet more evidence of Soviet aggression.

In Greece, there was a civil war between monarchists and communists. Britain had been helping the monarchists but, in February 1947, they told the Americans that they could no longer afford to be involved. Truman believed the Greek communists were backed by the USSR. He felt the Americans had to prevent communist expansion in Greece and in Turkey (where the Soviet Union had soldiers stationed on the border). In fact, Stalin was abiding by the Yalta agreement and was not interfering in Greece, but the affair allowed Truman to make containment official American policy.

In a speech to Congress in May 1947, Truman said 'it must be the policy of the United States to support free peoples who are resisting **subjugation** by armed minorities or by outside pressures'. In other words, the United

Subjugation: Conquest; being taken over by force.

Extract from Truman's speech to Congress

The gravity of the situation which confronts the world today necessitates my appearance before a joint session of the Congress. The foreign policy and the national security of this country are involved.

The United States has received from the Greek Government an urgent appeal for financial and economic assistance.

The very existence of the Greek state is today threatened by the terrorist activities of several thousand armed men, led by Communists, who defy the government's authority at a number of points …

Meanwhile, the Greek Government is unable to cope with the situation. The Greek army is small and poorly equipped. It needs supplies and equipment if it is to restore the authority of the government throughout Greek territory. Greece must have assistance if it is to become a self-supporting and self-respecting democracy.

The United States must supply that assistance.

The peoples of a number of countries of the world have recently had totalitarian regimes forced upon them against their will.

At the present moment in world history nearly every nation must choose between alternative ways of life. The choice is too often not a free one.

One way of life is based upon the will of the majority, and is distinguished by free institutions, representative government, free elections, guarantees of individual liberty, freedom of speech and religion, and freedom from political oppression.

The second way of life is based upon the will of a minority forcibly imposed upon the majority. It relies upon terror and oppression, a controlled press and radio, fixed elections, and the suppression of personal freedoms.

I believe that it must be the policy of the United States to support free peoples who are resisting attempted subjugation by armed minorities or by outside pressures.

I believe that we must assist free peoples to work out their own destinies in their own way.

I believe that our help should be primarily through economic and financial aid, which is essential to economic stability and orderly political processes.

It is necessary only to glance at a map to realise that the survival and integrity of the Greek nation are of grave importance in a much wider situation. If Greece should fall under the control of an armed minority, the effect upon its neighbour, Turkey, would be immediate and serious. Confusion and disorder might well spread throughout the entire Middle East.

I therefore ask the Congress to provide authority for assistance to Greece and Turkey in the amount of $400,000,000 for the period ending 30 June 1948. In addition to funds, I ask the Congress to authorise the detail of American civilian and military personnel to Greece and Turkey …

The free peoples of the world look to us for support in maintaining their freedoms.

If we falter in our leadership, we may endanger the peace of the world – and we shall surely endanger the welfare of our own nation.

In this speech to Congress, what reasons does Truman give for providing financial help to the Greek government?

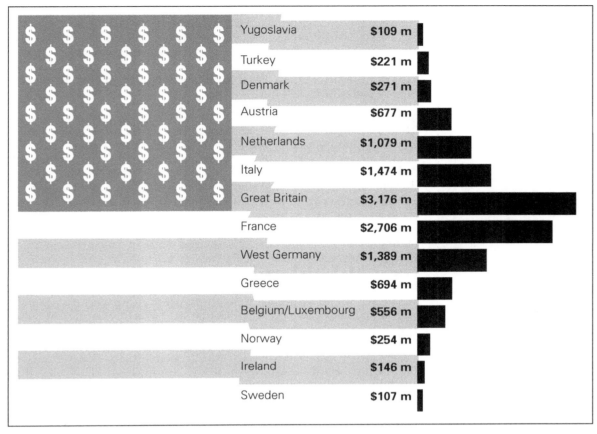

Marshall Aid to Europe
1947–1952

States was promising to help any country to fight communism, whether it was from internal revolution or from outside attack. This promise is known as the Truman Doctrine.

To enforce the Truman Doctrine and to help Greece and Turkey, Truman asked Congress for $400 million. The Republican Congress was reluctant to spend this kind of money even to fight the communists, so Truman had to play up the communist threat. (This was an important factor in the rise of McCarthyism – see Chapter 8.) It worked. Congress approved the money and the communists in Greece were defeated. The Truman Doctrine was the basis of American foreign policy for the next 40 years.

In what ways was the Marshall Plan also part of containment?

After the First World War, America had insisted that countries which were still weak repaid money owed to them. This had been one of the contributing factors to the Depression, as economically weak nations could not trade. After the Second World War, this did not happen. The United Nations Relief and Rehabilitation Administration and the World Bank poured $9 billion into the shattered European economies. For economic, moral and political reasons, the United States also gave money to help Europe recover. This was known as Marshall Aid. Seen as the economic counterpart of the Truman Doctrine, the idea came from George Marshall, the US Secretary of State.

Under the Marshall Plan or European Recovery Programme, the United States gave money to European states to rebuild their economies (see diagram). Over the next five years, $13.5 billion was paid out to 16 countries through the Organisation of European Economic Cooperation

(OEEC). Aid was given in cash and in goods, some of which the USA controlled. For example, the OEEC asked for 67,000 tractors but got only half because American farmers feared European competition. In return for aid, recipients had to share some information about resources.

Why did Britain, France, West Germany and Italy receive the most money under Marshall Aid?

Marshall Aid was also offered to Eastern European countries including the USSR, but the Soviets would not accept it and would not allow their allies to accept. The Americans knew the USSR would never share economic information, so it was clear that they never wanted them to get Marshall Aid. George Marshall said the Plan was aimed against 'hunger, poverty, desperation and chaos'. Although he denied it, there was an element of anti-communism in it. Strengthening Western Europe would help it to stand up to the Soviet Union.

Truman was also concerned for US trade. As European states were trading with each other, Truman was afraid America would be kept out of European markets. A third of the world's exports, in 1947, were from America: if Europe had more dollars to spend they might use them to buy more US goods. In fact, it became a condition of receiving aid that a certain percentage would be spent on American goods. Congress clearly agreed with him as the Economic Cooperation Act, which set up the Marshall Plan, was passed easily in both Houses of Congress (69–17 votes in the Senate and 329–74 in the House of Representatives).

The USSR retaliated with its own economic bloc, Cominform (the Communist Information Bureau). It was a propaganda effort more than anything because, in reality, they could not afford to give much to their allies. Marshall Aid was very important to Europe in helping the recovery from the Second World War. It also helped American trade. The aid was also about containing communism. Truman called the Marshall Plan and Truman Doctrine 'two halves of the same walnut'. By 1951, 80 per cent of American aid to Europe was military.

---

1. What agreements were made between the USA and the USSR at Yalta?

2. Explain the reasons why the Grand Alliance had broken apart by 1947. Which factors do you think were most important? Give reasons for your answer.

5.2 How far was Truman responsible for the development of the Cold War?
A CASE STUDY IN HISTORICAL INTERPRETATION

During the Cold War itself, writers in the West blamed the Soviet Union for the disintegration in relations between East and West. It was argued that the USSR was aggressive and determined to build an empire in Europe, therefore the West had to stand up to them. There was a fear of Soviet expansion in both the USA and in Western Europe. Stalin had imposed communist governments on Eastern Europe. Also, the Red Army was the largest army in the world and, unlike the American army, had not been demobilised at the end of the war. This fear was also influenced by the Kennan memorandum and by American experience of the Second World War. Stalin was seen as the new Hitler. As Hitler had tried to do, Stalin would take over Europe if the United States did not stand up to him. The lesson many Americans learned from the war was that they must not appease dictators. Instead, they must be confronted and contained.

The collapse of communism, in 1991, and the opening up of Soviet archives have led many historians to see a pattern of aggression in Soviet behaviour in Europe. They argue that it was this aggression and America's response to it which created the Cold War. For instance, John Lewis Gaddis, a historian from Yale University, argues that Truman understood Russia's need to protect itself. He accepted that it should have a sphere of influence in Eastern Europe, but that Soviet behaviour increasingly convinced the President and the American people that the USSR could not be trusted. (See 'Soviet Unilateralism and the Origins of the Cold War' in *Major Problems in American History Since 1945* [2001] edited by Robert Griffith and Paula Baker.) The failure of the Soviet Union to help the Poles in Warsaw in 1944 shocked the American people. They were further disturbed by Stalin's behaviour in Eastern Europe and other parts of the world, such as Iran. Even if the USSR did not intend to attack the West, its behaviour was aggressive and untrustworthy so it must be restrained.

Gaddis also points out that one of the reasons for the Cold War was that the American people disliked communism, which they, like Truman, saw as totalitarian. The Soviet Union and the Americans had a history of mistrust going back to the 1917 Russian Revolution. Their two political systems were virtually opposites. In 1919, the Americans had – along with the French, British and Japanese – sent troops to fight against the communists during the Russian Civil War (see Chapter 4). This War of Intervention meant that the Soviets believed America wanted to destroy communism.

Popular front: In this instance, a joining together of all kinds of governments and parties to oppose to the Nazis.

This belief was encouraged, in the 1930s, when Stalin proposed a '**popular front**' to fight against the rise of Nazi Germany. The West refused, so Stalin responded by signing the Nazi–Soviet Pact in 1939, where the USSR and Germany agreed to split Poland between them and not to fight each other. The Pact was greeted with shock in the West. Both sides thought, therefore, that the other could not be trusted. Even though they worked together successfully after 1941, these suspicions never went away and, as soon as the common enemy was removed, they resurfaced.

Historian Ralph B. Levering accepts, in *The Cold War, 1945–1987* (1988), that the Soviets believed the USA wanted to destroy communism, and that the two opposing world views were elements in the Cold War. He also points to the domestic pressure on Truman as an important factor. Levering quotes newspapers from the 1940s, which printed many anti-Russian articles and editorials. In a survey conducted in September 1945, almost 50 per cent of the American public said that although Russian friendship was desirable the government should not make too many concessions to it. Almost 10 per cent wanted as little as possible to do with the USSR. Anti-Russian groups, such as Polish-Americans and German-Americans, also put pressure on the Administration. Above all, the Republicans in Congress criticised Truman for being 'soft on communism'. Given the other problems he had with the unions, inflation and with McCarthyism, Truman could not afford to be seen as weak when dealing with Stalin.

Dean Gooderham Acheson (1893–1971)
A lawyer who first worked for FDR in the Treasury Department. He was Secretary of State (1949–53), helping to develop the Truman Doctrine and the Marshall Plan. Acheson was a strong supporter of NATO and of America's support for the Nationalist Chinese. He returned to practising law after the 1953 presidential election but was an advisor on foreign policy to succeeding presidents.

Even though there was pressure on Truman at home, he did deliberately play up the threat of communism to get support for his policy in Greece and to get the the Truman Doctrine passed. He and Secretary of State, Dean Acheson, exploited the Soviet threat as they wanted the United States to take a more active and forceful role in the world. This included 'getting tough with Russia', as Truman put it in 1946. It was time he said to 'stop babying the Soviets'. The fact that only the USA had the atom bomb allowed Truman to be hostile, not caring that this only made the USSR more fearful and therefore less likely to cooperate. So, although FDR had expressed worries about Stalin's trustworthiness just before his death in April 1945, there is no doubt that American foreign policy took a much tougher stance once Truman took over. This worsened relations between East and West.

However, perhaps the fundamental problem was one of understanding. The USSR failed to understand that in a democracy an American President had to take note of voters and opposition parties. Stalin also refused to see how his behaviour in Eastern Europe worried and dismayed the West. On the other hand, the Americans did not fully understand what the Second World War had cost the Soviet Union and why they were so determined to protect themselves. Americans also had a tendency to blame all communist activity, such as in Greece, on the Soviet Union, when far more frequently it was a product of local influences.

1. What reasons did the USA and the USSR have to mistrust each other?

2. How far do historians agree on who was to blame for the Cold War?

'The confrontation between the United States and the Soviet Union derived from differing post-war needs, ideology, style and power of the two rivals and drew on an historical legacy of frosty relations. Each saw the other, in mirror image, as the world's bully.'

(*American Foreign Relations: a history since 1895* by Thomas G Paterson *et al* [2000])

5.3 Why was Germany central to the Cold War in Europe?

Does this map show any potential problems in the settlement for Germany in 1945?

Between 16 July and 2 August 1945, Truman, Stalin and Churchill, accompanied by Attlee, met at Potsdam, to discuss what to do with Germany now that it had surrendered and Hitler was dead. The problem was whether or not to punish Germany and, if so, how severely. They did not want to repeat the mistakes of 1919 when it was believed Germany had been punished enough to create resentment but not severely enough to prevent it starting another war. Henry Morgenthau, the Treasury Secretary, put forward a plan in 1944, which proposed removing industrial facilities and reducing Germany to a purely agricultural economy. This plan was initially approved, but later rejected, by Truman. There were also those who felt it would be useful to build Germany up as a barrier against Soviet expansion in Europe. (Truman himself had said in July 1941, about the war in Europe, 'if we see that Germany is winning we should help Russia, and if Russia is winning we ought to help Germany.') There were fierce arguments about which policy to pursue.

In the end, it was agreed that Germany would be divided into four zones, each administered by one of the Big Three plus France. Berlin, in the Russian zone, would be divided into four sectors. All decisions regarding the sectors and zones were to be made jointly and all of the powers would be able to take reparations from their zone. The country was also to be de-Nazified – that is, the Nazi leaders removed and many put on trial, and an Allied Control Commission (ACC) set up to administer German affairs.

Divided Germany: occupation zones immediately after the Second World War.

At first, the West punished Germany, and they took reparations. As this was a drain on the US economy, having to feed the thousands of German refugees, it was decided to start giving aid instead. America decided on this change in policy **unilaterally**. Secretary of State Byrnes simply announced the change of policy in a speech in Stuttgart, in September 1946. This was only the beginning of the change in American policy towards Germany. By 1948, Marshall Aid was pouring into the western zones and the Allies were secretly discussing a new government and constitution for their zones, which they planned to join together.

In some ways, these actions were no more than an acknowledgement of reality. Britain, France and the USA had been working together,

Unilaterally: Done without consultation. In this case, it had been agreed that any change in Germany would be agreed by the occupying powers jointly, but America changed its policy on reparations without consulting the Soviets.

administratively and politically, and they all knew that the economic recovery of Germany was essential to the economic recovery of Europe. However, there were also Cold War considerations at work. The Americans believed a weak Germany could be infiltrated or taken over by communism. Conversely, a strong Germany was felt to be a barrier against Soviet expansion into Western Europe. By creating a single, strong western Germany they would be able to preserve democracy and capitalism at the centre of Europe.

How did the Berlin Airlift come about?

The Soviets knew of the secret talks being held by the Allies and were angry. The Americans failed to understand Soviet fears of a German military revival or the sense of betrayal that they felt at these secret negotiations, which went against the principles laid down at Potsdam. In March 1948, the Soviet delegation walked out of the ACC talks.

In June, the Allies joined their zones together and introduced a new currency, the Deutschmark. A few days later, it was extended into the Allied zones of Berlin. They also planned to introduce a democratically elected council into the western half of the city. In retaliation, the Soviets blocked all access from western Germany to Berlin by closing all roads and railways. This cut off two million West Berliners from the rest of Western Europe.

Stalin was hoping that this would force the Allies to leave the city: he argued that he could not see why the Allies would want to stay now they were creating their own West German state. But Truman felt that the United States could not abandon Berlin. Not only would this present the Soviets with a terrific propaganda coup, but it would also see his policy of containment fail at the first hurdle. Stalin's actions confirmed Truman's belief in communist expansionism. That same year the Soviets had forced a communist government on Czechoslovakia and, in China, the communists were on the verge of winning the civil war (see Chapter 6). Truman felt that to back down would be like Chamberlain's capitulation (surrender without much of a fight) to Hitler in the 1930s.

There were some in the Democratic Administration who advised the President that Berlin was not worth fighting for, but others saw the city as having a crucial role in the Cold War. Berlin was the only frontier where Soviet and American troops faced each other directly. For many, this alone was enough reason to stay. The overriding factor was to contain Soviet expansion. If the Allies did not stand up to the Russian threat here, where would be next?

General Clay, the American military commander in Berlin, said:

> 'When Berlin falls, western Germany will be next. If we mean to hold Europe against communism we must not budge ... If we withdraw, our position in Europe is threatened. If America does not understand this now ... then it never will, and communism will run rampant. I believe the future of democracy requires us to stay.'

Truman himself put it more simply: 'We are going to stay, period.'

Clay felt that the army should fight its way into Berlin if necessary, but Truman and the British believed this was too risky. So Ernest Bevin, the British Foreign Secretary, suggested that they should supply Berlin by air.

Under 'Operation Vitals', British and American planes took off every three minutes. They carried 2,000 tons of supplies to the city each day. At the height of the Airlift, this rose to almost 10,000 tons. Two million Berliners were fed and supplied from the air for the next 11 months. By any measure, it was a tremendous military achievement.

1. What message is the cartoon trying to make about the Berlin Airlift Crisis of 1948–49?

2. How useful is this cartoon to a historian writing about the early Cold War between 1945–49?

A 'Punch' cartoon, July 1948

In May 1949, Stalin called off the blockade. The Allies joined their zones together to create the Federal Republic of Germany (FDR). The Soviets responded by creating the German Democratic Republic (DDR). Germany was divided into two separate countries for the next 40 years.

Containment had worked and the Americans had won. Yet Truman had risked war with Russia. If the USSR had shot down an American plane either by accident or by design, the United States would have had to respond. Truman felt that backing down would have been worse. Besides, would the Soviets risk war when the Americans had a monopoly of atomic weapons? To ensure the Soviets understood how serious he was, Truman had stationed B-29 bombers in Britain. Everyone knew that these planes carried nuclear weapons. The crisis had enabled America to strengthen its military position in Europe, and this was to be strengthened still further with the creation of NATO.

'Eastern bloc': The countries in the east of Europe and in the Soviet Union that had communist regimes in the post-Second World War period.

The victory for Truman's policy of containment, however, did not solve the 'problem' of Berlin. While, for the West, it continued to be a beacon of democracy in the **'Eastern bloc'**, for the Soviet Union it continued to be a thorn in their side. Crises were to arise again over the city in 1958 and 1961.

Why was NATO created?

The Berlin Blockade convinced the United States of the need to strengthen Europe against the Soviet Union. In March 1948, Britain, France, Belgium, Holland and Luxembourg had signed a mutual defence treaty. Acheson was able to build on this to create the North Atlantic Treaty Organisation (NATO) in April 1949. Given the success of the Airlift and the seeming

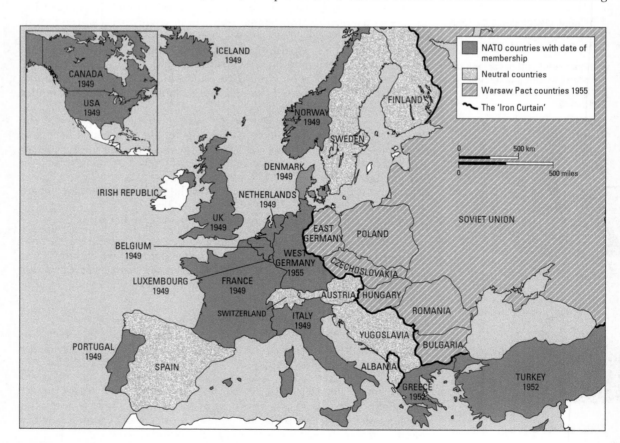

North Atlantic Treaty Organisation (NATO), 4 April 1949

success of Truman's containment policy, the Senate approved the signing of the NATO agreement by 82 votes to 13.

NATO was the first peacetime military alliance in US history. It consisted of 13 European states plus the USA, Canada and Iceland. Under its terms, an attack on one member was an attack on them all. However, the United States and Europe interpreted it differently. The United States saw it mainly as a 'nuclear umbrella' for Europe (i.e. America's nuclear weapons would give Europe all the protection it needed). Truman told the American public that large numbers of US soldiers would not be sent to Europe. But the Europeans and many of Truman's critics believed the USA was committing itself to protecting Europe militarily. When the Soviets exploded their own atom bomb in September, NATO was strengthened and the USA soon stationed soldiers in bases throughout Europe, backed by $1.5 billion in military aid.

In 1952, NATO was extended to include Greece and Turkey. As early as 1950, the Americans had wanted to bring Germany into NATO in order to strengthen its position within the western sphere of influence. They were also concerned that, with the outbreak of the Korean War, American troops would be stretched too far. They hoped that a rearmed Germany would lift some of the burden in Europe. Needless to say, the French, the British and the Soviets were very unhappy when Acheson announced his proposals to create ten German divisions. To ease European fears, the French Prime Minister René Pleven proposed that West Germany should be rearmed as part of a European army, where it could be controlled. So the European Defence Community was established in 1952, consisting of France, Italy, Germany, Belgium, Holland and Luxembourg.

However, this solution satisfied no one and the Americans continued to press for West German entry into NATO. To forestall this, the USSR even proposed a united, neutral Germany but this suggestion was never taken seriously. Continued pressure from the Eisenhower Administration finally led to West Germany joining NATO on 9 May 1955. In response to what they saw as a renewed military threat, the Soviet Union brought together its Eastern European allies into the Warsaw Pact five days later. It seemed that Germany had once again divided Europe into two armed camps.

Although the USSR feared a German military revival, it did not do as much damage to the new policy of peaceful co-existence which Eisenhower and Khrushchev were entering into, as it might have done. Just a few weeks after the creation of the Warsaw Pact, the Geneva Summit took place. The Soviet attempt to prevent West German entry into NATO had produced agreement over Austria.

Austria, like Germany, had been occupied by the four powers at the end of the Second World War. The Soviet Union had always insisted that a final agreement over Austria must go hand in hand with agreement over Germany. To show their moderation and therefore, hopefully, persuade the Americans to give way over Germany, the Soviets dropped their demand. This led to the signing of the Austrian State Treaty, which ended the ten-year occupation and created an independent, neutral Austria. Both sides could present this as a 'victory' as it kept Austria out of both NATO and the Warsaw Pact. The agreement helped the improving relationship between the USA and the USSR. However, it did not prevent West Germany joining NATO, as the Soviets had hoped, and it did not stop Germany being a problem for the two powers.

What was NSC-68?

From the late 1940s, Truman's advisors were saying that the United States would need to change its defence policy. The new demands of the Cold

War and the commitments of the Truman Doctrine meant that the organisation of the American military and its security system needed to be updated. The 1947 National Security Act created a Department of Defense to oversee all the armed forces, instead of having separate departments for the different services. It also set up the National Security Council to advise the President on defence and security issues, and the Central Intelligence Agency (CIA) to gather information. This was primarily an administrative measure, but it illustrates how far the United States had moved from the isolation of the inter-war years, and how important foreign policy now was.

Along with the Truman Doctrine and NATO, the USA would be spending much more on defence. In 1950, the National Security Council passed a resolution, NSC-68. This document analysed the international situation given the explosion of the Soviet bomb and the 'fall' of China to communism the year before. According to NSC-68, the Soviet Union was intent on spreading communism throughout the world – as China had shown – so it was up to the United States to prevent them. This would mean massively increasing military spending. When the Korean War broke out later that year, it seemed to confirm what the National Security Council was saying. The US defence budget rose rapidly from around $13 billion per year in the 1940s to $50 billion in 1953.

The professionalisation of the Defence Department and the increase in military spending under NSC-68 had important domestic effects on America. Companies involved in arms production throughout the USA now had far greater opportunities to gain government contracts. The aerospace industries of the south-western states, for example, saw their production levels and profits rise rapidly. The politicians from these states tried to ensure that continued to be the case. This growth in the defence industry's wealth and influence worried some people: they referred to it as the military-industrial complex and felt that no one area of industry should be so politically and economically powerful. When he left office in 1961, it was one of the things Eisenhower warned the American public about.

Some critics, including George Kennan, argued that the government was wrong and had exaggerated the Soviet threat. Others worried about the amount of money and effort that was now going into fighting the Cold War. By stressing the communist threat, NSC-68 unintentionally gave a boost to McCarthy's anti-communist campaign (see Chapter 8). What NSC-68 had done was to confirm and strengthen containment of communist expansion as America's number one foreign policy priority.

1. Why did Truman refuse to back down to the Russian blockade of Berlin in 1948?

2. How far had American military influence in Europe increased between 1945 and 1950?

Source-based questions: Containment in Europe, 1947–1949

SOURCE A

The Marshall Plan was an economic extension of the Truman Doctrine. American Secretary of State George Marshall produced his European Recovery Programme (ERP) which offered economic and financial help wherever it was needed. 'Our policy,' he declared, 'is directed not against any country or doctrine but against hunger, poverty, desperation and chaos.'

From *Mastering Modern World History* by Norman Lowe, 1982

SOURCE B

Most of the countries of Europe and Asia today are in a state of physical destruction or economic dislocation or both … two of the greatest workshops of Europe and Asia – Germany and Japan – upon whose production Europe and Asia were to an important degree dependent before the war have hardly been able even to begin the process of reconstruction … unforeseen disasters – what the lawyers call 'acts of God' – have occurred to the crops of Europe. For two successive years unusually severe droughts have cut down food production …

Your Congress has authorised and your government is carrying out a policy of relief and reconstruction today chiefly as a matter of national self-interest. For it is generally agreed that until the various countries of the world get on their feet and become self-supporting there can be no political or economic stability in the world and no lasting peace or prosperity for any of us.

From a speech by Dean Acheson on 8 May 1947
(Department of State Bulletin, 18 May 1947)

SOURCE C

Certainly there is no 'precedent' for today's worldwide cleavage [deep split] between democracy and communism. Perhaps, however, there is something of a parallel in remembering what occurred prior to a similar cleavage between democracy and Nazism when we surely learnt that we cannot escape trouble by trying to run away from it and when 'appeasement' proved to be a fatal investment. Of course we shall never know if history would have been different if we had all stood up to the aggressor at Munich. But at least we know what it cost to 'lie down'.

Senator Arthur J. Vandenberg Jr, March 1947 (from the 'Private Papers of Senator Vandenberg', 1952)

SOURCE D

My objection, then, to the policy of containment is not that it seeks to confront the Soviet power with American power, but that the policy is misconceived, and must result in a misuse of American power … [It] commits this country to a struggle which has for its objective nothing more substantial than the hope that in ten or fifteen years the soviet power will, as a result of long frustration, 'break up' or 'mellow'.

Walter Lippmann writing in 1947, from *The Cold War: A Study in US Foreign Policy Since 1945* by Walter Lippmann (1973).

SOURCE E

Soviet power, unlike that of Hitlerite Germany … does not work by fixed plans. It does not take unnecessary risks. For this reason it can easily withdraw – and usually does – when strong resistance is encountered at any point. Thus, if the adversary has sufficient force and makes clear his readiness to use it, he rarely has to do so. If situations are properly handled there need be no prestige-engaging showdowns …

Many foreign peoples, in Europe at least, are tired and frightened by experiences of the past, and are less interested in abstract freedom than in security. They are seeking guidance rather than responsibilities. We should be better able than the Russians to give them this. And unless we do, the Russians certainly will.

From George Kennan's telegraphic message from Moscow of 22 February 1946, published in *Kennan's Memoirs, 1925–1950* (1967).

---

1. Study Sources A and B.

How far do the sources agree on the motives for Marshall Aid to Europe?

2. Study Source A and use your own knowledge.

What was the Truman Doctrine?

3. Study Source D.

How useful is this source to an historian studying the origins of the Cold War?

4. Study all the sources and use your own knowledge.

Why did the United States develop the policy of containment in 1947?

5.4 How far did American–Soviet relations in Europe improve under Eisenhower?

Dwight David 'Ike' Eisenhower (1890–1969)
34th President of the USA (1953–60), a Republican. A professional soldier, he served as Commander of the Allied invasion of North Africa during the Second World War, and as Supreme Commander of the Normandy landings. After the War, he was president of Columbia University and chair of the Joint Chiefs of Staff (1949–50), before being asked to become head of NATO in 1950. Resigned from the army in 1952 to run for the presidency. His Vice-President was Richard Nixon.

John Foster Dulles (1888–1959)
Secretary of State under Eisenhower (1953–59). His brother Allen was head of the CIA. John Dulles was a strong influence on foreign policy, even though he and the President frequently disagreed. He had been a lawyer and worked for the Federal Council of Churches. Dulles was a strong **Presbyterian** and very anti-Communist: he saw the fight against communism as a fight between good and evil. He was against containment as it abandoned people to '**despotism** and Godless terrorism'.

Presbyterian: A branch of Protestant Christianity, often seen as quite strict in terms of morality.

Despotism: A way of being ruled without freedom and without a say in how you are governed.

Joint Chiefs of Staff: The heads of the military services.

Republican Dwight D. Eisenhower won the 1952 presidential election in the USA with 55 per cent of the vote. 'Ike' was a famous soldier who had been commander of the Normandy invasions and head of NATO. He was widely liked by people of all parties and by Congress, and was very popular with the public. 'Ike' talked about a new kind of Republicanism and introduced some new ideas into foreign affairs. Even though he was the first Republican president since Hoover in 1932, there was never any attempt to go back to the Republican isolationism of the 1920s; the world had changed too much for that. In many ways, Eisenhower was to continue what Truman had done, but he also added some new elements.

The world situation was more promising under Eisenhower than at any time since the Second World War. In some ways, it seemed that he might be able to build an easier relationship with the Soviet Union than Truman had been able to do. In 1953, Stalin died, the Korean War ended and Eisenhower was concerned to improve international relations. Yet the world was getting more complex and as communism spread to other areas there was more potential for conflict.

During the election campaign, 'Ike' and his Secretary of State, John Dulles, criticised Democratic foreign policy, saying that Truman did not do enough to stand up to communism. Containment was criticised as 'negative, futile and immoral'. Instead of merely containing the communists, Dulles talked about 'rolling back' the frontiers of communism and 'liberating' people from communist rule. As events were to show, this was not a realistic possibility. Without war the USSR was hardly likely to give up its influence in Eastern Europe, and Eisenhower was not prepared to go to war to remove them. In many ways, the Eisenhower Administration simply continued Truman's policy of containment.

What was the 'New Look'?

As a Republican, 'Ike' was committed to cutting government spending, including the defence budget which was around $40 billion per year. At the same time, lack of success in Korea showed the limitations of US ground forces. Eisenhower, therefore, wanted an effective way of fighting wars that was also cheap. The **Joint Chiefs of Staff** came up with the Radford Plan, or 'New Look'.

The 'New Look' proposed cutting conventional forces; therefore the USA would be more dependent on nuclear weapons. This would be cheaper than conventional forces. However, nuclear weapons, especially the hydrogen bomb, would be just as threatening to America's enemies – if not more so. As it was crudely but simply expressed, they were going to get 'more bang for the buck [US dollar]'.

Cutting defence spending could send the wrong signal and make the United States look weak, so it had to be clear that it was not worth anybody's while starting a fight with the America. In fact, Dulles said that other powers should realise that, if they took on the USA, they would 'be made to suffer … more than [they] can possibly gain', that there would be 'massive retaliation'. In other words, if anyone attacked the USA then the USA would strike back with far more force than the original attack deserved. The problem, as historian Stephen Ambrose sees it, was that 'since it was his only weapon, Dulles had to flash a nuclear bomb whenever he wanted to threaten the use of force'. This made every conflict a potential nuclear war and encouraged the spread of nuclear weapons. By 1956, the USA had 1,400 planes capable of dropping hydrogen bombs on the

Central Europe, 1955

Soviet Union. In a world so dangerous, Eisenhower also pursued a better relationship with the Soviet Union to make sure that he never had to practise massive retaliation.

How successful was the Geneva Summit of 1955?

The 'New Look' was only part of Eisenhower's foreign policy. His aim was not just to go round the world threatening people, he also believed in personal diplomacy in working with other powers and trying to remove the sources of conflict. Luckily, the Soviet leadership was also willing to talk. Nikita Khrushchev had replaced Stalin and, like Eisenhower, he wanted to cut military spending. If relations with the West were better, there should be less need for troops to be stationed in Europe. In 1953, Khruschev talked about 'peaceful co-existence' with the West. The idea of 'peaceful co-existence' was also attractive to the Americans because the Warsaw Pact had just been formed as the Russian counter-balance to NATO, and the USSR was catching up with American nuclear technology.

Given this desire on both sides for an improved relationship, a **summit** meeting was arranged between the USA, the USSR, Britain and France in Geneva. They gathered in the Swiss resort from 18–23 July 1955.

At the summit, 'Ike' proposed free communications between the two countries, and agreements on the peaceful use of atomic power and on disarmament. He also proposed an 'open skies' policy, whereby the two superpowers would exchange information on military installations and then be allowed to fly over each other's territory to check. The Soviet Union rejected this idea, but the Americans started spy flights anyway – a policy that was to end in disaster five years later.

In fact, the summit achieved almost nothing concrete. Yet it was a great success for Eisenhower personally, and journalists spoke of the 'spirit of Geneva'. The same year, an agreement was finally reached allowing for the removal of occupying forces from Austria, and guaranteeing the country's neutrality. Also, the Soviets officially recognised the Federal Republic of Germany. It seemed as though a new era in East–West relations might be beginning.

In 1958, Khrushchev became the first communist leader to visit the United States. Crowds gathered, sometimes in virtual silence, to glimpse a real, live Russian Communist. Vice-President Richard Nixon paid a visit to Moscow the next year, where he engaged Khrushchev in the so-called 'kitchen debate' at a trade fair. The two men argued the merits of their nation's technology. However, by 1959, there were already clouds darkening this new horizon.

Why did Cold War tensions continue after Geneva?

During the 1956 presidential election campaign, Dulles again talked about 'roll back' in Europe. He said there was little support among ordinary people for communism in the countries where it existed. Dulles believed, mainly correctly, that people living under communism did not want it and that, where possible, the USA should liberate people from its grip. The frontiers of the communist world should be 'rolled back'.

In October 1956, a revolt broke out against the communist government in Hungary. The revolt had been sparked by a speech made by Khrushchev in February of that year. It had also been encouraged by CIA broadcasts on Radio Free Europe. These broadcasts encouraged the Hungarians to believe, wrongly, that they would get American support. The revolt spread quickly. It led to the withdrawal of the Red Army and the establishment of a new government under Imry Nagy. 'Ike' made a speech sympathising with the revolt and Dulles expressed admiration for the rebels taking on

---

Nikita Khrushchev (1894–1971)

From a peasant family, he joined the Communist Party and Red Army, fighting with distinction in the Second World War. Eventually, he succeeded Stalin as leader in 1958. He pursued policies of reform at home, or peaceful co-existence with the West and tried to ease tensions with Eastern Europe. Failures in agriculture and foreign policy led to his removal in 1964.

Summit: A diplomatic meeting between the leaders of the foremost nations, especially the United States and the Soviet Union.

Imry Nagy (1895–1958)

Communist politician who wanted to reform the system in Hungary. He intended to maintain a communist system, but his intention to leave the Warsaw Pact was seen as a security threat to the USSR. He was arrested after the Hungarian Revolt and taken to the Soviet Union where he was shot two years later.

A 'Punch' cartoon published during the Hungarian Uprising of October 1956.

1. What message is the cartoon trying to make about Soviet policy in Eastern Europe in the 1950s?

2. Does the cartoon portray an accurate view of Soviet policy? Explain your answer.

the Red Army. In November, when the Hungarians talked of leaving the Warsaw Pact, the Red Army returned and crushed the revolt. Seven thousand Soviets and 30,000 Hungarians died; a further 200,000 were made refugees. The last message out of Budapest was a plea for help from the West. The USA allowed 25,000 refugees to come to America, but did no more. They knew that, geographically, there was little they could do to help. More importantly, they accepted the political reality that Eastern Europe was a Soviet sphere of influence. The Hungarian Revolt graphically illustrated the unrealistic ambition of liberation as a policy in the Cold War.

Berlin also continued to be a focus of tension between the two superpowers. Thirteen years after the War, there had been no peace treaty signed with Germany and the situation was pretty much the same as it had been left in 1949. The western sectors had developed and grown, as American aid continued to flow into the city, while progress in the Soviet-controlled half was very slow. This not only made the USSR look weak, there was also a constant stream of people fleeing to the West looking for a better life – many of whom were skilled people who were desperately needed in the East. Therefore, in November 1958, Khrushchev gave the Americans an ultimatum: there should be a peace treaty and American troops should leave Berlin by May the following year, or the USSR would sign its own treaty with East Germany. If America accepted Khrushchev's demands they would have to recognise East Germany, accept the permanent division of Germany, end the post-war occupation and leave Berlin.

There was pressure on 'Ike' to send troops, but he did not want to push Khrushchev into a corner. At the same time, he made it clear America would not leave Berlin.

The deadline passed and nothing happened. Khrushchev came to America in September 1959 and, at talks at Camp David (the US President's summer home in Maryland), the Soviets appeared to back down. The two leaders agreed to hold a summit in Paris in 1960, where the matter would be discussed. The crisis had passed away with nothing changing in Berlin, but it showed how the city remained a problem and continued to be central to the Cold War in Europe.

Why did the Paris Summit of 1960 fail?

Because of the relative success of Geneva and of Khrushchev's visit to the USA in 1958, a second summit was arranged between 'Ike' and Khrushchev in Paris, in May 1960. The summit also came about as a result of arguments about Berlin in 1958. On the eve of the conference, the USSR announced it had shot down a U-2 spy plane.

The build-up of the Soviet military and the failure of the 'open skies' proposal had led the USA to increase its spying with U-2 fights over Russia. They denied the plane was theirs, then said that it was a research plane which had gone missing. The Soviets then produced the pilot, Francis Gary Powers – alive and well. The summit broke up as American lies were exposed and, when 'Ike' left office a few months later, US–Soviet relations were at a very low ebb.

How did the space race contribute to the Cold War?

One aspect of the Cold War was propaganda. In one particular area in the 1950s the USSR took a big lead over America, scoring a massive propaganda victory: that was in space. However, the space race also had military implications as rocket and missile technology are so closely linked.

On 4 October 1957, the Soviet Union launched 'Sputnik', the world's first man-made satellite. This was followed by 'Sputnik II' the following year. The Americans were shocked by the launches and immediately stepped up their own space programme and spending on science education (see Chapter 8). 'Explorer I', America's own satellite, was launched in January 1958. The National Aeronautics and Space Administration (NASA) was created later in the year. Although it was part of the propaganda fight in the Cold War, NASA was put under civilian control, not military.

In August 1957, the Soviets also launched the first inter-continental ballistic missile (ICBM). This meant the USSR could now hit Western Europe with nuclear weapons. It would only be a matter of time before they would be able to hit America itself. The USA soon had its own ICBMs, but the myth of American technological superiority was over. The Gaither Report showed that the USA still had a military lead, but urged an arms build-up.

Also, the USSR was financing the arms and space programmes from economic growth of 7 per cent – twice that of the USA. In spite of this, Eisenhower refused to get into an arms race. His Republican economic views led him to want to keep defence spending low. He also feared that an arms race would intensify the Cold War and make it more dangerous.

Although 'Ike' refused to join an arms race in the way in which Kennedy would later, the USA did continue to develop its weapons programme (e.g. Polaris submarines). By the end of his presidency, 'Ike' had warned about the growth of what he called the 'military-industrial complex'. Too much of the economy was tied into defence spending. This meant the military and industries involved in defence production had little interest in peaceful co-existence; it was in their economic interests for the Cold War to continue. Politicians were involved too: if you represented a state or area where the main industry was defence, such as southern California, then the pressure was there from the defence companies in the area and from your constituents. Kennedy ignored this warning and built up America's arms production massively.

1. What were the aims of Eisenhower's foreign policy in Europe?

2. How far did Eisenhower's policy differ from Truman's?

3. How successful was Eisenhower's foreign policy in Europe?

5.5 How effectively did Kennedy pursue the Cold War in Europe?

John F. Kennedy was a decorated war hero and an anti-Communist who voted for the Truman Doctrine. During the presidential election campaign in 1960 he had accused the Republicans of letting things 'drift', saying that the Communists were winning the Cold War. In Cuba, Indo-China and West Africa it seemed as though communism was on the increase, and the U-2 crisis had humiliated the United States. Coming from a very competitive family, Kennedy was determined to 'win' the Cold War.

When he became President in 1961, his inauguration speech was entirely about foreign policy. His intention to take a forceful stand in the Cold War was made clear when he said:

'Let every nation know, whether it wishes us good or ill, that we shall pay any price, bear any burden, meet any hardship, support any friend, oppose any foe, in order to assure the survival and the success of liberty.'

One way Kennedy wanted to 'ensure liberty' was to build up America's nuclear deterrent. The fact that the U-2 flights showed it not to be true did not stop Kennedy from asserting that there was a 'missile gap' between the East and West, which must be made up. Consequently, he embarked on the biggest military build-up in US peacetime history so far. The defence budget was increased in 1961 by 15 per cent and Kennedy introduced a policy of 'flexible response', which would enable the USA to fight any kind of war. This entailed the building up of conventional forces, special forces such as the Green Berets and, of course, nuclear weapons. The number of ICBMs, for example, rose from 63 in 1961 to 424 in 1963. The irony of this policy was that the Soviet Union had to respond and build up its own arsenal. So rather than establish American superiority, Kennedy started an arms race making the world less secure.

John Fitzgerald Kennedy (1917–1963) 35th President of the USA (1961–63), the first Roman Catholic and the youngest person to be elected US President at 43 years old. 'JFK' made his name as a supporter of civil rights' legislation and as a prominent internationalist. He was the symbol of the new changes many American wanted to see. Perhaps most controversially , he involved the USA in the military defence of South Vietnam. In foreign affairs he had a great triumph in the Cuban Missile Crisis of October 1962 when Soviet missiles were withdrawn from Cuba. However, he also had many failures. In April 1961, a C.I.A. plot to invade Cuba, named the Bay of Pigs fiasco, failed badly. On 22 November 1963, JFK was assassinated in Dallas, his death causing worldwide grief. It is difficult to know whether JFK would have succeeded in foreign affairs had he lived.

How did the Berlin Wall affect Soviet–American relations?

The most potent symbol of the Cold War era was the Berlin Wall. Built in 1961, it was a massive propaganda victory for the West. In many ways, though, it stabilised the Cold War in Europe.

Ever since the War, West Berlin had continued to get richer because of its links to the western economies, while East Berlin remained poor. By 1961, 4,000 people a day were crossing from East to West through the city. This was both a propaganda problem for the Communists and a genuine economic issue, as most of those leaving were skilled and educated, and East Germany could not afford to lose its best minds.

Khrushchev had put pressure on Eisenhower to do something. Then, when he met with Kennedy at the Vienna Summit, in June 1961, he raised the matter again. Kennedy refused to stop this movement of people. Khrushchev then resurrected the 1958 proposals, but Kennedy took the same stand as Eisenhower: there would be no change in the status of Berlin.

In an attempt to halt the flow of people, the East Germans threatened to cut off the city entirely. JFK sent 40,000 troops to Europe, called up the **reserves** and asked Congress for $3.25 billion for military spending. Kennedy had just had a disaster in Cuba with the failure at the **Bay of Pigs** so he needed a foreign policy victory. It was also about enforcing containment. Just like Truman and Eisenhower, Kennedy believed the United States had to maintain its presence in Berlin or it would lose influence in Europe as a whole.

Then, on 13 August 1961, the Germans sealed West Berlin off from the East with wire fences, which they then replaced with a 30-mile wall with just four crossing points. This wall cut the city in half, dividing

Reserves: Military forces which are not permanently ready for action but which can be used in emergencies.

Bay of Pigs: In 1961 the Americans backed an invasion of Cuba by CIA-trained Cuban exiles. The aim of the invasion was to topple the communist government of Fidel Castro, but it failed and most of the exiles were arrested. It was a humiliation for Kennedy. The fear of another invasion led Castro to invite the Russians to build missile bases on the island. When the Americans discovered the missile sites in October 1962, it started a crisis which took the world to the brink of nuclear war. The US navy blockaded Cuba and the Soviets were forced to remove the missiles.

President John F. Kennedy stands on a platform looking over the Berlin Wall into the Eastern sector.

streets and families. General Clay sent tanks to the Wall and, for a while, Soviet and American troops were face to face waiting for the other to move. The military advised Kennedy to destroy the Wall by force, but he was not prepared to go to war with the USSR over a wall which they had built in their own sector of the city. He spoke to Khrushchev and both sides backed off.

The Wall stopped the flow of refugees to the West, allowing the East to rebuild its economy. In reality, there was nothing the Americans could do about it. For the Soviet Union it was a practical solution. For the West it provided powerful propaganda, showing to the world that under communism people had to be walled in.

It might not have been a solution either side liked, but the building of the Wall did ease tensions. Berlin ceased to be a major issue in the Cold War for the next 30 years. In fact, after the Wall went up the focus of the Cold War moved away from Europe. For Kennedy, Cuba took up far more of his time – with the failed Bay of Pigs invasion in 1961 and the Missile Crisis of 1962. Increasingly for Kennedy and particularly for President Johnson, American involvement in Vietnam was their major foreign policy concern. While the superpowers had their eyes fixed on South East Asia, their relations in Europe remained steady.

1. In what ways was the Berlin Wall a failure for both the Americans and for the USSR?

2. Had the Cold War in Europe eased under Kennedy? Explain your answer.

5.6 How successful was Nixon's policy of détente?

When Richard Nixon became president in 1968, the United States was still trying to achieve a victory in Vietnam. Johnson had focused what little interest he had in foreign affairs almost totally on the war, but then made a start with the Soviets on exploring the possibility of arms limitation. It was to be Nixon who would see this through.

Richard Nixon was hard working and intelligent. He was also suspicious, resentful and ruthless. In foreign policy, his best and worst traits were shown. He could be manipulative and dishonest, and he could also be **pragmatic** and adaptable.

Pragmatic: Dealing with things in a practical way; accepting things the way they are.

Although William Rogers was the Secretary of State, a much more important figure was Henry Kissinger, Nixon's National Security Advisor (NSA). Kissinger had taught international relations before he entered politics, and so was considered an expert on world affairs. As NSA, and later as Secretary of State for President Ford, Kissinger travelled all over the world talking personally to leaders of many nations. As early as 1969, Kissinger began secret meetings with Anatoly Dobrynin, the Soviet Ambassador to the United States. These so-called 'back channels' allowed Kissinger to do much of the preparation for Nixon's visits to the Soviet Union and China

Richard Milhous Nixon (1913–1994)	Henry Kissinger (1923–)	
37th President of the USA (1969–74), a Republican. He was Vice-President to Eisenhower (1953–61). As President, he was responsible for US withdrawal from Vietnam, and the improvement of relations with Communist China.	A German Jew born in Bavaria, he fled to the USA in 1938 to escape the Nazis. Appointed National Security Advisor (1969) by President Nixon, and was Secretary of State (1973–77). His missions to the USSR and China improved US relations	with both countries. He also took part in negotiating US withdrawal from Vietnam (1973) and in Arab–Israeli peace negotiations (1973–78). Joint winner of the Nobel Peace Prize in 1973.

The Arms Race:
some terms

Atom bomb: A nuclear bomb. The part of the bomb that explodes and does the damage is the warhead. The missile or plane it is launched from is the delivery system.

Hydrogen bomb: A thermonuclear bomb, though usually also referred to as nuclear, equivalent to 750 atom bombs.

Strategic weapons: Long-range weapons, controlled in the USA by the US Air Force Strategic Air Command. Strategic weapons were sited in the USA and in US bases in Europe, such as in Turkey.

Strategic bombers: Planes capable of delivering nuclear weapons (e.g. B-52s).

ICBM: Inter-continental ballistic missiles with a range of over 3,000 nautical miles (e.g. Titan II).

SLBM: Submarine-launched ballistic missiles (e.g. Polaris).

Cruise missiles: Low-flying missiles that can be launched by air, land or sea.

Tactical weapons: Also known as theatre nuclear weapons. These are ones that are short range and for use on the battlefield.

MIRV: Multiple independently targetable warheads – one missile can carry several warheads, each of which can be aimed at a different target.

SDI: Strategic Defence Initiative; nicknamed 'star wars'. A theoretical defence shield that can detect missiles and destroy them in space before they hit.

in 1972. Kissinger was prepared to pursue whatever policies he felt necessary to benefit the United States' position in the world. This led to criticism from the right, who felt that arms limitation and talking to the Soviets was being soft on communism.

Criticism from the left, however, was stronger. Kissinger's secret negotiations made him untrustworthy; his willingness to support dictators made him a poor spokesman for American freedom and democracy; and his strong support for the bombing campaigns in Vietnam aroused great hostility. However, he was an important figure and, throughout the period of détente, Nixon and Kissinger worked closely together.

Nixon and Kissinger believed in maintaining America's position and influence in the world, and that meant continuing to contain Soviet power. However, the world had changed in the 20 years since the Truman Doctrine. The Soviet Union had far more weapons and America's moral leadership had suffered badly because of the Vietnam War. Nixon's response was a policy he called 'the Grand Design'. This consisted of détente (i.e. building a better relationship with the Soviet Union) and the Nixon Doctrine (i.e. getting America's allies to take on more of the burden of fighting communism themselves rather that expecting the USA to do it for them). Although the Nixon Doctrine was primarily aimed at South East Asia, many Republicans also felt that it was about time the NATO countries contributed more to the protection of Western Europe. As a Republican himself, Nixon hoped that détente would ease tensions sufficiently to enable him to afford cuts in military spending.

Kissinger also talked about 'linkage'. He argued that if closer economic, political and strategic ties were built between the USA and the USSR there would be less room for conflict. Linkage also meant that they could not build an agreement with the Soviets in one area while disagreeing in another, so the two should be linked. What this meant in practice was that Nixon and Kissinger would negotiate arms reduction with the Soviet Union while, in return, they wanted Soviet help in pressurising the North Vietnamese to end the war.

How did Nixon pursue arms reduction?

Between 1968 and 1973, the American armed forces were cut by 1.2 million. This was partly due to withdrawing from the war (see Chapter 6), but it was also to signal to the USSR that America was serious about arms reduction. In 1969, talks about reducing arms got under way in Helsinki, but the whole policy nearly fell apart when the Soviet Union and America backed opposing sides in the 1971 war in Bangladesh. They continued, however, and to encourage the Soviets further Nixon visited China in 1972. As well as hoping to improve American relations and trade with China, Nixon and Kissinger were shrewdly exploiting the mutual fears of the two communist powers. They knew that the USSR feared a friendship between China and the USA: it would leave the Soviet Union very vulnerable. The visit produced the desired result and, in 1972, a summit meeting was held in Moscow. The result was the Strategic Arms Limitation Treaty (SALT), signed on 26 May.

Under the SALT agreement, there were limits on certain types of nuclear weapons and systems. The number of ICBMs was frozen at 1,607 for the USSR and 1,054 for the USA, while SLBMs (see panel opposite) were limited to 740 and 656 respectively. This seemed to favour the Soviet Union, but there were no limits on the numbers of bombers or on MIRVs (a missile with several, independently-targetable warheads). In both of these categories, the USA had more than double the number held by the Soviets. Neither were there any restrictions on the development of new weapons systems, such as Polaris submarines or Cruise missiles.

In a sense, SALT was a failure. It was to last only five years. It left out major categories of weapons and those categories that did have limits were fixed at higher levels than had previously existed. In other words, the two countries could build up to those limits. The agreement did nothing to halt weapons production. In fact, this continued to increase over the next five years. However, SALT was a recognition by the superpowers that the arms race was getting out of control and, at the very least, it had to be slowed down. Further agreements were to follow: the negotiations for SALT II beginning in 1977, as soon as SALT I was starting to run out.

Perhaps even more important was that, like the Geneva summit in 1955, détente produced a new spirit in the Cold War in Europe. The same year that it was signed, the two Germanies formally recognised each other and exchanged ambassadors. There was a general recognition of the boundaries of Europe which had been in place since 1945. Three years later, the Helsinki Accords were signed, in which 35 countries formally recognised the post-war settlement and promised to respect **human rights**.

Human rights: Belief that every individual has certain rights which must be respected by their government whatever its political beliefs and system. They include such things as freedom of religion, freedom of speech, the right to a fair trial etc.

As well as the arms limitation treaty, the two sides also signed an agreement, in 1972, on the basic principles of relations between the USSR and the USA. This contributed to détente as the two sides were basically agreeing to work together to prevent conflict and to promote peaceful co-existence. Kissinger thought this was more important than SALT itself. However, the dangers to peaceful co-existence and détente were brought vividly to life the following year with the Arab–Israeli War.

The USA and the USSR had been backing different sides in the ongoing conflict in the Middle East – the Americans backing Israel and the Soviets backing the Arab nations and Egypt. Nixon and Kissinger saw this situation as part of the Cold War struggle but, when Egypt and Syria launched an attack on Israel in October 1973, they saw the danger of being dragged into a war themselves. To support his ally, Nixon sent arms to Israel. Kissinger was sent to Moscow to work with the Soviet Union on creating a truce and saving détente. A truce was agreed but when the Israelis refused to abide by it the Soviet Union proposed that it should be enforced militarily by the two superpowers. For Nixon this was unacceptable. Jewish voters at home would not stand for it and, more importantly, it would encourage a Soviet military presence in the Middle East. When the USSR said they would go it alone if necessary, the Americans were alarmed. To make their opposition clear, Nixon put the country and all its bases abroad on nuclear alert. Within a year of SALT, it all seemed to be falling apart. However, both sides were desperately keen to avoid war. The USSR dropped its proposals and the

The arms build-up

Strategic bombers	1956	1960	1965	1970	1975	1979
USA	560	550	630	405	330	316
Soviet Union	60	175	200	190	140	140

ICBMs	1960	1964	1968	1970	1974	1979
USA	295	835	630	1,054	1,054	1,054
Soviet Union	75	200	800	1,300	1,587	1,398

SLBMs	1962	1965	1968	1972	1975	1979
USA	145	500	656	655	656	656
Soviet Union	45	125	130	497	740	989

Warheads	1945	1955	1965	1975	1985	
USA	6	3,057	31,265	26,675	22,941	
Soviet Union	0	200	6,129	19,443	39,197	

Americans put more pressure on Israel. A truce was agreed in 1973, backed by the United Nations, and a final settlement agreed in 1975.

As the Middle Eastern conflict had shown, the basic underlying suspicions between the two countries had not gone away and the Cold War was not over. When Nixon was forced to resign in August 1974, his Vice-President, Gerald Ford, succeeded him (see Chapter 9). The continued presence of Henry Kissinger meant there was some continuation in policy (e.g. the arms reduction talks continued). However, the USSR's failure to abide by the Helsinki Accords and the fall of Saigon in 1975 (see Chapter 6), led to an increase in anti-Communist feeling in the USA and there was a noticeable cooling in the policy of détente.

5.7 How far did détente continue under Carter?

James Earl Carter (1924–)
39th President of the USA (1977–81), a Democrat. In 1976 he defeated Gerald Ford in the presidential election, becoming the first southern president since the American Civil War. During his presidency, control of the Panama Canal Zone was returned to Panama, an amnesty programme for deserters and draft dodgers of the Vietnam War was introduced, and the Camp David Agreements for peace in the Middle East were drawn up. Defeated by Ronald Reagan in 1980.

Dissidents : Those who oppose or criticise the government. Especially applied to the USSR in the 1970s when groups of intellectuals and writers criticised the Soviet government for signing the Helsinki Accords on human rights but denied free speech to their own citizens.

Democratic President Jimmy Carter wanted an ethical foreign policy. Nixon had left office in disgrace and Carter was determined to pursue a more honourable conduct in world affairs. Yet this presented a problem. On the one hand, he was keen to reduce arms but, at the same time, he was very critical of the Soviet Union for its treatment of **dissidents**, which the Soviets resented. He was very inexperienced in foreign affairs, and so depended heavily on the advice of his Secretary of State, Cyrus Vance, and Secretary of Defense, Zbigniew Brzezinski. These two men had very differing views on how to handle the USSR. All this meant that Carter's policies were frequently inconsistent. For example, he removed American missiles from South Korea to show good faith to the Soviets, but then sent Brzezinski on a visit to China, which angered and worried the Soviet government.

Arms reduction talks continued into 1978 and 1979, but this atmosphere of uncertainty made them difficult. It was also hard as Carter kept trying to link arms reduction to human rights issues. The Soviets saw this as the United States trying to interfere in Soviet internal affairs. However, an agreement was finally reached in June 1979 (SALT II). There was to be a limit on delivery vehicles (i.e. missiles and bombers) of 2,400, falling to 2,250 by 1982. There was also to be a limit on the number of warheads per vehicle. The measure was limited but important, as it actually seemed to introduce a reduction, not just a halt, in the arms build-up. In fact, both the USSR and the Americans carried on installing new missiles in Europe, such as the Pershing and the SS-20. SALT II was also widely criticised at home. The left felt it did not go far enough, while the right felt it gave too much away to the Soviets. Carter himself admitted that it was little, but it was better than nothing. In the end, the arguments were irrelevant as the USSR invaded Afghanistan in December 1979 and the Senate refused to ratify the SALT treaty.

How did the USA react to the war in Afghanistan?

From the Russian point of view, the invasion of Afghanistan was to protect themselves from Islamic fundamentalism and to support a friendly, neighbouring government. To the Americans, it was more proof of the basic aggression of communism: nothing had changed since 1945. Carter announced the 'Carter Doctrine' – extending the Truman Doctrine to the Middle East – but, in reality, there was little the Americans could do. They were certainly not prepared to go to war to protect the Afghans and military support was virtually impossible in this land-locked, mountainous region.

As well as abandoning SALT II, the American government stopped exports to the USSR and increased their defence budget by $17.1 billion. The President also boycotted the Olympics held in Moscow in 1980, but many athletes went ahead and competed, ignoring their president's wishes. Carter tried to get America's European allies to join in the trade and sports boycotts but, though there was little support for the invasion in Europe, there was also little support for a trade boycott of Russia. Europe did not see the issue as that important and felt that Carter was over-reacting, especially with America's own record in Vietnam. In the end, what removed the Red Army from Afghanistan in 1988 was their own realisation that, after eight years, they were not going to win.

1. Why did The USSR and America pursue détente in the 1970s?

2. How far had relations between the superpowers improved between 1968 and 1980?

5.8 Why did the Cold War in Europe come to an end?

Ronald Wilson Reagan (1911– 2004)
40th President of the USA (1981–89), a Republican with strong anti-communist views. He was a Hollywood actor before becoming governor of California. Reagan defeated Carter in the 1980 presidential election. During the 1980s, he launched the biggest peacetime military build-up in US history. Supporter of the 'Star Wars' initiative. However, from 1985 he negotiated with Soviet leader Gorbachev towards reducing nuclear weapons in START (strategic arms reduction talks). He was wounded in an assassination attempt in 1981. Re-elected in 1984, in a landslide victory.

Between 1979 and 1986, a new Cold War was emerging. The Soviet invasion of Afghanistan had increased the belief in the USA that the USSR had not changed after 30 years and was still intent on establishing its power over other countries. American deployment of new weapons in Europe – such as Cruise missiles – made the Soviets feel threatened once more. Third World conflicts also affected relations between East and West, particularly in the Middle East and in Latin America. Another factor was that new leaders had emerged in both countries. Leonid Brezhnev died in 1982 and was followed in rapid succession by Yuri Andropov and Konstantin Chernenko. Both men were old and ill and their unexpected deaths following so quickly created instability both in the USSR itself and in relations with the USA. The United States, too, had a change of leader in the election of 1980, which had a great impact on the Cold War.

Carter's indecisive and weak foreign policy, not just in Europe but around the world, gave way to the patriotic and aggressive foreign policy of Republican President Ronald Reagan. He believed the USA should support its friends, even if they were dictators, oppose their enemies and be prepared to use military force where necessary. He referred to the Soviet Union as the 'evil empire' and said that all the troubles in the world could be traced back to the USSR, a country bent on world domination.

How much Reagan really believed that the USSR was an evil empire is debatable. His supporters argue that he knew the Soviet Union was getting weak internally, its economy was in bad shape and the war in Afghanistan was putting more strain on it and on Russian society. Therefore, by putting the Soviet Union under further pressure, Reagan would force it to negotiate over arms and to begin reforming the USSR.

Others feel that Reagan did believe the USSR was behind most of the world's troubles. He was a fervent capitalist who detested the communist system. The Soviets had been increasing their influence in Africa and Latin America, so Reagan was convinced they were trying to take over the world. Whatever the truth, Reagan certainly pursued an uncompromising Cold War policy.

How far did Reagan pursue arms reduction?

The United States, under Ronald Reagan, embarked on the biggest arms build-up in its history. In the 1980s, $550 billion a year was being spent on conventional and nuclear weapons. New systems were being developed, such as the stealth bomber and the neutron bomb (the Soviets called this the capitalist bomb as it was supposed to destroy biological matter, such as people, but not property). In 1983, Cruise missiles were shipped to bases in Europe. This made those areas targets. It sparked several protests, including a seven-year protest by women at Greenham Common, in

Britain. In spite of this phenomenal build-up, Reagan was also prepared to talk about arms control. He believed that America had to negotiate from a position of strength, otherwise it would be seen as weak and would be vulnerable to attack.

In 1982, the Strategic Arms Reduction Talks (START) began in Geneva but they failed to produce an agreement. The basic problem was that the two sides did not trust each other. During the talks, the Soviet Union clamped down hard on 'Solidarity', a democratic trade union movement which had developed in Poland. In 1983, they shot down a Korean passenger plane killing 269 people. As far as Reagan was concerned, this was typically aggressive communist behaviour. The Soviets had equal reason to be mistrustful of the Americans. During negotiations, the American side refused to discuss the possibility of including NATO in arms reduction and seemed to be asking for more than they were willing to give up. In March 1983, Reagan announced the development of the Strategic Defence Initiative (SDI), nicknamed 'star wars'. This programme was supposedly a defence shield which would destroy any missiles fired at the USA while they were still in space. In fact, most scientists believed it was unworkable. However, if it did work it would mean that many Russian missiles were effectively useless, while leaving the USSR still open to attack. To them, it seemed that the USA was talking about peace but its actions were very different.

How did Gorbachev affect the Cold War?

In 1985, Mikhail Gorbachev became the new Soviet leader and set about a new programme of reform in the USSR. This raised fears in the United States that the reforms would strengthen the USSR and improve its position in the Cold War. Although Britain's Prime Minister, Margaret Thatcher, said she could 'do business' with him, early encounters between Reagan and Gorbachev did not go well. Meetings in Geneva in 1985 and Reykjavik in 1986 produced no real agreement on arms. They argued about the types of weapon to be limited and whether current agreements were being abided by, but the real stumbling block continued to be SDI. In 1987, they signed the Intermediate-range Nuclear Forces Treaty (INF). This was a major achievement as, for the first time, there were to be actual reductions in weapons. Intermediate-range weapons were to be dismantled and there were to be inspections to ensure that each side was fulfilling its obligations. The first weapons were dismantled in 1988.

Why had this improvement happened? Many credit Reagan's military build-up with forcing the USSR into a position where it simply could not afford to carry on trying to keep up with the United States. The build-up had also worried both America's allies and the general public about the sheer number of nuclear weapons now in existence. This concern about nuclear proliferation was increased in 1986 with the accident at the Chernobyl nuclear reactor in the Ukraine, which contaminated the land and atmosphere as far away as Wales. A major factor was that the relationship between Reagan and Gorbachev had become very productive. Reagan realised that Gorbachev was genuinely looking for a better relationship with the West, and Reagan himself was more willing to compromise than his talk about the 'evil empire' implied.

Relations continued to improve with a visit by Reagan to Moscow in 1988. Yet the INF treaty only cut out one class of missile. The build-up Reagan had instigated meant there were still thousands of nuclear weapons in the East and West pointed at each other, and he had taken the USA into enormous debt to pay for them.

Mikhail Sergeivich Gorbachev (1931–)
Son of a peasant family, he became a law graduate and joined the Communist Party in 1946. He rose through the Party to become Secretary for Agriculture in 1978 and at 41 the youngest member of the Politburo, the USSR's governing body, in 1980. In March 1985, he was elected General Secretary of the Politburo, making him in effect the leader of the USSR. He wanted to modernise the country and make it more efficient but soon realised that to do this there had to be serious reform of the Soviet system. He embarked on policies of perestroika (restructuring) and glasnost (openness), which ended in creating a democratic system in the Soviet Union. His work to democratise the USSR and the freedoms he introduced into Eastern Europe won him the Nobel Peace Prize in 1990.

Why did communism in Eastern Europe collapse?

The true roots of the collapse of communism in the USSR and Eastern Europe lay in Soviet and Russian history, but the Cold War was a contributing factor. By maintaining a policy of containment for 40 years, the USA had ensured that the Soviets had to spend a lot of money on arms – money they were not able to spend improving conditions for their people. Reagan's spending made this even worse. To execute his planned reforms, Gorbachev had to reduce the Russian military. This gave encouragement to Eastern European states that they could also reform and that the Red Army would not stop them this time. From 1989, change began to happen rapidly. The border between Austria and Hungary was opened up, allowing people to travel from East Germany to the West, through Hungary and Austria. The numbers of people passing through became a flood. Gorbachev advised the East Germans to open the Berlin Wall and allow direct travel from East to West.

On 9 November 1989, the East Germans opened up the Berlin Wall. Citizens of the city, who had been divided from friends and family for four generations, poured through. All over the world, millions watched the events unfold on television, knowing that they were witnessing a turning point in history. The end of the Cold War had begun.

What was the US response to events in Europe?

The new President, George Bush, reacted slowly to events in the East. There were some who advised him to move quickly, especially when the Warsaw Pact collapsed at the end of 1989. An intelligent and well-travelled man, George Bush felt that, as the situation in the USSR and Eastern Europe was changing so rapidly, it was best for the USA to move slowly and avoid making any costly errors. The Warsaw Pact might have ended, but the USSR still possessed its nuclear weapons and one of the largest armies in the world.

George Herbert Walker Bush (1924–)
41st President of the USA (1989–93), a Republican. Director of the CIA (1976–81) and Vice-President (1981–89). As President, sending US troops to depose General Noriega of Panama was popular at home. Success in the 1991 Gulf War against Iraq further raised his standing. However, despite signing START I (July 1991) and reducing US nuclear weapons, Bush's popularity at home began to wane. Defeated by Democrat Bill Clinton in the 1992 presidential elections.

What does this celebration on top of the Berlin Wall tell historians about the collapse of the Wall and the end of the Cold War?

Protesters on the Berlin Wall on 9 November 1989.

Meetings were arranged throughout 1989 between Secretary of State James Baker and Russian Foreign Minister Eduard Shevardnadze. They discussed the ongoing changes in the Soviet Union and the East, and raised the possibility of beginning the START talks again. This time, the Soviets made it clear they would accept America's development of SDI, thus removing one of the major obstacles to an agreement.

In June 1990, Bush and Gorbachev met in Washington. They agreed to cuts in both chemical weapons and long-range nuclear weapons. This was made formal in July under START I, which limited both countries to 1,600 nuclear delivery vehicles (i.e. bombers, submarines etc.) and 6,000 nuclear devices. As with the INF treaty, this represented a reduction in the number of weapons and allowed for verification (checking by the other side). The two men also agreed to greater contacts between the two countries and to increased trade.

The situation in Europe continued to develop rapidly. In the spring of 1990, the Baltic States of Latvia, Estonia and Lithuania declared their independence from the USSR, followed by the Ukraine. All over the East – in Romania, East Germany and elsewhere – Communist dictators were being pressured by the people into resigning and were being replaced by democratic governments. In the USSR itself, Gorbachev was a victim as he was too closely identified with the old regime. Boris Yeltsin replaced him in December 1991 and the Union of Soviet Socialist Republics became the Commonwealth of Independent States. On Christmas Day 1991, the red flag bearing the hammer and sickle was removed from the Kremlin (central government building).

Perhaps the most important change of all came in Germany. Once the Berlin Wall was opened, demands for re-unification began. In July 1990, a new West German Chancellor, Helmut Kohl, was elected promising to re-unite his country. Bush and Gorbachev discussed the situation at their meeting in June and afterwards. America wanted the new united Germany to be a member of NATO, but Gorbachev was reluctant to accept this and wondered what NATO's purpose was now that the Cold War was over. Some other states were also concerned by the re-unification of Germany, having suffered two world wars in the 20th century which were both, arguably, due to German militarism. The Americans and Germans worked to remove these fears by pledging that the latter would not have nuclear or biological weapons and that their army, which now numbered 1.8 million, would be held in check by membership of NATO.

In September 1990, the armies of occupation were removed from Germany. In October, the Federal Republic and the Democratic Republic were joined together, re-uniting Germany 45 years after Potsdam. Perhaps Truman's policy of containment had held the line and maintained peace in Europe for all this time. Perhaps Kennan was right when he looked back in the 1960s and said that he had been wrong and that America should have tried to find a way of working with the USSR. The Cold War in Europe had cost the United States billions of dollars and decades of tension. Yet it was only after its end, in the former Yugoslavia, that NATO troops had to be sent into the field to contain a war on European soil.

1. In what ways was SDI threatening to the Soviet Union?

2. How consistent was President Reagan's arms policy?

Further Reading

Texts designed for AS Level students

The Enduring Vision by Paul Boyer and others (D.C. Heath & Co., 1993) – easy to read and well-illustrated narrative.

The USA and the Cold War by Oliver Edwards (Hodder & Stoughton, 1997) – clear narrative with practice exercises and note-making guide.

The Limits of Liberty by Maldwyn James (Oxford University Press, 1995) – clear narrative account.

The Cold War by Bradley Lightbody (Routledge, 1999) – clear chapters covering whole period, with lots of source questions.

Texts for A2 and advanced study

Rise to Globalism by Stephen Ambrose and Douglas Brinkley (Penguin, 1997) – fascinating and detailed account of post-war policy, quite critical of the USA.

Major Problems in American History Since 1945 edited by Robert Griffith and Paula Barker (Houghton Mifflin, 2001) – sets of documents on major issues, followed by interpretative essays by leading historians.

American Foreign Relations: A History Since 1920 edited by Thomas G. Paterson, J. Garry Clifford, Kenneth J. Hagan (Houghton Mifflin, 2000) – detailed narrative, well illustrated.

The Truman Years 1945–1975 by Mark Byrnes (Longman, Seminar Study series, 2000)

Television and video

'The Cold War' – CNN production shown on the BBC (1999–2000). Divided into six videos: (1) Iron Curtain; (2) Reds; (3) M.A.D.; (4) Dirty wars; (5) Third World wars; and (6) Final Countdown. Available from DD Video, 5 Churchill Court, Station Road, North Harrow, Middlesex HA2 7SA.

'Truman' – a video written and produced by David Grubin for 'The American Experience' series (1994). It is divided into three one-hour episodes: the first covers Truman's political rise and the dropping of the atom bomb on Japan in 1945; the second episode covers Truman's Administration in domestic and foreign affairs up to 1949; the third episode concentrates on the Korean War.

Useful websites

The Cold War has hundreds of websites. The following are just a few:

http://history1900s.about.com – lists lots of other sites and has a quiz.

HTTP://WWW.GWU.EDU/~NSAARCHIV – the US National Security Archive containing lots of sources and the international Cold War history Project.

HTTP://WWW.EAGLE3.AMERICAN.EDU/~MM5860A/ORIGINS – description of the Cold War but also lots of links.

HTTP://WWW.CNN.COM/SPECIALS/COLD.WAR – site for CNN television series, but has interesting photographs and bits of information including some animated summaries.

6 The USA and the Cold War in Asia, 1945–1973

Key Issues

- Why did the Cold War spread to Asia after 1945?

- With what success did the USA contain the spread of communism in Asia, 1945–1975?

- How far did US policy towards Asia change, 1945–1975?

Framework of Events

1945	US occupation of Japan begins
1946	Truce in Chinese Civil War
1948	China Aid Act
	Two separate governments set up in North and South Korea
1949	Communist victory in Chinese Civil War
1950	USSR and China sign mutual defence pact
	June: Outbreak of war in Korea
1951	US–Japanese treaty
	US treaty with the Philippines
1952	US occupation of Japan ends
1953	End of Korean War
1954	Fall of Dien Bien Phu
	Geneva Accords on French Indo-China
	Defence Pact between USA and Taiwan/Formosa
	September: Signing of SEATO
1955	First Formosa/Taiwan Crisis
1958	Second Formosa/Taiwan Crisis
1962	Neutrality of Laos agreed in Geneva
1963	2 November: Assassination of President Diem of South Vietnam
	22 November: Assassination of President Kennedy
1964	August: Gulf of Tonkin Incident
1965	February: Attack on US military base at Pleiku
	March: Marines land at Da Nang in South Vietnam
	Anti-war protests by Students for a Democratic Society

1968	January: Tet Offensive in South Vietnam
	16 March: My Lai Massacre
1969	May: Paris peace talks begin
	15 October: March Against Death
1970	30 April: Invasion of Cambodia
	4 May: Students killed in protest at Kent State University
1972	Linebacker bombing campaigns
	22 February: Nixon visits China
1973	27 January: Paris Peace Agreement
	March: Americans withdraw from South Vietnam
1975	April: Fall of Saigon.

Overview

WHILE President Truman focused his attention on Europe after the end of the Second World War, there were those in government who argued that equal attention needed to be paid to the East. After all, it was the attack on Pearl Harbor by the Japanese that had brought the Americans into the War and the USA had a long history of friendship with the Chinese going back to the 1890s. As America also got rubber and oil from the East and had bases in the Pacific, the Far East was also strategically important. These 'Asia-firsters' argued that Europeans could take care of themselves and that the government should pay more attention to the East. But as the chief adversary in the Cold War was the Soviet Union, Europe tended to play a larger role in American foreign policy. At times, events in Asia forced themselves to the forefront.

At the end of the Second World War, the Americans took on the role of main occupiers in Japan, hoping to turn it into a democratic and peaceful power. It was to be weakened so that it would never again threaten America's interests in the Pacific. Events in China forced a change of attitude. When China 'fell' to communism in 1949, Japan was turned into the United States' foremost ally in the region and was built up to be a balance against communist expansion in Asia. By 1951, the Americans had a formal alliance with their recent enemy.

The threat of the world's most populous nation falling to communism led to the extension of the Truman Doctrine to the Far East. However, geographical, as well as political, realities prevented the USA from helping the Nationalist forces in China to halt the advance of Mao's Communists. By continuing to back Chiang Kai-Shek and the Nationalists, the Americans found themselves on the verge of war with China in 1955, and again in 1958. The disagreements were over the fate of the islands of Formosa (now known as Taiwan), to which the Nationalists had fled in 1949. Disputes over the islands have continued to damage American relations with China ever since.

The policy of containment, embodied in the Truman Doctrine in 1947, could be said to have prevented war in Europe for 40 years, yet that same policy found the Americans getting into a war in the Far East in 1950. At the end of the Second World War, Korea had been divided into a Communist North and a Democratic South, led by Kim Il Sung and Syngman Rhee respectively, who both wanted to re-unify their nation. In 1950, the North Koreans invaded the South to do just that.

President Truman, supported by the United Nations, decided to take a stand. An army from 16 countries went to Korea to throw out the invaders. Rather than achieving a quick and easy victory, American arrogance led to the Chinese entering the war and a two-year stalemate resulted. The war finally ended in 1953, with Korea still divided.

Even more damaging was the American involvement in Vietnam. When the former French colony of Indo-China attempted to gain its independence, in 1945, they hoped the Americans, as former colonials themselves, would help. Instead the Americans chose to back their NATO ally in their unsuccessful attempt to hold on to power. After the French defeat at Dien Bien Phu, Indo-China was divided into four areas, with Vietnam divided, like Korea, into a communist North and a non-communist South. Unlike Korea, however, there was widespread support in Vietnam – North and South – for the Communist leader Ho Chi Minh. As in Korea, the Americans tried to enforce containment. The so-called 'Domino Theory' convinced them that, if South Vietnam were allowed to fall to communism, then the rest of Asia would follow.

Over the next two decades, American involvement in South Vietnam was gradually increased. By 1965, combat troops landed at Da Nang, the first marines sent abroad to fight since Korea: America was again at war. This time though they were fighting a jungle war, with no clear enemy in a different uniform, and they were fighting without the support of the majority of the population or of their allies. The conduct of the war in Vietnam and American losses led to an anti-war movement at home which actively opposed the governments of Johnson and Nixon. The war divided American society like no other since the Civil War. It was a war which the country was not winning. Finally, in 1973, a peace treaty was agreed and the United States pulled its troops out of Vietnam. The 'fall' which they had tried so hard to prevent happened just two years later with a North Vietnamese invasion followed by the unification of the country under Communist leadership.

American conduct of the Cold War in Asia was far less successful than its policy in Europe. In many ways, containment was an inappropriate response to events in the Far East. It assumed that the Soviet Union was behind all communist movements and, when China became communist, it was assumed the two powers acted as one. In both these assumptions, the Americans were wrong. The Soviet Union was undoubtedly involved in the spread of communism to Asia, and it did sometimes work hand in hand with China. More often the rise of communism was the result of local conditions. Revolutionary groups such as the Vietcong were frequently more nationalist than communist. This failure to understand the Far East was affected by the McCarthyism of the 1940s, which saw the removal of many experts from the State Department because of accusations of communist sympathies. It was also due to seeing policies work in Europe and falsely believing that they could be applied elsewhere. Some argue it was also due to American racism going back to the 19th century which underestimated Asian peoples. The USA did have some successes in the Far East, in fact they achieved their aims much of the time. It was the disaster in Vietnam which was the major weakness in US policy in the Far East during the Cold War.

1. Identify the developments mentioned in the mind map which you regard as a failure in US policy. Give brief reasons for your choice against each development.

2. 'Until 1965, US policy in Asia was a success.' How far do you agree with this view?

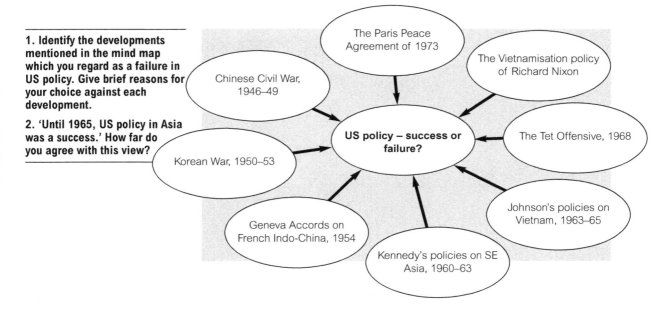

6.1 How successful were US policies towards Japan, 1945–1952?

Douglas MacArthur (1880–1964)
Professional soldier who served in France during the First World War and in the Philippines in the 1930s. He commanded US forces in the Pacific during the Second World War and after a retreat from the Philippine Islands he organised the 'island hopping' campaign which helped to recapture the Pacific. He was in command of UN forces in Korea until removed by Truman.

Feudalism: A system of organising society based on land ownership and obligation. In return for protection and being able to farm the land, the peasant gives obedience and service to the landowner. This system had been widespread in Europe but had died out in the 18th and 19th centuries. A type of feudalism had continued in Japan, and the Americans believed it held Japan back from developing democratic institutions. Also, because it emphasised obedience, it had allowed the military to lead Japan into war. The Americans hoped that abolishing it would speed up Japan's modernisation.

After the surrender in August 1945, the United States occupied Japan in order to establish a new, democratic government. As in Germany, there was a council of the four powers to discuss Japanese issues, but only US troops occupied the country. The USA also took control of several Pacific islands including the Marshall Islands, the Marianas and the Carolinas. They also occupied the islands of Okinawa and Iwo Jima which they had fought so hard to capture during the War. This American dominance angered the Soviets but, as they had entered the war against Japan so late, they could do little more than protest. In respect for their contribution to the war and for their strategic concerns in Asia, they were given a role in the occupation of Korea instead. The USA did as much as possible to limit Soviet and, therefore, communist influence in the Far Eastern settlement.

General MacArthur, the American commander in Japan, was given almost dictatorial power to turn Japan from a militaristic state into a democratic one. Communists were banned from government posts, the military was drastically reduced and **feudalism** was ended. MacArthur encouraged reform with votes for women, legalisation of trade unions, a democratic constitution that outlawed war, and a democratically elected government. The kind of democracy the Americans wished to create in Japan between 1945 and 1952 was very much in their own image. Communists were banned from government positions or from posts in the universities where they might influence future leaders, and restrictions were placed on trade unions. While trade links with other Asian states were encouraged, the Americans did not wish to see Japan regain its former position. It would be taught by the USA to be democratic and peaceful and content within its own islands.

Why did American policy towards Japan change?

Originally, the USA had seen China as its main trading and military partner in the Far East, but 1949 changed that. When the communists won the civil war in China, it became important to build Japan back up as a strong

Chinese troops march through Beijing in 1949. The soldiers on the lorry are holding up a photograph of Mao Ze-dong and a propaganda poster.

power to counter-balance 'Red' China. Building up the Japanese economy would also have the added benefit of providing a market for US goods now that much of the former trade with China was lost. Also, as in Europe, there was the fear that if Japan remained a poor country it would be more susceptible to communism itself. All these factors turned American policy towards Japan around. It would continue to be developed as a democratic nation, but from 1950 onwards there would be help and support for its rapid economic redevelopment. The occupying forces did much to rebuild Japanese industry and Congress gave $500 million in aid. America's allies in the East – Thailand, the Philippines and Indonesia, for example – were encouraged to trade with Japan and open up their markets to Japanese exports. The Americans were determined that as the old colonial powers lost their influence in Asia, America would not lose its and it would not see communism take over. In the words of historian Richard Crockatt, in *The United States and the Cold War 1941–1953* (1989), 'Japan became the keystone of containment in Asia.'

The decision to strengthen Japan was given added urgency in 1950 when war broke out in Korea between the communist North and the western-backed South. Japan could now be useful as a base from which to run operations in Korea and as a place for 'R and R' (rest and recuperation away from the war) for American soldiers. To reinforce the new friendship a treaty was signed, in 1951, formally ending the war between the USA and Japan. The occupation ended on 28 April 1952. Also, in September 1951, a Mutual Security Treaty was signed allowing the USA to maintain military bases and troops on Japanese territory. Japan was allowed to develop an army of 110,000 men for its own defence.

Although they had been part of the war against Japan, the Soviets refused to sign the treaty. Relations between the USA and the Soviet Union had deteriorated badly in Europe since 1945 and conflicts in the East made things worse. Understandably, they took differing positions with regard to the revolution in China and the war in Korea. The USSR also resented the way it had been edged out of all decisions relating to Japan. The Soviets felt that they had a valid interest in the area. (Japan and Russia had fought a war, 1905–06, and had several historical disputes over territory.) They knew that Japan was being built up as part of American containment policy and, to the USSR, it looked as if they were being encircled.

The Soviets were not the only ones less than happy with these developments. Those countries which had suffered Japanese attack during the War were very uneasy and, within Japan itself, there were several demonstrations against the American bases. In 1954, anti-American riots forced Eisenhower to cancel a proposed visit to Japan.

In spite of the concerns, Japan quickly became economically powerful and was one of America's strongest allies in the East. Continued support and aid built Japan up from a defeated nation to one that was competing economically with the United States itself by the 1960s. The constitution which the USA had given it meant that they never supplied military help to the Americans in places such as Korea or Vietnam but, ironically, this also meant that they spent their money on economic growth not war. The thriving capitalist economy was a stronger protection against communist infiltration than any number of US bases.

1. In what ways was the political system of Japan changed under the Allied occupation?

2. Why was the USSR excluded from the Japanese settlement?

3. Why and how did American policy towards Japan change?

6.2 Why did the United States fail to prevent a Communist victory in China?

* Chinese names can be spelled a number of ways. Chiang Kai-Shek is sometimes seen as Jiang Jei-shi and Mao Ze-dong as Mao Tse-Tung.

What was American policy towards the Chinese Civil War, 1945–1949?

In 1927 a civil war broke out in China between the Nationalists, led by Chiang Kai-Shek* and the Communists, led by Mao Ze-dong. The USA had ties of trade and immigration with China going back into the 19th

Chiang Kai-Shek (1887–1975)
The son of a middle-class family who became a professional soldier in 1906. While in the military he became a republican and revolutionary. When the empire fell apart, Chiang joined Sun Yat-sen's Nationalists who were trying to re-unite China. Jiang went to Moscow in 1923 to study the Soviet system, but in 1927 he threw the communists out of the Nationalist Party. In 1928, he established a government in Nanking, but it was in conflict with the communists and then the Japanese. When Chiang lost the civil war in 1949 he took his forces to Taiwan where, with the backing of the USA, he established an economically successful state.

Mao Ze-dong (1883–1976)
Born into a peasant family, he studied at Beijing University and worked for a while as a primary teacher. Mao was a founding member of the Chinese Communist Party (CCP) in 1921. He worked on labour organisations. Unlike most communists, who said that the urban working classes were the foundation of the revolution, Mao argued that the peasants were also potential revolutionaries. When Chiang threw the communists out of the Nationalist Party (1927), Mao and his followers began to organise the peasants in the countryside. In 1934, he led the 'Long March' during which his followers fled 6,000 miles across China to escape attack by the Nationalists. Under Mao's leadership, the CCP grew to over a million strong by 1945. During the 1950s, Mao attempted to modernise China with the 'Great Leap Forward' programmes of industrialisation and **collectivisation** of agriculture, but they produced much hardship for the Chinese people. As rivalry for the leadership of world communism intensified, Chinese relations with the USSR deteriorated in the 1960s, while in the 1970s friendship with the USA grew.

Collectivisation: The bringing under state ownership and control of farms and factories. The usual method is to combine a number of small firms or factories into one larger one.

century and China was therefore seen as culturally and economically important to the USA. Their isolationist policies of the 1920s meant they watched with interest but took no real part in events. When the Japanese attacked China in 1937, the various groups in the civil war put aside their differences to fight the invader. At Yalta, Roosevelt had persuaded Stalin to support Chiang and to keep Mao under control so that they could focus on defeating Japan. However, conflict broke out again in 1945.

Clearly, the Americans did not want the Communists to win. A communist victory, they felt, would endanger the 'open door' trade policy which they had fought so hard to establish in China decades before. There was also a danger of communism spreading to Japan, where the USA was working hard to establish a democratic government. On the other hand, State Department officials warned Truman of the danger of identifying the Americans too closely with Chiang who was both corrupt and unpopular. Ideally, what Truman wanted was a negotiated peace which would allow the Nationalists a part in government, as well as remove the need for US intervention. An American-backed conference between Chiang and Mao, in 1945, failed to find a solution. Chiang refused to make concessions, particularly over the industrialised area of Manchuria, which both sides wished to control. Truman sent 50,000 US troops to try to help Chiang establish control once the Soviets had pulled out. This encouraged Chiang to believe that he would have American support for whatever policies he chose.

The following year, President Truman sent George Marshall to try and find a solution. He managed to negotiate a truce in January 1946, but it fell apart within three months when Chiang's forces attacked Manchuria after the Soviets had pulled out leaving Mao in control of the area. American support failed to help the Nationalists take the province and as popular resentment against Chiang grew, it was also turned against the United States. In 1946, the Americans started to withdraw.

In the USA, Truman was criticised, especially by the Republicans, for not applying the principles of containment to Asia. General Wedemeyer advised giving further financial support to the Nationalists and, in 1948, the China Aid Act gave $400 million to Chiang, bringing to $3 billion the amount of aid given by the US since 1945. However, the aid was having little effect. Even as the Act was being passed, the Communists were moving towards victory. The outbreak of the crisis in Berlin meant that American attention was focused firmly on events in Germany. By October 1949, the Communists had won and Chiang Kai-Shek and and his two million followers had fled to the island of Formosa/Taiwan. The Americans refused to recognise the communist government of the People's Republic of China. Instead they continued to refer to Taiwan and its government as Nationalist China.

Why did the USA not intervene in China?

When General Wedemeyer gave his advice to President Truman, he said that the USA should send another 10,000 troops to help Chiang, but Truman refused. Secretary of State, Dean Acheson, pointed out that sending advisors or military chiefs would lead to more troops being sent and America had neither the men nor the desire to get into a land war in China. The defeat was also happening at the same time as problems were increasing in Berlin, so the government did not want to tie up troops in the Far East when they might be needed in Europe.

Acheson also had to admit that it was largely Chiang's own fault that he had lost. The Nationalist leader was corrupt and undemocratic, so support for Mao was strong among the poor in China. The Nationalists

---

Albert Coady Wedemeyer (1897–1989)

A professional soldier, Wedemeyer served in China and Germany between the wars and spoke Mandarin Chinese. During the Second World War he worked with General Marshall and helped to plan the Normandy landings. In 1944, he was sent again to the Far East and advised support for the Nationalists in China. He retired in 1951.

refused to support land reform and therefore failed to gain the support of the peasants, who made up 80 per cent of the population. They even lost middle-class support by letting inflation run at 700 per cent, wiping out people's savings and businesses. In 1945, Chiang had an army of 2½ million, outnumbering the Communists five to one but, by 1949, the Nationalist forces had halved through defections to the Communist side.

China lobby: Politicians, businessmen and others who tried to pressure the government over their policy on China. They were usually the 'Asia-firsters' (see page 177) but included others who wanted the government to do more for China.

American political sympathies might have been with the Nationalists, but nothing either Truman or the **China lobby** could say or do would alter the realities of the situation. The USA simply could not send tens of thousands of men across an ocean to face an enemy of several millions, or do this in support of a government which was unpopular among many of its own people. As Acheson wrote, in the so-called 'China White Paper' published in 1949, 'Nothing this country did or could have done within the reasonable limits of its capabilities would have changed the result [of the civil war].'

The geographical and political realities did not stop Truman's critics from accusing him of 'losing' China. To many Americans, it seemed that communism was indeed spreading. The signing of a mutual defence pact between China and the USSR, in 1950, confirmed the belief that the Soviet Union was bent on world domination and had now added the world's most populous country to its sphere of influence. Together the USSR and China formed a massive bloc, cutting off a huge market for US trade and spreading communist dominance into the Far East.

What was the effect of the 'loss' of China on US policy?

John Dulles called it 'the worst defeat the United States has suffered in its history'. In many ways the United States over-reacted to the events in China. Firstly, for all the politicians might argue, China had not been America's to 'lose' – as many historians have pointed out. Acheson was right when he acknowledged that there was nothing the USA could have done to affect the outcome of the Civil War. It was a fight over which they had no control and which was about China, not about the Cold War as they believed (a lesson America might well have learned before Vietnam). The Americans also overestimated the strength of the bonds between China and the USSR. They might have signed an alliance, but there were deep-seated rivalries over territory in Manchuria and over the nature and leadership of worldwide communism. The USA assumed that the two communist states acted together, and in this they were frequently wrong. However, the 'loss' was very damaging for Truman and did affect both foreign and domestic policy.

The Republicans blamed Truman for the fall of China to communism. It helped to fuel the rise in McCarthyism as they accused spies in the State Department of being responsible. Their accusation of spies in the government was given added weight when the Soviet Union exploded its own atom bomb the same year that China fell. This not only cost many State Department officials their jobs, losing valuable expertise on far Eastern affairs, but also meant that Truman had to respond to the criticism by being seen to be equally tough on communism – which fuelled the anti-communist hysteria still further.

In spite of an early attempt by Mao Ze-dong to build a relationship with the United States, the Truman Administration refused to see Communist China as anything other than a Soviet puppet. Internationally, they tried to weaken Mao's position. They blocked the entry of the People's Republic into the United Nations and tried, largely unsuccessfully, to persuade their allies not to recognise Mao's government. They continued to give financial

1. In what ways did President Truman support the Nationalist Chinese?

2. How successful was American policy towards China in the years 1945 to 1949?

and moral support to the Nationalists in Taiwan. This support was to cause continuing problems for Eisenhower in the 1950s.

American policy in Asia was deeply affected by the loss of China. It led to a complete turn around in its conduct towards the Japanese, who now became the United States' most valued ally in the region. It also meant that, when Truman was faced with further communist aggression in Korea, he could not afford to back down.

6.3 How and with what consequences for foreign policy in Asia did the USA get involved in war in Korea?

Syngman Rhee (1875–1965)
Korean nationalist who was imprisoned by the government in his youth for his political activities. He studied in the USA, returning briefly to Korea before Japan occupied it in 1912. He returned to the USA to campaign for Korean independence. He was elected president of South Korea four times between 1948 and 1960. Although in theory South Korea was a democracy, Rhee's rule was very dictatorial. Student-led protests in 1960 led to his resignation and exile.

Kim Il Sung (1912–1994)
As a young man he fought in the guerrilla movements against Japanese occupation. In the 1930s, he went to train in the USSR and during the Second World War he served in a Korean unit in the Red Army. He became the Soviet-backed leader of North Korea in 1948. After the war he made North Korea into a one-party dictatorship. Even after the fall of communism in Europe in 1989, North Korea remained firmly **Stalinist**. He remained leader of the country until his death in 1994, when his son succeeded him.

Stalinist: A political system based on the type of communism developed by Stalin in the USSR 1929–53. It is highly centralised, the leader has great authority, and there is widespread use of terror.

During the Second World War, Korea had been occupied by the Japanese. As a result of agreements at Potsdam, the Soviet Union had joined the war against Japan and helped to liberate Korea. Consequently, the country was divided at the end of the war into two zones, occupied by the Americans and the Soviets, with the border being the 38th Parallel (see map on page 178). As in Germany, the division was meant to be temporary and elections were to be held to unify the country. However, when the Americans submitted the issue to the United Nations in 1947, the USSR refused to go along with it. The Americans decided to go ahead and hold elections in their zone the next year. The two superpowers then pulled their troops out, leaving a divided Korea with Syngman Rhee leader of a democratic South and a communist-backed North under Kim Il Sung.

The Soviets had opposed the elections, as they believed Korea would vote to be a capitalist democracy. The USSR wanted to extend their power into the Far East, so a united, non-communist Korea was not in their interests. With China about to fall under communist control, Korea would add to the strength of communism in the area and extend Soviet influence. For similar reasons, the Americans did not want a united Korea if it were under communism. So, when the Soviet Union refused to go along with the elections, the Americans just held elections in their own zone. Though they wanted free elections they were not prepared to fight the USSR over the issue, especially when Berlin and China were of more immediate concern.

How did the war break out?

On 25 June 1950, North Korean troops invaded the South. Almost 100,000 men, equipped with Soviet-made tanks and aircraft, poured into the South capturing Seoul (the southern capital) and most of the country down to Pusan. The attack came without warning and was totally unexpected by the USA. In fact, diplomats heard the news first from journalists and refused to believe it. The South Koreans turned to America for help.

Truman felt he had no choice but to take a stand. Morally, the South Koreans had suffered an unprovoked attack and deserved aid from their allies. On a domestic political level, he had to take action. He was low in the opinion polls and there were mid-term elections coming in November. Truman had already been heavily criticised by McCarthy and by the Republicans for 'losing' China: he could not afford to lose Korea too. He also believed in the need for containment. He was convinced that the Soviet Union was behind the attack and, if the United States did not stop them in Korea, they would 'swallow up one piece of Asia after another'.

Two days after the attack, Truman ordered military supplies to be sent to South Korea from the American bases in Japan and ordered US planes and ships to the area. The 7th Fleet was sent to the China Sea to ensure the Chinese did not take advantage of the situation and attack Taiwan. Truman had decided that America would fight but, to avoid lengthy debate in

Congress, he went to the United Nations for support for his action. He asked the UN Secretary General for a meeting of the Security Council. The UN Charter said that all the members would support any fellow member who suffered an unprovoked attack. It seemed that South Korea was in that position so the United Nations authorised the USA to organise and coordinate military action by 16 member nations against the North Koreans to get them out of the South.

Of the 11 members of the Security Council, only Communist Yugoslavia voted against the Korean operation. The Soviets could have exercised their veto in the Security Council to prevent the action, but the USSR was boycotting the UN at the time in protest at America blocking Communist China's entry to the organisation, so the vote passed. They did not make this mistake again.

How effectively did the UN pursue the war?

In July 1950, the first American troops landed in Korea. The counter-attack began in September when UN troops under General Douglas MacArthur landed at Inchon, behind the North Korean lines. The invasion quickly collapsed and by 8 October they had forced the North Koreans back behind the 38th Parallel. At this point, the Americans had achieved containment. They had done what the UN had authorised them to do (i.e. get the invaders out of South Korea). Instead of calling a ceasefire, the American-led forces invaded the North and, by October, had captured the northern capital, Pyongyang. With victory seeming so easy, the Americans decided to try and retake the initiative in the Cold War and regain some territory from the Communists.

An invasion of North Korea would be seen by the Chinese as a threat to their security. Urged on by Stalin, they warned the Americans not to invade North Korea. Neither the Americans nor their allies took the warning seriously. As American troops neared the Yalu River, the border between Korea and China, the Chinese invaded. On 19 October, 250,000 Chinese troops poured over the border. The UN forces were completely

---

The United Nations

Set up in 1945 in San Francisco to remove sources of conflict and to preserve peace.

The General Assembly	**The Security Council**	**The Secretariat**
Each member state has a representative. It meets once a year and debates issues and allocates the budget.	It has five permanent members – Britain, USA, USSR, France and China – and originally had six non-permanent members. These are elected for two years by the Assembly, and the number has increased as the UN has grown. The permanent members have a veto over Council decisions.	This is the UN civil service and does the day-to-day work. In charge of it is the Secretary General, elected for five years by the Assembly. He (there has been no female Secretary General yet) is the face of the UN and can bring any matter to its attention.

The UN also has many agencies which deal with specific issues, such as the UNHCR for refugees, UNESCO for education and culture, WHO for health etc.

The UN has only twice organised peace enforcement operations: Korea in 1950–53 and the Gulf War in 1992.

overwhelmed and within four months they had been pushed back and Seoul was once again in Communist hands. The Americans and the UN forces stood their ground and pushed northwards once again and, by late spring, the fighting settled around the 38th Parallel and got bogged down – almost like First World War trench warfare.

How was the war brought to an end?

Neither power wanted the war to spread to an all-out fight between America and China, nor did they want to involve the Soviets. Yet neither side wanted to back down. The Chinese knew the Americans would continue to support Chiang in Taiwan and that if they also controlled the Korean peninsula it would threaten Chinese security. While the Americans would not pull out of Korea, leaving it all in communist hands, containment meant they had to protect the South. Two years of attrition was the result.

To break the deadlock, General MacArthur wanted Truman to 'unleash Chiang' (i.e. to support an attack on the People's Republic by Nationalist forces from Taiwan). The British urged the Americans to be cautious about extending the boundaries of the war. Any direct attack on Chinese territory ran the risk of bringing the Soviet Union in to protect China. The danger was a third world war, and the British knew full well that the Soviets would probably launch an attack in Europe. The United Nations had only given them a mandate to remove the invaders from South Korea; they had not given permission for an attack on Communist China. President Truman knew that at home the people were growing tired of a war which had seemed to promise a short and easy victory, but had so far dragged on for over a year with no end in sight.

MacArthur, however, continued to press his arguments and even suggested that Truman use the atom bomb on China. In the spring of 1951, when Truman refused to see things his way, MacArthur complained to Joseph Martin, a Republican Congressman. Martin then went to the press and made public the disagreement over policies. In spite of the popularity of MacArthur, Truman had no choice but to sack him. A military commander could not be allowed to flout the will of the President and dispute his orders in public. MacArthur was replaced. The Joint Chiefs of Staff fully supported Truman's decision, but MacArthur was welcomed home as a hero. His dismissal did nothing for Truman's falling popularity.

It was obvious, even before 1951 was out, that the war was not going to be over quickly. Negotiations for an armistice began in Panmunjon but they dragged on for two years, while the fighting continued to claim lives from each side and from among the Korean civilian population. Then, in 1953, world circumstances changed, allowing for progress in the war. Stalin died and Eisenhower became President of the USA. During the election, 'Ike' had promised to end the war. Stalin's death meant the Soviet Union also had an excuse to improve relations with the USA and with a new government which genuinely wanted the war to end.

During the 1952 presidential election campaign, 'Ike' had promised to go to Korea personally to end the war. The death of Stalin meant that there was a more sympathetic attitude in the Soviet Union and a willingness to put pressure on China for a settlement. The negotiations, however, were not smooth. Twice nuclear war was threatened by US Secretary of State John Dulles who wanted to ensure the Chinese knew America was serious about ending the war one way or another. He threatened a second time when China stalled the talks because Syngman Rhee had released 25,000 prisoners when it had been agreed that the UN would do all prisoner repatriation. In order to get negotiations going again, Dulles threatened China with nuclear weapons, and they backed down.

A ceasefire was finally agreed in 1953, with the border being the 38th Parallel, where it remains today between communist North Korea and democratic South Korea. A de-militarised zone keeps the two sides apart.

The three-year war had ended with the situation pretty much as it had been before the war started. With the new border, the South Koreans gained 1,500 square miles of land. The cost of those 1,500 square miles was two million lives. During the course of the Korean War, 54,246 American soldiers died – only 4,000 fewer than in the 12-year conflict in Vietnam – and another 106,000 were wounded. The financial cost has been estimated as, at least, $20 billion. Containment in Asia was proving to be very expensive.

What were the effects of the Korean War on US policy?

Apart from the millions of dead and wounded, as well as the damage done to the villages and people of Korea, the war had important domestic and foreign policy effects on the United States.

Bipartisan: Supported by both parties. The parties put aside their differences for a while (e.g. in a war or over a piece of legislation on which they both agree).

Initially, the war had **bipartisan** support in Congress, but it quickly turned to criticism of Truman. The dragging out of the war after 1951 began to raise serious questions at home, which once again fuelled McCarthyism. The United States was the most powerful nation in the world and it was fighting, along with 15 other nations, a small Asian state. Why had they not won easily? Even when the Chinese entered the war, many Americans still could not understand their failure to secure victory against a country far less developed than theirs. Rather than look for real causes in the nature of the fighting or in the fact that a country of two billion people could absorb massive losses in battle, they looked for a scapegoat. Many found it by continuing to believe that traitors in the State Department and in government were to blame.

Many Republicans also blamed Truman for the war happening in the first place. The 'Asia-firsters' maintained that, if he had shown more resolve over China, Communist expansion would have been halted before it even reached Korea. They were still assuming that the Democratic Administration could have affected the Chinese civil war. Since Truman had proclaimed his Doctrine, the USA had been faced with having to decide whether or not to enforce it in Berlin, in China and in Korea. In the first it had succeeded, in the second it had not really been attempted, and in the third situation it had in fact succeeded by getting the North Koreans and the Chinese out of South Korea. But, as far as many Republicans were concerned, Truman's containment policy was failing in Asia.

When President Truman bypassed Congress and went to the United Nations to get support for a military operation in Korea, he was not going beyond his powers. As a member of the UN and signatory to the Charter, the USA could be expected to help a fellow member. As Commander-in-Chief of the US armed forces, Truman could send soldiers to fight abroad. Taking military action without fully consulting Congress was a further growth in Presidential power which began under Roosevelt and was to develop still further under Kennedy and Johnson with regard to Vietnam – and with more dire consequences.

The Korean War also had a serious impact on foreign policy. Korea had shown Truman the necessity of strengthening America's military position in the Far East. Truman set about forming treaties to put this right. Two defence treaties were signed in 1951, with Japan and with the Philippines. The same year, a defence pact was signed between Australia, New Zealand and the USA – the ANZUS Pact. This meant the USA was now more closely

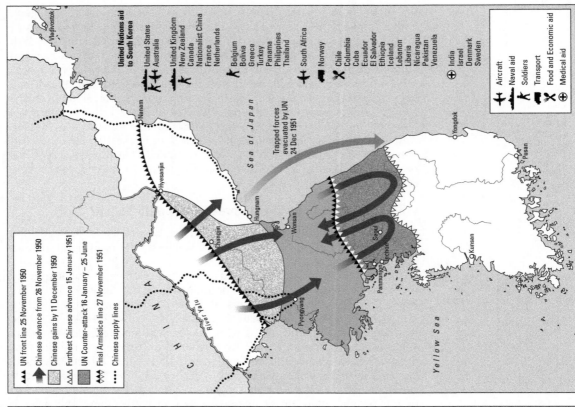

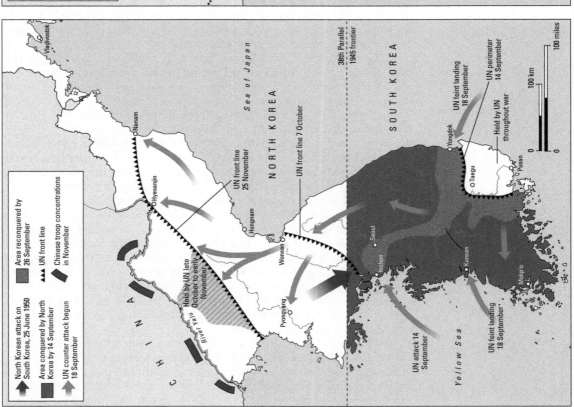

The Korean War: (left) June–November 1950; (right) November 1950–November 1951

involved in Asian affairs. The Truman Doctrine, it seemed, was going to be applied to the East as well as to Europe. Although to Truman himself, Europe would always be more important, America built up bases and friendships in the East. Both military and economic aid was sent to its allies in Japan, the Philippines and Thailand.

The experience of the Korean War led the United States to be more active in its pursuit of containment in Asia. Not only did America build a system of alliances throughout the region, but there was a much firmer approach to crises in the area. When emergencies arose in Taiwan and when the French found themselves facing communist-led rebellion in Indo-China, the American position was firm. It seemed that military action was no longer ruled out. In fact, the military was deployed more frequently in Asia during the Cold War than in Europe.

President Truman not only strengthened America's military position in the Asia, he also strengthened NATO and built bases in North Africa. Eisenhower extended the system of treaties and bases creating the South East Asian Treaty Organisation (SEATO) and the Baghdad Pact in 1954. According to historian Stephen Ambrose, in *Rise to Globalism* (1997), 'Truman extended American bases around the world, hemming in both China and Russia.' The result of this containment was massive military spending. The defence budget, in 1953, was $52.6 billion. Kennan had thought of containment in primarily political and economic terms, but it was now firmly a military policy.

1. Why did the Korean War last three years?

2. General Omar Bradley famously said of MacArthur's plan to attack China that it would be 'the wrong war, in the wrong place, at the wrong time, against the wrong enemy'. How valid is this view when applied to US involvement in the Korean War?

6.4 Why did the Korean War take place?
A CASE STUDY IN HISTORICAL INTERPRETATION

The Korean War is often referred to by veterans as the 'forgotten war'. Sandwiched between the slaughter of the Second World War and the nightmare of Vietnam, its importance and its costs are often overlooked. In some ways, it is a simple war to explain: the North launched an unprovoked attack on the South; the UN came to the defence of the South and threw out the armies of the North. The intervention of the Chinese was a mistake. Unfortunately, it meant the war took longer than it should have.

The issues of the Korean War are much more complex than that. Whose fault was the war? Some blame Truman for not backing the South more forcefully, while others blame the South because there were many border incidents caused by the South which could have led to war. The North Koreans invaded, but would Kim Il Sung have dared to start a war without consulting Stalin?

Coming as it did just after the 'fall' of China, many people at the time saw the Korean War in the context of the Cold War in Asia. Many on the right, such as the 'Asia-firsters', blamed Truman for the war, arguing that his policies encouraged it. Firstly, they argued that by removing American troops in 1948 he had left South Korea defenceless against the Communists. Secondly, they pointed out that Secretary of State, Dean Acheson, had made a speech in January 1951 saying that Korea was outside the US 'defence perimeter' (i.e. the parts of Asia important to US defence). This encouraged the North Koreans and the Soviet Union to believe that South Korea was not important to America and it would not fight to defend it: a belief encouraged by America's unwillingness to fight in China.

The historian Stephen Ambrose also blames Truman, but for very different reasons. He is critical of American foreign policy and argues strongly that Truman wanted to 'sell' NSC-68 to the people and to Congress, and the Korean War was perfect. Ambrose also maintains that the President wanted to increase US involvement in Asia and that his rapid reaction to events was evidence of this policy.

James Patterson, in *America in the Twentieth Century* (1994), is much more sympathetic to the US government. He points out that Truman's military advisors, including MacArthur, had recommended removing troops from Korea. It had little strategic value and the military needed the resources being used in Korea to strengthen NATO. If Truman had conveyed the message that South Korea did not matter to the USA it was certainly not his intention and he should not take the blame for a war. Patterson also argues that although the military might suggest higher spending through NSC-68 they would hardly want a war to get it. The war did, in fact, enable a massive build-up in the US military with spending rising from $14 billion in 1949 to $52.6 billion in 1953 – 60 per cent of the federal budget. (Though this fell again after the war.) Patterson also points out the obvious fact that it was the North who invaded the South. Therefore, whatever else might be said, they had started the war.

Gary Reichard, in *Politics as Usual: the Age of Truman and Eisenhower* (1988), looks at the personalities of the men involved as well as their policies. He agrees that Truman did react quickly when the invasion occurred, but says that this rapid reaction was simply typical of his quick, and even unthinking, response to crises.

The Americans themselves clearly believed that the Soviets were behind the attack. Kim Il Sung had visited Moscow in April 1950 and it now seems clear from the Soviet archives which have been opened recently to western historians, that Stalin did give his backing for the invasion. In May and June, the Soviets sent military supplies to North Korea, including 150 T-34 tanks. As has been pointed out – see Thomas G. Paterson et al, *American Foreign Relations: A History Since 1920* (2000) – the Soviet support was half-hearted, particularly once the war had started. It seems likely that the USSR gave its support to Kim Il Sung hoping for a quick victory in Asia after the failure in Berlin. Once the Americans made their position clear and the war began, the Soviets backed off. They were not willing to go to war with the United States in order to fulfil Kim's dream of a united Korea.

Perhaps some of the blame should go to Syngman Rhee, the South Korean leader. It may be argued that he was aggressive in his behaviour and attitude to the North, and he made no secret of the fact that he wanted to unite Korea. He encouraged border incidents hoping to bring about a war so that the USA would come to his defence and unite Korea under his leadership.

Peter Lowe's study, *The Origins of the Korean War* (1997), looks at how all the major players had an influence in the events leading to the war. He analyses each one of them in turn. Both the Americans and the Soviets played their roles. Lowe points out that Korea needs to be seen in the international context of the Cold War. In other words, the USA, the USSR and China each hoped to improve their international position by the stand they took in Korea. However, Lowe points out that what must not be forgotten is the Korean context. As well as a Cold War conflict, Korea was also a civil war and, at its heart, were the desires of Kim Il Sung and Syngman Rhee.

Inflammatory rhetoric: Speeches and statements made deliberately to annoy and anger, in this case, the North Koreans.

Although the UN investigation just after the war found that Rhee was not to blame for the invasion, it was only looking at immediate events. There was a history of border skirmishes, harassment and **inflammatory rhetoric**. Rhee had constantly looked to the United States for aid and support, and believed that he had it. Though he might not have started the war, he did welcome it.

1. What would have been the advantages to the USSR of supporting Kim Il Sung in the invasion of South Korea?

2. How far and for what reasons do historians differ on their interpretations of the causes of the Korean War?

Both Lowe and Paterson agree on the central role of Kim Il Sung in events. Like Rhee, he also wanted to unite the two Koreas, but he is the one who did something about it. The visit to Moscow, in 1950, was to secure Soviet support for his plans. Kim misled Stalin over how easy the victory would be to ensure his backing and to get the necessary supplies. If Stalin had refused, he would have gone to Mao to try and secure the backing of the Communist Chinese. As Paterson puts it: 'The initiative, and probably the timing, of the war came from Pyongyang not from Moscow or Beijing.'

6.5 What problems did China/Taiwanese relations pose for the United States after 1949?

When Eisenhower became President in 1953, the Nationalist Chinese still held Taiwan, as well as the neighbouring islands of Quemoy, Matsu and Tachen. American support for the Nationalists had continued after 1949, and had been increased after the Korean War as the USA put more emphasis on its Asian alliances. Aid to Taiwan was averaging $250 million per year. The US 7th fleet, sent by Truman in 1950, was still blockading Taiwan in order to keep the peace between the Nationalists and the Communist Chinese. In 1954, Secretary of State John Dulles signed a treaty promising US protection to defend Taiwan and its islands.

At home, 'Ike' was under great pressure from the 'Grand Old Party' (as the Republican Party was nicknamed) to continue to support Chiang and not recognise communist China. The Republicans and the 'Asia-firsters' did not want another victory for Mao. Partly because of this pressure and partly because of the need to force China to negotiate over the Korean armistice, 'Ike' removed the fleet in 1953 to 'unleash Chiang'. Nationalists raided the coast of China, so in retaliation the Chinese bombarded Quemoy and Matsu and invaded the Tachen islands. Nationalist raids on the coast of China were a common occurrence and the Communists used this opportunity to retaliate. They were also keen to test how strong the defence treaty of 1954 was.

In fact, the Republican Administration in America saw Quemoy as crucial to the defence of Taiwan, and Taiwan as crucial to US security in

---

Timeline of Sino(Chinese)–USA relations

1949 US Ambassador in China refuses invitation to meet Chinese Communist Party (CCP) leaders in Beijing

1950 USA pledges itself to defend Taiwan against the CCP and recognises Guomindang (GMD) in Taiwan as official Chinese government
Chinese attack US troops on North Korean border

1950s USA and China on very bad terms: supported opposite sides during Korean War (1950–53); US citizens forbidden to buy anything from China

1960s Relationship still very poor: worsened by Vietnam War (1965–73) – support opposite sides again

1964 China tests first nuclear weapon; alarms the USA

1971 US advisor secretly visits Beijing
Communist China allowed into the United Nations

1972 President Nixon visits China
USA allows China to purchase a wide range of non-military goods.

Brinkmanship: This means taking arguments to the very brink to convince opponents you are serious, hence brinkmanship. Part of the problem with massive retaliation as a policy was that the enemy had to believe you were serious about using atomic weapons.

Asia. So, in January 1955, 'Ike' got approval from Congress to deploy troops to the area as he saw fit under the 'Formosa Resolution'. This was the first 'area resolution' which gave the President almost unlimited authority to use US forces in a certain area of the world. It passed both Houses of Congress with healthy majorities of 83–3 in the Senate and 410–3 in the House of Representatives. This was a very important extension of presidential power. As Dulles pointed out, at least 'Ike' was getting Congressional approval for his actions, unlike Truman in Korea.

As Eisenhower was now operating the 'New Look' policy with its doctrine of massive retaliation, the Americans threatened to use the atom bomb if China continued the bombardment. He also got the USSR to put additional pressure on China, and it finally backed down. As historian Stephen Ambrose says, '**Brinkmanship** held the line. In the process, however, it scared the wits out of people around the globe.' The United States was again enforcing containment and standing by its alliances. If Mao had been testing the defence treaty he had been given his answer.

Why did problems between China and Taiwan arise again in 1958?

In 1958, a crisis over Quemoy rose again. Chiang had increased the Nationalist army on the islands to 100,000 men, which the Chinese saw as provocative. Once again China commenced a bombardment and, once again, Chiang turned to the Americans for help. Eisenhower sent ships to the area to escort Nationalist ships in safety, but he resisted pressure from Republicans at home and from Chiang to use nuclear weapons. Dulles made it clear to the Communists that Chiang still had American support. He also made it clear to Chiang that the USA was under no obligation to help him every time he chose to provoke Mao. The USA would have fought for Taiwan itself, but did not want to get dragged into a war over Quemoy. Once again, timing was important.

In the same year, another crisis arose over Berlin. Khrushchev was paying a visit to the United States so the added problem of conflict in Asia was to be avoided. In October 1958, Chiang removed some of the troops and China ceased the bombardment.

What Taiwan showed, as did events in Korea and Indo-China, were the limitations on brinkmanship. It also showed how the USA was losing patience with Chiang who seemed to think the Americans would automatically help out no matter what he did. Eisenhower and Dulles had no intention of getting into a war with China for Chiang's sake. Like Truman, they also realised the growing importance of Asia as a Cold War arena and the need to build up American strength in the area.

The South East Asia Treaty Organisation (SEATO) was set up in September 1954. This organisation laid down that:

● all parties would consult if they felt threatened;

● they would act against aggressors if all agreed;

● and a separate protocol would guarantee the freedom of Cambodia, Laos and South Vietnam (the former French colony of Indo-China).

1. In what ways did Eisenhower use American military power in his policy towards the Far East?

2. How effective was Dulles' policy of brinkmanship?

The USA, Britain, Australia, New Zealand, France, Thailand, Pakistan and the Philippines signed SEATO. It was different from NATO in that it was only a promise to consult, not a promise to act. Unlike NATO, SEATO had no permanent organisation or military force. Yet, although Dulles assured Congress that SEATO was only about consultation, at the same time he told the Cabinet that the USA would act in Asia if necessary to protect American interests, even if that meant acting alone. The USA was committing itself to containment in Asia under Eisenhower just as much as it had under Truman.

6.6 Why did the USA become increasingly involved in South East Asia, 1945–1965?

Ho Chi Minh (1890–1969)
As a young man he travelled and worked in Europe. A strong nationalist, he campaigned unsuccessfully for Vietnamese independence at the Paris Peace Conference in 1919. He joined the Communist Party and trained in Moscow. Before returning to Vietnam, Ho worked in the USSR and China. He led the Vietminh to success against the French but then as leader of North Vietnam he fought against the Americans and the South Vietnamese for the rest of his life, never living to see an independent Vietnam.

The area of South East Asia which now covers Vietnam, Cambodia and Laos was taken over by the French Empire in the 19th century. In 1930, Ho Chi Minh formed the Indo-Chinese Communist Party, the Vietminh, to fight for independence from France. During the Second World War, the Vietminh, helped by the Allies, fought against Japan. When the war ended, they resumed their fight against France. As they had helped America against the Japanese, and since America was anti-colonial, Ho Chi Minh hoped the Americans would help them to get independence for Vietnam, but that did not happen.

Why did America support the French in Indo-China?

Even though the USA was anti-imperialist, Truman supported France financially, spending $2 billion which, at its peak, was 78 per cent of France's costs. He also gave $50 billion in economic aid to the region. Truman saw the conflict in Vietnam in Cold War terms. He believed the Vietminh were taking orders from Stalin, so supporting France was enforcing containment and the Truman Doctrine. This was especially important to Truman after 1949 as he was still being criticised for the 'loss' of China and did not want another communist country in the East. He had to show he was still tough on communism.

Many State Department officials pointed out that Ho was more of a nationalist than a communist. There were many Vietnamese who were not communists, but nevertheless supported Ho Chi Minh. Dean Acheson said this was irrelevant. However, by ignoring the fact that Ho was fighting for his country's independence, the Americans always continued to see Vietnam in Cold War terms – meaning that they dangerously misunderstood the nature of the war.

Historian Vivienne Sanders, in *The USA and Vietnam, 1945–1975* (1998), quotes a far-sighted Defence Department official, who said in 1950 about Truman's continued support for the French:

'We are gradually increasing our stake in the outcome of the struggle … we are dangerously close to the point of being so deeply committed that we may find ourselves completely committed to direct intervention. These situations, unfortunately, have a way of snowballing.'

Even though Truman gave financial aid to the French, he did not want military involvement or to send troops to South East Asia. He was more concerned with European affairs in the 1940s and Korea in the 1950s.

How did American involvement increase under Eisenhower?

By 1953, the Vietminh had 250,000 regular soldiers and a militia of nearly two million. Also, their promises of education, healthcare and land did much to win over the ordinary people. They were also getting supplies from the Chinese. The Vietminh were numerous, popular and well-supplied.

By 1954, France was losing the battle at Dien Bien Phu where the Vietminh surrounded their forces. There was debate in the US government about what to do and whether Vietnam mattered to US security. Dulles and Vice-President Nixon wanted to bomb the Vietminh, but 'Ike' refused. He had been elected partly on his promise to end the war in Korea, so the American public would not stand for US troops being sent to another war in Asia so soon after the ceasefire. Congress made it clear they would not support involvement and, when 'Ike' sounded out America's allies, he found that they also refused to back the idea of intervention.

Eisenhower, though, worried that if Indo-China fell to communism the surrounding countries would also fall, like a row of dominoes. He believed the USA had to give some support to the French. Therefore, he continued Truman's policy of financial support but he also sent 300 US personnel to help France as the Military Assistance Advisory Group. This put the first American personnel in South East Asia.

In spite of American help, in May 1954 the French surrendered with 7,200 dead and 11,000 taken prisoner. A peace settlement was agreed between the involved powers at Geneva. Under the Geneva Accords 1954, Indo-China was split into four: Laos, Cambodia, and North and South Vietnam, which were divided along the 17th Parallel.

It was intended to hold elections in all four countries in 1956 and to reunite the two Vietnams, but the USA was afraid if they held elections Ho Chi Minh would win. 'Ike' admitted in his diary that Ho Chi Minh would probably get 80 per cent of the vote. Therefore, the USA refused to sign the Accords and backed Ngo Dinh Diem as leader of South Vietnam, with North Vietnam being led by Ho Chi Minh. The USA invited South Vietnam to join SEATO and stepped up the amount of aid to $500 million a year. More advisors were sent, in contravention of the Geneva Accords. By 1960, there were more than 1,500 US personnel in South East Asia. As the anonymous diplomat had warned, the USA was gradually increasing its stake in Vietnam.

Diem was not a popular Prime Minister and even the USA admitted he was only the best of a bad bunch. He was Catholic in a country of Buddhists and gave jobs to his family. He made no attempt to win peasant support, as Ho did. Corruption and torture of prisoners became routine. 'Ike' urged Diem to introduce land reform to gain the support of the people, but Diem ignored him.

Many people in South Vietnam demanded the elections they had been promised and actively opposed the government of Diem. The opposition to Diem consisted of many groups and was known as the National Front for the Liberation of South Vietnam, or NLF. The Communists largely formed the military wing of the NLF, as they were the strongest group. These South Vietnamese communists were known as the Vietcong (VC). They were supported and equipped by Ho Chi Minh who, in turn, received support and help from the Chinese and the Soviet Union.

This communist backing convinced Eisenhower that this was, indeed, a Cold War conflict. His belief in the Domino Theory persuaded him that it was necessary to support Diem. Above all, Ho and the NLF were Vietnamese nationalists. They had not fought the French and the Japanese, and the French again, simply to come under American control. This misunderstanding of the nationalist nature of the Vietnam conflict was fatal for Eisenhower and his successors.

Why was the involvement in South East Asia intensified under Kennedy?

Under President Kennedy, foreign policy was very much controlled from the White House. He was more interested in foreign than domestic affairs. Military spending grew dramatically and Kennedy believed he also had to take a firm stand in South East Asia, for both foreign and domestic reasons. Having made Republican 'weakness' an election issue, he could hardly do less than they had, but his own views on the Cold War led him to increase American involvement.

Like Eisenhower, Kennedy also believed in the Domino Theory, especially in places like Vietnam. He believed that Third World areas were

Ngo Dinh Diem (1901–1963)
Aristocratic and catholic politician who served in the French-backed governments until 1933. He rejoined politics in 1954 as Prime Minister. In 1955, he declared himself President but refused to hold the elections as proposed at Geneva. His American-backed government was corrupt and dominated by his family. His failure to reform led to his assassination in 1963.

where the Cold War would now be fought. He was a strong supporter of the policy of containment, having entered Congress in 1946 and voted in support of the Truman Doctrine in his first days as a politician. In his own inauguration speech, in January 1963, he promised to 'bear any burden, support any friend and oppose any foe' to ensure liberty: Vietnam was an arena to put this into practice. JFK's advisors also encouraged further involvement in Vietnam. Robert McNamara, Secretary of Defence, was convinced that US military superiority would win and he advised sending 40,000 troops. Dean Rusk, Kennedy's Secretary of State, and National Security Advisor McGeorge Bundy also felt the USA should stand up to communism in South East Asia, as did the Joint Chiefs of Staff. No one was seriously suggesting to Kennedy that he might pull back from Eisenhower's position.

Like Eisenhower, Kennedy did not want to get the USA militarily involved in Vietnam, so he refused even though he was under pressure from the army to send troops. More money and more advisors were sent to help Diem so that, by 1963, 23,000 US personnel were in the country. Simply by being there it meant the US personnel were likely to get more involved.

Kennedy initially found himself involved in the affairs of Laos, where a civil war had also broken out, partly due to American backing for anti-government forces in the country. Kennedy sent some military supplies through Thailand, and sent advisors to Laos itself. An agreement, reached at Geneva in 1962, established a neutral government in Laos, but the USA continued to send arms and supplies as they felt that strengthening anti-Communist forces in Laos would improve their position in Vietnam.

How did military strategy increase involvement?

One of the difficulties preventing success against the NLF and VC was that the Army of the Republic of Vietnam (ARVN) and their American advisors were fighting a war against guerrillas. To combat the terrorist tactics used by the NLF and the VC, Kennedy wanted a policy of 'flexible response'. This entailed using several different methods of fighting, not just one, with particular emphasis on Special Forces such as the Green Berets. They were to train the South Vietnamese in counter-insurgency (i.e. how to defeat terrorists).

One policy used was 'strategic hamlets'. This entailed rounding people up and putting them into villages fortified and protected by the military to isolate them from the VC. However, this created resentment against the government and these hamlets could be infiltrated or taken over by VC guerrillas without the ARVN being aware.

Bombers and helicopters were sent to help, but the American crews often ended up doing the fighting.

The policies being pursued by the ARVN and the Americans were not very effective in military terms or in terms of gaining support from the people of South Vietnam. The VC, on the other hand, treated the people well, paying them for any supplies they took. Like Eisenhower, Kennedy failed to get Diem to appreciate the need to win the support of the people. In May 1963, there were widespread protests against Diem, including one by a Buddhist priest who set himself alight to show his opposition to the Diem regime.

In the same year, a plot to assassinate Diem was hatched by men within his own government. The CIA knew the plan, as did the American ambassador in Saigon, but they saw him as a liability so did not stop it. Diem was murdered just a few weeks before Kennedy himself was assassinated in Dallas. General Westmoreland, the American military commander in Vietnam, said that this involvement in assassination made the USA morally obliged to stay in the country to sort out the mess.

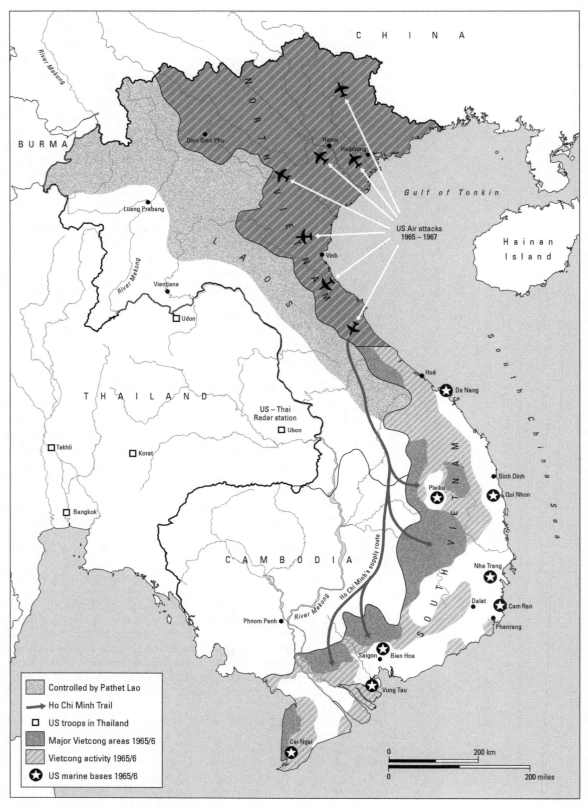

US involvement in Indo-China, 1965–1967

By 1963, there were 16,700 Special Forces troops and advisors in South Vietnam. There were American helicopters, planes and boats. The number of US personnel killed in 1963 was 489. Step by step, three presidents had increased American involvement in the war in South Vietnam.

Why did Vietnam become a military conflict under President Johnson?

The death of Kennedy provided a perfect opportunity for America to withdraw from the conflict. Instead, the new president, Lyndon Johnson (LBJ), immediately increased the number of personnel in South Vietnam by 30 per cent. Why?

The attitude of the Johnson Administration towards the growing involvement in Vietnam was made clear when Secretary of State, Robert McNamara, said: 'We want an independent, non-communist Vietnam.' To a strongly-held belief in the Domino Theory, Johnson added the belief that the USA had to stand by its allies such as South Vietnam because, if it did not, no one would trust it again. A retreat from Vietnam would send a signal to the world of American retreat elsewhere.

Johnson's own interest was really in domestic policy and the creation of the 'Great Society'. He believed that the United States could free South Vietnam from the Communist threat and then reform it just as he was reforming America. The reality, on the ground, was that the Vietcong controlled 40 per cent of the Vietnamese countryside and they were not going to give this up without a fight.

Having inherited Kennedy's Cabinet, Johnson also inherited Kennedy's advisors. They continued to support a military solution to the problem of South East Asia. Even when some cabinet members started to have second thoughts in the mid-1960s about American policy, LBJ's personality discouraged opposition. They were afraid to tell him the truth or disagree when he said he did not want to be 'the first president to lose a war'.

What was the impact of the Tonkin Incident on US policy in Vietnam?

At first, Johnson continued JFK's policies of sending aid and advisors, although the numbers increased greatly. In 1964, things changed. On 2 August, North Vietnamese patrol boats fired on the 'USS Maddox' while it was on patrol in the Gulf of Tonkin, but planes from the carrier 'Ticonderoga' drove them off. Two days later, the 'Maddox' and the 'C. Turner Joy' were again patrolling (a **euphemism** for spying on North Vietnamese coastal installations) when they reported being fired on by the North Vietnamese. They returned fire, but later investigations were unclear whether they had been attacked or had been mistaken. The incident gave Johnson the perfect opportunity he had been waiting for to escalate American involvement in the war.

In response to his request, Congress passed an area resolution. The Tonkin Resolution allowed LBJ to take 'all necessary steps including the use of military force' in South East Asia to protect US interests. It also allowed him to take the war to the North Vietnamese who were supplying the VC. By Johnson emphasising the attack and not the provocative patrols, the resolution easily passed both Houses (416–0 and 88–2).

The war now began to escalate dramatically. A US base at Pleiku was attacked, in February 1965, killing eight American servicemen and leading to air strikes on North Vietnam. In March 1965, US marines, the first combat troops sent to Vietnam, landed at Da Nang. The USA was slowly but surely taking over the fighting from the South Vietnamese. (By the end of 1965, there were 184,000 US military personnel in Vietnam.)

Euphemism: A polite word or expression which you can use instead of one that might offend or upset people (e.g. 'to pass on' is a euphemism for 'to die').

1. Why did Truman and Eisenhower support the French in Indo-China?

2. According to the 'Quagmire Theory', the USA got sucked into the conflict in Vietnam almost without realising it was happening. How far would you agree with this explanation of Kennedy and Johnson's increasing involvement in Vietnam 1961–1965?

6.7 A study in depth: Who was more responsible for US involvement in Vietnam: JFK or LBJ?

■ To what extent did Kennedy commit the US to involvement in Vietnam?

■ Did Johnson merely follow Kennedy's policies on Vietnam?

Framework of Events

1954	Geneva Peace Accords; temporary division of French Indo-China into four states
1956	Supported by the US, anti-communist Ngo Dinh Diem becomes leader of South Vietnam
1960	National Liberation Front (NFL) of South Vietnam is born; beginning of communist attempt to overthrow South Vietnam Government
1961	JFK increases number of US military advisers to South Vietnam
1962	International agreement of Laos, which declares that country 'neutral'
	Strategic Hamlets Programme begins
1963	Assassination of Ngo Dinh Diem
	Assassination of Kennedy three weeks later
	LBJ takes over US presidency
1964	Gulf of Tonkin incident and resolution
1965	Operation Rolling Thunder begins
	US ground troops sent to South Vietnam
1968	Communist Tet Offensive in South Vietnam
	US troop level reaches 565,000
	LBJ announces he will not seek re-election as president
	LBJ begins negotiations with North Vietnam

THE Vietnam War bitterly divided the USA in a way no other conflict had done since the Civil War of 1861–5. Over two and a half million Americans served in Vietnam. Fifty-eight thousand were killed. It was the first time in US history that America had lost a war.

Why did the USA become involved in a conflict 10,000 miles from the USA? Ever since the 1960s, contemporaries and historians have debated who was responsible for US military involvement. Did JFK lay the foundations for involvement? Had JFK lived would the involvement of US ground troops have been avoided? Was it really Lyndon Johnson's war?

Depending upon whom you believe, Vietnam destroyed the presidencies of both men. The plot of Oliver Stone's film, *JFK*, suggests that Kennedy was assassinated because he wanted to pull out of Vietnam. Johnson's presidency was clearly adversely affected. His decision not to seek re-election as president in 1968 was directly due to Vietnam.

Lyndon Baines Johnson (1908–1973)
He served as vice president until Kennedy's death, when he assumed the presidency (1963–69). In many ways Johnson's presidency was a continuation of JFK's. 'LBJ' became the most reformist president since the New Deal of the 1930s. He was also able to do more for African-American rights than any president had done since the US Civil War. LBJ's most controversial act was the commitment of ground troops to South Vietnam. So great was the financial cost of engagement in a vicious guerrilla ground war and the opposition to the war in the USA that, in 1968, LBJ decided not to seek re-election as president.

To what extent did Kennedy commit the US to involvement in Vietnam?

Kennedy and Indo-China in 1961

In his inaugural address as US president, made on 20 January 1961, JFK stated:

> 'Let every nation know … that we shall pay any price, bear any burden, meet any hardship, support any friend, oppose any foe, in order to assure the survival and success of liberty.'

To understand JFK's view towards Vietnam one must remember that he became president at the height of the Cold War. It was widely believed by decision makers in Washington DC at the time that the USA faced a communist conspiracy to extend communism across the globe. In this endeavour, the USSR, Communist China and North Vietnam all acted together. Opposing communism in Indo-China was part of a worldwide conflict.

The importance of the USA in the global conflict against communism was made clear by the outgoing President Dwight Eisenhower. In 1954, Eisenhower had stated:

> 'You have a row of dominoes set up, you knock over the first one, and what will happen to the last one is the certainty that it will go over very quickly … When we come to a possible sequence of events, the loss of Indo-China, of Burma [Myanmar], of Thailand, of Malaya and Indonesia following.'

Indo-China

This map shows Indo-China in 1954, after the Geneva Accords.

■ Indo-China is a region of South East Asia, once ruled by France until 1954. Between 1946 and 1954, France fought a major war against Vietnamese nationalists who wanted independence from France. By 1954, France had lost 78,000 people in the war.

■ In 1954, in Geneva, Switzerland, an agreement was made between the USA, USSR, China, Britain and France about the future of Indo-China.

■ Indo-China was divided into four states. Two states became monarchies: Laos and Cambodia. However, from the late 1950s, communist forces attempted to take over eastern Laos.

■ Vietnam was divided into two states. North Vietnam was communist and ruled by Ho Chi Minh. South Vietnam was non-communist. It was ruled by Ngo Dinh Diem, who acted as a dictator.

■ The Geneva Peace Accords (Agreement) planned to have elections throughout Vietnam in 1956 to decide its future. Under US pressure, Diem cancelled the elections. President Eisenhower feared Ho Chi Minh would win and create a united, communist Vietnam.

■ In 1960, communists in the South created the NLF, National Liberation Front. The USA called them Viet Cong (VC). They planned a guerrilla war, with Northern assistance, to unite Vietnam as a communist state.

In addition, when Eisenhower briefed Kennedy on foreign policy in 1961, he stated that the most important issue facing the USA in the conflict with communism at that time was the communist attempt to take over Laos. In fact, for most of his presidency, Kennedy spent more time dealing with Laos than South Vietnam. It was only in 1963 that Vietnam became a more dominant problem.

The case against holding Kennedy responsible for US military involvement in Vietnam

Ever since JFK's assassination, speculation has developed about exactly what he was willing to do to protect South Vietnam from a communist takeover.

Robert F. Kennedy, JFK's younger brother, who was attorney general between 1961 and 1963, said in a conversation in 1967:

'We saw the position the French were in [in 1954] and my brother was determined early that we would never get into that position.'

General Maxwell Taylor, who led several US missions to South Vietnam between 1961 and 1963, made a similar comment regarding JFK. After Taylor requested that the USA send 8000 ground troops to aid South Vietnam in 1961, he stated:

'I don't recall anyone strongly against this plan except one man, the President. It was really the President's personal conviction that US ground troops shouldn't go in.'

Some historians also believe that JFK was unwilling to make a large military commitment. Arthur M. Schlesinger, in *Robert Kennedy and His Times* (1978), believes JFK occupied a middle position between two opposing groups of advisers on Vietnam. On the one hand, there were 'hawks' such as the head of the **Joint Chiefs of Staff**, General Lyman Lemnitzer. He wanted strong military support for South Vietnam. On the other hand, there were those like US Ambassador to India J.K. Galbraith, who wanted a phased withdrawal of US support for Vietnam. This group tended to support a solution similar to that achieved over Laos in 1962. In that year US envoy, William Averell Harriman, was able to get an agreement with the USSR. Both sides agreed on the 'neutralisation' of Laos. This meant the creation of a coalition government that contained communist and non-communist elements. According to Arthur Schlesinger, Kennedy wanted a solution to the problem in South Vietnam that would avoid a large military commitment by the USA. He wanted to support the South Vietnamese Government in defeating the communist guerrillas.

On JFK's accession to presidency, there were 800 military advisers in South Vietnam. He increased this number to 3000 by December 1961, to 10,000 in 1962 and to 16,000 by the time of his assassination. Advisers included a contingent of Green Berets – an elite group of special forces trained to fight guerrilla war. JFK hoped that such forces could help defeat communism in **Third World** countries while avoiding a direct military confrontation with the USSR. In addition, JFK increased military aid to the South Vietnamese army (ARVN). In many ways, JFK was buying time. In 1961 and 1962, Vietnam was still a sideshow in US foreign policy. Crises over Berlin and Cuba absorbed much more attention.

According to historian Lawrence Freedman in his book *Kennedy's Wars* (2000), JFK planned to withdraw US advisers once he had won the 1964 presidential election. Senator Mike Mansfield remembers JFK saying, 'I can't depart until 1965 – after I'm re-elected.' When asked by his aide Ken

---

General Maxwell Taylor (1901–87)
Taylor was a Second-World-War general who led the 101st Airborne Brigade at the Battle of Arnhem. Between 1961 and 1965, he was a personal military adviser on Vietnam. He made several fact-finding missions to South Vietnam to appraise the situation. In the autumn of 1961, Taylor, with economic adviser Walt Rostow, visited Saigon and reported on the chaotic situation in South Vietnam. Taylor suggested sending ground troops. His wish was finally granted by LBJ in March 1965.

Joint Chiefs of Staff: the leading generals and admirals of the US armed forces.

O'Donnell how the USA would be able to withdraw from South Vietnam, JFK stated, 'Easy, put a government in there that will ask us to leave.'

Throughout 1961 and 1962, the Kennedy administration consistently stated that Ngo Dinh Diem was the strong man of Vietnam, who had to be supported in order to defeat the communist uprising. However, by 1963, Diem's regime had become very unpopular. He was a Roman Catholic in charge of a predominantly Buddhist country. His government was dominated by Catholics and was noted for corruption. Instead of using US aid to fight the communists, he used it to gain support for his own government.

Strategic Hamlets Programme: villagers in rural areas were rounded up and put in hamlets to isolate them from communist influences.

In 1962, the US suggested the creation of the **Strategic Hamlets Programme**. A similar programme had been used by the British in Malaya, where they successfully defeated a communist uprising in the 1950s. However, Diem and his brother Ngo Dinh Nhu did not create hamlets in areas threatened by communists but in areas where they could gain more political support. They believed the USA would always back them, no matter what they did, because the alternative was a communist victory.

By the spring of 1963, JFK's advisers were suggesting that Diem was in fact the cause of growing communist influence rather than the solution.

In November 1963, generals of ARVN, with CIA help, overthrew Diem, killing him and his brother in the process. This was part of JFK's plan to find a strong South Vietnamese Government that would allow the US to eventually withdraw.

In assessing what JFK might have done had he lived beyond 22 November 1963, several historians have passed comment. Lawrence Freedman, in *Kennedy's Wars* (2000), believes that JFK's advisers were badly divided about what to do in South Vietnam and that Kennedy's policy was aimed at healing rifts among them. Hugh Brogan, in *Kennedy* (1996), states:

> All that can be said is that Kennedy would have been more reluctant than Johnson in accepting a [military commitment] and might well have looked sooner, harder and more successfully for an alternative.

In *The Imperial Presidency* (1973), Arthur Schlesinger helps to explain why. In sending 16,000 advisers, JFK had merely followed actions taken by previous presidents in foreign policy. Also, by November 1963, only 100 US servicemen had been killed in South Vietnam. To most Americans, Vietnam was still a little-known sideshow.

The case for holding Kennedy responsible for US involvement in Vietnam

JFK fervently believed that the US faced a global communist threat. He accepted Eisenhower's 'domino theory'. JFK was faced with a communist uprising in a 'friendly country' and could not afford defeat. US prestige across the world was at stake. Only in this global context can JFK's actions be understood.

Even in 'neutral' Laos, JFK used the CIA to support anti-communist forces. Supplies were flown in, by CIA-owned 'Air America', from Thailand. In addition, US B52 bombers attacked communist positions in central and eastern Laos between 1962 and 1963. These actions were done secretly without Congressional approval.

Kennedy was determined to use South Vietnam as a testing ground for new theories on how to combat communist aggression. He placed great hope in counter-insurgency forces, which would fight guerrilla forces on their own terms. The Green Berets were the force that would be used across the globe for this purpose. According to historian Stephen E. Ambrose, in *Rise to Globalism: American Foreign Policy Since 1938* (1971), 'Kennedy was prepared to do anything to prevent a Viet Cong victory.'

JFK/LBJ advisers on Vietnam

The title 'The best and the brightest' was given to the members of the JFK/LBJ administrations because they were recruited from top universities and large businesses.

Dean Rusk: Secretary of State

- Rusk was a highly intelligent man, who had studied for three years at Oxford University before joining the State Department during President Truman's administration (1945–53).
- He was former Under Secretary of State whom JFK chose because he thought he would be a good second-in-command. JFK wanted to be his own Secretary of State. During the Kennedy years, Rusk was sidelined as JFK tended to get advice from his brother, Robert F. Kennedy. Rusk was given more freedom to operate under LBJ, but he was never in the position where he could have offered independent advice. In the debates on Vietnam, he was overshadowed first by Robert Kennedy and later by McGeorge Bundy.

Robert McNamara: Secretary of Defense

- McNamara had attended the University of California at Berkeley and also Harvard University. After one month as chief executive of the Ford Motor Company, he left his post, in January 1961, to become Defense Secretary. He became JFK's and LBJ's major adviser on Vietnam.
- With a razor-sharp mind and strong personality, McNamara became a central figure in developing US policy on Vietnam. Kept in the post by Johnson, he virtually ran US policy on Vietnam until August 1968 when he resigned to become president of the World Bank. He was described as aggressive and as being characterised by toughness, quickness, fluency, competence, incorruptibility and a force of personality.

McGeorge Bundy: National Security Adviser

- Bundy came from a very wealthy family in Boston, Massachusetts. He attended the best private schools: the Dexter School (where JFK also attended) and Groton (where Franklin D. Roosevelt had been a pupil). He then studied at Yale University. At 30 years old, he became a lecturer in Government at Harvard University.
- Although Bundy was a supporter of the Republican Party, he was strongly attracted to JFK's policies and willing to join his government. He was appointed National Security Adviser from 1961 to 1966, when he resigned to become president of the Ford Foundation. As National Security Adviser, he usually worked a 12—hour day and played a central role in all JFK's foreign policy decisions over Berlin, Cuba and Vietnam. His brother, William P. Bundy, Assistant Secretary of State for Far Eastern Affairs, led the Working Group in 1965 that advised LBJ to begin bombing North Vietnam.

The main strategy of the Kennedy administration until 1963 was to support Ngo Dinh Diem at all costs. He was believed to be the strong man, capable of defeating communism. Unfortunately, such a policy backfired. Diem was immensely unpopular. His leadership was in many ways the reason why the Viet Cong (VC) gained influence in 1961 and 1962. Diem feared a military coup against him by ARVN generals and was very suspicious of any general who won military victories. Instead of fighting the VC, ARVN generals tried to avoid conflict at all costs. A spectacular example was the Battle of Ap Bac in January 1963 when 2,000 ARVN troops with US helicopter support were ordered not to move forward and attack 350 lightly armed VC. Instead they were ordered to change their mission to one of blocking positions – a decision that had serious consequences.

Within the USA, opposition to Diem's regime came from journalists such as Neil Sheehan of *United Press International* and David Halberstam of *The New York Times*. The latter noted:

> [Diem] became more convinced than ever that it had its ally [USA] in a corner, that it could do anything it wanted, that continued support would be guaranteed because of the communist threat [and that] the US could not suddenly admit that it had made a vast mistake.

It was Halberstam who first put forward the 'quagmire theory' – the idea that the USA, without forethought, had been sucked into giving military support to Diem.

A key turning point came in August 1963 with the appointment of Henry Cabot Lodge as US Ambassador to South Vietnam. Lodge had been defeated by JFK in the Senate election of 1952. He had also been Nixon's vice-presidential candidate in 1960. From the moment Lodge arrived in Saigon, on 22 August 1963, he was convinced Diem had to be removed. Nationwide protests by Buddhists had brought the country to the point of revolt. From late August to November, Lodge worked with ARVN generals to remove Diem. On 1 November 1963, Diem was overthrown.

Diem's fall, however, led to increased instability in the Southern Government. Diem was first replaced by General Minh and then, in February 1964, by General Khahn. They both formed weak governments. Instead of improving the situation, JFK's policy had made matters worse.

When JFK was assassinated three weeks later, his Vietnam policy was in a mess. Although JFK had ruled out military action against North Vietnam in 1963, Lawrence Freedman in *Kennedy's Wars* (2000) suggests that, in 1964, he might have been forced to change his mind as the military situation deteriorated in the South. This is also the view held by several of today's historians. Historian William H. Chafe notes, in *The Unfinished Journey: America Since World War II* (1999):

> Kennedy and his advisers had charted a course that step-by-step involved the United States inextricably deeper in the Vietnam tragedy. As Ambassador Maxwell Taylor later recalled, 'Diem's overthrow set in motion a sequence of crises, political and military, over the next two years which eventually forced President Johnson in 1965 to choose between accepting defeat or introducing US combat troops.'

Historian James N. Giglio states, in *The Presidency of John F. Kennedy* (1991):

> Given what we know of President Kennedy, it is difficult to conceive of his pulling out of Vietnam without a reasonable honourable settlement.

So was Lyndon Johnson put in an impossible position over Vietnam when he became president on 22 November 1963?

Did Johnson merely follow Kennedy's policies on Vietnam?

When LBJ became president he did possess some knowledge of Vietnam. As vice president, he had visited South Vietnam during a tour of Asia. However, the situation was still regarded as a sideshow in the early months of Johnson's presidency and he concentrated on enacting domestic reform such as the Civil Rights Act and the Great Society Programme.

Nevertheless, it was difficult for LBJ to change Kennedy's policies on Vietnam. He had, after all, inherited Kennedy's foreign policy advisers. On

26 November 1963, a National Security Action Memorandum (NSAM) stated:

> The central object of the US to South Vietnam [is] to assist the people and government of that country to win their contest against the externally directed and supported communist conspiracy.

So, from November 1963 to the summer of 1964, US policy followed the line of offering financial and military aid to the South Vietnamese Government. Johnson openly stated that he would carry on JFK's work. He said:

> 'I swore to myself that I would carry on. When I took over I often felt as if President Kennedy was sitting in the room looking at me.'

However, by the time Johnson decided not to seek re-election, on 31 March 1968, the situation was transformed. There were 565,000 US ground troops stationed in South Vietnam. The US air force flew bombing missions against targets in North Vietnam. General Westmoreland, US commander in Vietnam, was requesting 200,000 extra troops. The war was costing the US $60 million a day and the USA was bitterly divided about supporting a war that had cost over 35,000 lives and wounded 175,000.

There is considerable evidence to suggest that LBJ would commit the USA to a major war in Vietnam. Historian William H. Chafe, in *The Unfinished Journey: America Since World War II* (1999), suggests that Johnson's Texan background made him determined not to be the first president to lose a war.

By mid-1964, the military and political situation in South Vietnam had deteriorated so much that LBJ's advisers feared the state might collapse. The USA could not afford to lose South Vietnam to communism at the height of the Cold War.

Like JFK, Johnson was a firm believer in the 'domino theory' and the need to stand up to communist aggression. On 27 April 1965, he made the comment:

> 'We are resisting aggression, and as long as aggressors attack, we shall stay there [Vietnam] and resist them – whether we make friends or lose friends.'

Yet, as late as 12 August 1964, Johnson was telling the American Bar Association:

> 'They [the South Vietnamese] call upon us to supply American boys to do the job that Asian boys should do. They ask us to take reckless actions which might risk the lives of millions. Moreover, such action would offer no solution at all to the real problems of Vietnam.'

Why did Johnson decide to escalate the war, between February 1964 and March 1965?

There are a number of differing interpretations as to why Johnson decided to escalate the war. One interpretation involves the presidential election of 1964 when Johnson faced an extreme anti-communist opponent in the Republican candidate Barry Goldwater.

At the height of the campaign, between 2 August and 4 August, an incident occurred in the Gulf of Tonkin, off the coast of North Vietnam. On 2 August, two US destroyers, the USS Maddox and the USS C. Turner Joy were allegedly attacked by North Vietnamese torpedo boats. A second, alleged attack occurred on 4 August. There is considerable confusion even today about what actually happened. In the confidential Department of Defense documents, the **Pentagon Papers**, released in 1971, there is a strong suggestion that no actual attacks took place. Johnson, however, used the incident to intervene directly in the Vietnam War. For most of the period since 1963, Secretary of Defense Robert McNamara had run the war. Johnson used the incident to get Congress to pass the South East Asia (or Gulf of Tonkin) Resolution. As historian Arthur M. Schlesinger notes, in *The Imperial Presidency* (1973), this was 'rushed through Congress in a stampede of misinformation and misconception, if not of deliberate deception'. Schlesinger and others such as journalist Neil Sheehan, whose book on Vietnam is called *A Bright Shining Lie: John Paul Vann and America in Vietnam* (1989), see Johnson as deliberately misleading Congress and the US public into escalating the war in Vietnam.

The Gulf of Tonkin Resolution gave the US President powers to wage limited war abroad. Initially, Johnson authorised air attacks against specific targets in North Vietnam. In February 1965, this policy was broadened into Operation Rolling Thunder. This was a systematic attempt to bomb North Vietnam and supply lines through Laos known as the Ho Chi Minh trail. Some historians believe that this was the turning point. Rowland Evans and Robert Novak state in their book *Lyndon Johnson and the Exercise of Power* (1966):

> From that moment the war that had been impersonal, distant and secondary became for Lyndon Johnson the consuming passion of his presidency. It became, more than any other war in the 20th century for any other president, a personal war.

On 8 March 1965, following a Viet Cong attack on a US air base at Pleiku, South Vietnam, Johnson committed ground troops for the first time. Three and a half thousand US Marines landed at Da Nang. By April, the numbers had risen to 18,000. On 28 July 1965, Johnson announced that troop levels would rise to 125,000. They had reached 200,000 by the end of the year.

Should Johnson be blamed personally for direct US military involvement?

To an extent, LBJ was a victim of circumstance. In his biography of Johnson, entitled *Big Daddy from the Pedernales* (1986), historian Paul K. Conkin notes:

> Johnson's policies flowed consistently from a series of decisions made by three earlier presidents [Truman, Eisenhower, Kennedy]. Continuity, not new departures, marked his choices, not because of a lack of experience on his part but because of his own belief and values. He wanted above all else to contain the Vietnam conflict.

It must be remembered that it took LBJ 18 months before he eventually committed ground troops to South Vietnam. In the period from November 1963 to March 1965, considerable debate took place among his advisers about what to do. Throughout this critical period, Johnson received pessimistic reports about the quality of ARVN and its inability to prevent communist infiltration of South Vietnam.

Johnson set up a Working Group to study possible options in South Vietnam. It was chaired by McGeorge Bundy's brother, William P. Bundy, and contained members from the Department of Defense, the Central Intelligence Agency, the State Department and the Joint Chiefs of Staff. William Bundy reported the findings of the Working Group to LBJ. He explained that the South Vietnamese Government was very weak. He advocated bombing the North as a way of taking pressure off the South

Defense Secretary Robert McNamara and President Johnson after receiving information of new problems in Vietnam in 1964.

Vietnamese Government. In 'The War in Vietnam' in *The Johnson Years* (1981), historian George C. Herring notes:

> The United States [was] primarily responsible for escalating the war [as a] desperate attempt to stave off the collapse of South Vietnam from within.

What Johnson and his major advisers failed to comprehend was the limited impact superior US military technology would have on an enemy determined to unite their own country.

The only dissenting voice from among the inner circle of advisers came from Under Secretary of State George Ball. He thought the commitment of US ground troops would be disastrous. He concluded that once the US was committed to militarily defending South Vietnam they were there for the long haul. His suggestion that up to 500,000 troops would have to be deployed was met with astonishment by the other advisers. However, historians Leslie K. Gelb and Richard H. Betts, in *The Irony of Vietnam: The System Worked* (1979), claim that LBJ and his advisers knew exactly what they were getting into when they escalated the war in February and March 1965.

In retrospect, it is perhaps easy to see the folly of the decision of Johnson and his advisers. However, as historian George Herring states, in 'The War in Vietnam', in *The Johnson Years* (1981):

> It must be stressed that the situation he inherited in Vietnam lent itself to no easy solution – perhaps no solution at all. Those who argue that a more decisive use of military power and a deeper commitment to negotiations would have brought the desired results conveniently overlook the harsh realities of the conflict: (1) a determined, fanatical enemy (2) the threat of Soviet and Chinese intervention (3) a weak ally (4) domestic consensus which wanted success in Vietnam without paying a high price.

Johnson and his administration are often criticised for having made crucial decisions on escalation without notifying Congress. The escalation into a major conflict, involving US troops, was done in an atmosphere of misinformation about what was actually happening. Only after the publication of the Pentagon Papers in 1971, did the degree of deception and misinformation become apparent. On this point, LBJ and his advisers should be held accountable.

Who was responsible?

Whether you believe the US stumbled into the quagmire of a land war in Vietnam or consciously and deliberately chose to do so depends upon the historical evidence available. However, the context of the 1960s needs to be taken into consideration when making your final decision. The USA was involved in a global struggle against communism. It was widely believed that Ho Chi Minh in Hanoi worked closely with Chairman Mao in China and the Soviet leadership. Any failure to stand up to communism in Vietnam would have worldwide consequences. The USA had already stood up to communist aggression in Europe in the late 1940s over Berlin. It had also done so in Asia in the Korean War. The war in Vietnam was a continuation of the same policy.

The arrogance of American power at the time also needs to be borne in mind. The USA, with its vastly superior military equipment, thought it could easily defeat an economically backward South East Asian state in North Vietnam. The USA greatly underestimated the nature of guerrilla warfare where lightly-armed troops could be very effective against US forces.

If US military involvement had been kept to aerial bombing, public opinion may have supported the war longer. By committing **conscript** ground troops, the loss of American lives in Vietnam helped turn public opinion against the war by early 1968.

President Johnson later assessed what had gone wrong. Historian Vaughn Davis Bornet, in *The Presidency of Lyndon B. Johnson* (1983), notes:

> President Johnson admitted that two 'key mistakes' had been made on Vietnam. 'Kennedy should have had more than 16,000 military advisers

US marines preparing to evacuate an area after an 11-day long battle.

Conscript: a person forced to do compulsory military service.

there in the early 1960s. And then I made the situation worse by waiting 18 months before putting more men in. By then the war was lost.'

This would suggest that, rather than showing reluctance in going to war, Johnson believed that more effective military action earlier would have succeeded.

Who was more responsible for US involvement in Vietnam: JFK or LBJ?

1. Read the following extract and answer the question.

Johnson and his advisers insisted that by intervening in Vietnam they were defending vital interests of the United States. It resurrected the 'domino theory' first publicised by Eisenhower in 1954, warning that the fall of South Vietnam would cause the loss of all South East Asia with disastrous economic, political, and strategic consequences for the United States. Johnson and his Secretary of State, Dean Rusk, repeatedly emphasised that the failure to stand up to aggression would encourage further aggression, upsetting the international order the United States had established since World War II and perhaps provoking a third world war.

Adapted from G.C. Herring, 'The War in Vietnam', in *The Johnson Years: Foreign Policy, the Great Society, and the White House*, edited by Robert A. Divine, University of Texas Press, 1981, p 28.

Using the information in the extract above, and from this section, explain why the USA increased its military commitment in Vietnam between 1961 and 1965.

2. 'Johnson, not Kennedy, was responsible for US military involvement in Vietnam by 1965.' How far do you agree with this statement?

6.8 Why did the USA fail to defeat communism in South East Asia, 1965–1973?

Defoliants: Chemicals used on trees and plants that make all their leaves fall off. This made it harder for guerrilla fighters to hide in the forests.

Napalm: A type of petroleum jelly which is used to make bombs that burn and destroy people and plants.

The number of American soldiers in Vietnam rose steadily from 200,000 in 1965 to 543,000 by 1969. Even though America largely took over the fighting from the ARVN, the war did not go any better. In fact, the way in which the war itself was fought often meant even greater involvement: if a policy failed they had to do more to make up losses. Therefore the intensity of the war increased. The desire to close down the Ho Chi Minh Trail, along which supplies were fed from North to South, led to Operation Rolling Thunder, a bombing campaign against North Vietnam. Although between 1965 and 1968 more bombs were dropped on North Vietnam than all the bombs dropped in the Second World War, they failed to have a significant effect. In the cities of North Vietnam production was moved out of Hanoi and spread around the country so that the raids did minimal damage. On the Trail, the North Vietnamese and Vietcong simply built another road in another part of the jungle.

Free-fire zones were designated, in which anyone could be a target. New technologies were brought into the fighting. For example, **defoliants** such as Agent Orange were sprayed to try and destroy the jungle cover of the VC, and **napalm** was used in raids. There was a policy of 'pacification' which meant that, where a village was suspected of helping the VC, it was destroyed. Because they were not fighting an easily identifiable enemy, success began to be measured by 'body count' and 'kill ratio'. A dead Vietnamese was presumed to be a dead VC, whether they were or not.

Understandably, rather than winning the 'hearts and minds' of the Vietnamese peasants, these kind of policies turned many of them against the Americans and pushed them into support for the Vietcong. Young American soldiers, drafted into the war, could not understand how they were not welcomed as liberating heroes as their fathers had been in Europe. Morale in the American army worsened, with drug taking and desertions becoming serious problems. Violence against civilians worsened most horrifically at My Lai in 1968 where 347 unarmed men, women and children were killed by American soldiers (see panel).

Yet all the time the generals were telling the President, and the President was telling the public, that they were winning the war and that victory was just around the corner. This fiction was dramatically exposed in January 1968, when the North Vietnamese Army (NVA) and the Vietcong launched the Tet Offensive.

NVA troops and the VC mounted a coordinated attack in 36 of the 44 provincial capitals throughout the South, hoping to spark off a mass uprising against Saigon. It was the largest engagement of the war. The death toll consisted of 58,400 Communists, 4,000 US troops, more than 2,000 ARVN and 14,300 civilians. The US Embassy itself was attacked. Four embassy staff were killed. It took three weeks to re-take Saigon. In military terms, Tet was a failure for the NVA. Their losses were massive, far more devastating than the Americans realised, and they had failed to launch an uprising against the South Vietnamese government. However, psychologically, it was a turning point for the Americans. Seeing the television pictures of VC in the embassy compound brought home to the

The My Lai Massacre

On 16 March 1968, soldiers from the 11th Infantry brigade entered the village of My Lai as part of a search and destroy mission in Vietcong-held territory. During the raid, the men of 'C' company killed over 300 men, women and children, including 70 who were gathered into a pit and shot. Soldiers shot or bayoneted children as young as two years old. For over a year, the army covered up the massacre. Then it was leaked to the 'New York Times' and an investigation and trial were launched. Thirteen soldiers were charged with war crimes, but only the platoon commander, Lieutenant William Calley, was convicted. He served three years of a ten-year sentence, then he was pardoned.

The average age of the American soldiers in Vietnam was just 19. One soldier spoke of the war 'wearing us down, driving us mad, killing us'. In spite of this and in spite of the fact that the majority of soldiers did not commit atrocities, the My Lai Massacre had a profound effect on the war at home. American people were revolted by it and thought the sentences were far too lenient. Many were angry at the military cover-up. Others saw it as simply part of the madness of the war. It contributed significantly to the growing divisions in the United States over the war in Vietnam.

Murdered women and children at My Lai, 1968

public that, in spite of what the government was telling them, they were not winning the Vietnam War.

Despite their superior technology and money, it seemed the United States could not win this war. The Americans were still backing an unpopular corrupt government that lacked the support of the majority of the people. With the help of the peasants, the VC and NVA could use the jungle and the country villages to hide out and continue their guerrilla warfare. Many military men at the time and since have argued that part of the problem was that the wrong approach was used to meet this challenge. After Tet, the army asked for a further 206,000 men. To defeat the Communists, the American government had to commit itself to total war and fully use the resources of the world's most powerful nation, as they had in the Second World War. But Johnson was not prepared to do this. Vietnam was already taking finance away from his beloved Great Society programmes and by 1968 the government was $25.3 billion in debt. There were already half a million men in Vietnam and it is doubtful if the American public would have allowed him to raise the money and manpower necessary to achieve a complete military victory. In fact, the American public was increasingly turning against the war, especially after the 1968 Tet Offensive.

While the majority of Americans had supported government policy throughout the war, an increasing number were questioning why they were in Vietnam. It was among students that the anti-war movement started, with the first 'teach-in' at the University of Michigan in 1965. The anti-war movement then spread among students, organised by Students for a Democratic Society (SDS). Their protest was about the morality of the war as much as its effectiveness. It was taking money away from Johnson's poverty programmes. In their view, the United States had no right to tell other countries how to run their governments. The students organised protest marches, burned draft cards, held debates, broke up classes etc. During the March Against Death in 1969, 300,000 filed past the White House in silence for 40 hours each carrying the name of a dead soldier or a destroyed village. At Kent State University, in 1970, four students were killed and 11 injured when National Guardsmen opened fire on a protest against Nixon's invasion of Cambodia.

Opposition was not just from students. The growing 'credibility gap' between what the government was telling people about the war and what was actually happening concerned many Americans. Among liberals especially, hostility to the war increased in the 1960s. President Kennedy's brother, Robert Kennedy, came out against the war in 1968 when he decided to run for the Democratic presidential nomination against another anti-war candidate, Eugene McCarthy. The architect of containment himself, George Kennan, was also a critic of the war. There were also protests in other countries and much criticism of US policy. Whether the anti-war movement had any real impact on the conduct of the war is an area of current debate. It is doubtful that the protests in themselves forced the government to make peace but, in a democracy, no government can ignore totally the protests of a large and growing section of the population.

There had been a halt in bombing as early as 1965 in order to explore peace talks, but the USA would not accept any Communists as part of the government of Vietnam so they failed. By 1968, President Johnson realised that the war had to end. Opposition was increasing at home and abroad, the war was costing billions of dollars and thousands of lives, and Tet had shown them they were not winning. The opposition and failure to make any headway in the war led Johnson to announce on television to the American public that the USA would be seeking peace talks. He also made the surprise announcement that he would not be seeking re-election in 1968. Peace talks began in May 1968 in Paris. Nothing was agreed before Johnson left office.

Why did Nixon take action between 1969–1973 to end the war?

Nguyen Van Thieu (1923–2001)
A soldier who for a while fought with the Vietminh but then sided with the French. He served under Diem and then under his successor Nguyen Cao Ky. Thieu was involved in Diem's assassination in 1963. He was elected President in 1967, a post he held until the fall of South Vietnam in 1975. His rule, like Diem's, was undemocratic and corrupt.

When Nixon came to office, in 1969, he wanted to end the war for the same reasons as Johnson. But Nixon also had other foreign policy aims, especially building friendship with China, which demanded peace in Vietnam. He formulated the so-called 'Nixon Doctrine': the USA would give aid to countries facing internal revolt but not ground troops. This meant withdrawal from South East Asia and no more Vietnams. Nixon felt that he could not just pull out, as this would look like a defeat. He wanted 'peace with honour'. Nixon hoped for a Korean-style solution with Thieu in charge of South Vietnam. In the meantime, while negotiations were going on, US troops had to be removed without South Vietnam collapsing. The solution was the policy of Vietnamisation (i.e. getting the ARVN to take back the responsibility for the fighting).

Historian Stephen Ambrose says that this 'proved to be a disastrous choice, one of the worst decisions ever made by a Cold War president'. The policy bought the Americans time for negotiation and withdrawal, but it worsened the situation on the ground. The US troops saw little point in fighting when it was clear they were going to leave and the ARVN felt betrayed. Desertions increased in both armies. At the same time, the USA had to pour more supplies into Vietnam in order to equip them to fight the NVA; so the costs of the war increased.

TNT: Abbreviation for the most famous high explosive: trinitrotoluene.

To put more pressure on North Vietnam in the peace talks, and to cover the withdrawal of US troops, the bombing intensified. For example, Operation Linebacker I dropped 155,000 tons of **TNT** on North Vietnam in 1972. Nixon's bombing campaigns were part of his 'mad man' strategy: he wanted North Vietnam to believe he was mad enough to use an atom bomb if they did not negotiate. In 1969, the secret and illegal bombing of neighbouring Laos and Cambodia began, followed in April 1970 by an invasion to try and destroy the Ho Chi Minh Trail and communist bases in these countries.

Look at the picture here, the photograph on pages 199 and Source B on page 209. How do these events help to explain why so many people in the USA opposed US involvement in South East Asia?

A student screams in horror. Soldiers shot dead four students at Kent State University who were part of a protest against the Vietnam War in 1970.

Cartoon by Nicholas Garland, which appeared in 'Daily Telegraph' on 3 April 1970, entitled 'The good samaritan ...'.

1. What message is this cartoon making about Nixon's policy?

2. Do you think the cartoonist believed that Nixon's Vietnam policy was likely to be successful? Explain your answer.

Khmer Rouge: Communist guerrilla forces in Cambodia whose leader was Pol Pot, a man of mystery who fought in jungles for five years before 1975 without making any clear statement of his political intentions. For more on the actions of the Khmer Rouge and Pol Pot see page 204.

When the 'New York Times' leaked the story about Cambodia, there were forceful protests at home and abroad. Congress reacted by repealing the Tonkin Resolution and passing the Cooper–Church Amendment cutting off any military aid that was being used against Cambodia. Nixon backed off, but the damage to Cambodia was immeasurable. The destabilisation of the country allowed the **Khmer Rouge** to seize power in 1975. The murderous regime, led by Pol Pot, wiped out a quarter of the entire population before it was stopped in 1979, by the Vietnamese.

Throughout 1968–1972, negotiations took place, but with little success. The USA wanted North Vietnam to accept Thieu in the South, but it refused. As the negotiations dragged on so, therefore, did the war. An attack by the North Vietnamese, in March 1972, led Nixon to launch Linebacker II – a ten-day bombing raid so fierce that the Swedish Prime Minister likened it to the crimes of the Nazi death camp at Treblinka.

In the end the negotiation, the continued fighting and pressure from the Soviet Union and China, who also wanted an end to the war, finally worked. The peace treaty was signed in Paris on 27 January 1973. Under its terms, the USA would withdraw from South Vietnam, all prisoners of war were to be returned, and there were to be negotiations to decide the future of North and South Vietnam. A Committee of National Reconciliation was to organise free elections, which included representatives of the South Vietnamese, the Communists and neutrals. In effect, Nixon had got a treaty which he could have had in 1968. Each side had made compromises but, in the intervening four years, 20,553 more Americans and half a million more Vietnamese had died.

Paris Peace Agreement, 27 January 1973
- US troops to be withdrawn from Vietnam, Laos and Cambodia.
- Establishment of a National Council for Reconciliation in South Vietnam which would include the Communists and which would organise free elections in the South.
- An international commission to oversee the ceasefire.
- Full exchange of prisoners.

The USA continued to give aid to the government of South Vietnam after 1973. They had withdrawn their troops, but had not given up hope of seeing South Vietnam remain non-communist. CIA advisors, as well as military personnel, remained behind. In 1974, Congress voted $700 million in aid for Thieu's government. But the North Vietnamese had no more intention of abiding by the ceasefire agreement than the Americans. In 1975, they launched an attack which quickly over-ran the country. The ARVN collapsed, with thousands deserting or changing sides. Thieu's government fell and, in April, Saigon was captured. Vietnam was united under communist leadership.

What were the effects of the Vietnam War on the USA and on South East Asia?

The social and psychological costs of the Vietnam War were enormous, as were the costs in people and material. The USA had spent at least $150 billion on the war, taking badly needed resources away from social policies at home. Eighty thousand Americans and at least two million Vietnamese were killed. Added to this were hundreds of thousands wounded and disabled in the USA and in Asia. The social problems of veterans returning home having lost a war they were expected to win were ignored for decades.

More bombs were dropped on Vietnam, Laos and Cambodia during the war than had been dropped in the entire history of the world. The physical damage to these countries caused suffering for many years afterwards. Thousands were disabled, thousands more developed cancer from the defoliants used by the Americans. The rebuilding of the economies and infrastructures of South East Asia would take years.

The American government and its political system were also affected badly by the war. The politicians were shown to have consistently lied to the public (e.g. over troop numbers and over the bombing of Cambodia). After the war there was a lack of faith in government. (This was made much worse by the Watergate scandal happening shortly after.)

Congress was also very concerned about the way they, too, had been misled. They also worried about the way succeeding presidents had increased America's commitments in Vietnam largely through their own office rather than through consulting Congress. JFK had used executive power to send Green Berets; LBJ also did the same and lied about the numbers of soldiers sent. The Tonkin Resolution extended presidential power in South East Asia, and Nixon illegally bombed and invaded Cambodia. To reassert its authority, Congress passed the War Powers Act in 1973 requiring that it be consulted before the President sends US forces into a war or consulted within 48 hours in an emergency. The President also had to get Congress' approval for continuance of a war beyond 60 days. In fact, the War Powers Act has never been invoked, but it symbolised how far Congress thought the Executive had sidelined them during the war.

There was disillusionment with the United States' world role among both the public and politicians, at home and abroad. The Americans were no longer the 'good guys' in the Cold War. Their role as 'world's policeman' was questioned and their willingness to act militarily was severely undermined in case it became 'another Vietnam'.

Truman had extended the policy of containment from Europe to Asia. Eisenhower's belief in the domino theory had convinced him to follow Truman's lead. Kennedy and Johnson had increased American involvement to the level that it became an all-out war to determine the political future of Vietnam. What the Americans never understood was that Vietnam was not about the Cold War: it was a nationalist war about Vietnam finally getting its independence from colonial or occupying powers in order to determine its own future. The Americans also consistently underestimated how much punishment the Vietnamese were willing to take to get that independence. When they did finally realise in 1968 that they could not win, they got out. But their determination to try not to make it look like the defeat it was kept the war going for an unnecessary five more years, at immense cost to both sides.

---

1. In what ways did the fighting intensify between 1968–1973?

2. Why were the Americans unable to win the 'hearts and minds' of the Vietnamese people?

3. How successful was Nixon's policy of Vietnamisation?

6.9 What impact did the Nixon presidency have on US policy towards Asia?

What was the impact on Laos and Cambodia?

As well as presiding over the American withdrawal from Vietnam, the military policies pursued by the Nixon government affected the states bordering Vietnam. The NVA sent supplies to the South through Laos and Cambodia. They had bases in both countries from which they operated. To destroy these lines of communication, both countries were bombed and invaded. In Laos, the ARVN was put into the field and it performed very poorly, being defeated by Laotian troops. The bombing of the country, however, caused much damage and cost many lives.

The effects in Cambodia were much more serious. In March 1969, the Cambodian ruler, Prince Norodom Sihanouk, was toppled in a **coup** by military leader Lon Nol. Sihanouk had tried to maintain neutrality in the war in Vietnam in spite of the Ho Chi Minh Trail passing through Cambodian territory. Nixon saw the coup as an opportunity. The Cambodian government had its own problems with the Khmer Rouge. Nixon believed that he could join with Lon Nol in the crusade against communism and that the Cambodians would, in turn, close down Vietnamese operations in Cambodia. The American invasion, however, destabilised the country and when the USA pulled out of South East Asia they also pulled out of Cambodia, allowing the Khmer Rouge to take power in 1975.

Under the leadership of dictator Pol Pot, the Khmer Rouge set about building a new society in the renamed country of Kampuchea. This involved wiping out all opposition, all intellectuals, all those corrupted by western influences etc. Over the four years of the Khmer Rouge terror, a quarter of the Cambodian people were killed, including almost all the country's doctors, nurses, teachers and engineers. In 1979, the Vietnamese army invaded and removed Pol Pot, setting up a pro-Vietnamese government. The Americans were not to blame for the genocide of the Khmer Rouge but their interference in Cambodia, while it tried to stay out of the war, was a major factor in creating the conditions which allowed the Khmer Rouge to take over. What was just as damaging was that the American vote in the United Nations stopped UN aid going to Cambodia for many years because it had a Vietnamese-backed government. In many ways, the suffering of Cambodia was worse than that of Vietnam.

Coup: An attempt by a group of people, often army officers, to get rid of the ruler or government of a country and to seize power for themselves.

How did Nixon and Kissinger attempt to improve relations with China?

In July 1971, President Nixon shocked the American public by announcing his intention to visit the People's Republic of China. Henry Kissinger had arranged the visit secretly a few months before and it turned out to be a tremendous success.

Nixon had decided, on taking office, that he would modify US policy towards China. He would be able to do this in a way no Democrat could, because as a Republican and with his background of support for McCarthy no one could accuse him of being soft on communism. He could count on the support of his Republican colleagues while, at the same time, getting the endorsement of Democrats who desired better relations with China. That this would gain him votes in the 1972 presidential election was certainly a factor in his policy. He ensured that the television coverage of the visit was extensive and extremely favourable.

However, the election was only one factor in Nixon's change of strategy. A major factor was the war in Vietnam. Better relations with China might encourage the Chinese to reduce their aid to the North Vietnamese. In this he was unsuccessful as communist aid continued to flow into Vietnam. Though when peace talks started, they did have more support from the Chinese than they might otherwise have had.

Monolithic: Like a single, large block.

A visit to China would also have the added advantage of worrying the Soviets. Where Truman had seen communism as **monolithic**, in fact relations between the USSR and China had always been tense. By 1969, the split had come out into the open. Nixon believed he could play the two states off against each other. Both would fear the other making an alliance with the United States, leaving them isolated. The longer he could keep them guessing, the stronger America's position would be. It would also make them each more likely to cooperate with his policy of *détente*. For China and Russia the advantage of friendship with the US was obvious, as it would strengthen their position against the other.

In the early 1970s, Nixon pursued a policy of *détente* towards the USSR, by which Nixon and Kissinger were able to build much better relations with the Soviet government. This led to a visit by the President to Moscow, in 1972, and to the signing of the Strategic Arms Limitation Treaty (SALT). Through the policy of *détente* and 'triangular diplomacy' between the USA, USSR and China, President Nixon was able to achieve two things. Firstly, he was reducing the amount of support available to the North Vietnamese. The Soviet Union would not stop supporting its ally altogether, but the new relationship with the USA would encourage it to limit that support. For example, when Nixon launched the Linebacker operations the Soviets did not respond directly as they did not want to damage *détente*. Secondly, Nixon was able to play the Soviets and the Chinese off against each other. Each was fearful of isolation. That also gave Nixon more support and freedom of action in Vietnam.

Recession: A temporary decline or setback in economic activity or prosperity.

The state of the economy was also a factor in Nixon's calculations. In the early 1970s, the world was entering a deep **recession**. As it had for a century, China promised new markets for American goods.

The Americans made steps towards improved relations early on in the Administration with the lifting of restrictions on trade and travel to China. Nixon also gave permission for the American table tennis team to visit the People's Republic. Although this led to many jokes about 'ping-pong diplomacy', it was an important step in improving relations. The actual visit lasted seven days and was a great success. There were meetings between Nixon, Kissinger, Mao and the Chinese premier Zhou En-lai. There were banquets and visits to the Great Wall – all broadcast throughout the world.

What impact did demonstrations like the one shown in this photograph have on US policy towards Vietnam?

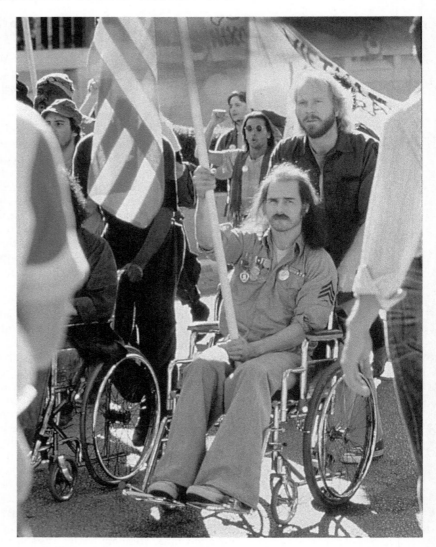

From the film 'Born on the Fourth of July', starring Tom Cruise as Vietnam veteran Ron Kovik.

The visit produced only a slight change in policy in Vietnam, notably pressure from China on the North Vietnamese delegation in Paris to come to an agreement. It was another six years before the Chinese and Americans resumed full diplomatic relations, but it did have some important effects. Trade between China and the USA increased to $700 million by 1973 and, just after Nixon's visit, the People's Republic was granted the Chinese seat in the United Nations. Both Japan and Taiwan were concerned by the growing friendship between the USA and the Communists so, to ensure that they were not left behind, both countries made their own efforts to build closer ties with Communist China. The problems had not gone away. Taiwan's fate remained a problem for the two countries and the two political systems were still opposed, but Nixon's trip had done much to increase understanding between the two nations and to ease some of the tensions of the Cold War.

Source-based questions: Opposition to the Vietnam War

SOURCE A

A poster entitled 'Cooperation in battle. Shoot down any enemy aircraft in order to launch the offensive.' It was produced in North Vietnam in 1972

SOURCE B

Newspaper picture of 8 June 1972. The nine-year-old South Vietnamese girl, Kim Phuc, was the victim of a napalm attack.

SOURCE C

Generally ... the media were instinctively pro-war and only shifted when sharp elite divisions had already become apparent. Undoubtedly, the famous photographs and film footage of napalm and bomb damage did have an impact. Analysis of television and press coverage, however, does not support Nixon's charges of anti-war bias. White House communication failures ... were more damaging to the Administration cause than any activities of crusading journalists.

From *Vietnam: American Involvement at Home and Abroad* by John Dumbrell, 1992

SOURCE D

By the end of February [1968], the most respected figures of American journalism had placed themselves on record in opposition to the administration policy, creating in the process [approval for opposition to] the war that would ultimately compel the government to reassess its position.

From *The Unfinished Journey* by William H. Chafe, 1986

Source-based questions: Opposition to the Vietnam War

SOURCE E

Traditional history portrays the end of wars as coming from the initiative of leaders – negotiations in Paris or Brussels or Geneva or Versailles – just as it often finds the coming of war a response to the demand of 'the people'. The Vietnam war gave clear evidence that at least for that war (making one wonder about the others) the political leaders were the last to take steps to end the war – 'the people' were far ahead. The President was always far behind.

From *A People's History of the United States*
by Howard Zinn, 1980

SOURCE F

I remember sitting on this wretched outpost one day with a couple of my sergeants ... This one sergeant of mine, Prior was his name, said, 'You know Lieutenant, I don't see how we're ever going to win this.' And I said, 'Well Sarge, I'm not supposed to say this to you as your officer – but I don't either.'

Philip Caputo, quoted in *Cold War* by Jeremy Isaacs and
Taylor Downing, 1998

1. Study Source A.

Explain what is meant by the term 'propaganda'.

How might this photograph be used as propaganda?

2. Study Source B.

What impact did images such as this have on the anti-war movement?

3. Study Sources C and D.

How far do they agree on press support for the war?

4. Using all the sources and your own knowledge, assess the importance of domestic opposition on America's withdrawal from the Vietnam War.

Further Reading

Texts designed for AS Level students

JFK & LBJ by Derrick Murphy (Collins Historymakers, 2004)

The Enduring Vision by Paul Boyer and others (D.C. Heath and Co., 1993) – easy to read and well-illustrated narrative.

The USA and Vietnam, 1945–1975 by Vivienne Sanders (Hodder and Stoughton, Access to History series, 1999).

The Cold War by Bradley Lightbody (Routledge, 1999) – good, clear chapters covering whole period with lots of source questions.

Texts for A2 and advanced study

Rise to Globalism by Stephen Ambrose and Douglas Brinkley (Penguin, 1997) – fascinating and detailed account of post-war policy; quite critical of the USA.

Vietnam by John Dumbrell (British Association for American Studies, 1992) – an easy-to-read pamphlet covering the war 1945–1975 at home and abroad.

A Noble Cause? America and Vietnam by Gerard de Groot (Longman, 1999) – covers the military, strategic, political and cultural aspects of the war as well as looking at the legacy for both countries.

Dispatches by Michael Herr (Picador, 1991) – a journalist's account of the war from talking to soldiers that truly brings home the nightmare quality of Vietnam.

America's Longest War by George Herring (McGraw-Hill, 1996) – detailed analysis of American policy from the 1950s onwards in Indo-China.

Vietnam: A History by Stanley Karnow (Pimlico, 1991) – detailed and comprehensive analysis of the war.

The Korean War by Peter Lowe (Longman, Origins of Modern Wars series, 1997) – looks at the war from the perspective of all the countries involved.

The Limits of Liberty by Maldwyn Jones (Oxford University Press, 1995) – clear narrative account.

American Foreign Relations: A History Since 1920 edited by Thomas G. Paterson, J. Garry Clifford, Kenneth J. Hagan (Houghton Mifflin, 2000) – detailed narrative, well illustrated.

Television and video

'The Cold War' – CNN production shown on the BBC (1999–2000).

'Vietnam: A Television History' – 13-part series produced by PBS shown on Channel Four in 1982.

'Truman' – a video written and produced by David Grubin for 'The American Experience' series (1994). It is divided into three one-hour episodes: the first covers Truman's political rise and the dropping of the atom bomb on Japan in 1945; the second episode covers Truman's Administration in domestic and foreign affairs up to 1949; the third episode concentrates on the Korean War.

Websites

The Cold War in Asia has hundreds of websites. The following are just a few.

http://www.gwu.edu/~nsaarchiv – the US National Security Archive containing lots of sources and their international Cold War history project.

http://www.eagle3.american.edu/~mm5860a/origins – description of the Cold War but also lots of links.

http://www.cnn.com/specials/cold.war – site for CNN televison series, but has interesting photographs and bits of information including some animated summaries.

http://hometown.aol.com/veterans/warlib6k – websites for the Korean War.

http://hometown.aol.com/veterans/warlib6v – websites for the Vietnam War.

www.yale.edu/lawweb/avalon/coldwar.htm – a site for primary documents on the Cold War in Asia.

http://www.lbjlib.utexas.edu/shwv/shwvhome.html – internet project on Vietnam with images and links.

www.pbs.org/wgbh/pages/amex/vietnam/- – website for 13-part series 'Vietnam: A Television History' containing the scripts of each one-hour episode.

7 Civil rights, 1865–1992

Key Issues

- What role did African-Americans play in the achievement of political and civil equality in the USA?

- How significant was opposition to the achievement of full civil rights for African-Americans?

- How important was the federal government in the development of African-American civil rights, 1865–1992?

- In what ways did the civil rights of Native, Hispanic and Oriental Americans change, 1865–1992?

7.1 How important was the Reconstruction period (1865–1977) for the development of African-American civil rights?

7.2 Why were the Southern states able to introduce segregation in 1877–1919?

7.3 What did African-Americans do to improve their position in US society, 1877–1945?

7.4 How successful were African-Americans in their attempt to gain civil and political rights, 1945–1968?

7.5 Historical interpretation: The role of Dr Martin Luther King Jr and the civil rights movement

7.6 How important was the federal government in the achievement of African-American civil rights, 1945–1992?

7.7 How far did African-Americans achieve full civil rights by 1992?

7.8 In what ways did the civil rights of Native Americans change, 1865–1992?

7.9 How far did civil rights for Hispanic and Oriental Americans improve, 1865–1992?

7.10 An in-depth study: Who did more for African-American civil rights – JFK or LBJ?

Framework of Events

1865	Freedman's Bureau is established
	Civil War ends
	13th Amendment of the Constitution
1866	Civil Rights Act
	Freedman's Bureau Act
	Ku Klux Klan founded
	Riots in southern cities against African-Americans
1867	Reconstruction Act
	Howard University founded
1868	President Johnson impeachment trial
	14th Amendment of Constitution
	President Grant is elected
1870	15th Amendment to Constitution
	First Enforcement Act
1871	Second Enforcement Act
1872	Ku Klux Klan Act
1875	Civil Rights Act
1877	End of Reconstruction
1883	Civil rights cases in Supreme Court
1887	First Jim Crow laws passed in Florida
	Dawes Severalty Act
1895	Booker T. Washington's Atlanta Compromise Speech
1896	'Plessy v Ferguson' case in Supreme Court

1898	'Williams v Mississippi' case in Supreme Court
1909	NAACP founded
1915	Ku Klux Klan refounded at Stone Mountain, Georgia
1917	UNIA founded by Marcus Garvey
1919	Race riots across America in 'Red Summer'
1924	All Native Americans made US citizens
1934	Indian Reorganisation Act
1938	Supreme Court case of 'Missouri ex rel. Gaines v Canada'
1942	Congress on Racial Equality founded by James Farmer
1948	US armed forces desegregated
1954	'Brown v Board of Education' case
1955	Montgomery Bus Boycott begins
1957	Southern Christian Leadership Conference founded
	September: Central High, Little Rock
1960	Lunch counter protests; SNCC founded
1961	Freedom Rides by CORE
1963	Birmingham demonstrations; March on Washington
1964	Civil Rights Act; Poll Tax amendment
1965	Selma to Montgomery March; Voting Rights Act
	Malcolm X is assassinated
	Rise of Black Power
	Riots in Watts District of Los Angeles
1966	Black Panther Party founded by Newton and Seale
1968	Martin Luther King is assassinated
	American Indian Movement founded
	Race riots across USA
1969	'Alexander v Holmes County' case
	AIM activists occupy Alcatraz
1971	'Swann v Charlotte Mecklenburg Board of Education' case
1974	Indian Self-Determination Act
1978	Bakke case on affirmative action
1984	Jesse Jackson runs for Democratic nomination for President
1988	Jesse Jackson again runs for Democratic nomination for President
1992	Rodney King riots in South Central Los Angeles.

Overview

THE issue of civil rights is essential to understanding the establishment and development of the United States. The idea appears in the Declaration of Independence (1776), when the Founding Fathers declared:

'We hold these truths to be self-evident, that all men are created equal, and that they are endowed by their Creator with inalienable rights, that among these are Life, Liberty and the Pursuit of Happiness.'

When the Constitution was produced in 1787, many states refused to ratify it until civil and political rights were incorporated in it. In 1791, the first ten amendments – known as the Bill of Rights – were included. These allowed the Constitution to be accepted by all 13 states. Included in the Bill of Rights were freedom of speech, freedom of religion and the right to trial by jury.

Since its creation, the United States of America (USA) has faced the continuing problem of civil, political and social equality. Even though the Constitution included the Bill of Rights, from 1791, it also allowed slavery. The only time slaves are mentioned in the Constitution is for the purpose of calculating state representation in the House of Representatives. For this purpose, a slave was calculated to be worth three-fifths of a free man.

The issue of slavery eventually split North and South to create the conditions which led to the outbreak of Civil War in April 1861. Although the war began on the issue of a state's right to secede from (leave) the USA, by 1862, President Lincoln transformed the conflict into a moral crusade to end slavery. The Emancipation Proclamation of September 1862 declared that, from 1 January 1863, slaves would be 'forever free'.

Even though the Civil War may have brought an end to slavery, it did not bring civil, political and social equality for African-Americans. From 1865 to 1992, a central feature of US society was the struggle of African-Americans to achieve these rights. For most African-Americans, the Northern victory in the Civil War proved to be a false dawn. It would take another 100 years before they could achieve civil and political equality. White opposition in the South, where most African-Americans lived, was able to regain control of state government by the end of the Reconstruction period (1877).

Jim Crow laws: 'Jim Crow' was a music-hall character invented by Thomas D. Rice in the 1820s. Dressed in rags and with his face blacked up, 'Jim Crow' came to represent a white view of happy-go-lucky blacks; his name was later applied to the laws regulating the lives of black Americans in the South.

Vigilante groups: These are formed when people join together to catch and punish anyone who they think is doing wrong or breaking the law. Such groups are unofficial, and often form when the people concerned think the police are not keeping order properly.

Once in control, they were able to force African-Americans into a position of second-class status. This was achieved by a variety of methods. **Jim Crow laws**, passed by the government in Southern states, introduced segregation. This created separate public facilities for blacks and for whites. African-Americans were also barred from voting by a variety of methods. These actions received support from the US Supreme Court, which upheld segregation in a number of court cases in the 1890s.

These actions were supplemented by the use of terror and intimidation. White **vigilante groups,** such as the Ku Klux Klan, engaged in general acts of violence against African-Americans. By the 1920s, African-Americans had become the invisible men of US society and politics. Disenfranchised, forced to use separate facilities and to occupy low-paid jobs, they were the racial underclass of America.

Faced with this predicament, African-Americans reacted in a number of ways. The leading African-American spokesman in the South in the last quarter of the 19th century was Booker T. Washington. Born a slave, he advocated social advancement at the expense of civil and political equality.

Criticised for accepting segregation, the sociologist Gunnar Myrdal, in *The American Dilemma* (published in 1944), stated:

'For his time, and for the region where he worked and where nine-tenths of all Negroes live, his policy of abstaining from talks on rights was entirely realistic.'

However, Washington's views were challenged by a leading northern African-American, W.E.B. Du Bois. As the first African-American to receive a Doctor of Philosophy (PhD) degree from Harvard, he dismissed Washington's acceptance of civil and political inferiority. In 1910, he helped found the National Association for the Advancement of Colored People (NAACP). The NAACP fought, primarily through the legal system, to gain full civil rights.

By the 1920s, another leading African-American advocated a different course. West Indian-born Marcus Garvey supported the development of a strong black identity. This would be achieved through separate development from whites and through support for the African heritage of black Americans. Garvey's 'black nationalism' was a forerunner for the Black Muslims of the Nation of Islam, Malcolm X and the Black Panthers.

However, for the vast majority of African-Americans political action had little impact or support. Instead, the most attractive way to avoid the **legal segregation** of the South was to migrate North. The Great Migration, in the first three decades of the 20th century, saw thousands of African-Americans move north to cities such as Chicago, Detroit and New York. Nevertheless, they still lived in poor segregated housing.

Legal segregation: The deliberate creation by law of separate facilities for whites and African-Americans, mainly in the former Confederacy states.

A major turning point for African-Americans was the Second World War. Thousands worked in war industries. Large numbers served in the armed forces in the defence of democracy against German and Japanese tyranny. They fought for democracy and freedom but faced second-class status on their return from military duty.

From 1945, the civil rights movement began to take shape across America. In 1948, President Truman desegregated the armed forces. In 1954, the NAACP successfully brought public school segregation to an end by taking the 'Brown versus Board of Education' case to the Supreme Court. Within the South, African-American and civil rights bodies fought segregation in a wide variety of places and in a number of different ways. In Montgomery, Martin Luther King led a campaign to end bus segregation. In the 1960s in North Carolina, students of the Student Non-Violent Co-ordinating Committee (SNCC) helped to end lunch counter segregation. In 1961, students of the Congress for Racial Equality helped to bring an end to inter-state bus segregation.

Through their own efforts, African-Americans challenged legal segregation and won. However, to achieve civil and political equality they needed the support of the federal government. The Supreme Court provided legal support by declaring segregation unconstitutional. The President and Congress passed laws that enforced civil rights and guaranteed voting rights. In jobs, they established the principle of **affirmative action**.

Affirmative action: Policies introduced by the federal government from J.F. Kennedy's Administration (1961–63) onwards, for people and for firms employed by the government. The aim was to reserve a certain number of jobs for people from ethnic minority backgrounds, such as African-Americans and Oriental Americans.

By 1970, legal segregation had come to an end. However, unofficial segregation still existed in the North because of the creation of ethnic neighbourhoods. Enforced bussing and affirmative action proved a controversial way of redressing decades of discrimination. Nevertheless, by the 1980s, African-Americans had achieved full civil and political equality. Many had also achieved social equality. Unfortunately, many more still lived in relative poverty in inner-city **ghettos** in the North or in rural poverty in the South. This bifurcation of African-American society still created major problems in US society, as the Rodney King riots in South Central Los Angeles in 1992 proved.

Ghettos: Areas in a city or town where poor people or people of a particular race, religion or nationality live in isolation.

Although African-Americans stand out as the largest ethnic group to have faced sustained discrimination and denial of civil rights over a long period of US history, they are not alone. Native Americans faced similar problems. By 1865, Native Americans east of the Mississippi river had been defeated by the USA and either forced westward into Indian territory or into reservations.

Between 1865 and 1890, the remaining Native Americans west of the Mississippi were defeated and also forced into reservations. The Dawes Act of 1887 helped to transform Native-American society. Under the Act, collective tribal ownership of land came to an end and Native Americans were to be educated along Christian, western lines. This helped to destroy Native-American culture. In 1924, all Native Americans became US citizens.

By the 1960s, most Native Americans on reservations faced poverty, unemployment and alcohol and drug abuse. On the back of the black civil rights movement, an American Indian Movement was formed in 1968 to fight for Native-American rights. Using direct action and the courts, Native Americans began to gain civil and social equality from the 1970s onwards.

Similarly, Oriental Americans faced discrimination and social inequality over the same period. Although large numbers of Chinese labourers were used to construct the transcontinental railroad, they faced discrimination. In 1882, the Chinese Exclusion Act drastically limited Chinese immigration. Most Oriental Americans lived on the West Coast of the USA. These comprised Chinese, Japanese and, more recently, Korean and Vietnamese Americans.

The most notorious act of discrimination against Oriental Americans came in the Second World War, when the entire Japanese-American population was placed in concentration camps.

Like other ethnic minorities, Oriental Americans have benefited from the broader civil rights movement since the 1950s. In particular, they have benefited from affirmative action programmes.

Hispanic Americans have comprised some of the more historic and recent waves of non-white immigration into the USA. In the border states, Hispanic Americans faced social discrimination. In the 1960s and 1970s, their cause was championed by the Hispanic-American union leader Cesar Chavez. However, Hispanic American illegal immigration has become a major issue in the USA since the 1960s.

The historian Maldwyn A. Jones entitled his study of US history from 1607 to 1992 *The Limits of Liberty* (published in 1995). For much of the period 1865 to 1992, large parts of US society faced civil, political or social inequality. Yet the underlying theme of the period has been the achievement of civil and political equality for the vast majority of US citizens.

1. What are civil and political rights within the context of US history?

2. What factors limited the development of African-American civil rights between 1865 and 1992?

3. Explain why Native Americans, Oriental Americans and Hispanic Americans have faced discrimination within the USA between 1865 and 1992?

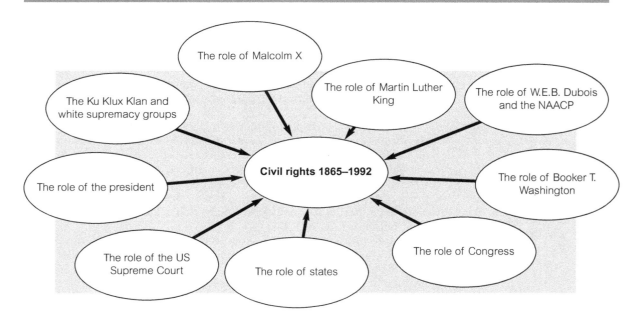

1. **From the factors mentioned in the mind map, what do you regard as the most important obstacles to the achievement of African-American civil rights in the period 1865–1992? Give reasons for your answer.**

2. **Identify the contributions of the following to the advancement of African-American civil rights: Booker T. Washington, W.E.B. Dubois, Martin Luther King and Malcolm X.**

   Who do you regard as the most influential African-American in the advancement of civil rights? Give reasons for your answer.

3. **Which of the factors mentioned in the mind map were both an obstacle and a help to the achievement of African-American civil rights at different times during the period 1865 to 1992?**

   Identify the periods and any incidents when you think they were obstacles and where they helped African-American civil rights.

7.1 How important was the Reconstruction period (1865–1877) for the development of African-American civil rights?

The end of the Civil War should have been a major turning point in the history of African-Americans. The North's victory brought an end to slavery. In addition, the three Civil War Amendments – the Thirteenth, Fourteenth and Fifteenth (see page 217) – seem to have guaranteed African-Americans full civil and political equality.

However, the end of the Civil War and the beginning of the Reconstruction era (1865–1877) proved to be a false dawn for the four million slaves in the former Confederacy and border states. During this period, attempts were made to improve the civil, political and social position of the former slaves.

In March 1865, before the end of the Civil War, the Freedman's Bureau was created by the federal government to give food, shelter, medical aid and land to ex-slaves. In 1866, a Freedman's Bureau Act was passed, over President Johnson's veto, which extended the work of the Bureau. It also included the right of military courts in the South to hear cases of **racial discrimination**. Although poorly resourced, the Freedman's Bureau did help the creation of schools for African-Americans. It was aided in this task by charity workers from the North and by religious organisations. In 1865, 95 per cent of ex-slaves were illiterate. This had dropped to 81 per cent in

Racial discrimination: Actions which deliberately penalise a person because of their racial background.

1870 and to 64 per cent by 1890. African-American education was enhanced further with the creation of higher education institutions, such as Howard University and Fisk University in 1866–67.

African-Americans also benefited from the Civil Rights Act of March 1866. This gave them citizenship and outlawed racial discrimination. However, the most important reforms were the three Civil War amendments – 13, 14 and 15.

Nevertheless, attempts to improve the position of African-Americans in the former Confederacy faced considerable opposition. In 1865 and 1866, all the former Confederate states had passed 'black codes' which replaced the old slave codes. Although their content varied from state to state, the underlying aim was to keep the freed slaves in a second-class position. The most oppressive 'black code' was against **vagrancy**. Homeless freedmen were fined and imprisoned. To counter the black codes, Congress passed the Civil Rights Act of 1866.

A more sinister form of white opposition came in the form of vigilantes and the use of violence. In 1866, ex-Confederates in Pulaski, Tennessee formed the Ku Klux Klan (KKK). The KKK used violence and intimidation against African-American and white supporters of Reconstruction governments in the South. In May 1866, white crowds in Memphis, Tennessee, attacked African-Americans who had served in the Northern Army, killing 46. In Mississippi, Klansmen mutilated a leading black Republican. In 1870, in Georgia, the Klan murdered three scallywag Republicans.

Congress reacted to the rise of white vigilante groups by passing a series of acts between 1870 and 1872. In May 1870, the First Enforcement Act protected black voters. In February 1871, the Second Enforcement Act provided federal supervision of southern elections. Finally, in 1872, the Third Enforcement Act gave federal troops the power to suspend habeus corpus and arrest suspected KKK members. The combined result of this federal action was to remove the threat, albeit temporarily, of white intimidation of African-Americans.

The Reconstruction era has been portrayed, in the past, as a period of African-American domination of southern politics. In some ways, this is true. The Reconstruction Acts of 1867 and 1868 completely altered the electorate in the former Confederacy. In the 1868 presidential election, the Republican candidate, Ulysses Grant, won by 300,000 votes. It is clear that, without the 700,000 African-American votes from the South, he would not have achieved a majority of votes.

Yet within the Southern states, black political control was a fiction. Only one African-American became a Lieutenant (Deputy) Governor of a state, Pinckney Pinchback of Louisiana. Two blacks became US senators, both from Mississippi: Hiram Revels and Blanche Bruce. Fourteen blacks became Congressmen. Even when 600 blacks were elected to state legislatures, they did not always work together.

A greater failing of the Reconstruction period was in social matters. As the African-American leader Frederick Douglass noted, the former slaves were 'left free from the individual master but a slave of society'. Without education, money or property, the ex-slave faced a new type of social inferiority. Only 4,000 freed slaves gained land under the Southern Homestead Act of 1866. During the Reconstruction period, work on the plantation was replaced by sharecropping. With very high rates of interest for borrowing money, African-American sharecroppers were kept in a cycle of poverty and dependence upon whites. Following the economic crash of 1873, their position deteriorated further.

A development which became a recurrent feature of African-American life was the desire to leave discrimination and intimidation in the South by moving North and West. During the 1870s, over 15,000 African-Americans

Vagrancy: A way of life in which someone goes aimlessly from place to place and does not have a home or a job, or who often begs or steals in order to live.

Civil War Amendments to the US Constitution passed during Reconstruction		
Thirteenth Amendment	Ended slavery in the USA	Became law in December 1865
Fourteenth Amendment	Provided equal protection under the law for all citizens Extended right to due process of law to the individual states	Became law in July 1868
Fifteenth Amendment	Guaranteed right to vote to all citizens irrespective of race, colour or previous condition of servitude (slavery)	Became law in March 1870

Homesteaders: The people who claimed land for free in the West, following the 1862 Homestead Act. They were also called 'sodbusters' because many used eastern farming methods which did not work in the climate of the West.

White supremacists: Whites who believe that the white race was superior to all other races. In particular, they regard African-Americans as biologically and intellectually inferior.

1. In what ways did the lives of African-Americans change during Reconstruction?

2. How did Southern whites oppose Reconstruction?

3. To what extent did Reconstruction fail?

left the South and moved to the Free State of Kansas to set up as **homesteaders**. When they arrived, they still faced racial discrimination. As long ago as the 1830s, the French political observer Alexis de Tocqueville noted: 'race prejudice seems stronger in those states where slavery no longer exists'.

Although African-Americans faced the most severe discrimination in the Old South, it did not mean that there was racial tolerance elsewhere.

In 1877, Reconstruction came to an end with the Compromise of 1877. To get elected president, Republican candidate Rutherford B. Hayes needed southern electoral college votes. To acquire these, he abandoned Reconstruction. This allowed **white supremacists** in the Democratic Party to gain control of all of the Old South, inaugurating a new 'dark age' for African-Americans.

7.2 Why were Southern states able to introduce segregation in 1877–1919?

White opposition to civil and political equality for African-Americans is a major theme in the history of civil rights in America. Even though the Confederacy lost the Civil War, the changed status of African-Americans was accepted with extreme reluctance. The black codes of 1865–66, and the formation of vigilante groups such as the Ku Klux Klan, were ways in which Southern whites attempted to maintain their superiority in politics and society.

Radical Republican: Member of the Republican Party, more than likely in Congress, who wanted to bring about fundamental change in the Southern states following the Civil War. Radical Republicans were responsible for the impeachment of President Johnson in 1968.

Even before the end of Reconstruction, in 1877, the rights of African-Americans in the former Confederacy were being eroded. By 1876, **Radical Republican** governments existed in only three Southern states: South Carolina, Florida and Louisiana. In spite of restrictions placed on former officials of the Confederacy in the Fourteenth Amendment, white supremacist governments were already appearing. This was the result of the 1872 Amnesty Act, which had restored the political rights of all but a few hundred former Confederates.

Northern support for Reconstruction had clearly faded before the Compromise of 1876. The Senate rejected the 1875 Enforcement Bill,

against southern white vigilantes. The Civil Rights Act of the same year, which guaranteed equal rights in theatres and other public places, was never enforced.

What was of considerable significance was the role of the US Supreme Court on the issue of civil rights. In the 'Slaughter House Cases' of 1873, the Court declared that the Fourteenth Amendment rights only covered national citizenship. This covered issues such as inter-state travel. The Court declared that the federal government did not safeguard civil rights against violation by individual states.

In 1875, in the 'United States versus Cruikshank' case, it was decreed that the civil rights in the Fourteenth Amendment did not protect African-Americans against discrimination by individuals, only by state governments. In the following year, in the 'United States versus Reese' case, the Court refused to put on trial officials in Kentucky who had prevented African-Americans from voting. Taken together, these actions show that northern politicians and the Supreme Court had abandoned African-Americans to their own devices before 1877.

However, the Compromise of 1876 is significant in that it shows clearly that, in return for control of the national government, the Republican Party was willing to abandon the South to the white supremacist Democratic Party. From the 1870s until the 1960s, the former Confederacy became the 'Solid South' of the Democratic Party.

Once whites were in control of southern state governments, African-Americans faced the creation of a society which placed them firmly in a position of inferiority. Beginning in Florida, in 1887, laws were passed which created legal segregation of the races. The Florida law created separate accommodation on railroad carriages. Similar laws in Mississippi in 1888, Texas in 1889, Louisiana in 1890 and Alabama, Arkansas and Georgia in 1891 followed this. Known collectively as 'Jim Crow laws' (see panel), they created a segregated society not dissimilar to apartheid in South Africa – which existed from 1948 to the early 1990s.

Examples of Jim Crow laws across the USA

Alabama	**Buses**: All passenger stations shall have separate waiting rooms for the white and coloured races.
Florida	**Education**: The schools of white children and the schools of Negro children shall be conducted separately.
Georgia	**Burial**: The officer in charge shall not bury any coloured persons upon ground used for burial of white persons.
Louisiana	**The blind**: The Board of Trustees shall maintain a separate building on separate ground for the care and instruction of all blind persons of the black race.
Mississippi	**Inter-marriage**: The marriage of a white person with a Negro or person who shall have one-eighth or more Negro blood, shall be unlawful.
North Carolina	**Textbooks**: Books shall not be inter-changeable between white and coloured schools, but shall continue to be used by the race first using them.

In introducing Jim Crow laws, the southern states were accused of violating the civil rights of African-Americans under the Fourteenth Amendment. However, in a number of Supreme Court cases, the highest legal authority in the USA upheld these developments. In 1883, in three civil rights cases, the Court threw out the 1875 Civil Rights Act on the grounds that the Fourteenth Amendment applied to governments not individuals.

Of greater significance was the 1896 case of 'Plessy versus Ferguson'. Homer Plessy, a person of mixed race, challenged the legality of the Louisiana railroad company which had created separate railroad cars for whites and for blacks. The Court declared that Louisiana had not violated the Fourteenth Amendment because it had created 'separate but equal' facilities for the races. In 1899, in 'Cumming versus the Board of Education', the separate but equal principle was extended to schools. These cases laid the foundation for legalised segregation, which lasted until the 1950s and 1960s.

The loss of civil rights was not limited to the Fourteenth Amendment rights of 1868. African-Americans were also denied voting rights which had been guaranteed under the Fifteenth Amendment of 1870. In 1890, Mississippi became the first state to impose new voting qualifications which had the effect of taking the vote away from most African-Americans in that state. These voting restrictions included literacy tests and residential qualifications. They also included **poll taxes**, which disenfranchised poor whites. However, it also took the vote away from large numbers of African-Americans. In 1898, in 'Mississippi versus Williams', the US Supreme Court upheld these new voting regulations. Later, states such as Louisiana, introduced the 'grandfather clause' into voting regulations. This declared that a person could vote only if his grandfather had the vote. This excluded the vast majority of African-Americans, whose grandfathers had

Poll taxes: These were taxes, introduced first in Mississippi, which had to be paid if someone wanted to vote. Poor whites became disenfranchised, as did large numbers of African-Americans.

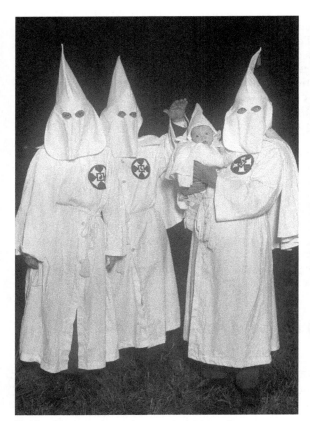

Ku Klux Klan members at a secret night meeting.

After being accused of murder, these two young African-American men were taken from the county jail and lynched in the public square in Marion, Indiana, on 9 August 1930.

been slaves. Texas also introduced the 'whites only' primary election. In a state where Democrats always won the election, this effectively removed African-Americans from the political system.

The effect of these new regulations on African-American voter registration was dramatic. In Louisiana, for example, there were over 130,000 African-Americans registered to vote in 1896. Within four years, by 1900, the figure had fallen to just 5,300.

To reinforce legal segregation and disenfranchisement, whites also engaged in the use of terror. Although the Ku Klux Klan had declined, attacks on African-Americans increased. Between 1890 and 1899, 187 African-Americans were lynched on average each year. The vast majority of these were in the Old South. Between 1887 and 1917, a total of 2,734 African-Americans were lynched. There were also outbreaks of serious race riots. In 1917, in East St Louis, Illinois, African-Americans were murdered by white mobs.

By 1919, the position of African-Americans in the Old South had changed little since the end of the Civil War. In political and civil rights, African-Americans faced legal segregation, violence and intimidation. This latter aspect of life was exemplified by the re-founding of the Ku Klux Klan at Stone Mountain, Georgia, in 1915 by William Simmons.

In social terms, most southern African-Americans lived in poverty. Most worked as sharecroppers or in menial, low-paid jobs. Outside the Old South, the plight of African-Americans was only slightly better. Jim Crow laws also existed in states such as Oklahoma and Kansas.

African-Americans who lived in northern cities such as Chicago and New York faced unofficial segregation. This occurred mainly in jobs and housing, but also included schooling. In Chicago, for instance, in 1919, Irish-American and Polish-American workers, in league with the police, attacked African-Americans. It would seem that nowhere in the United States did African-Americans achieve full civil rights.

The inferior position of African-Americans was reinforced by academic views about racial superiority. The popularity of social darwinist thinking suggested that academics, such as Carl Brigham and Luther Burbank, attempted to use biological science to prove African-American inferiority.

1. In what ways did the federal government undermine the civil and political rights of African-Americans between 1877 and 1919?

2. What do you regard as the most important reasons for the deterioration in the position of African-Americans within US society 1877–1919?

Give reasons for your answer.

Even in the White House, President Woodrow Wilson seemed to sympathise with opponents of African-American rights. He attempted to segregate the federal civil service during his presidency (1913–21). He also applauded D.W. Griffth's film 'The Birth of a Nation' and had the film screened at the White House. The film had an enormous effect on the American public. It portrayed the Civil War and Reconstruction period, showing the Ku Klux Klan in a heroic light and African-Americans as incapable of acting responsibly.

Within this hostile political and social environment, African-Americans did attempt to improve their position.

7.3 What did African-Americans do to improve their position in US society, 1877–1945?

During the period 1877 to 1945, African-Americans attempted to improve their civil, political and social position within US society. For the majority of African-Americans, life involved poor living and working conditions in the Old South. They faced the daily problem of legal segregation, as well as the possibility of violent retaliation from the white community if they challenged the status quo.

In such conditions, three leading African-Americans offered differing ways of dealing with the situation. In the last quarter of the 19th century, the dominant black voice was a former slave, Booker T. Washington. In the first decade of the 20th century, his views were challenged by a northern-educated academic W.E.B. Du Bois. In the 1920s, black nationalism was supported by Jamaican-born Marcus Garvey. He supported the idea of black separateness in US society. In the 1930s and 1940s, A. Philip Randolph, an African-American trade union leader, became an important voice in the search for greater rights. During the New Deal era (1933–45), important gains were made in federal employment by African-Americans.

Perhaps African-Americans made the most significant development. Beginning with the First World War, the 'Great Migration' of African-Americans began. Tens of thousands left the Old South to move north. By 1945, cities such as Philadelphia, Chicago and New York had large African-American populations.

How important was Booker T. Washington in the advancement of African-American rights?

Booker T. Washington had been born a slave in 1856. For the first nine years of his life, he lived on a plantation in Virginia. He came to represent the hopes and aspirations of southern blacks who had been freed because of the northern victory in the Civil War. Until his death in 1915, Booker T. Washington was widely regarded as the leading voice in the African-American community. He was the first black to receive an honorary degree from Harvard University. He was also the first black person to be invited for a meal with the President at the White House.

For all his high profile, Booker T. Washington was a controversial figure. To many African-American activists at the time, and since, he has been portrayed as someone who accepted the inferior status of African-Americans in US society. He represented the hopes and aims of the majority of southern blacks after the Civil War. In an era of 'rugged individualism', he advocated self-help, self-reliance and social advancement.

He was aided, during the Reconstruction period, by the efforts of northerners to improve African-American education in the South. From 1872 to 1875, Booker T. Washington attended the Hampton Normal and Agricultural Institute, in Virginia, which had been founded in 1868 by Samuel Chapman Armstrong.

For the rest of his life, Washington actively supported attempts to improve the education of African-Americans in the South. However, this education was to be practical and vocational rather than academic.

The crowning glory of Washington's educational efforts came after 1881 when he was made Principal of Tuskegee Institute in Alabama. Tuskegee specialised in practical subjects such as wagon-making, wheel-making and learning to be a blacksmith or a good housekeeper. It also helped to develop studies in new agricultural techniques. Later, in the 1890s, the Tuskegee Institute developed extension courses in the area around the college.

Washington reached national prominence, in 1895, at the Atlanta International Exposition. In what became known as his 'Atlanta Compromise' speech, Booker T. Washington laid out his vision of the African-American in US society. He told the African-Americans in the audience that:

> 'Our greatest danger is that in the great leap from slavery to freedom we may overlook the fact that we shall prosper as we learn to … glorify common labour. No race can prosper till it learns that there is as much dignity in tilling a field as in writing a poem.'

Booker T. Washington (1856–1915)
Black educator and leader. Born into slavery in Virginia. Attended Hampton Institute in 1860s. Became first Principal of the black Tuskegee Institute in 1881. Washington was a supporter of black self-help and self-reliance. His aim was to improve black education, which would lead to social advancement. He avoided openly campaigning for equal civil and political rights. His 'Atlanta Compromise' speech of 1895 contains his main aims and vision for the African-American in US society.

He went on to stress the opportunities for African-Americans in economics, rather than mention the lack of civil and political rights. He called on African-Americans to:

> 'cast down your bucket where you are – cast it down in making friends … of the people of all races by whom we are surrounded. Cast it down in agriculture, mechanics, in commerce, in domestic service, and in the professions.'

The speech reflected the views of the vast majority of African-Americans in the Old South. They wanted to improve their social and economic position within the framework of white supremacy and segregation.

It was Washington's implied acceptance of white supremacy which made him an influential African-American leader accepted by white America. White newspapers applauded his 'Atlanta Compromise' speech across America. It also enabled Washington to get white supporters for African-American education. It allowed him to become adviser on African-American affairs to Presidents McKinley and Theodore Roosevelt. In 1896, on a visit to Europe, he even met and had tea with Queen Victoria in Britain.

Yet, for all his national and international fame, Washington lived in an era of increasing persecution and discrimination against African-Americans. From the 1890s until his death in 1915, Jim Crow laws were passed across the South, the US Supreme Court upheld segregation and thousands of blacks were lynched. While he was adviser to Theodore Roosevelt, the Brownsville affair occurred in 1906. Black troops stationed

Does this map show how the 'Great Migration', beginning at the time of the First World War, had little impact on the geographical distribution of the black population?

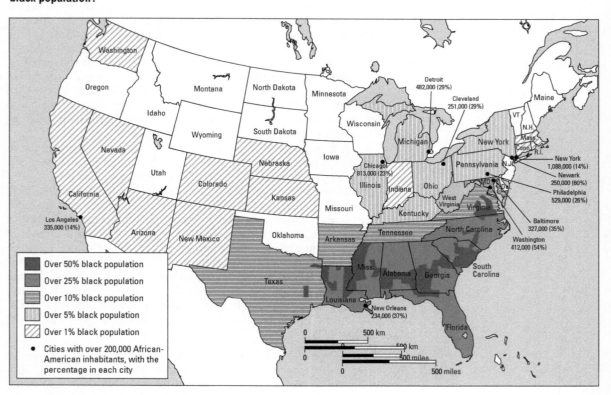

African-American population in the USA, 1965

Court-martialled: To be tried by a military court. Martial law – the law governing the armed forces – is stricter than either civil or criminal laws that affect civilians.

in Brownsville, Texas, were accused of rioting. Washington could not prevent a whole black regiment from being **court-martialled**.

Privately, Washington financially supported attempts to bring court cases to challenge segregation. However, he was unwilling to jeopardise his relationship with white America by adopting a radical stance. Such a strategy would have created a violent white backlash, which could have had serious consequences for African-Americans, particularly in the Old South.

Booker T. Washington was heavily criticised, by later generations of African-American activists, as a person who seemed to turn a blind eye to civil and political rights. However, Washington was a realist. As Gunnar Myrdal stated, in *The American Dilemma* (1944):

> 'For his time and for the region where he worked and where nine-tenths of all Negroes lived, his policy of abstaining from talks of rights and of "casting down your buckets where you are" was entirely realistic.'

Washington's practical approach to improving the economic position of African-Americans was the central feature of his adult life. In 1900, he helped found the National Negro Business League to encourage business skills and to show what African-Americans had achieved in commerce and the economy. In 1911, the National Urban League was created. This organisation campaigned for equal conditions and opportunities in industry and commerce for African-Americans. This approach reflected Booker T. Washington's approach to the position of African-Americans in a society dominated by whites.

How did the views of Du Bois differ from the views of Booker T. Washington?

W.E.B. Du Bois (1868–1963)
Black historian, sociologist and civil rights leader. Professor of Latin and Greek at Wilberforce University, Ohio (1894–96); Professor of Sociology at Atlanta University, Georgia (1897–1910). Founder of the NAACP in 1909. Editor of 'The Crisis', NAACP magazine (1910–34). Left NAACP in 1948 because of its lack of radicalism. Joined the American Communist Party in 1961.

W.E.B. Du Bois came from a completely different background to Booker T. Washington. Born in Massachusetts in 1868, he was brought up in the North in a middle-class family. He received a PhD degree from Harvard University – the first African-American to do so. His thesis was entitled 'The Suppression of the Atlantic Slave Trade to the United States 1638–1870'. Du Bois was also a socialist who wanted to see radical social and economic change in America. In later life, he joined the American Communist Party. It was whilst at Atlanta University that he had published, in 1903, *The Souls of the Black Folk* – a study of African-Americans.

Initially, Du Bois supported Washington's efforts to raise the economic position of African-Americans. He regarded the 'Atlanta Compromise' speech of 1895 as a 'phenomenal success – it was a word fitly spoken'. Later, he criticised Washington's views as narrow and pessimistic. This was due primarily to Washington's acceptance of the lack of civil and political rights for African-Americans.

In 1905, Du Bois directly challenged Washington's position with the creation of the Niagara Movement. Du Bois led a group of African-American activists in demanding full civil and political rights for African-Americans. Initially, they met in Buffalo in upstate New York. However, they were forced to move to the Canadian side of Niagara Falls to found their movement.

The Niagara Movement had paved the way for the formation of the National Association for the Advancement of Colored People (NAACP) in 1909. The aim of the organisation was to campaign peacefully for full civil and political rights. These would be achieved through educating the public, but mainly through the courts. By 1914, the NAACP had 6,000 members. In 1915, it achieved its first court success. In 'Guinn versus the

United States', the 'grandfather clause' used as a voting qualification in Oklahoma was declared unconstitutional. In 1917, in 'Buchanan versus Warley', segregationist housing regulations were also declared unconstitutional.

Du Bois was an elitest. As editor of the NAACP publication 'The Crisis' from its inception in 1910 until 1934, he campaigned for the top 'talented tenth' of the African-American population to lead the campaign for full rights. In his autobiography, Du Bois claimed that 'if "The Crisis" had not been a personal organ and expression of myself, it could not possibly have attained its popularity and effectiveness!'

Du Bois' greatest contribution to the development of African-American rights was his role as a propagandist, using 'The Crisis' to highlight discrimination and black achievement. However, his lasting contribution was the creation of the NAACP, which played such an important role in the achievement of civil rights in the 1940s and 1950s.

What impact did Marcus Garvey have on the development of African-American society?

Throughout his career, Du Bois kept his distance from ordinary African-Americans. His campaigns for better rights fell far short of a mass movement. Yet, in the 1920s, Marcus Garvey, under the banner of 'black nationalism', was able to achieve a mass following in the northern cities of the USA. In his study of the USA from 1920 to 1941, entitled *The Anxious Decades* (1992), Michael Parrish calls Marcus Garvey 'the black Messiah'.

Although brought up in the British West Indies, Garvey is closely identified with African-Americans in northern cities such as New York. On the eve of the First World War, he founded the Universal Negro Improvement Association (UNIA). This supported the creation of a strong, independent economic base for African-Americans. This was followed, in 1919, by the creation of the Negro Factories Corporation. It reflected the views of Booker T. Washington to some degree. Garvey's aims were to reclaim Africa from the white man. In this sense, he was one of the first effective black critics of European colonialism. Garvey supported black nationalism and a separate black identity. He declared integration, as supported by the NAACP, as 'the greatest enemy of the Negro'. Under the UNIA, a black star shipping line was created. Its shares were available only to African-Americans. By 1920, the UNIA had over two million members.

> **Marcus Garvey (1887–1940)**
> Jamaican political thinker and activist. Formed the Universal Negro Improvement Association in 1914, and moved to the USA in 1916, where he established branches in New York and other northern cities. He was an early advocate of black nationalism. He led a 'back to Africa' movement for black Americans to establish a black-governed country in Africa. The cult of Rastafarianism is based largely on his ideas.

> **Study the aims of the UNIA.**
>
> a) In what ways are they similar to the ideas of Booker T. Washington?
>
> b) In what ways do they different from Washington's views?

> ### The aims of the Universal Negro Improvement Association
>
> 1 To champion Negro nationhood by the liberation of Africa from colonial rule
>
> 2 To make the Negro race conscious
>
> 3 To breathe the ideals of manhood and womanhood into every Negro
>
> 4 To advocate self-determination
>
> 5 To make the Negro world-conscious
>
> 6 To print all the news that will be interesting and instructive to the Negro
>
> 7 To instil racial self-help
>
> 8 To inspire racial love and self-respect.

> ### An address made by Marcus Garvey in New York City:
>
> 'The white man of the world has been accustomed to deal with the Uncle Tom cringing Negro. Up to 1919 he knew no other Negro than the Negro represented through Booker T. Washington. Today, he will find a new Negro is on the stage. Every American Negro and every West Indian Negro must understand that there is but one fatherland for the Negro, and that is Africa.'

Garvey's black nationalist and separatist views were opposed by the NAACP. They also brought the UNIA under FBI investigation. In 1923, Garvey was convicted of mail fraud. He was fined $1,000 and sentenced to five years in prison. When he left prison in 1927, he was deported as an undesirable alien.

Yet, in his short career, Garvey had created a mass following and had laid the foundations for the black nationalism of the 1960s which would be associated with the Nation of Islam and the Black Panthers.

What contribution did A. Philip Randolph make to African-American rights?

A. Philip Randolph's contribution was primarily in the field of labour relations. In 1925, he was the founding president of the African-American Brotherhood of Sleeping Car Porters on the railroad. In 1938, he took his union into the Congress of Industrial Organisations – a new national union structure. Randolph did so because he disliked the segregationist views of the other national union organisation, the American Federation of Labor.

Randolph's greatest triumph was his planned March on Washington in early 1941, as a means to force President Franklin D. Roosevelt (FDR) to make concessions to African-Americans. As he stated in January 1941: 'We loyal Americans demand the right to work and fight for our country.'

The march on Washington movement was an all-black protest. It was a forerunner of the type of protest associated with the civil rights movement in the 1950s and 1960s. But the planned march never took place. Instead, FDR issued Executive Order 8802, in June 1941. It outlawed racial discrimination in the defence industries. This enabled tens of thousands of African-Americans to gain employment during the Second World War.

Inspired by Randolph's action, James Farmer founded the Congress of Racial Equality, in 1942. The aim of this organisation was to engage in non-violent protest in order to help gain civil and political rights for African-Americans. In 1943, this involved a 'sit-in' protest at a Chicago restaurant which had refused to serve African-Americans.

How important was the 'Great Migration' for African-Americans?

While leaders such as Du Bois, Garvey and Randolph helped to devise strategies to improve the position of African-Americans in US society, individual blacks 'voted with their feet' to improve their lives. As a result of the outbreak of the First World War in Europe, in 1914, European immigration dropped sharply. In its place came the migration of African-Americans from the Old South northward. Between 1915 and 1925, 1.25 million African-Americans sought employment in the North. Between 1925 and 1940, a further one million migrated north. From 1910 to 1930, the African-American population of Chicago rose from 44,000 to 234,000. In New York, over the same period, the population rose from 91,000 to 328,000.

A. Philip Randolph (1889–1979)

Black trade unionist. Socialist Party candidate in the early 1920s. In 1925, he founded the Brotherhood of Sleeping Car Porters – an African-American union. Got union to join Congress of Industrial Organisation (CIO) in 1938. In 1940–41 Randolph organised the March on Washington Movement to campaign for civil rights. The march was called off following the President's decision to end discrimination in the defence industry. In 1948, Randolph helped to persuade President Truman to end segregation in armed forces. In 1955, became Vice-President when the CIO merged with American Federation of Labor to form the AFL/CIO.

Most African-Americans moving north were forced to live in black ghettos. In Chicago, blacks lived on the South Side in places such as Calumet City; in New York they lived in Harlem and in Philadelphia on the north and west of the city.

This large-scale population movement had important cultural consequences. It led to the development and growth of jazz. Black singers and musicians became known nationally. In the Cotton Club, in Harlem, New York singers such as Cab Calloway and band-leaders such as Duke Ellington were given their opportunity. African-American musicals appeared on Broadway, such as 'Shuffle Along' in 1922, and 'Blackbirds' from 1926–28. The two most prominent black artists in the period were trumpet player and singer Louis Armstrong and singer-actor Paul Robeson. These performers helped to raise the national profile of African-American culture.

It was these groups which were most receptive to Marcus Garvey's crusade for black nationalism and A. Philip Randolph's call for black membership of trade unions.

However, the arrival of large numbers of African-Americans in northern cities also increased racial tension. In 1919, race riots occurred across America in 25 cities. In 1942, a major race riot in Detroit led to the deployment of troops to restore order.

How far had the position of African-Americans changed within US society by 1945?

By 1945, the geography of African-American society had changed drastically. No longer were they concentrated in the Old South, engaging in subsistence agriculture. African-American education had expanded dramatically. Black schools, agricultural colleges and universities were firmly established across the Old South. However, for the vast majority of African-Americans, social advancement was segregated from whites.

Nevertheless, the foundations of what was to become the civil rights movement had been laid. Beginning in 1915, the NAACP had successfully reversed discriminatory legislation in the Supreme Court. In 1938, in the case of 'Missouri ex rel. Gaines versus Canada', the Supreme Court made its first attack on the 'separate but equal' interpretation of the Fourteenth Amendment when it declared that Missouri had failed to provide law school places for African-American students.

In addition, during the New Deal, FDR had begun to offer government positions to African-Americans. In the Second New Deal (1935–37), Mary McLeod Bethune was appointed director of the Division of Negro Affairs of the National Youth Administration. During the Second World War, Robert Weaver was made an adviser to the Department of the Interior. Eleanor Roosevelt, the President's wife, supported civil rights. She resigned from the Daughters of the American Revolution when they refused to allow African-American Marian Anderson to sing in Constitutional Hall, Washington. During the Second World War, Eleanor Roosevelt gave active support to the creation of the African-American 90th fighter group based at Tuskegee.

The NAACP, the National Urban League and the Congress for Racial Equality had all been created by 1945. Between 1940 and 1947, African-American voter registration in the Old South had increased from 2 per cent to 12 per cent.

When tens of thousands of African-American servicemen returned from the Second World War, hopes were high for greater civil, political and social rights.

1. Explain in what ways Booker T. Washington and W.E.B. Du Bois differed in their views on the improvement of the position of African-Americans in US society?

2. Why do you think Marcus Garvey's views were popular with northern African-Americans?

3. Who do you regard as the most important influence on the development on African-American rights between 1877–1945: Booker T. Washington, W.E.B. Du Bois, Marcus Garvey or A. Philip Randolph?

Explain your answer.

7.4 How successful were African-Americans in their attempt to gain civil and political rights, 1945–1968?

The years 1945 to 1968 represent the most significant years in the movement for African-American civil and political rights. During this period, thousands of African-Americans across the USA took it upon themselves to fight for an improvement in their position. Their efforts placed African-American civil rights at the centre of US politics.

The quest for greater equality must be seen against the background of the Cold War. From 1945, the USA and its allies were engaged in a global ideological and military struggle with communism. The USA portrayed itself as the defender of the Free World against communist tyranny. It was also a period of rapid decolonisation by the European powers, most notably Britain and France. As the former colonies received independence, they became a battleground in the conflict between East and West. Against this backdrop of world events, the existence of legal segregation in the Old South seemed to be a major embarrassment for the United States' position in the world.

Also during this period, a revolution occurred in the mass media. The development of television and, in particular, television news, brought the issue of civil rights into every American living room. No longer could the African-American be regarded as America's 'invisible man', suffering discrimination in silence.

In their struggle for full civil and political rights, African-Americans used a variety of methods and worked through a variety of institutions. Already in existence was the National Association for the Advancement of Colored People (NAACP), founded in 1909. It used legal challenges in the courts to overturn discrimination. In 1941, A. Philip Randolph had used the threat of a march on Washington to force the federal government to take action on behalf of African-Americans in employment. In the following year, the Congress for Racial Equality was founded by James Farmer. It supported the non-violent political protest put forward by the Indian nationalist leader, Mahatma Gandhi.

These groups had to fight against legal segregation in the Old South backed up by violence and intimidation by groups such as the Ku Klux Klan. Elsewhere in America, African-Americans faced discrimination in jobs and housing. In 1947, the Brooklyn Dodgers Baseball team caused a sensation by playing an African-American, Jackie Robinson, in major league baseball for the first time. In Hollywood films and popular novels, African-Americans were usually portrayed as poorly educated, doing menial jobs and always in a supporting role. The first African-American to win an Oscar was Hattie McDaniel, as Scarlett O'Hara's African-American maid in 'Gone With the Wind', in 1939.

In popular cartoons, the only part of an African-American to appear were the legs of a maid in the 'Tom and Jerry' cartoons. Even though the USA had fought to defend freedom against Nazi Germany and Japan, it had done so with segregated armed forces. In 1945, the obstacles to African-American equality seemed enormous.

The NAACP, the US Supreme Court and legal challenges to segregation in education

The challenge to legal segregation was rooted in the US Constitution. Under the Bill of Rights of 1791 and the Fourteenth Amendment of 1868, African-Americans were guaranteed equal civil rights. However, the Supreme Court had interpreted the Constitution in such a way as to allow legal segregation. The most important Supreme Court judgements had been 'Plessy versus Ferguson' of 1896 and 'Cumming versus the Board of Education' in 1899. These established the principle of 'separate but equal' facilities.

However, the interpretation of the Constitution was dependent upon the composition of the Supreme Court. In the late 1930s and early 1940s, FDR had appointed justices, such as Felix Frankfurter, who were sympathetic to black civil rights. A turning point was the appointment of Earl Warren, former Republican Governor of California, as Chief Justice in 1953. President Eisenhower later claimed that this was 'the biggest goddam mistake I ever made'. Warren was to lead the Supreme Court into its most liberal, radical phase between 1953 and 1969.

The 'Brown versus Board of Education' case, 1954

On 17 May 1954, the Supreme Court declared separate but equal educational facilities unconstitutional, in a 9–0 unanimous decision. In 'Brown versus the Board of Education, Topeka, Kansas', the Supreme Court declared that 'separate but equal' educational facilities were not of equal standard and that African-American children had been psychologically affected by such a system. The case had been brought to the Supreme Court by the NAACP legal team, headed by Thurgood Marshall, in 1953. It was the culmination of a series of cases which had been brought before the Court since 1945. For instance, in the 'Sweatt versus Painter' case in 1950, the Court had already demanded a $3 million upgrading of the African-American Prairie View University in Texas, because its facilities were inferior to those of white colleges in the state.

What was also significant about the Brown case was the fact that legal segregation had taken place in a state outside the former Confederacy. In 1955, in what became known as the 'Brown II' case, the Supreme Court demanded the integration of all public schools 'with all deliberate speed'.

Although the NAACP had won over the Supreme Court, it faced massive resistance from whites in the Old South. White citizens' councils were created across the South to oppose integration. State governors such as Ross Barnett in Mississippi actively supported these councils. Faced with possible integration, states such as Virginia merely closed down the public school system. In 1955, 100 southern Congressmen signed 'The Southern Manifesto' declaring that the 'Brown case' was a 'clear abuse of judicial power'. By the end of 1956, not one school had been integrated in the 'Deep South'.

Central High School, Little Rock, 1957

In September 1957, matters were brought to a head at Central High School, in Little Rock, Arkansas. A moderate southern state with a moderate governor, Orval Faubus, Arkansas refused to allow school integration. When nine students attempted to enrol at Central High, a white mob surrounded the school. It was only when President Eisenhower sent 1,000 members of the 101st Airborne Division that the students were able to attend school.

James Meredith and 'Ole Miss.', 1962

Another crisis over educational integration occurred when African-American James Meredith attempted to enrol in the all-white University of Mississippi in Oxford. Opposed by Governor Ross Barnett and the state citizens' council, Meredith was only admitted after President Kennedy sent in hundreds of US **marshals** and thousands of troops to maintain order. Meredith was admitted to university, but was later wounded in a shooting (see photo opposite).

Marshals: Police officers in the USA who control and organise a particular area or district.

'Alexander versus Holmes County', 1969

Even after Earl Warren had retired from the US Supreme Court in 1969,

James Meredith lying on a Mississippi highway, 6 June 1966, after being shot by a sniper.

De facto: [Latin] Existing in fact, whether legal or not.

the Court continued to champion the cause of school integration. In the 1969 case of 'Alexander versus Holmes County', the Court declared that all public schools should be desegregated immediately. The claim was that the Brown II case had demanded 'all deliberate speed' in 1956, and no further delays could be tolerated by 1969. Between 1969 and 1974, the proportion of African-American schoolchildren in the Old South who were educated in segregated schools, dropped from 68 per cent to 8 per cent.

'Swann versus Charlotte Mecklenburg Board of Education', 1971
Although legal segregation of public schools was being brought to an end following the Brown decision of 1954, schools were still divided into black and white elsewhere in America as a result of segregated housing. In the 'Swann' case, this *de facto* segregation of schools was to end.

This case led to the need to bus black and white students across urban areas in order to integrate schools racially. In the North, this involved bussing black students from inner-city ghettos into white suburbs, and vice versa. This created widespread resistance. Serious rioting occurred in Boston, Massachusetts, in 1974. It became part of a nationwide campaign called ROAR (Restore our Alienated Rights). Opposition led a more conservative Supreme Court, in 1974, to moderate its position on compulsory bussing in 'Milliken versus Bradley'.

Ending the reign of 'Jim Crow' in the Old South, 1955–1965

While the NAACP had fought a long campaign to persuade the US Supreme Court to end segregation in education, the campaign to end segregation in transportation produced new organisations and new African-American leaders.

The Montgomery bus boycott of 1955–1956
The Montgomery bus boycott is of great significance to the civil rights movement for several reasons. It saw:

- the creation of an important grassroots African-American organisation – the Montgomery Improvement Association (MIA);

- the rise to national prominence of a young Baptist minister, Dr Martin Luther King Junior;

- the growth of a concerted, well-organised and successful, peaceful resistance by African-Americans to bus segregation in the heart of the Old South. (Montgomery, in 1861, had been the Confederate capital for a brief period.)

The person who sparked off the boycott was Mrs Rosa Parks, a NAACP activist, when she was arrested in March 1955 for not giving up her seat to a white man while sitting at the front of a bus. Bus boycotts had occurred before across the South, in places such as Baton Rouge, Louisiana. Rosa Parks had previously refused to give up her seat, but this was the first time she had been arrested. Local members of the NAACP, such as E.D. Nixon, wanted to use the Parks case to launch a campaign to end bus segregation in Montgomery and, ultimately, across the South.

The choice of Martin Luther King to 'front' the protest proved prophetic. A supporter of non-violent political protest, King was influenced by the example of Mahatma Gandhi, the Indian national leader. King was an excellent speaker. As a minister, he reflected a central feature of African-American leadership in the South. Using their churches, ministers had led the way in protesting against segregation and discrimination. At the Dexter Avenue Baptist Church in Montgomery, Alabama, King preached his non-violent political message. Before him, the Reverend Vernon Johns had used his position to highlight injustices against blacks.

As an outsider, as a minister and as an effective speaker, Martin Luther King was able to forge links between different African-American groups into the MIA. Initially, the MIA did not want an end to bus segregation. Instead, it wanted a more humane enforcement of segregation. For instance, it wanted drivers to be more polite to African-American customers.

However, due to white intransigence and the almost universal acceptance of the boycott by African-Americans, bus segregation was brought to an end on 21 December 1956.

The Montgomery bus boycott was successful only partly because of King's leadership. The boycott also received considerable sympathy from the white press, in particular outside the Old South. It was also made possible because on 13 November, in 'Browder versus Gayle', the US Supreme Court had declared bus segregation unconstitutional in Montgomery.

The successful boycott, in the face of widespread white opposition, encouraged further action by African-Americans. In 1957, the Southern Christian Leadership Conference (SCLC) was formed in Atlanta, Georgia. Martin Luther King became its leader and spokesman. The SCLC reflected the importance of African-American ministers as the focal point of opposition to discrimination. It also planned to be an **umbrella organisation** providing central direction to different civil rights groups and organisations.

SNCC and the lunch counter protests, 1960

Martin Luther King and the SCLC may have had a powerful national profile, but the civil rights movement was a broader, more diverse affair. In *Bearing the Cross: Martin Luther King Jr and the Southern Christian Leadership Conference* (1986), David Garrow quoted African-American activist Jo Ann Robinson about the nature of the movement. She states:

'The amazing thing about our movement is that it is a protest of the people. It is not a one-man show. It is not a preachers' show. It's the people.'

To prove this point, on 1 February 1960, a group of African-American students entered the Woolworth's department store in Greensboro, North Carolina and sat down at the 'whites only' lunch counter waiting to be served. This sparked off a wave of non-violent lunch counter protests in 54 cities across nine states in the Old South (see photo). In April 1961, at Shaw University, Raleigh, North Carolina, black activist Ella Baker founded the

---

Martin Luther King (1929–68)
King was born in Atlanta, Georgia. By the time he became a Baptist minister, in 1954, he was a civil rights campaigner for African-Americans and a member of the National Association for the Advancement of Coloured people. He first came to national attention as leader of the Montgomery bus boycott of 1955/6. In 1957, he was elected president of the Southern Christian Leadership Conference – an organisation formed to provide new leadership for the civil rights movement. Target of intensive investigation by federal authorities, chiefly the FBI under J. Edgar Hoover. Luther King was one of the organisers of the march of 20,000 people on Washington DC (1963) to demand racial equality. King was a brilliant speaker and between 1957 and his death in 1968 he spoke over 2,500 times about injustice, protest and action. In 1964, he was awarded the Nobel Peace Prize. On the evening of 4 April 1968 his life was brought to an untimely end when he was assassinated by a lone, white gunman in Memphis, Tennessee.

Umbrella organisation: An organisation which tries to unite a variety of different organisation under its leadership.

A Caucasian (white) woman bars the way as African-Americans are about to enter the lunch counter of a department store in Memphis, Tennessee, on 10 June 1961.

Student Non-violent Co-ordinating Committee (SNCC). The aim of the organisation was to give a voice to African-American students. Martin Luther King encouraged SNCC, hoping that it would be a student wing of the SCLC. However, the students stayed independent of the SCLC.

The sit-in protests were reported in the national press. Attacks by whites on sit-in protestors were seen on television. Student involvement was central to the protests against discrimination. The success in desegregating lunch counters laid the foundation for greater student protest. Joining with students from CORE, the Congress for Racial Equality, SNCC activists engaged in the Freedom Rides of 1961.

CORE and the Freedom Rides of 1961

The Freedom Rides, on inter-state buses through the South, reflect an important feature of the civil rights movement. The aim was to shame the federal government into action which would safeguard African-American rights. As James Farmer, founder of CORE, stated:

> 'We planned the Freedom Rides with the specific intention of creating a crisis. We were counting on the bigots of the South to do our work for us. We figured that the government would have to respond if we created a situation that was headline news all over the world, and affecting the nation's image abroad. An international crisis that was our strategy.'

All CORE planned to do was to find out if the law against segregation on inter-state bus travel really existed in the South. Already in two decisions – in 1946 in 'Morgan versus Virginia' and in 1960 in 'Boynton versus Virginia' – the Supreme Court had outlawed segregation on inter-state bus travel.

On 4 May 1961, four white and four African-American students took inter-state buses from Virginia to Mississippi to test the law. At Anniston, Alabama, the **Greyhound bus** in which they were travelling was fire-bombed. Other freedom riders were attacked by a mob in Birmingham, Alabama, and in Jackson, Mississippi.

Greyhound bus: A bus company providing long-distance travel services across the USA.

The media coverage of these events had the desired effect. It forced the Inter-state Commerce Commission and the Justice Department, under

Attorney General Robert F. Kennedy, to enforce segregation on inter-state transportation.

What the lunch counter protests and the freedom rides achieved was to add a new dimension to civil rights protests. Although professing non-violence, the students of SNCC and CORE forced Southern whites into violent retaliation by their actions. They had actively encouraged violent white resistance to highlight their case to American and world public opinion. In doing so, they forced the Kennedy Administration to act.

Birmingham and the march on Washington in 1963

The need to emulate the success of African-American and white students of SNCC and CORE was not lost on Martin Luther King. Following his success in the Montgomery bus boycott of 1955–56, he had experienced mixed success. An attempt by SCLC to double the level of black voter registration in the 'Crusade for Citizenship', between 1958 and 1960, had limited success. Also, during 1961–62 King had become involved in civil rights protests in Albany, Georgia. However, the white Police Chief, Laurie Pritchett, avoided violence and forced King to abandon his campaign in August 1962.

In 1963, King was able to find the confrontation he required in Birmingham, Alabama. The Police Chief, Eugene 'Bull' Connor, played into the hands of the civil rights demonstrators who wanted to end segregation in the city. Using schoolchildren as demonstrators, the civil rights organisers were able to provoke Connor into using police dogs and water cannon – all filmed and shown on primetime television.

In August 1963, A. Philip Randolph's dream of a march on Washington took place. Over 250,000 civil rights supporters met at the Lincoln Memorial to hear Martin Luther King make the keynote speech. In his 'I have a Dream' speech, King put forward his own vision of an integrated, tolerant society. It confirmed him in the position of both leader and conscience of the civil rights movement. It also propelled him into the centre of the international stage and led, in 1964, to his being awarded the Nobel Peace Prize.

Freedom summer and the Mississippi Freedom Democratic Party, 1964

In the summer of 1964, SNCC organised communities across the South to develop local civil rights groups to campaign for greater equality. SNCC members, both white and black, faced considerable white opposition. Several were murdered. These events formed the background for the 1988 film 'Mississippi Burning', starring Gene Hackman and Willem Dafoe.

When SNCC organisers could not register black voters through normal methods, they encouraged African-Americans in Mississippi to form the Mississippi Freedom Democratic Party (MFDP), as an alternative to the white-dominated state party.

At the Democratic National Convention in August 1964 in Atlantic City, New Jersey, both the official state Democratic Party and the MFDP demanded to represent the delegation from Mississippi. Lyndon Johnson and his aides were able to offer a compromise by allowing the MFDP two representatives at the Convention. Johnson's action led to the official state delegation leaving the Convention in protest.

The incident at the Democratic National Convention made many SNCC members disillusioned with the Johnson government and helped force them towards a more radical stand in 1965.

Selma and the Voting Rights Act of 1965 – the high tide of Martin Luther King's influence?

King's ability to pressure federal government into action is illustrated by his participation in the Selma to Montgomery peace march of 1965. His actions came after the failure of black activists during Freedom Summer of 1964 to increase African-American voter registration.

Deliberately marching through the most racist part of Alabama, the marchers faced violent reaction from state troopers and white protestors at Pettus Bridge, Selma. Known as 'Bloody Sunday', the incident on 7 March 1965 forced President Johnson to intervene. He placed state troopers under federal control. They allowed the march to continue to Montgomery. The publicity created sufficient pressure to help Congress pass the Voting Rights Act of 1965, which guaranteed the voting rights originally provided by the Fifteenth Amendment of the Constitution in 1870. As a result of the passage of the 1964 Civil Rights Act, the Twenty-Fourth Amendment and the Voting Rights Act of 1965, legal segregation was brought to an end in the United States. The civil and political rights first granted to African-Americans in the Civil Rights Amendments of 1865 to 1870, now became a reality.

After Selma, Martin Luther King's authority as the spokesman for African-American civil rights declined. In August 1965, serious rioting by African-Americans in the Watts district (now South Central) of Los Angeles left 34 people dead. In July and August, King attempted to lead a civil rights campaign in Chicago. However, attempts to desegregate the Gage Park housing district led to massive white resistance and King was forced to call off his campaign.

The 'March against Fear' was organised in June 1966. The event was to commemorate James Meredith's admission to the University of Mississippi in 1962. Early in the march, Meredith was wounded by a sniper and had to withdraw (see photograph on page 229). However, when the SCLC and SNCC became involved, splits about tactics and aims began to appear. The

1. Which states had the lowest African-American voter registration before the Voting Rights Act of 1865? Give reasons.

2. Which state displayed the greatest increase in African-American voter registration after the passage of the 1965 Voting Rights Act?

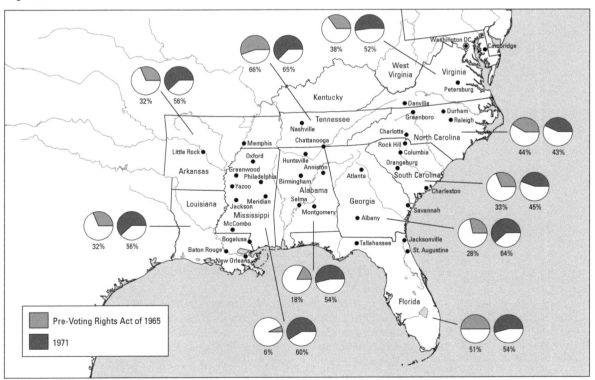

Map showing the major cities of the southern civil rights movement and the percentage of black voting-age population registered.

Civil rights legislation, 1964–1965

The Civil Rights Act, 1964

- Discrimination on the basis of race was outlawed in all places of public accommodation including restaurants, theatres, motels, sports stadia, cinemas and concert halls.

- The Attorney General of the USA was given power to start federal court action against any violation.

- The federal government had the power to withhold federal funds from any state not complying with the Act.

- It set up the Equal Employment Opportunities Commission with powers to outlaw job discrimination.

Twenty-Fourth Amendment to the Constitution, 1964

- Outlawed the use of poll taxes in federal elections.

The Voting Rights Act, 1965

- Banned literacy tests for voter registration.

- Appointed federal examiners to ensure voter registration.

'March against Fear' represents the beginning of a split within the civil rights movement, which saw the end of Martin Luther King's dominance.

In 1967, Martin Luther King made the momentous decision to speak out openly against American participation in the Vietnam War. His criticism of the Johnson Administration ended his links with the federal government, which had led to the passage of the civil rights legislation of 1964 and 1965.

In the same year, Martin Luther King broadened his campaign beyond civil and political rights. His 'Poor People's Campaign' aimed at achieving social equality. This change in direction led to a fall in support from white, middle-class liberals. When King was assassinated in Memphis, in April 1968, he was speaking in support of the sanitation workers' strike. Yet by that date, the civil rights movement had begun to fracture, revealing more radical and militant groups and aims.

The rise of radical black activism, 1965–68

Throughout its existence, the civil rights movement had been a loose coalition of groups. For a period up to 1965, Martin Luther King had acted as national spokesman. However, by then, the coalition had begun to fall apart. More radical voices than Martin Luther King's began to appear.

Malcolm X

Born in 1925, Malcolm X continues to be a figure of controversy. He presented a completely different vision of the position of the African-American in US society from that of Martin Luther King. From excerpts of speeches they made, compare the views of these two figures.

Malcolm X (1925–1965)
Born Malcolm Little in Nebraska. Black radical who joined Nation of Islam. Split with Nation of Islam in 1964 and was murdered in Harlem by Nation of Islam supporters.

Martin Luther King's 'I have a Dream' speech, August 1963, encapsulates his philosophy:

'I have a dream that one day this nation will rise up and live out the true meaning of its creed "We hold these truths to be self-evident, that all men are created equal."

I have a dream that my four little children will one day live in a nation where they will not be judged by the colour of their skin but the content of their character …

Let freedom ring. When we let freedom ring … we will be able to speed up that day when all God's children, black men and white men, Jews and Gentiles, Protestants and Catholics, will be able to join hands.'

From a speech by Malcolm X to the Northern Negro Leadership Conference, Detroit, November 1963:

'The white man knows what revolution is. He knows that the black revolution is worldwide in scope and in nature. The black revolution is sweeping Asia, is sweeping Africa, is rearing its head in Latin America.

Revolution is bloody, revolution is hostile, revolution knows no compromise, revolution overturns and destroys everything that gets in its way.

Whoever heard of a revolution where they lock arms, singing "We shall overcome"? You don't do that in a revolution. Those Negroes aren't asking for a nation – they're trying to crawl back to the plantation.'

King's speech is optimistic and tolerant, looking forward to an integrated society. Malcolm X, on the other hand, supports black revolution. It is intolerant and threatening.

Part of the difference comes from the fact that Malcolm X was brought up in a northern ghetto. He was from a poor background and had spent time in jail for drug offences. King came from a middle-class Southern background.

By 1963, Malcolm X had become a member of the Nation of Islam, the Black Muslims. He supported black nationalism. As a result, he had more in common with Marcus Garvey (see section 7.3) than with Martin Luther King. Malcolm X wanted to go beyond mere civil and political rights. He supported social revolution.

In November 1963, Malcolm X decided to split from the Nation of Islam and establish his own organisation. From then until his death, in February 1965 at the hands of Nation of Islam assassins, Malcolm X began to moderate his views on whites, but maintained his support for revolutionary movements in Africa and Latin America.

Unlike King, Malcolm X had virtually no influence outside the ghettos of the North. However, he did represent a more intolerant, radical view which found expression in other groups.

Black Power and the Black Panthers

Malcolm X is less important for what he personally achieved than for his influence on other black radicals. Floyd McKissick became chairman of CORE in January 1966. In SNCC, Stokely Carmichael became chairman

Stokely Carmichael (1941–2000)
West Indian-born, radical black activist. Emigrated from Trinidad to USA in 1951. Joined SNCC at university. Was a freedom rider in 1961. Chairman of SNCC in 1966. Became supporter of Black Power. Left SNCC in 1968 and opposed the Vietnam War. Later helped found the All-African People's Revolutionary Party and changed his name to Kwame Toure.

later in the same year. Both figures supported liberation movements in the Third World. They also wanted to adopt a more radical approach to civil rights. The idea associated with both chairmen was Black Power. It emerged from a growing belief and pride in being African-American. Opposition to the Vietnam War also affected it. By 1967, Carmichael and McKissick had rejected the tolerant, non-violent strategy used by Martin Luther King. Instead, they sought solidarity with Africa and the development of a separate and distinct black identity. An offshoot of the development of Black Power was the adoption of the Afro hairstyle by many northern blacks.

The most extreme manifestation of Black Power was the Black Panther Party for Self-Defense. This was founded in October 1966 in Oakland, California, by Huey Newton and Bobby Seale. The Black Panthers identified more with Cuban revolutionary Che Guevara than with Martin Luther King. Their demands included reparations to the black community for the discrimination faced by African-Americans since their arrival as slaves. They also wanted blacks to be exempt from military service. Wearing

> **Huey P. Newton (1942–1989)**
> Co-founder in 1966 with Bobby Seale of Black Panther Party in Oakland, California to protect blacks against police brutality and racial discrimination. Convicted of the manslaughter of a policeman in 1967. Conviction was later overturned. Fled to Cuba in 1974 to avoid a murder charge, but returned to USA in 1977. Murdered in Oakland (1989).

Explain why posters like this would attract African-Americans to support 'Black Power'?

'Power to the People' poster produced by the Black Panthers, 1960s

distinctive black berets, black leather jackets and black gloves, the Panthers represented the most extreme phase of the civil rights movement.

The high point in the publicity for Black Power came with the Mexico Olympics in 1968. At the 400 metres men's final award ceremony, African-Americans Tommy Smith and John Carlos made the Black Power salute with black leather gloves. After the demonstration, neither athlete represented the USA again. In 1969, 27 Black Panthers were shot by the police and 750 were arrested. By 1970, FBI infiltration had broken the back of the Black Panther leadership. Never numbering more than 5,000 members, the Black Panthers gained publicity far greater than their real influence deserved.

How far had African-Americans gained their civil and political rights by 1968?

1. What methods did African-Americans use to advance their case for civil rights?

2. Why was legal segregation brought to an end by the mid-1960s?

3. How far was the achievement of civil rights due to actions of African-Americans?

By the time of Martin Luther King's assassination, legal segregation was rapidly coming to an end in the Old South. However, *de facto* segregation of schools still existed across America because of racially separated housing areas. Although African-Americans could now vote freely, many still faced severe economic hardship. Poorly educated compared with whites and living in poor housing, African-Americans still faced far greater social and economic problems than the majority of the white population.

Instead of being a year of triumph for African-Americans, 1968 became a year of riots in almost every major city across the USA.

7.5 The role of Dr Martin Luther King Jr in the civil rights movement
A CASE STUDY IN HISTORICAL INTERPRETATION

The case for King

To many people, both within and outside the United States, Martin Luther King personified the civil rights movement. Today, his memory is celebrated in the USA by a national holiday on the day of his birth. In the Auburn District of Atlanta, the Martin Luther King National Historic Site has been created. It has, as its centrepiece, a history of the civil rights movement.

When King was assassinated by a lone, white gunman, he instantly became the martyr of the civil rights movement. His funeral in Atlanta, on 9 April 1968, was attended by political leaders from around the world and across America. After all, it was an election year. In his funeral oration to Dr King, Benjamin Mays, his former teacher, claimed that King had:

> 'contributed largely to the success of the student sit-in movements in abolishing segregation in downtown establishments. His activities contributed mightily to the passage of the civil rights legislation of 1964 and 1965.'

Later, in 1977, when King received the posthumous award of the Presidential Medal of Freedom, the citation stated: 'Martin Luther King Jr was the conscience of his generation. A Southerner, a black man, he gazed upon the great wall of segregation and saw that the power of love could bring it down.'

Clearly, Dr King had a large impact on how the civil rights movement was perceived by other Americans and by people around the world. His ability to speak eloquently and thoughtfully gave him a high profile in the age of television. His speeches during the Montgomery bus boycott maintained morale among the local African-American community. His 'I have a

Dream' speech in August 1963 is widely regarded as one of the finest speeches in US history.

However, it was not just the delivery of speeches that made King so significant, it was also the message. His support for non-violent, peaceful protest was the only realistic strategy open to African-Americans at the time, if they were to achieve their civil and political rights. Any other strategy would have resulted in a more violent backlash. King's strategy elevated the civil rights cause to a high spiritual and religious level. As a Baptist minister, he turned the civil rights cause into a religious movement in the way Lincoln had transformed the conflict between the states into a moral crusade into end slavery in the Civil War.

King's strategy was effective because African-Americans, in theory at least, already had equal civil and political rights. These had been guaranteed by the three Civil War amendments of 1865–70. What King and his supporters were able to do through their peaceful protests was to shame America into recognising that fact. Through the use of the media and by linking the civil rights cause directly with the Declaration of Independence and the Constitution, King occupied the high moral and political ground.

In many ways, King was fortunate in facing opponents who, themselves, reflected the intolerance of which he spoke. In 1955, during the Montgomery bus boycott, African-Americans were attacked and churches bombed. Then Emmet Till, a young African-American boy from Chicago, was brutally murdered by two white men in Money, Mississippi, for the crime of having talked to a white woman. His mother demanded an open casket funeral back in Chicago, where the nation's media photographed Till's badly mutilated body.

From a media point of view, Eugene 'Bull' Connor, the police chief of Birmingham, Alabama, offered the most striking example of white intolerance, in the full glare of national publicity at the civil rights demonstrations of 1963. Arresting schoolchildren and pregnant women, brutally attacking the demonstrators with dogs and water cannon, Connor was the personification of everything that was wrong with legal segregation in the South.

King's contribution was also important in organisation. In 1957, he was elected president of the Southern Christian Leadership Conference. King

Martin Luther King delivers his 'I Have a Dream' speech in front of the Lincoln Memorial during the Freedom March in Washington DC, 28 August 1963.

used the organisation as an umbrella organisation to unite the various civil rights groups across the South. From 1957 to 1965, King was the unofficial leader of the civil rights movement.

He also inspired others to participate in the movement. His non-violent protest strategy inspired the lunch counter protesters of 1960, which led to the formation of SNCC. King also inspired liberal whites to take part in the civil rights cause. His moral, non-violent stance helped to create this fragile coalition of interests.

Due to his high media and national profile, King was able to act as the link between the civil rights movement and the White House during the Kennedy and Johnson years. King met Kennedy twice during the presidential campaign of 1960. It was Robert F. Kennedy, the brother of the presidential candidate, who helped get King out of an Atlanta jail after he had been arrested for the first time during a voter registration drive. These events helped to forge a link between King and the Kennedy White House, in particular with Robert Kennedy, the Attorney General. During the Kennedy Administration (1961–63), Robert Kennedy intervened decisively on a number of occasions to help the cause of educational integration in the South.

During and after the Montgomery bus boycott, King served as a catalyst of increasing symbolic and charismatic significance. He was able to direct attention onto, and support for, protests started by others.

Until the emergence of the Black Power slogan, King, through his prestige and force of personality, was able to hold together an obviously fragmenting civil rights coalition. In this respect, he served as the vital centre of the movement, standing between the 'conservatism' of the NAACP and National Urban League, and the 'radicalism' of SNCC and CORE.

A testimony to King's role in the civil rights movement is to assess what happened to the SCLC after his assassination. Under the Reverend Ralph Abernathy and then the Reverend Jesse Jackson, the organisation declined rapidly in significance.

The supporters of Black Power, who criticised King's campaign strategy, achieved far less for African-Americans. It is significant that many historians conclude their studies of the civil rights movement in 1968 with King's death.

The case against Martin Luther King

Ella Baker, a former staff member of the SCLC and a founder of SNCC claimed that 'the movement made Martin rather than Martin making the movement'. It is clear that the civil rights movement, in its broadest sense, was already in existence by the time Dr King became actively involved. The NAACP had already won the historic Brown case in the US Supreme Court in 1954. King was not involved in the events surrounding the enrolment of nine black students at Central High School, Little Rock in 1957, nor was he involved in James Meredith's application to attend the University of Mississippi in 1962. In fact, on the whole issue of desegregation in education, Martin Luther King had played a marginal role.

When he was asked by E.D. Nixon to front the Montgomery Improvement Association during the bus boycott of 1955–56, he was chosen because he was an outsider and a person not associated with the civil rights struggle in Montgomery.

Andrew King, a member of SCLC and, later, Mayor of Atlanta claimed that:

'everything [Martin Luther King] did he was pushed into. He went to Montgomery in the first place because … he wanted a nice quiet town where he could finish his doctoral dissertation … and got trapped into the Montgomery Improvement Association. It wasn't until the time of Birmingham [1963] that he kinda decided that he wasn't going to be able to escape.'

King was more a spokesman than a leader of a wide and diverse movement. The lunch counter protests of 1960 and the Freedom Rides of 1961 were devised and executed by students outside his control. King's attempts to make the SNCC the student wing of SCLC came to nothing. From 1960 to 1965, SNCC and CORE had an uneasy relationship with King and the SCLC.

Unlike the students of SNCC and CORE, King faced a number of embarrassing failures as leader of SCLC. The campaign for increased voter registration, from 1958 to 1960, had virtually no impact. His attempt to desegregate Albany, Georgia, in 1961–62 also came to nothing. When faced by a shrewd police chief, like Laurie Pritchett in Albany, who avoided violent confrontation, King's tactics did not work.

Above all, King's area of influence was the Old South. The SCLC had its headquarters in his home town of Atlanta. In the North, King's role was marginal. On the few occasions King became involved in the civil rights movement in the North, he faced failure. In 1966, King went to Chicago to lead a demonstration against slum housing, *de facto* school segregation and poor employment opportunities for African-Americans. He came across hostile reaction from Polish Americans in Cicero who stoned his march. King was injured by a brick thrown during his attempt to march through the white housing area of Gage Park.

It seems clear that King's influence was centred on the South in the years 1955–66. After that date, SNCC and CORE became detached from King's control. They looked for inspiration from the writing of Malcolm X and the lure of black nationalism. King also lost support from the Johnson White House when he began to speak out openly against the Vietnam War. This was made clear in a speech, on 4 April 1967, at Riverside Church, New York City, when he claimed:

'We have supported the enemies of the peasant of Saigon. What do they think as we test our latest weapons on them, just as the Germans tested out new medicine and new tortures in the concentration camps of Europe?'

Also in 1967, King began to lose white, middle-class support when he embarked on 'The Poor People's Campaign'. Having gained civil and political equality for African-Americans, King was attempting to gain social equality. Through support for Third World revolutionary movements and social justice at home, King had ceased to be a liberal and was perceived to be a socialist.

King did not help his alienation from white, liberal America. He kept as a close aide a known communist, the white Stanley Levinson. This made King and the civil rights cause vulnerable to attacks from FBI chief J. Edgar Hoover, who always contested that King was a communist sympathiser.

Martin Luther King has come to symbolise the civil rights years of 1955–68. The nature of his death elevated King to a national hero. However, as King's own sister, Christine Farris, noted: 'My brother was no saint [but] an average and ordinary man.'

SNCC activist, Diane Nash, claims that:

'If people think that it was Martin Luther King's movement, then today they – young people – are more likely to say, "gosh, I wish we had a Martin Luther King here to lead us today." If people knew how the movement started, then the question they would ask themselves is, "What can I do?"'

1. What do you regard as Martin Luther King's main contribution to the civil rights movement? Explain your answer.

2. Why do you think there are so many differing interpretations of Martin Luther King's role in the civil rights movement?

7.6 How important was the federal government to the achievement of African-American civil rights, 1945–1992?

The federal government occupies a central role in the achievement of full civil rights for African-Americans. It was the federal government, during the Civil War, that freed the slaves. However, from the end of Reconstruction, in 1877, the federal government turned a blind eye to the introduction of legal segregation in the Old South.

The federal government in the USA comprises the President, the Congress and the US Supreme Court. Each branch of the government has played a different role in the achievement of civil rights.

In the Congress, the dominance of the Democratic Party in the Old South, from 1877 to the late 1960s, meant that important committees were run by Southern Democrats, who were completely opposed to full civil rights for African-Americans. Southern Democrats proved to be an obstacle to the introduction of effective civil rights legislation up to the 1960s.

The Presidency has also had a mixed role in the achievement of civil rights. Democrat Presidents Truman, Kennedy and Johnson all played an important role in the advancement of civil rights. However, they faced opposition from within their own party. On two occasions – in 1948 and again in 1968 – Southern Democrats put forward their own anti-civil rights presidential candidate, to stand against the official Democrat candidate.

Finally, the US Supreme Court played a central role in the achievement of civil rights. As the highest judicial body in the land, its power to interpret the Constitution was central to the ending of legal segregation in the South.

A fair deal for African-Americans under Truman, 1945–1953?

During FDR's long presidency (1933–45) very little was done at federal level to aid African-Americans. Attempts to make lynching a federal offence failed in the Congress. During the New Deal, alphabet agencies did aid poor African-Americans. In the Youth Administration, Mary McLeod Bethune, an African-American, became director of the Negro Affairs Department. However, in the Second World War era, African-Americans benefited from FDR Executive Order 8802, which forbade racial discrimination in the defence industry.

Although Truman came from the border state of Missouri, he had earned a reputation for fairness during the Second World War. When peace came, Truman put the Fair Employment Practice Commission on a permanent, peacetime footing. Truman also met members of the National Emergency Committee against Mob Violence in September 1946. The Committee highlighted the extent of legal segregation in the South and of discrimination against African-Americans.

In the 1948 election, Truman made civil rights an issue. In Executive Order 9980, Truman ended racial discrimination in federal employment. This order created the Fair Employment Board. In August 1948, in Executive Order 9981, he desegregated the US armed forces.

All of these actions helped to alienate Southern Democrats. In retaliation, they put forward Senator Strom Thurmond as a states' rights ('Dixiecrat') candidate for the presidency.

Truman made tentative steps towards providing better rights for African-Americans. He was aided by two Supreme Court decisions – one, in 1946, which outlawed segregation on inter-state buses. He was also supported by the liberal Democrat pressure group, Americans for Democratic Action. However, he was bitterly opposed by Southern Democrat and Republic Congressmen. This group dominated the 80th Congress of 1947–49.

Reluctant player: Dwight D. Eisenhower, 1953–1961

The election of a moderate Republican, in 1952, did not augur well for the civil rights movement. Eisenhower was loath to upset the conservative coalition which had brought him to power. However, his appointment of Earl Warren as Chief Justice of the Supreme Court in 1953 helped to bring about a revolution in that institution. Under Warren's leadership, the Supreme Court became a proactive force in bringing about full civil rights. In the Brown Case of 1954, it declared unconstitutional the 'separate but equal' interpretation of the Fourteenth Amendment.

In response to this development, Eisenhower declared that:

> 'I am convinced that the Supreme Court decision set back progress in the South at least 15 years. It's all very well to talk about school integration – if you remember that you may also be talking about social disintegration.
>
> We can't demand perfection in these moral things. All we can do is keep working toward a goal and keep it high. And the fellow who tries to tell me that you can do these things by force is just plain NUTS!'

However, Eisenhower was forced to act, in September 1957, when Governor Orval Faubus opposed school integration and a white mob attempted to prevent the enrolment of black students. The 1,000 troops from the 101st Airborne Division were sent to enforce integration.

Attempts to aid African-American voter registration were made during Eisenhower's second administration. In the first civil rights acts since Reconstruction, the 1957 and 1960 Acts attempted to give federal judges more power in enforcing black voter registration. However, Southern Democrat resistance in Congress made both Acts ineffectual.

Kennedy and the New Frontier, 1961–1963

John F. Kennedy (JFK), like Martin Luther King, has gone down in history as a martyr – gunned down in his prime, promises unfulfilled. However, the Kennedy Administration had no strategy on civil rights when it entered office. For most of his presidency, JFK displayed a reluctance to get involved in civil rights, an attitude which mirrored the views and actions of his predecessor.

Kennedy was also hampered by the fact that he had won the narrowest of victories over Nixon in the 1960 election, gaining 49.5 per cent of the vote. He also faced a hostile Congress in which a coalition of Southern Democrats and Republicans blocked much of his legislative programme.

Like Eisenhower, Kennedy was forced to act because of actions by African-Americans. The lunch counter protests of 1960, the Freedom Rides of 1961 and James Meredith's attempt to enrol at the University of Mississippi forced federal action. Attorney General, Robert F. Kennedy (RFK), proved to be the most active member of the Administration. Through his actions, lunch counters were desegregated and the Supreme Court ruling on inter-state bussing was enforced. The Justice Department under RFK also helped to desegregate the universities of Mississippi and Alabama.

The intensity of African-American protest and the adverse publicity it gave at the height of the Cold War forced JFK to introduce a Civil Rights Bill, in 1963, to end legal segregation. However, there was little chance of its passing through Congress. JFK's assassination, in November 1963, changed all that.

Johnson and the end of legal segregation, 1963–1969

Ironically, it took a Southern President, from Texas, to bring legal segregation to an end. On the wave of emotion following JFK's assassination and by using his excellent powers of persuasion, Lyndon B. Johnson (LBJ) was able to pass through Congress the Civil Rights Act of 1964 and the Voting Rights Act of 1965. Together with the Twenty-Fourth Amendment of 1964, these enforced the civil and political rights which had been promised to African-Americans in the Civil War amendments of 1865–70. The 1968 Omnibus Housing Act helped to end racial discrimination in housing.

In addition, LBJ's 'war on poverty' brought much needed federal aid to inner city areas. The education, medical and social reforms of the Great Society (see Chapter 8) gave many African-Americans a chance for social and economic advancement.

However, the Johnson years also witnessed the riots of 1965 in Watts and of 1968 across the USA, as African-Americans living in the ghettos of northern cities showed their frustration at decades of discrimination and social deprivation.

Nixon, Ford and Carter, 1969–1981 – a return to conservatism?

Richard Nixon won a narrow election victory over his Democrat opponent Hubert Humphrey in 1968. He was aided by the entry into the race of Alabama Governor, George Wallace, as the American Independent Party candidate. Wallace won the Old South. However, Nixon also received considerable votes in the area. During his presidency, he adopted the 'Southern strategy' of winning the 'solid South' away from the Democratic Party to his own Republican Party.

As part of his plan, he nominated but failed to get appointed two southern conservatives to the Supreme Court, C. Harold Carswell and Clement F. Haynsworth. However, when Chief Justice Earl Warren retired in 1969, he was able to replace him with the conservative Warren E. Burger. Although supposedly more conservative, the Supreme Court under Nixon expanded the scope of school desegregation. In 'Alexander versus Holmes County', school integration in the Old South was speeded up. In 1971, in 'Swann versus Charlotte Mecklenburg Board of Education', bussing was ordered across America to end *de facto* school segregation.

In addition, Nixon greatly reduced direct federal aid to inner cities. Instead, he introduced 'creative federalism' in which federal money was given directly to the states.

Nevertheless, beginning in 1969 with the Philadelphia Plan, Nixon extended the affirmative action programme on federal-funded projects. He wanted firms on government contracts to put aside 26 per cent of their jobs for ethnic minorities within four years. By 1972, affirmative action was extended to embrace over 300,000 firms. In taking this action, Nixon wanted to split the New Deal coalition. He hoped to benefit African-Americans and to damage the power of the AFL/CIO trade union movement. In 1971, the Supreme Court upheld Nixon's right to insist on affirmative action in 'Giggs versus Duke Power Company'.

Jimmy Carter's one-term Democratic Administration (1977–81) made little impact on the plight of African-Americans. For much of Carter's Presidency, the USA faced economic recession. However, Carter did appoint 14 African-Americans as ambassadors. The most high-profile appointment was that of SCLC's Andrew Young to be US ambassador to the UN.

The most significant developments in the Carter years involved legal defence of affirmative action. In the Bakke case of 1978, the Supreme Court retreated on the issue – upholding a white student's right to enter the University of California. Nevertheless, in 1980, in 'Fullilove versus

Klutznick' the Court upheld the need to allocate 10 per cent of jobs to ethnic minorities.

The New Conservatism of Reagan and Bush, 1981–1992

During the Reagan years (1981–89), serious attempts were made to limit federal government support for civil rights programmes and legislation. Reagan limited the power and authority of the US Commission on Civil Rights by appointing more conservative personnel. He did the same in the federal judicial system. In his two terms, he appointed around 25 per cent of the federal judiciary. However, his most significant appointment was that of the conservative William Rehnquist as Chief Justice to the Supreme Court in 1986.

In 1982, Ronald Reagan supported the segregated Bob Jones University in the South in its attempt to get tax exemption status. In 1988, Reagan also vetoed the Civil Rights Restoration Bill which aimed to enforce federal support for affirmative action. However, Republicans and Democrats united in Congress to override his veto. In addition, Reagan opposed the renewal of the Voting Rights Act of 1965.

Perhaps the most significant action by Reagan was his attack on the welfare state, which had been established under the New Deal in the 1930s. 'Reaganomics' (see Chapter 9) saw dramatic tax cuts and cuts in federal programmes to aid the poor. An example was the 1988 Family Support Act, which forced people on welfare to do community service work or to take part in government training schemes. These changes in welfare hit African-Americans particularly badly. In 1980, African-Americans comprised 11.7 per cent of the population but made up 43 per cent of those receiving welfare under Aid to Families with Dependent Children, 34.4 per cent of those in subsidised housing and 35.1 per cent of those using food stamps.

During the Reagan and Bush years, the Supreme Court became more conservative. In 1971, following the retirement from the Court of former NAACP member, Thurgood Marshall, George Bush nominated the conservative African-American, Clarence Thomas. In addition, under both presidents, the Justice Department took a hostile stance towards affirmative action programmes. In 1992, in 'Freeman versus Pitts' the Supreme Court weakened school desegregation orders. By the time of Bill Clinton's election as President in November 1992, many of the gains of the civil rights years of 1954–70 were under threat.

1. Which branch of the federal government was most supportive of African-American civil rights?

Explain your answer.

2. Was the US Presidency more of a hindrance than a help to the cause of African-American civil rights?

Explain your answer.

7.7 How far did African-Americans achieve full civil rights by 1992?

In his study *Black America, 1992, An Overview* (published in 1993), John E. Jacob, President of the National Urban League, declared:

'I would categorise the state of Black America in 1992 as one of bleak despair countered by fresh hope.

The despair was rooted in the effects of a long, debilitating recession that drove many black families deeper into poverty and diminished already stagnating employment opportunities.

The hope was based on the election of a new administration pledged to chart a different course for the nation.'

Many African-Americans faced a life of poverty. On average, they earned 61 per cent of what white families received. Proportionately larger numbers of African-Americans were on welfare and in prison.

The feeling of discrimination and desperation came to a head in South

Central Los Angeles, in the Rodney King affair. An African-American, Rodney King, was videoed being brutally attacked by members of the Los Angeles Police Department. When the police were acquitted, a riot ensued in which 54 people were killed, 2,400 injured and 17,000 arrested. Ten thousand businesses were destroyed, with the loss of 50,000 jobs. Other outbreaks of rioting occurred in Atlanta, San Francisco and Madison, Wisconsin.

1. Describe the changes in average incomes of blacks and whites in the USA between 1967 and 1991.

2. Does the data suggest that the economic position of blacks had improved between 1967 and 1991? Explain your answer.

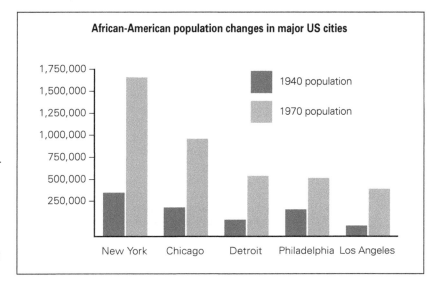

African-American population changes in major US cities

1940 population
1970 population

New York   Chicago   Detroit   Philadelphia   Los Angeles

Average income of persons with income, by race and sex (1991)

	Male			Female		
	Black	White	B/W	Black	White	B/W
1991	$12,962	$21,395	60.6	$8,816	$10,721	82.2
1990	13,409	22,061	60.8	8,678	10,751	80.7
1989	13,850	22,916	60.4	8,650	10,777	80.3
1988	13,866	22,979	60.3	8,461	10,480	80.7
1987	13,449	22,666	59.3	8,331	10,199	81.7
1986	13,630	22,443	59.9	8,160	9,643	84.6
1985	13,630	21,659	62.9	7,945	9,312	85.3
1984	12,385	21,586	57.4	8,080	9,109	88.7
1983	12,335	21,092	58.5	7,615	8,912	85.4
1982	12,591	21,011	59.9	7,498	8,501	88.2
1981	12,851	21,611	59.5	7,412	8,343	88.8
1980	13,254	22,057	60.1	7,580	8,187	92.6
1979	14,019	22,648	61.9	7,358	8,085	91.0
1978	13,844	23,110	59.9	7,480	8,307	90.0
1977	13,560	22,850	59.3	7,446	8,622	86.4
1976	13,719	22,785	60.2	7,791	8,268	94.2
1975	13,475	22,538	59.8	7,530	8,288	90.9
1974	14,397	23,235	62.0	7,385	8,180	90.3
1973	14,754	24,392	60.5	7,352	8,146	90.3
1972	14,519	23,970	60.6	7,497	8,025	93.4
1971	13,639	22,870	59.6	6,778	7,736	87.6
1970	13,709	23,121	59.3	6,803	7,473	91.0
1969	13,603	23,386	58.2	6,361	7,543	84.3
1968	13,432	22,641	59.3	5,957	7,511	79.3
1967	12,554	21,935	57.2	5,478	6,960	78.7

The Rodney King affair shows that African-Americans still had not received full civil rights. However, there had been major changes in US society. Legal segregation had gone by the end of the 1960s in the Old South. Desegregation in schooling outside the Old South was brought to an end with bussing during the 1970s. Affirmative action programmes had enabled tens of thousands of African-Americans to get jobs and places at university. In the 1994 mid-term election, over 40 African-Americans were returned to Congress. The number included the first African-American woman to be elected to the Senate, Carol Brown of Illinois. African-Americans had become mayors of large cities, such as Tom Bradley in Los Angeles and Marion Barry in Washington DC. In 1991, the Commander of the US armed forces in the Gulf War was Colin Powell, who later became Secretary of State under George W. Bush in 2001.

In popular culture, African-Americans have developed a much higher profile. On television, Oprah Winfrey has hosted one of the most popular 'chat shows'. In the cinema, actors such as Eddie Murphy, Morgan Freeman and Denzel Washington have became major stars. In popular music, Tamla Motown became an avenue for many black artists to gain national fame, such as Diana Ross and Michael Jackson.

It seems clear that many African-Americans have benefited from the advancement in civil and political rights. In 1978, African-American sociologist William J. Wilson published *The Declining Significance of Race*. In this study, Wilson points out that a new black economic and social elite had appeared.

However, in the 1990 US Census nine out of 31 million African-Americans lived in households with an income less than $35,000 per year. What had taken place was the bifurcation of African-American society into rich and poor.

The civil rights struggle had benefited many African-Americans. Unfortunately, it had still left a large number living in poverty. In the third edition of *The Unfinished Journey* (1995), American historian William Chafe notes:

> 'one of the primary consequences of this process was the increasing bifurcation of black America into a two-class society. While 35 to 45 per cent of black families succeeded in achieving a middle-class lifestyle during the 1970s, another 30 per cent of the black population experience a steady decline into ever deeper poverty.
>
> As a consequence of bifurcation, the lives of inner-city blacks became a montage of unmitigated blight, depression and hopelessness.
>
> In middle-class America Martin Luther King's "dream" of August 1963 seems to have come true. For African-Americans living in inner city areas their social and economic position deteriorated in the 1970s and 1980s.'

David Swinton of Jackson State University sums up the problem in 'Economic Progress for Black Americans in the Post Civil Rights Era' published in *US Race Relations in the 1980s and 1990s* (1990):

> 'The civil rights strategy focused on the development of laws and programs to eliminate discrimination. The basic decision in these policies was to ignore differences in wealth and ownership. This strategy contains the assumption that individual black initiative is sufficient to eliminate racial inequality within a reasonable period of time.'

Unfortunately, individual black initiative benefited only a minority of African-Americans.

1. Explain the meaning of the 'bifurcation' of African-American society.

2. To what extent did the civil rights movement fail to get full civil rights for African-Americans by 1992?

7.8 In what ways did the civil rights of Native Americans change, 1865–1992?

Plains Indians: A collection of tribes which lived between the Mississippi river and the Rocky Mountains. The most notable being the Sioux and the Cheyenne.

In 1865, Native Americans were divided into over 250 tribes, speaking 35 major languages. At no time in American history to that date did Native Americans provide a united ethnic group. Many Native Americans remained outside government jurisdiction. Around 250,000 **Plains Indians** occupied the West. Many of the larger tribes in the East had been transported westward in the 1830s to occupy Indian territory which was later to become the state of Oklahoma in 1907.

To many in the US government in 1865, the Plains Indians were an obstacle to national development. It was the 'manifest destiny' of the US government to dominate the continent. Native Americans were seen as a primitive branch of humanity who needed the benefits of Christianity and western civilisation if they were to progress.

Between 1865 and 1890, the Plains Indians were defeated by US armed forces. The basis of US policy towards Native Americans was embodied in the Dawes Severalty Act of 1887. The Act aimed to end the nomadic life of the Plains Indians. They were given land and US citizenship. With the latter came the civil rights of all US citizens. In 1901, US citizenship was extended to the five civilised tribes living in Indian territory – Creek, Choctaw, Chickasaw, Seminole and Cherokee. In 1924, all Native Americans became US citizens.

In reality, the Dawes Act helped to destroy Native-American culture. Children were educated to become US citizens. Property and land speculators were able to buy Indian land. By 1934, the total land area given to Indians in 1887 had been reduced by two-thirds. Much of what remained for Native Americans was poor farm land. This placed Native Americans in a **cycle of poverty** in which most would remain. Riven by disease, the Plains Indians population had fallen to 100,000 by 1900.

Cycle of poverty: The social and economic position in which people cannot get out of poverty no matter how hard they try.

At federal level, the white-dominated Bureau of Indian Affairs dealt with Native-American issues. Generally, Native-American views were ignored. It took until the New Deal for changes to be made. Under a new Commissioner for Indian Affairs, John Collier, the Dawes Severalty Act provisions were abandoned. In the 1934 Indian Reorganisation Act, Native-American culture was safeguarded for the first time. Tribes were reorganised into self-governing bodies which could adopt their own legal systems, police and constitution.

In spite of these changes, 75 of the 245 Indian tribes opposed the Act, including the largest tribe, the Navajo of Arizona and New Mexico.

Collier also ensured that Native Americans benefited from New Deal agencies such as the Civilian Conservation Corps (CCC) and the Public Works Administration (PWA).

Even with these changes under the New Deal, most Native Americans lived in abject poverty. It was not until 1944 that they began to organise a campaign to gain greater equality. In that year, the National Congress of American Indians (NCAI) was founded. It was the first organisation to include all Indian tribes. During the Eisenhower Administration (1953–61), the NCAI helped prevent the President ending Indian rights on reservations. Like the NAACP, the NCAI used the courts to protect Native-American rights.

In 1972, a landmark Supreme Court decision was made in 'Passamquaddy versus Morton'. The Passamaquaddy Indians of Maine received substantial damages from the US government for having broken the treaty of 1790 between the tribe and the US government. In 1980, the Sioux nation received $107 million for land taken away from them illegally

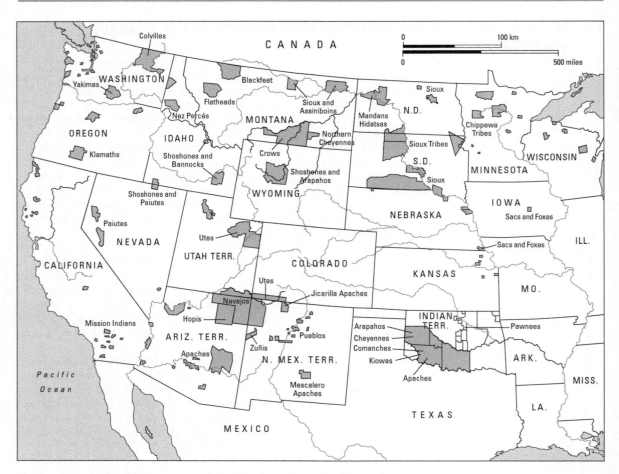

Western Indian reservations, 1890

in South Dakota in the late 19th century. In 1988, the tiny Puyallup tribe of Washington state was given $162 million in compensation for land taken away by the city of Tacoma in the 1850s.

Since that time, Native-Americans have used their position as 'independent nations' within the United States to introduce gambling from which they have benefited financially. However, decisions on gambling have not been welcomed by all Native Americans. The issue led to a major split within the Mohawk nation in upstate New York in the late 1980s.

Like the African-American civil rights movement, the Native-American rights movement produced its radical wing. In 1968, the American Indian Movement (AIM) was founded in Minneapolis, Minnesota. One of the founders, Dennis Banks, explained why it was created:

'We started because of the slum housing conditions, the highest unemployment rate in the whole of this country; police brutality against our elders, women and children.'

AIM activists made headline news in 1969, when 14 members occupied the derelict Alcatraz jail in San Francisco Bay. In 1972, AIM militants occupied the Wounded Knee battle site in South Dakota. At the same time, the actor Marlon Brando refused to accept in person his Oscar for Best Actor in the film 'The Godfather'. Instead he sent an Indian princess to Hollywood to pick up the award.

Militant action seemed to work when the federal government passed the 1974 Indian Self-Determination Act. This granted tribes control over federal aid programmes on reservations, as well as control of their schools.

1. How far have Native-American civil rights changed between 1865 and 1992?

2. Why do you think it has taken so long for Native Americans to gain full civil rights?

7.9 How far have the civil rights of Hispanic and Oriental Americans improved, 1865–1992?

Cesar Chavez (1927–1993)
Leading trade union organiser for Mexican-American migrant farm workers. Born in Arizona. Chavez was able to force producers to agree to trade union contracts after nationwide grape and lettuce boycotts in 1960s and 1970s.

For much of the period from 1865 to the end of the Second World War, Hispanic Americans formed a minority of the populations of California, Arizona, New Mexico and Texas. They were divided from mainstream American society by their language, Spanish, and their religion, Catholicism. The vast majority of Hispanic Americans worked as agricultural labourers. During the Depression, the Hispanic workers in California formed the CUCOM (Confederation of Unions of Mexican Workers and Farm Labourers) to fight for better conditions. Strikes occurred across southern California and in the Salinas valley of central California. Again in the 1960s and 1970s, Cesar Chavez led the Hispanic farm workers in a series of strikes in order to improve their working conditions.

From 1945, increasing numbers of Hispanic Americans arrived in northern cities from Mexico, Puerto Rico and Central America. Like African-Americans, they were forced to lived in ghettos and to work in low-paid jobs. In New York City, Spanish Harlem began to rival African-American Harlem.

The Leonard Bernstein musical 'West Side Story', first performed in the 1950s, used Hispanic-American gang warfare in New York City as a modern interpretation of the Shakespeare play 'Romeo and Juliet'.

As European immigration has declined in the USA, Hispanic immigration has increased greatly. Driven by economic hardship, Hispanic Americans have entered the USA both legally and, increasingly, illegally.

The rapid increase in Hispanic immigration has created tension, particularly in the states that border Mexico. In 1970, the Hispanic population stood at nine million. By 1990, it had risen to 20 million but it is hard to calculate the number of illegal immigrants. Spanish has become the second language of the USA. It is predicted that by the middle of the 21st century Spanish speakers may well outnumber English speakers in many states. In 1990, almost 20 per cent of Mexican Americans and 30 per cent of Puerto Rican Americans lived below the poverty line.

Oriental Americans were also economic migrants to the USA. Initially, they were centred on the Pacific coast but eventually most large cities had a 'China town'. San Francisco possessed the largest China town outside Asia. It also has its own distinctive 'Japan town'.

1. Describe the changes in ethnic make-up of the USA between 1980 and 1990.

2. Does the data below suggest that ethnic problems have got worse between 1980 and 1990? Explain your answer.

Chinese labourers formed the backbone of the workforce on the western part of the transcontinental railroad in the 1860s. However, by 1882, opposition to Oriental immigration had grown so much that Congress passed the Chinese Exclusion Act.

The greatest violation of civil rights faced by Oriental Americans came in the Second World War when the entire Japanese-American population,

Resident population distribution for the USA by race and Hispanic origin

	1990 Number	%	1980 Number	%	Change (+)
Total population	248,709,873	100.0	226,545,805	100.0	9.8
White	199,686,070	80.3	188,371,622	83.1	6.0
Black	29,986,060	12.1	26,495,020	11.7	13.2
American Indian, Eskimo or Aleut	1,959,234	0.8	1,420,400	0.6	37.9
Asian or Pacific Islander	7,273,662	2.9	3,500,439	1.5	107.8
Other race	9.804,847	3.9	6,758,319	3.0	45.1
Hispanic origin	22,354,059	9.0	14,608,673	6.4	53.0

numbering 400,000, was forced into concentration camps for the duration of the war. It took until the Presidency of George Bush Senior (1989–93) for the federal government to make a public apology for the treatment which Japanese Americans received in the War.

Since the 1960s, Oriental immigration has included Koreans and Vietnamese. In the Rodney King riots of 1992, African-American rioters attacked stores owned by Korean Americans, as well as attacking the police.

Both Hispanic and Oriental Americans have benefited from federal government affirmative action programmes since the 1960s. In politics, Oriental-American Congressmen have been elected from California and Hawaii, where Oriental Americans form the majority of the population.

1. In what ways has Hispanic immigration to the USA changed between 1865 and 1992?

2. How have Hispanic and Oriental Americans been discriminated against between 1865 and 1992?

Source-based questions: The civil rights movement in the 1960s

SOURCE A

We affirm the ideal of non-violence as the foundation of our purpose and the manner of our action. Non-violence seeks a social order of justice permeated by love. Integration of human endeavour represents the crucial first step towards such a society.

Through non-violence, courage displaces fear; love transforms hate. Acceptance dissipates prejudice; hope ends despair. Peace dominates war; faith reconciles doubt. Justice for all overthrows injustice.

Love is the centre of non-violence. Love is the force by which God binds man to himself and man to man.

By appealing to conscience and standing on the moral nature of human existence, non-violence nurtures the atmosphere in which reconciliation and justice become actual possibilities.

The Student Non-violent Coordinating Committee (SNCC) Statement of Purpose, 15 April 1960

SOURCE B

Let us continue our triumph and march to the realisation of the American dream. Let us march on segregated housing, until every ghetto of economic depression dissolves and Negroes and whites live side by side in decent housing. Let us march on segregated schools until every vestige of segregated and inferior education becomes a thing of the past and Negroes and whites study side by side in the socially healing context of the classroom.

Let us march on poverty until no starved man walks the streets of our cities.

Let us march on ballot boxes, until we send to our city councils, state legislatures and the United States Congressmen who will not fear to do justice, love mercy and walk humbly with their God.

For all of us today the battle is in our hands. The road ahead is not altogether a smooth one. There are no broad highways to lead us easily and inevitably to quick solutions. We must keep going.

'Our God is Marching On' – a speech made by Dr Martin Luther King Jr on the steps of the Alabama State Capitol in Montgomery at the conclusion of the Selma to Montgomery Civil Rights March, 25 March 1965.

SOURCE C

White America will not face the problem of color, the reality of it. The well-intended say: 'We're all human, everybody is really decent, we must forget color.' But color cannot be 'forgotten'. White America will not acknowledge that the ways in which this country sees itself are contradicted by being black. Whereas most of the people who settled in this country came here for freedom, blacks were brought here to be slaves. Our vision is not merely a society in which all black men have enough to buy the good things in life. When we urge that black money go into black pockets, we mean the communal pocket. We want to see money go back to the community and used to benefit it. We want to see black ghetto residents demand that an exploiting storekeeper sell to them, at minimal cost. The society we seek to build among black people is not a capitalist one. It is a society in which the spirit of community and human love prevail.

'What We Want' – an essay by Stokely Carmichael, elected Chairman of SNCC in May 1966, writing in September 1966.

Source-based questions: The civil rights movement in the 1960s

---

1. Use Source B.

How do the language and style of Martin Luther King's speech suggest he supports an integrated tolerant society?

2. Use Sources A and B.

In what ways do these two sources put forward similar aims?

3. Use Source A and information from this chapter.

How useful is this source to a historian writing about the methods used by the civil rights movement in the 1960s?

4. Use Sources A and C.

How have the aims of SNCC changed between its formation in 1960 and 1966?

5. Use all the sources and information from this chapter.

'The use of non-violent protest had only limited success in improving the position of African-Americans in US society during the 1960s.'

Assess the validity of this statement.

7.10 Who did more for African-American civil rights – JFK or LBJ?

7.10.1 Was JFK forced by African-American activists to take action on civil rights?

7.10.2 Did Johnson merely fulfil Kennedy's legacy on civil rights?

Framework of Events

1960	February: Lunch-counter protests begin, by SNCC members, in Greensboro, North Carolina
1961	May: 'Freedom rides' begin by CORE members
1962	October: James Meredith is first African-American student to enrol at University of Mississippi
1963	February: Kennedy proposes Civil Rights Bill
	April: Demonstrations in Birmingham, Alabama, led by Martin Luther King
	June: JFK goes on national television to support a strong Civil Rights Bill following murder of NAACP leader, Medgar Evers
	Civil Rights Bill sent to Congress
	August: 'March on Washington' and Martin Luther King's 'I have a dream' speech
1964	January: Poll tax amendment to US Constitution
	July: Congress passes the Civil Rights Act
1965	March: Martin Luther King leads Selma-to-Montgomery march against segregation
	August: Congress passes Voting Rights Act
	Black riots in Watts district of Los Angeles
1967	July: Black rioting in Newark, New Jersey and Detroit, Michigan
	Kerner Commission set up by Johnson to investigate causes of riots
	October: Thurgood Marshall becomes first African-American member of US Supreme Court
1968	April: Assassination of Martin Luther King followed by rioting in cities across America
	Congress passes Civil Rights Act

Overview

T HE 1960s were a momentous decade in the history of African-American civil rights. Not since the Civil War (1861–5) and the Reconstruction era (1863–77), did African-American rights hold centre stage in US domestic politics. The decade was associated with a concerted attempt to end legal segregation and discrimination against African-Americans. This occurred predominantly in the **Old South**, which had comprised of the Confederacy during the Civil War. Action consisted of demonstrations and direct action by African-Americans. More noted among the **pressure groups** that fought for equal rights were the NAACP (National Association for the Advancement of Colored People), the CORE (Congress of Racial Equality) and the SNCC (Student Non-violent Coordinating Committee). These groups forced the USA to accept the moral dilemma that it was the leader of the free world against communism but denied a large proportion of its citizens full civil and political rights. Kennedy and Johnson had to confront this issue and played an integral part in gaining full civil and political rights for African-Americans.

Old South: the former States of the Confederacy (1861–5). It comprised of Mississippi, Louisiana, Arkansas, Texas, Alabama, Georgia, North and South Carolina, Virginia, Florida and Tennessee.

Pressure groups: political organisations that do not seek election to office but that attempt to influence or pressure politicians to follow a particular policy.

African-Americans in 1961

In 1961, African-Americans numbered 18.8 million or 10.5 per cent of the US population. Traditionally they had lived in the Old South. However, by 1960, following the 'great migration' of the 1920s–40s, African-Americans also comprised an important proportion of the population of the cities outside that area. In 1960, they comprised 53.9 per cent of Washington DC, the capital. They also comprised 34.9 per cent of Baltimore, Maryland, 28.9 per cent of Detroit, Michigan and 22.9 per cent of Chicago, Illinois. The African-Americans outside the Old South tended to live in inner-city ghettoes. In 1965, 43 per cent of all African-American families were living below the poverty line, earning under $3000 per year.

Under the US Constitution, African-Americans should have had the same political and civil rights as all other Americans. The thirteenth, fourteenth and fifteenth amendments of the Constitution, passed between 1865 and 1870 gave them full rights. However, from 1877, state governments in the Old South had led the way in passing Jim Crow laws. These laws provided separate facilities for African-Americans in virtually everything from education, to housing and recreation. A landmark decision by the US Supreme Court in 1954 led the way towards ending this system. In Brown versus Board of Education of Topeka, the Court declared that having separate schools for black and white students was unconstitutional. However, by 1961, only very limited change had occurred in removing Jim Crow laws. African-Americans across most of the Old South were still second-class citizens.

7.10.1 Was JFK forced by African-American activists to take action on civil rights?

The Kennedy and Johnson record on civil rights before 1961

There is little evidence to show that either JFK or LBJ had a strong desire to support civil and political equality for African-Americans. According to journalist and family friend of the Kennedys', Arthur Krock, JFK 'never saw a Negro on social-level terms'. Kennedy came from Massachusetts, which possessed only a small African-American population. Johnson was similar. The main ethnic minority that Johnson had contact with, before starting his political career, were Hispanic Americans in San Marcos, Texas.

Both politicians had the ambition to rise to the top of the Democratic Party. To do so they needed the support of Southern white Democrats. Throughout the 1950s, Kennedy sought to avoid upsetting Southern Democrats – so much so that the NAACP regarded Senator Kennedy with suspicion.

In 1957, Kennedy went so far as to criticise President Eisenhower's dispatch of troops to protect the African-American students who wished to enrol at Central High School, in **Little Rock**. In the same year, JFK voted with Southern Democrats for the **pro-jury trial amendment** to the Civil Rights Bill. This greatly reduced the Act's effectiveness in defending African-American civil rights. Even when he won office in 1960, Kennedy informed black leaders that he did not plan to introduce any civil rights legislation in 1961.

Johnson also avoided conflict with the people who were his natural constituency. LBJ's great mentor in the Senate was Richard Russell of Georgia. He was a leading segregationist. Also, from 1955 to 1960, Johnson was Senate majority leader and to be successful he had to keep Southern Democrats on his side. Southern Democrats held the chairs of the most important Senate committees. Although two civil rights Acts were passed, in 1957 and 1960, when Johnson was Senate majority leader, he made sure that the legislation made little difference to white domination of Southern politics.

How did Kennedy defend civil rights during his presidency?

There is considerable evidence to suggest that Kennedy reacted to events rather than took a positive stand on African-American civil rights. During the presidential election year of 1960, civil rights became national news with lunch-counter protests by black students. Starting at the F.W. Woolworth department store in Greensboro, North Carolina, students of the SNCC began a sit-down protest to force Woolworth's to serve black as well as white customers. In February 1961, other black and white students adopted similar non-violent protests against segregation in inner-state bus travel. Students of CORE tested federal law by travelling through the Old South on 'Greyhound' interstate buses. When they reached Anniston, Alabama, white protesters firebombed their bus.

Little Rock: in the autumn of 1957, nine black students attempted to enrol at Central High School, Little Rock, Arkansas. The governor of Arkansas, Orvil Faubus, attempted to prevent their enrolment and was supported by white segregationists. To allow the students the right of enrolment, President Eisenhower sent the 101st Airborne Division to Little Rock to force compliance with federal law, which forbade segregation in public schools.

Pro-jury trial amendment: white juries in the Old South could amend legislation against African-American voter registration.

Lunch-counter protest by African-American students at Woolworth's, Greensboro, 1960.

Confronted with an inflammatory situation, JFK relied on his brother, Attorney General Robert F. Kennedy, to deflate the situation. He sent federal marshals to aid the students. In *Sweet Land of Liberty?: The African-American Struggle for Civil Rights in the Twentieth Century* (1998), historian Robert Cook notes:

> The dispatch of US marshals revealed the extent to which the Kennedys had been embarrassed by media coverage of the 'freedom ride'.

The 'freedom rides' and Robert Kennedy's involvement are explained in some depth in episode 3 of the television series *The Eyes on the Prize*. Kennedy had almost daily telephone contact with the state authorities in Alabama. However, the Kennedys were reluctant to force the issue of desegregation. Arthur M. Schlesinger, in *Robert Kennedy and His Times* (1978), notes that by protecting the 'freedom riders' but not forcing desegregation, Robert F. Kennedy 'became almost as unpopular among civil rights workers as he was among segregationists'.

Schlesinger's critical view of the Kennedy stance on civil rights is borne out by other historians. In *The Civil Rights Movement: Struggle and Resistance* (1997), William T. Martin Riches notes:

> Although the election of JFK was largely due to the African-American vote, his appointment of his brother Robert as attorney general did not augur well for those involved in the civil rights movement.

Irving Bernstein, in *From Promises Kept: John F. Kennedy's New Frontier* (1991), notes:

> ... [JFK] had not known many black people, knew little about segregation, and had not considered the federal role in promoting desegregation.

Nevertheless, pressure was placed on the Interstate Commerce Commission, by the administration, to ban segregation in interstate bus terminals. This enforced the 1958 US Supreme Court decision of Boynton versus Virginia, which had declared such practices unconstitutional.

Following the 'freedom rides', John Kennedy wanted to avoid any other confrontation in the South that would force him to act. JFK had major problems with the conservative coalition in Congress. The Southern white Democrat committee chairman was stalling much of his New Frontier domestic programme. Kennedy feared another Little Rock episode.

Unfortunately, in 1962, Kennedy was faced with this type of problem when African-American James Meredith applied to take a law degree at the all-white University of Mississippi. The Democrat Party within Mississippi was split between moderates and extremists. Governor Ross Barnett, who was completely against desegregation, led the latter. Attempts at peaceful enrolment came to nothing. In the television series *The Eyes on the Prize*, Kennedy is shown telephoning Ross Barnett as part of a plan to find a peaceful solution to the problem. In the end, Robert F. Kennedy decided to send 170 US federal marshals and Deputy Attorney General Nicholas Katzenbach to Mississippi University. An all-night riot on 1 October 1962 between white segregationists and the US marshals left two dead and over 100 people injured. The Kennedys sent in 30,000 troops to restore order.

JFK was equally reactive in his attitude to the civil rights movement when Martin Luther King organised demonstrations in Birmingham, Alabama in April–May 1963. The televised scenes of police dogs and water hoses to disperse demonstrators, who included children and pregnant women, shocked the people. It also acted as a major landmark in the education of the Kennedy brothers in the extent of discrimination against African-Americans in the Old South. In *To Redeem the Soul of America: The*

Southern Christian Leadership Conference and Martin Luther King, Jr. (1987), historian Adam Fairclough states:

> The success of Birmingham should not be judged according to its impact on Congress. The evidence strongly suggests that the SCLC's demonstrations played a decisive role in persuading the Kennedy administration to introduce legislation.

As shown in *The Eyes on the Prize*, JFK gave a nationally televised speech on 11 June 1963 in support of further civil rights for African-Americans.

However, historian James N. Giglio, in *The Presidency of John F. Kennedy* (1991), believes JFK began to change his view earlier. He believes JFK's proactive view on civil rights dates from late 1962, which was:

> … a time of frustration for the administration over growing Southern violence, the slowness of civil rights advances, and criticism from virtually all civil rights groups.

He believes 'Kennedy recognised the discontent and perceived need for action'.

Action took the form of a very modest Civil Rights Bill sent to Congress in February 1963. This aimed to improve African-American voting rights and to assist the desegregation of public schools. However, the chance of even this surviving the opposition of the conservative coalition looked slender. Nevertheless, JFK supported the '**March on Washington**', in August 1963, which brought the whole civil rights issue to the seat of government.

Kennedy was fortunate that his presidency coincided with two constitutional amendments that benefited African-Americans. On 29 March 1961 the United States ratified the twenty-third amendment, which had been proposed in June 1960. This gave the citizens of the district of Columbia the right to vote in presidential elections. Washington DC had a black majority by late 1961. On 27 March 1962, the twenty-fourth amendment was submitted to Congress. When ratification was completed, on 23 January 1964, poor black and white people were no longer prevented from voting 'by reason of failure to pay any poll tax or other tax'.

'**March on Washington**': civil rights campaigner A. Philip Randolph organised a 'March on Washington' to publicise the cause of African-American civil rights. Two hundred and fifty thousand people participated. Martin Luther King was the keynote speaker.

Attorney General Robert Kennedy talks to civil rights marchers in Washington in 1963.

Politics is the art of the possible. Given the political conditions of Kennedy's presidency, it could be argued that he achieved what was possible in black civil rights. He won the narrowest of election victories in 1960. He needed the support of Southern white Democrats in Congress to support his domestic and foreign policies and so he needed to move cautiously on civil rights. According to his British biographer, Hugh Brogan, in *Kennedy* (1996):

> Kennedy entered the White House at a moment when the issue of racial oppression could no longer be dodged. He had to act, and did so effectively and (in the main) willingly. There is no reason to believe that any other man who could have been elected president in 1960 would have done better and perhaps none could have done so well.

On his inaugural day, Kennedy spotted that the guard of honour of the US Coast Guard contained no African-Americans and so he later pressured the Coast Guard to recruit black people. On deeper investigation, Kennedy found that, in the State Department, only 15 out of 3,467 people in the foreign service were African-Americans. Robert F. Kennedy found only 10 out of 995 Justice Department employees to be black. As a result, by Executive Order, JFK created, in March 1961, the President's Committee on Equal Employment Opportunity (PCEEO). Chaired by Vice President Lyndon Johnson, the PCEEO aimed to prevent discrimination for all those doing business with the Federal Government. Given the size of the Federal Government, this involved thousands of employers. Kennedy also forced the Civil Service Commission to appoint more black employees. If it had not been for conservative opposition in Congress, he might well have appointed the first African-American to a Cabinet post – Robert C. Weaver in the Department of Housing and Urban Development. This became reality during Johnson's presidency. In 1961, Secretary for the Interior Stewart Udall was able to persuade the national football team, the Washington Redskins, to end their ban on hiring African-American players.

Finally, Kennedy became the first president to appoint an African-American as a Federal Circuit judge when he appointed NAACP lawyer Thurgood Marshall to the Court of Appeals for the Second Circuit in New York. However, politics is full of compromises. To obtain Southern white support for Marshall's appointment, Kennedy had to agree to the appointment of Harold Cox to the Federal Circuit Court in Mississippi. Cox was a noted white supremacist.

By the time of his assassination, Kennedy had begun to address the noted imbalance of African-Americans in government employment. The PCEEO began the first steps to affirmative action, ensuring that places were set aside for ethnic minorities in companies wishing to gain government contracts. This was called Plans for Progress. Although, in retrospect, this was a modest measure, Kennedy's Civil Rights Bill had been carefully crafted to give black people more rights without alienating the conservative coalition in Congress.

7.10.2 Did Johnson merely fulfil Kennedy's legacy on civil rights?

Did Lyndon Johnson bring about the second Reconstruction?

Between 1963 and 1969 the Jim Crow laws, which had made African-Americans second-class citizens in the Old South, were abolished. This was achieved primarily through three Acts of Congress: the Civil Rights Act 1964, the Voting Rights Act 1965 and the Civil Rights Act 1968. To many contemporaries, this process seemed like a second Reconstruction era. The first Reconstruction era, 1863–77, had seen the abolition of slavery and the granting of full civil and political rights to African-Americans. Following 1877, white supremacy was re-established across the South. Then, from 1963 to 1969, the hopes of the first Reconstruction era were put into practice. Does Lyndon Johnson deserve all the credit in achieving this transformation in American race relations? Doris Kearns Goodwin, an early biographer of LBJ, states in *Lyndon Johnson & the American Dream* (1976):

> His position on racial issues was more advanced than that of any other American president: had he done nothing else in his entire life, his contributions to civil rights would have earned him a lasting place in the annals of history.

Bruce Miroff, a radical critic of both Kennedy and Johnson, quoted by Steven F. Lawson in *The Johnson Years* (1981), stated:

> No other administration accomplished so much in the way of civil rights legislation; no other president undertook such a commitment to the black cause.

Civil rights legislation passed by Congress 1963–9

Civil Rights Act 1964
- Title I: Introduced tough new controls over state voting laws and included guidelines for the use of literacy tests.
- Title II: Outlawed racial segregation for all public facilities and accommodation.
- Title III: Outlawed racial segregation for all government facilities.
- Title IV: Provided federal assistance for the desegregation of public schools.
- Title V: Expanded the powers of the federal Commission on Civil Rights.
- Title VI: Forbade racial discrimination in any federally assisted programme.
- Title VII: Forbade all discrimination in employment, including race, colour, religion, national origin and sex. (This was an important move towards equality of men and women.)
- Also set up the Equal Employment Opportunities Commission (EEOC) to ensure that the Act was followed.

The Voting Rights Act 1965
- Banned literacy tests for voter registration.
- Appointed federal examiners to ensure that voter registration was fair and legal.

Civil Rights Act 1968
- Outlawed discrimination on the basis of colour, race, religion or national origin in the rental or sale of housing, except in owner-occupied or owner-managed units.
- Outlawed racial discrimination in jury selection.
- Made it a federal crime to interfere with voting, work, schooling and participation in federally assisted programmes.
- Made it illegal to interfere with civil rights workers.
- Introduced fines and imprisonment for anyone who travelled across state lines to foment or participate in a riot.

On paper, Johnson's achievements do look very impressive. When he became president on 22 November 1963, JFK's Civil Rights Bill had been held back by the Rules Committee of the House of Representatives. As a tribute to the memory of the murdered President, LBJ used all his persuasive skills to get the Civil Rights Act passed into law by 2 July 1964.

According to historian Kevern Verney, in *Black Civil Rights in America* (2000), 'the Civil Rights Act brought to fruition the Bill introduced by Kennedy in 1963'. In the administrative history of the Justice Department, Kennedy's contribution is seen as significant. Even though the House Rules Committee had delayed the Civil Rights Bill of 1963, Justice Department civil rights lawyers had ensured that when the Bill emerged from the House Judiciary Committee for consideration by the whole House of Representatives it still contained JFK's proposals for strong federal action on civil rights. Johnson was able to ensure a smooth passage through Congress once he became president. His supporters in the Senate broke a 57-day **filibuster** by anti-civil rights senators. Johnson also met with leaders of civil rights groups such as CORE and SNCC who agreed to suspend major demonstrations until after the presidential election of November 1964. LBJ hoped to prevent a white backlash that would have benefited his Republican opponent for the presidency, Barry Goldwater.

In the passage of the Voting Rights Act, Johnson's support for further action has been called into question. According to Professor Stephen F. Lawson, in 'Civil Rights', in *The Johnson Years* (1981):

> Johnson preferred to postpone further legislative action on civil rights, but the resumption of mass protests in Selma, Alabama, in 1965, forced him to change his mind.

Under the leadership of Martin Luther King, African-American civil rights activists had decided to highlight the plight of voter registration problems for black people in the Old South. A civil rights march, from Selma to Montgomery, Alabama, was met with violence by Alabama state police at Pettus Bridge on Sunday 7 March. The media coverage of 'Bloody Sunday' helped force Johnson to federalise the Alabama **National Guard** to protect the marchers. From 17 March to 25 March, over 25,000 civil rights protestors completed the march. During the march, two white civil rights supporters, Viola Liuzzo and Protestant Minister James Reeb were murdered. These events prompted Johnson to convene a joint session of Congress where he announced his intention to introduce a Voting Rights Bill.

The Civil Rights Act 1964 and the Voting Rights Act 1965 effectively brought to an end racial discrimination against African-Americans in public facilities and in voter registration. In his book, *The Vantage Point: Perspectives of the Presidency, 1963–1969* (1971), Lyndon Johnson said:

> With the passage of the Civil Rights Act 1964 and [the Voting Rights Act] 1965, the barriers to freedom began tumbling down. At long last the legal rights of American citizens – the right to vote, to hold a job, to enter a public place, to go to school – were given concrete protection.

Could Johnson have done more?

The Acts did not, however, bring an end to African-American discontent. As the Voting Rights Bill passed through Congress a major race riot occurred in the Watts district of Los Angeles, now known as South Central LA. Between 11 and 15 August 1965, 34 people were killed and over 1,000 were injured. Almost 3,500 rioters and looters were arrested. According to historian Kevern Verney, in *Black Civil Rights in America* (2000):

Frightened African-American girls fleeing from police during a riot in Brooklyn, 1964.

Watts was one of the first of 239 outbreaks of racial violence in over 200 US cities in the five 'long hot summers' from 1964 to 1968. Almost every large American city outside of the South was affected, including Oakland in California in 1965 and 1966, Cleveland, Ohio, 1966 and 1968, Chicago, Illinois, 1966 and 1968, Newark, New Jersey, 1967, and Detroit, Michigan, in 1967. In 1964 there were 16 serious outbreaks of violence in 16 cities, but the first five months of 1968 alone saw 65 riots in 64 cities.

Johnson was both perplexed and angry at inner-city African-American rioting. He stated 'that all that crazy rioting almost ruined everything'. It seemed to him that African-Americans were ungrateful for his efforts in civil rights and inner-city regeneration. It clearly slowed any further plans Johnson had for legislative action. Plans to introduce a further Civil Rights Bill in 1966 were curbed. James Harvey, in *Black Civil Rights During the Johnson Administration* (1973), believed that Johnson did not push the 1966 Bill because 'he was thinking about a growing white backlash'. When the Civil Rights Act 1968 was finally passed, it contained a section that was aimed at rioters and at those who fomented race riots. Such a section had to be included to placate Congressional concerns about the 'long hot summers' of rioting.

Johnson can be criticised for his reaction to the riots. On 29 July 1967, he set up the Kerner Commission to investigate the causes of the rioting. The Commission presented its findings in February 1968. The report regarded white racism as an important contributory factor. It called for sweeping reforms in housing, employment, education and welfare. Johnson ignored its proposals. The costs of such proposals came at a time when the administration was finding it increasingly difficult to fund the Vietnam War.

There was also another problem regarding the Vietnam War and the civil rights movement. Martin Luther King began to attack US policy on Vietnam. On 4 April 1967, Martin Luther King delivered an address at the Riverside Church in New York City. In the speech, he compared American action in Vietnam with Nazi action in the Second World War. He said:

'We have destroyed their [the Vietnamese's] two most cherished institutions: the family and the village. We have destroyed their land and crops. We have supported the enemies of the peasants of Saigon [capital of South Vietnam]. We have corrupted their women and children and killed their men. What do you think as we test our latest weapons on them, just as the Germans tested out new medicine and new tortures in the concentration camps of Europe?'

Later in April, King attended the 'Spring mobilisation to end the war in Vietnam'. From 1966, Vietnam was inreasingly coming to dominate Johnson's presidency and so King's anti-war actions hit Johnson's own policy position hard. King also launched the Poor People's Campaign in 1967. He wanted Congress to enact a Bill of Rights for the Disadvantaged. This would involve a massive federally funded programme of aid to the poor. Again, this hit Johnson's policy position hard as it was a direct criticism of his own 'war on poverty'. As a result, the close relationship Martin Luther King had developed with the Johnson White House came to an end.

In addition, as inner-city violence escalated in the North, more militant groups began to represent African-American opinion. In 1966, the Black Panther Party was formed. It adopted a more confrontational and aggressive stance in support of African-American rights. It wanted African-American rights to incorporate social and economic rights as well as civil and political rights.

In the last years of his presidency, Johnson became increasingly remote from the African-American community and has been criticised for not enforcing the civil rights legislation he helped to pass. Historian Allan Wolk, in *The Presidency and Black Civil Rights: Eisenhower to Nixon* (1971), claims that Johnson handed over enforcement to the Justice Department, which was led by the cautious Attorney General Nicholas Katzenbach. Wolk claims that LBJ should have given enforcement to Hubert Humphrey, his vice president, who had briefly acted as civil rights coordinator in the administration and had been very effective.

Even within his own political party, Johnson faced criticism. At the Democratic National Convention, in August 1964, Johnson faced two delegations from Mississippi. On one side, was the all-white, segregationist official delegation. On the other, was a delegation representing the Mississippi Freedom Democratic Party. This had been organised by the SNCC and represented African-Americans. Johnson allowed the official white delegation to represent Mississippi. However, he gave the Freedom Democratic Party two votes at the Convention as a compromise. This angered the official delegation into leaving the Convention.

By 1968, Johnson was soundly condemned by Southern white people. In that year, former Democrat governor of Alabama, George Wallace, ran against the Democrats for the presidency. He formed the American Independent Party. He polled 9.9 million votes and carried five Southern states with a combined Electoral College of 46.

Overall, Johnson was proud of his achievements. He had appointed the first African-American Cabinet member, Robert C. Weaver, and the first African-American US Supreme Court judge, Thurgood Marshall. In December 1972, shortly before his death, Johnson held a conference on civil rights at the Johnson Library in Johnson City, Texas. Several civil rights leaders took part and congratulated him on his efforts. In his own conversations with his biographer Doris Kearns Goodwin, he regarded his record in civil rights to be his greatest achievement.

Assessment

In terms of actual achievement, Johnson clearly did more than Kennedy to aid racial equality. The Civil Rights Act 1964 and the Voting Rights Act 1965 stand out as great legislative achievements. However, in achieving these momentous changes Johnson had a number of advantages. He benefited from the wave of sympathy following Kennedy's assassination. He also built on work carried out during Kennedy's presidency. After all, as vice president, he had chaired the PCEEO. The Civil Rights Act of 1964 was, in essence, Kennedy's Civil Rights Bill of the previous year. Johnson also benefited from a pliant, supportive Congress. The eighty-ninth Congress, elected in 1964, was dominated by Liberal Democrats who supported Johnson's stance on legislative action.

Yet, Johnson clearly deserves praise for the speed and effectiveness of his intervention to aid African-Americans. His command of Congress meant the two landmark Acts of 1964 and 1965 became law. Johnson's 'war on poverty' also aided poor and disadvantaged black people. However, what had begun so promisingly in 1963/4 began to face problems by 1966/7. The increase in inner-city racial violence highlighted the social and economic plight of Northern African-Americans. Also, Johnson's growing preoccupation with the Vietnam War drew him away from domestic problems such as civil rights. In the end, Johnson's triumph was a flawed triumph.

Both Kennedy and Johnson benefited from the dynamism of the civil rights movement. Leaders such as Martin Luther King and organisations such as CORE and SNCC made black civil rights the major domestic issue facing both presidents. In the television era, no president could stand idle when peaceful demonstrators were beaten by police in Southern states such as Mississippi and Alabama. Both JFK and LBJ were placed in a position where they had to confront what sociologist Gunnar Myrdal termed the 'American dilemma' – the issue of race. When confronted, both presidents acted positively to address civil rights.

Who did more for black civil rights: JFK or LBJ?

1. Read the following extract and answer the question.

We are confronted primarily by a moral question. It is as old as the Scriptures and is as clear as the American Constitution. The heart of the question is whether all Americans are to be afforded equal rights and equal opportunities: whether they are going to treat our fellow Americans as we want to be treated.

We face a moral crisis as a country and a people. It cannot be met by repressive police action. It cannot be left to increased demonstrations in the streets. It cannot be quieted by token moves or talk.

From a nationally televised speech by President John F. Kennedy on 11 June 1963.

Using information from the extract above, and from this section, explain what Kennedy and Johnson did to give African-Americans equal rights and equal opportunities.

2. 'The Civil Rights Act of 1964 was a turning point in the development of African-American rights during the Kennedy-Johnson years.' How far do you agree with this statement?

Further Reading

Texts designed for AS Level study

Race Relations in the USA by Vivienne Sanders (Hodder & Stoughton, Access to History series, 2000)

Martin Luther King Jr. and the Civil Rights Movement in America by John White (British Association for American Studies, 1991)

JFK & LBJ by Derrick Murphy (Collins Historymakers, 2004)

Texts for A2 and advanced study

The Civil Rights Movement by William T. Martin Riches (Macmillan, 1997)

Black Civil Rights in America by Kevern Verney (Routledge, 2000)

Black Leadership in America from Booker T. Washington to Jesse Jackson by John White (Longman, Second edition 1990)

Sweet Land of Liberty? by Robert Cook (Longman, 1998)

Bearing the Cross: Martin Luther King and the Southern Christian Leadership Conference by David Garrow (William Morrow, 1986) – Pulitzer Prize Winner.

Parting the Waters: Martin Luther King and the Civil Rights Movement 1954 to 1963 by Taylor Branch (Macmillan, 1991)

Pillar of Fire: America in the King Years, 1963–1965 by Taylor Branch (Simon & Schuster, 1998)

Video

'Eyes on the Prize: the Civil Rights Years in the USA, 1954–1970' – PBS.

Websites

www.worldbook.com/fun/aajourny – these give a good introduction to topics such as the Civil Rights Act 1964, the Equal Employment Opportunities Commission and Affirmative Action.

WWW.WATSON.ORG/~LISA/BLACKHISTORY – provides introductory coverage of topics such as school integration.

WWW.BLACKHISTORY.EB.COM/MICRO/727/78 – provides pen portraits of black leaders such as Stokely Carmichael.

INFO.GREENWOOD.COM/BOOKS/0313250 – contains encyclopaedia of African-American civil rights.

WWW.NPS.GOV/MALU/DOCUMENTS – contains information on Jim Crow laws, Martin Luther King and the civil rights issue in general.

WWW.TOPTAGS.COM/AAMA/VOICES/SPEECHES/NEGROCON – contains African-American almanac covering broad range of African-American history.

HOMETOWN.AOL.COM/KLOVE01 – contains excerpts from Martin Luther King's speeches.

HOMETOWN.AOL.COM/NOWACUMIG/BACKGRND – contains information on the American Indian Movement and Native-American civil rights.

8 US domestic history, 1945–1969

Key Issues

- How far was this period one of social and political change?

- How strong was the US economy in this period?

- How far did the power and role of federal government increase in this period?

8.1 What problems did Truman face in his first administration of 1945–1949?

8.2 How far did Truman build on the New Deal in social policy?

8.3 What impact did McCarthyism have on the USA?

8.4 How far did Eisenhower continue the policies of his Democratic predecessors?

8.5 How far were the 1950s an 'Age of Affluence'?

8.6 Why did Kennedy achieve so little in domestic reform?

8.7 Why did Johnson embark on the Great Society?

8.8 Historical interpretation: How successful was the Great Society?

8.9 An in-depth study: Who was more effective in domestic reform – JFK or LBJ?

Framework of Events

1945	Truman becomes president
	GI Bill
1946	Price Control Act
1947	Taft–Hartley Act
	House Un-American Activities Committee hearings start
1948	Truman defeats Dewey in presidential election
1949	Truman proposes Fair Deal
1950	McCarthy's speech at Wheeling claiming there were 57 Communists in the State Department
1951	Twenty-Second Amendment to the Constitution
1952	Eisenhower elected first Republican president since Hoover
1954	McCarthy is censured by the Senate
1958	National Defence Education Act – first federal money for education
1961	Kennedy takes office
1963	Kennedy talks about a 'war on poverty', but is assassinated before putting it into action
1964	Johnson wins landslide election and launches the Great Society
	Economic Opportunity Act
1965	Elementary and Secondary Education Act
	Medical Care Act
1966	Demonstration Cities and Metropolitan Development Act
	Clean Water Restoration Act
1967	Air Quality Act
1968	Wild and Scenic Rivers Act

Overview

B y the end of the Second World War, in 1945, the United States had been through tremendous change. The Depression had seen millions of Americans lose their jobs, their savings and their homes. The economy had almost collapsed. Franklin Roosevelt (FDR) and his New Deal policies had seen federal government take on a new role in running the economy to try and bring the country out of the slump. They made fundamental changes to the welfare structure to ensure that no crisis like it could happen again. The coming of war in Europe brought jobs to American people, and its own entry into the war in 1941 finally ended the Great Depression. Federal power, particularly the power of the President, had been further extended by the needs of the Second World War. Once peace returned, two questions arose:

● Would the American economy return to depression?

Laissez-faire **attitudes**: The belief that federal government should interfere as little as possible in the economy, but leave business to get on with it.

● Would federal government return to the *laissez-faire* **attitudes** of the 1920s?

Although the Second World War had brought the United States out of the Depression, once the War was over the Depression did not return. Far from returning to Depression, the USA experienced massive economic growth and the majority of Americans saw living standards rise steadily through the 1950s and the 1960s. New technologies were a major factor in this growth but, unlike the 1920s, federal government also worked hard to build economic wealth. The business of American government was business. Both Democrats and Republicans now routinely used tax and spending policies to control economic growth.

However, this growth in government power worried many. Congress felt that its power had declined relative to that of the Executive. President Truman was to have many battles as Congress tried to reassert its authority. There was even the Twenty-Second Amendment to the Constitution, added in 1951, to ensure that no future president could have the amount of power which FDR was believed to have had. But there could be no return to the 1920s. In spite of constraints, Truman attempted to build on and develop the New Deal. Even when the Republicans returned to power in 1953, Eisenhower accepted many of the social changes the Democrats had made. Later on, in the 1960s, both Kennedy and particularly Johnson would extend and develop the idea that federal government should protect and care for those in need.

While the majority of Americans saw their living standards rise, there were also millions who did not. It was estimated that a quarter of Americans lived in poverty. Although there was no direct crisis such as in the 1930s, Kennedy declared a 'war on poverty' as part of his New Frontier programmes. He began a programme of measures concerning welfare, health and education, but conflict with Congress and his untimely death meant he was able to achieve little. His successor, Lyndon Johnson, was a man who had served under FDR and was determined to go further than Roosevelt had done in ending poverty in America. The Great Society was the biggest programme of social legislation in US history. Its success is disputed, but it was unquestionably an attempt to use the power of federal government to achieve improvements in the lives of millions of Americans.

Politically, the Democrats continued to hold power for most of the 1960s following eight years of a Republican administration (1953–1961). The Democrats' hold on both houses of Congress was just as strong. However, there were conflicts between the various branches of government and within the parties themselves, especially in the Democrats, which limited the achievements of the Presidents. The 'conservative coalition' of Southern Democrats and Republicans was to prove a particular problem.

The biggest political crisis of the era – apart from civil rights (see Chapter 7) – was the anti-Communist hysteria that became known as McCarthyism.

The quarter century that followed the Second World War saw the United States experience economic growth and political conflict. It also saw the growth of federal government and a real attempt to deal with poverty and injustice.

1. Write a brief account on the aims and policies in the mind map.

2. Who do you regard as the most successful president in domestic policy in the period 1945 to 1969? Give reasons for your answer.

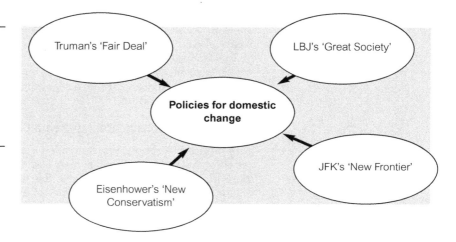

8.1 What problems did Truman face in his first administration of 1945–1949?

Truman's Administration: leading domestic posts

Secretary of the Treasury:	Henry Morgenthau Jr (1945) Frederick Vinson (1945–46) John W. Snyder (1946–53)
Attorney General:	Francis B. Biddle (1945) Thomas C. Clark (1945–49) J. Howard McGrath (1949–52)
Secretary of the Interior:	Harold L. Ickes (1945–46) Julius A. Krug (1946–49) Oscar L. Chapman (1950–53)
Secretary of Agriculture:	Claude R. Wickard (1945) Clinton P Anderson (1945–48) Charles F. Brannan (1948–53)
Secretary of Commerce:	Henry A. Wallace (1945–46) William Averell Harriman (1946–48) Charles Sawyer (1948–53)
Secretary of Labor:	Frances Perkins (1945) Lewis B. Schwellenbach (1945–48)

In April 1945, the strains of fighting the Great Depression and the Second World War finally took their toll and Franklin D. Roosevelt, America's longest-serving President, died. His Vice-President, Harry S. Truman, succeeded him.

Truman's job was not going to be easy. Although he had experience in Congress and as Vice-President, he had not been prepared for the office of President. When he unexpectedly found himself in the Oval Office (US President's official work place) he said that he felt as though the moon, stars and planets had fallen in on him. Not only did he have to follow the greatest president the 20th century had produced, but the **political machine** of Kansas City, in the state of Missouri, was known for its corruption. Many felt that they were going to get another Harding. Others, who knew him from Congress, liked and respected him.

Political machine: The various party committees, groups and individuals that control elections in a certain area. Often associated with corruption.

Being from a poor background, and having worked with Roosevelt, Truman wanted to build on the New Deal to take social reform into new areas, particularly healthcare. He also knew that the American public was weary of change. After the upheavals of the Depression and of the Second World War, the public craved stability, in domestic politics at least. In fact, under Truman, there was conflict between the White House and Congress, conflict in industry and conflict over communism. It was to be a far from tranquil Administration.

Why did Truman have problems with Congress?

Although the Republicans controlled Congress from 1946 to 1948, for much of his time in office Truman had a Democratic Congress, yet they were by no means a united party. There were 'New Deal liberals' who wanted Truman to continue the work of his predecessor. They blamed him when things went wrong, conveniently forgetting the problems FDR had with Congress in 1938. There were the Southern Democrats, frequently referred to as 'Dixiecrats', who disliked Truman's stand on civil rights, and who had more in common with the Republicans over issues such as union rights. They frequently voted with the Republicans in Congress. This meant that, although Truman had a Democratic Congress for much of his Administration, he did not have an easy job getting legislation through. For example, one of his first actions was to put forward a 21-point programme calling on Congress to pass a series of social reforms. They were almost all rejected. Not only was Congress concerned about the potential cost of the proposals, they also resented the way Truman was demanding so much so soon. FDR had been granted 'broad executive power' in a time of crisis: Truman was going to have to work much harder for his policies to be passed.

The mid-term elections of 1946 only made the situation worse as, for the first time since 1930, the Republicans had a majority in Congress. They held 246–188 seats in the House of Representatives and 51–45 in the Senate. The Republican Party had not been in control of Congress since Herbert Hoover was in the White House and they were determined to make the most of their opportunity.

The economic problems caused by the War, particularly inflation and the increasing number of labour disputes, had encouraged people to turn against the Administration. The Republican slogan of 'Had enough?' captured the mood of many disillusioned voters and the Democrats did badly everywhere outside the South. This was largely a protest vote, rather than a real turning away from the Democrats. It can be illustrated by the fact that both Houses returned to Democratic control in 1948. However, in the meantime, Congress did much to block several of Truman's measures.

One measure which the Republican Congress did manage to get

through was the Twenty-Second Amendment to the Constitution, which limited a president to two terms. The fact that this was passed by Congress and ratified by the states shows that there was real concern over how much the power of the President had increased under FDR in the 1930s and 1940s. The determination of Congress to re-assert its power to pass or reject legislation made life hard for the Truman Administration and made relations between the two very difficult. In seven years, the President vetoed 250 bills passed by Congress and they, in turn, **overrode** 12 of those vetoes. It was one of the worst records of conflict over legislation in American history.

Overrode: If the President vetoes a bill, Congress can still pass it into law if two-thirds of the members of each house agree. This is called overriding.

How serious were the economic problems facing Truman?

At the end of the War, Truman was afraid that the USA would slide back into depression. His polices were aimed at preventing that and at encouraging real growth.

Firstly, he wanted a slow de-mobilisation of the military, because he was afraid of the effect on the economy of 12 million men suddenly flooding the job market. He also felt that given the developing Cold War it was important for the USA to keep a credible armed force. Clearly, this would be unpopular with the families who wanted their men home as quickly as possible. As the mid-term elections were approaching, the soldiers and their families used political influence to get home. There was a campaign of sending postcards to the White House with the slogan 'No boats, no votes!' The threat worked. The army was reduced from 12 million, in 1945, to 3 million within a year, and was halved again over the next year. Although there was a lot of short-term unemployment, the feared recession did not return. Unemployment never rose much above 4 per cent during the Truman presidency.

Businessmen and the public also wanted a quick return to normality. So plants were returned to peacetime production and government-controlled factories were privatised. With all these men returning home, there would be a demand on goods and it would take time for the factories to produce enough. The economic effect, therefore, was 25 per cent inflation in 1945–46, made worse by Congress's $6 billion tax cut. Truman's fear had been realised, and this high level of inflation was one of the reasons the Democrats lost support in the 1946 mid-terms.

To deal with this and to try and stabilise prices, the President wanted to continue the Office of Price Administration (OPA) which had controlled prices during the War. However, the **conservative coalition** in Congress wanted to abolish the OPA and return to letting business have more say over its own affairs.

Conservative coalition: The voting or working together of conservative Democrats and Republicans in Congress.

Truman proposed a price control bill, in 1946, to extend the life of the OPA. However, when the Bill reached Congress it was amended and watered down so much that the OPA would have been powerless, and so Truman vetoed the amendments. His supporters in Congress warned him that the Bill was the best he could get, and he was eventually forced to accept it. Congress had, effectively, ignored his veto and had made Truman accept an Act in which he had no faith. Although some prices, such as rents, rose dramatically, by the end of 1946 the economy was stabilising and the OPA was no longer needed.

In 1946, Congress did accept Truman's proposal for a Council of Economic Advisors (CEA). The CEA's job was to watch the economy and recommend government action, if necessary. Congress also passed an Employment Act, which gave a commitment to maximum employment and productivity. It required the President to give an annual report to Congress on the state of the economy, with recommendations. However, the Employment Act did not go as far as Truman wanted. He had hoped for a bill demanding 'full' employment, but it showed that America now accepted more government involvement in the economy and that it would not go back to the *laissez faire* of the 1920s. It was the job of the government to exercise a guiding hand, at the least, to the economy of the country.

With 12 million soldiers returning home, there would be a need for housing and for jobs to prevent a recession such as that which followed the First World War. Truman hoped to provide housing through the Federal Housing Agency, which provided government-backed mortgages at good rates of interest. However, he was unable to get money from Congress for more public housing, and construction companies were keener to build commercial properties than homes. Nevertheless, the construction boom that followed the Second World War did provide many jobs for the returning men.

GI: Stands for 'government issue'; a GI is an American serviceman who wears government issue clothes and carries government issue weapons.

Of more help was the 'GI Bill', passed by Congress as compensation for those who had served their country. Ex-servicemen were allowed 52 weeks' unemployment relief if needed; loans were given for education, farms, housing and business. Between 1945 and 1955, $20 billion was given out to help 7.8 million veterans.

By the end of the 1940s, the economy began to pick up. In 1947, half the world's manufacturing output was from the USA. By the mid-1950s, America would be experiencing massive economic growth. As industry got back into peacetime production it was able to meet demand, and demand was high. The GI Bill and wages from the War meant that the returning soldiers had a lot of money to pump into the economy. A baby boom created a massive market for domestic products. Even the outbreak of the Korean War in 1950 was also an impetus to growth, as was new technology. So although the first few years of Truman's Administration were not economically successful, the last couple of years were and the growth would continue into the following two decades.

What problems did the Truman Administration face with organised labour?

By the 1940s, trade unions were much stronger than they had been in the 1920s and 1930s. The Wagner Act of 1935 had encouraged union growth, and the need for labour during the War increased the power of the unions dramatically. By 1945, 15 million workers belonged to trade unions – approximately 36 per cent of the non-agricultural work force.

> There were two major labour organisations in the USA in the 1940s – the American Federation of Labor (AFL) and the Congress of Industrial Organisations (CIO).
>
> The AFL was formed in 1886. It represented unions of mainly skilled workers and craftsmen. It did little for women or the less skilled workers of the factories, so in 1935 the leader of the United Mine Workers, John L. Lewis, broke away to form the CIO. Lewis did a great deal to encourage union membership among industrial workers.
>
> In 1955, the two organisations merged into the AFL–CIO to fight for workers' rights, education, beneficial legislation etc.

The high inflation after the War meant that the trade unions began demanding wage rises. In 1946, there were strikes in most major industries. A government-organised conference, in November 1945, did little to bring management and unions together. The President mediated the strikes, but at the cost of 19 per cent price rises and 18–19 per cent wage rises, which all worsened the inflation problem.

For Truman this was a political problem – for when workers got pay rises management put up prices to pay for them, which only encouraged further inflation. Truman knew that the unions were vital to Democratic Party finances. He also knew that there was widespread public hostility to union demands and, within the party, the Southern Democrats were also hostile. The President was caught in the middle.

In April 1946, a coal strike began involving 400,000 miners and looked like spreading to other areas. The railwaymen then came out. Such a widespread strike in these areas would have severely damaged American industry. So, to prevent it, Truman asked Congress for emergency powers to use troops in the dispute and even to draft strikers into the army. Congress sensibly refused. Truman had overreacted and risked a major crisis in industry, far worse than the one he was trying to resolve.

Although Congress held Truman back in this instance, the Republicans and conservative Democrats were increasingly anti-union, and they took measures to reduce union power. In 1947, the Republican Congress passed the Taft–Hartley Act.

The Taft–Hartley Act of 1947

- Listed various 'unfair' labour practices
- Outlawed the **closed shop**
- Required union officers to sign non-communist oaths
- Allowed bosses to sue unions under certain conditions
- Authorised the President to demand an 80-day 'cooling-off' period before strikes.

Closed shop: The right of a union to prevent non-union members being hired by the company. It protects the union members from being outnumbered by non-union workers and therefore losing their power to protect their members.

Needless to say, the unions were furious and wanted the Act repealed. What the unions wanted were federal guarantees for the closed shop and free collective bargaining (i.e. the right to represent their members and their interests). Truman vetoed the Act, but Congress again overrode the veto. Truman felt the Taft–Hartley Act was vindictive, even though he had had his own quarrels with the unions. However, under the American Constitution, Congress passes the laws even if the government does not want them.

Truman's problems did not end there, even though the power of the union was reduced. In April 1952, a strike was threatened in the steel industry where the workers demanded an increase in wages because of increased production caused by the Korean War. Because he did not want to appear weak and he was concerned about a strike in wartime, Truman seized control of the mills under Executive Order, claiming **Executive Privilege**. Although they did not want the strike, the steel companies did not want the government taking control of their factories either, so they challenged the President's authority to do this in the Supreme Court. The Court agreed with the mill owners. Truman had to hand the mills back. A seven-week strike followed, resulting in shortages and higher steel prices. Yet again, when Truman tried to act tough, he had ended up backing down and looking weak.

Executive Privilege: The right of the President to take action in an emergency.

1. Why did Truman have poor relations with Congress in his first administration?

2. How successfully did Truman handle labour issues in his first administration?

8.2 How far did Truman build on the New Deal in social policy?

Why did Truman win the 1948 presidential election?

Truman had had many problems with the Republican-controlled Eightieth Congress, particularly over labour issues and the economy. There had also been conflict over the race issue and over social reform. The Democratic Party itself continued to be split, especially over race, and it was not enthusiastic about re-nominating Truman, the 'accidental president'. Therefore, when the elections came everyone, including the Democrats, expected the Republicans to win. Yet Truman surprised everyone and gained a victory with 49.5 per cent of the vote.

The Democratic Party went into the election badly divided. So much so that there were, in effect, three Democratic candidates: Henry A. Wallace from Iowa ran as a progressive candidate and J. Strom Thurmond ran as a states' rights candidate. Wallace was a New Dealer disappointed by the lack of social reform from Truman. He was a well-respected man with wide political experience as Secretary for Agriculture under FDR, and Vice-President before Truman (1940–44). It was feared that he could take sufficient liberal votes away from Truman to give the election to the Republicans. In the end, Wallace took less than 2.5 per cent of the vote. Thurmond, Governor of South Carolina, led the Southern Democrats who disagreed with Truman's positive civil rights stand in the election. Like Wallace, he polled less than 2.5 per cent of the vote but, as his votes were concentrated in the South, he managed to win four states, and tied with Truman in Tennessee. In fact, having these two candidates worked in Truman's favour, as he was able to present himself as the moderate in between Wallace on the left and Thurmond on the right.

So why, in spite of a divided and unenthusiastic Party, did Truman win? Firstly, organised labour and 'blue collar' working-class Americans

The 1948 Presidential Election results

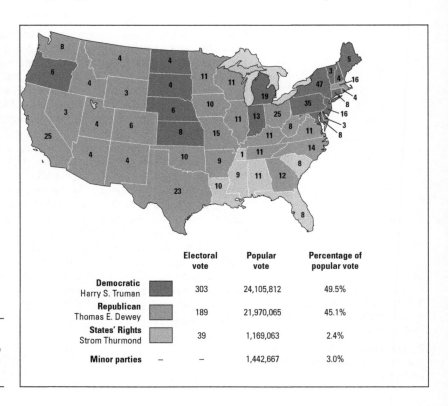

	Electoral vote	Popular vote	Percentage of popular vote
Democratic Harry S. Truman	303	24,105,812	49.5%
Republican Thomas E. Dewey	189	21,970,065	45.1%
States' Rights Strom Thurmond	39	1,169,063	2.4%
Minor parties	–	–	1,442,667	3.0%

Study the map.

Explain why Truman was able to win the election even though he won a minority of states.

supported him, in spite of the problems of 1946, because they did not want the Republicans to win. Unions had been a strong foundation of Democratic support for over 20 years and they were not now going to turn to the Party that had given them Taft–Hartley.

Likewise, black support for the Democrats remained strong. If anything, Truman's stand on civil rights tied African-Americans more closely to the Democrats than the New Deal had. The votes of northern blacks more than made up for the losses to Thurmond and, on the whole, the South remained fairly solidly Democrat.

Truman's standing up to Russia in the Cold War was also popular. Throughout the election, he stressed the anti-Communist theme and the need to continue his policy of containment. Events in Berlin and Czechoslovakia added to the President's warnings and enhanced his reputation for handling foreign policy (see Chapter 5).

Elections are not only won, they are also lost. There is no doubt that Truman's victory was in part due to the poor showing by the Republicans. The Republican candidate was Thomas E. Dewey, a moderate but rather dull candidate. Dewey criticised the government for inaction and called for unity, but the Republican Party could offer little in the way of real policies. Like the Democrats, they too were divided. Many Republicans would have preferred Senator Robert Taft of Ohio as their candidate, but he was considered too conservative. Taft was an isolationist in foreign policy which, at the height of the Cold War, was not a popular position. There were also divisions in the Party as to how far, or even whether, they should try to reverse the New Deal. These divisions meant that they could offer little to the electorate that was positive and that they had no real strategy for victory. Truman, on the other hand, travelled 22,000 miles around the country putting across his message. That message was largely designed by his special advisor Clark Clifford.

Clifford encouraged Truman to appeal to the various groups who might support the Democrats, particularly ethnic groups. Blacks and Jews were singled out as large minorities who could win the election for them. Truman's insistence on action on civil rights forming part of the Democratic platform was undoubtedly influenced by Clifford, as was the Administration's decision to recognise the newly established state of Israel. (Though, in both cases, Truman was also taking decisions he believed to be right.) The strategy was extremely successful and both groups contributed significantly to Truman's victory.

Truman also emphasised that he was on the side of the 'people' against the 'special interests', such as the corporations. Being a Missouri farm boy he found the role of the 'little man' taking on the 'big guys' an easy one to play. But, as with civil rights and Israel, Truman was also taking policy stands in which he believed. He called for action on housing, healthcare, education and the minimum wage. Truman accused the Republican Congress of blocking progress, calling it the 'do nothing Congress'. It was especially successful as the Republican election programme contained many measures which Truman had wanted but which Congress had refused to pass. He challenged them to a special session in July 1948, saying that if they were serious about social reform they would get their chance to pass the measures. The bluff worked and the Republican promises of social reform from then on seemed hollow.

In addition to winning against all predictions, the Democrats also regained control of Congress, 54–42 and 263–171. Truman believed that this gave him a mandate for the social reform he had attempted in 1945.

Thomas E. Dewey (1902–1971)

Lawyer and US attorney who gained prominence prosecuting gangsters, successfully convicting 72 of them. He was Governor of New York for three terms between 1943–55. Chosen as presidential candidate by the Republican Party in 1944 and 1948. He was a well-liked and competent man. Failing to win the White House, he continued as Governor of New York and then returned to practising law. He was offered a Supreme Court job by Nixon, but turned it down due to his age.

Clark Clifford (1906–1998)

Lawyer. Served in navy during the Second World War. Special advisor to Truman, he helped formulate the Truman Doctrine and helped Truman win the 1948 election. Clifford worked for Kennedy as advisor during JFK's time in the Senate and the White House, and he was Johnson's Secretary of Defense 1968–69. He was also an advisor to Democratic president Jimmy Carter.

How successful was the Fair Deal?

When Truman had presented his 21-point programme to Congress after the War, it was clear that he wanted to build on the New Deal, protecting the vulnerable in society. In his State of the Union address to Congress in January 1949, he said that:

> 'the foundations of a healthy economy cannot be secure so long as a large section of our working people receive substandard wages' and he asked for 'comprehensive housing legislation ... [and] a national health programme to provide adequate medical care for all Americans'.

To pay for all this, he asked for a $4 billion tax increase. Both the Democratic and Republican Congresses rejected his proposals. Now he was no longer just the man who succeeded FDR, but had been elected in his own right, he returned to what became known as the Fair Deal. In his State of the Union address, he also called for:

- an increase in the minimum wage

- repeal of the Taft–Hartley Act

- the expansion of **social security**

- the setting up of public works schemes

- and a healthcare programme.

All of this was to be paid for out of taxation.

Social security: A system by which the government pays money regularly to people who have no other income or only a very small income.

In some areas, Truman was successful. Social security was extended to one million more Americans and the minimum wage went up from 40¢ to 75¢ an hour. Farmers benefited from measures for soil conservation, flood control and rural electrification. To deal with the housing shortage, the National Housing Act 1949 provided for the building of 810,000 subsidised, low-income homes over six years, though only about half the proposed number were, in fact, built. It also included measures for slum clearance and urban renewal. Congress also set up the National Science Foundation in order to encourage research and development in science which, although motivated by Cold War considerations, was a boost to education. But many of Truman's proposals were still rejected; notably, measures for federal healthcare and education – two crucial areas which FDR and the New Deal had not touched.

Truman proposed a national health insurance system based on a tax of 4 per cent on the first $6,300 of a person's income. The proposal was attacked in Congress not only as a tax-raising measure, but also because it was felt that it was not the job of the federal government to tell people how to arrange their own healthcare. The American Medical Association, which represented doctors, attacked the proposal as 'socialised medicine'. It saw any attempt by government to interfere in this area as little short of communism. A Hospital Construction Act was passed, but it benefited the building industry more than medicine. It was to be almost 20 years before a federal healthcare programme would be passed.

Likewise, little was done in education in spite of increasing evidence of the poor state of American schools. Education was seen as a state issue, not a federal one. Democratic Congressmen knew that any attempt to interfere would run into problems, especially in southern states, because of the issue of segregation. Like healthcare, it would be the Johnson Administration that would eventually provide federal support for education.

Although Truman's relations with Congress had improved, they still blocked his measures. Conservative Democrats and Republicans worked against him on many major issues and he was no Roosevelt who could inspire Congress to agree with his wishes. Truman had a background in congressional politics but he had little tact when dealing with Congress, which was increasingly concerned with issues like Communist subversion and, from 1950, the war in Korea. To get support on these issues, he had to give up the Fair Deal.

Given these problems, Truman's Fair Deal had little chance of being enacted. For many, the New Deal had done enough and they did not want to take federal government into these areas of policy. Truman was trying to push further than either Congress or the public was prepared to go. There were some 'New Deal liberals' who saw FDR's policies as only a beginning. They had faith in the power of federal government to effect real change in people's lives and in society. But this was being replaced by a new 'Cold War liberalism' which, although it supported federal government's role, also felt that Roosevelt had tackled the most serious problems. The key now was to consolidate what they had, rather than go further. It was this mood that held the American public. So, although Truman achieved much in strengthening measures like social security, he was unable to take the Fair Deal further.

Why did the Democrats lose the 1952 election?

When the 1952 election came, the economy was picking up and Truman had had a few successes with the Fair Deal. But in election year there were crises, which damaged the chances for the Democrats. The steel strike, the war in Korea (see Chapter 6) and the difficulties with McCarthy all pointed to a poor election showing. To add to Truman's problems, hearings began in 1951 into corruption in the Reconstruction Finance Corporation and the Internal Revenue Service. Stories of bribes and 'gifts' came out involving friends of the President. These hearings were televised and did much damage to Truman's Administration.

Given these circumstances, the Democratic Party did not want Truman to stand again and was relieved when he announced his retirement. It chose the intellectual Adlai Stevenson as their candidate to take on Eisenhower. However, he was no match for the popular war hero and, for the first time since 1932, there was a Republican in the White House.

It is easy to see only the negative side of the Truman Administration. There can be no question that, domestically at least, he was not one of the more successful presidents of the post-war era. He was in constant conflict with Congress, whether it was controlled by the Republicans or by his own party. On at least two occasions he collided head-on with the unions, who were natural supporters of the Democratic Party. His Administration ended amid charges of corruption. Above all, he contributed to the rise of the anti-Communist hysteria of the period which was so damaging to the United States. Yet Truman did preside over the relatively calm transition from war to peace and, in spite of Congress, handled the economy successfully. Though he came nowhere near to achieving all he wanted, he was able to extend the social provisions of the New Deal to millions more Americans. Truman's presidency was not a shining success domestically, but neither was it one of abject failure. Like Truman himself, it could be said to have been moderately successful.

1. Why did Truman win the 1948 election?

2. How successful was Truman in domestic affairs in the years 1945 to 1953?

8.3 What impact did McCarthyism have on the USA?

According to historians such as William Chafe, there is a traditional intolerance in America which surfaces periodically, such as in the early 1920s (see *The Unfinished Journey*, published in 1991). Chafe sees the rise in

Subversion: The destruction or overthrow of a government.

anti-communism of the late 1940s and early 1950s as an example of this 'seasonal allergy'. Some historians, however, view the episode as a reaction by conservatives to the New Deal and all it stood for. Others stress a fear of enemies all around which grew up as a result of the Second World War and the Cold War, coming together with a fear of internal **subversion**. Some historians see it more in psychological terms, as America coming to terms with a period of massive and frightening change and looking for someone or something to blame for their fears. Whatever the reason, the anti-Communist hysteria of the Truman and Eisenhower administrations witnessed a massive attack on the civil liberties of American people and it is looked upon as a black period in American history. What started it and what was going on?

How did the development of the Cold War affect the domestic history of the USA?

Although the United States and the Soviet Union had been allies in the Second World War, by the late 1940s there was a growing fear of Communism and its expansion. A raid, in 1945, on the offices of 'Amerasia', a Communist magazine, revealed several documents from the US State Department and one from an official in the US navy. Shortly afterwards, the Canadian government uncovered a spy network operating in America, which was sending information to the Russians. Americans knew that communism preaches the overthrow of other political systems. Given that the Russians had established Soviet governments in most of Eastern Europe, a real fear grew that there was a danger of Communist subversion inside the USA. In 1945, the Communist Party of the United States had only around 80,000 members, in a country of 140 million, but it did take money and directions from Moscow.

The passing of the National Security Act in 1947 (see Chapter 5) further increased fears of Communism and of the USSR. The Act set up a Department of Defence by joining together the Departments of the Navy, Army and Air Force. It created the National Security Council to advise the president on security issues. That the Administration felt the need for such action created a fear that there really were weaknesses in American security. To get the Act through Congress, Truman had played on this fear, making it more real.

Truman received a letter from the Director of the Federal Bureau of Investigation (FBI), J. Edgar Hoover, saying there was a real problem with Communist conspiracies in America and that the government had to act. In March 1947, Truman issued Executive Order 9835, which established Federal Loyalty Boards.

The Order allowed for the removal of federal employees if 'reasonable grounds exist for belief that the person involved is disloyal to the government of the United States'. Although the Order did contain safeguards, these did not seem particularly effective. Individuals could be 'considered' a threat if they were members of any group which the Attorney General named as subversive. People's beliefs could get them fired as much as any actual activity and the principle of innocent until proven guilty seemed to have been abandoned. Estimates vary, but between 1947 and 1951 up to 3,000 employees were forced to resign and 300 were fired. No evidence of actual subversion was ever uncovered.

The 'Amerasia' case had clearly worried the government, and the President had no reason not to believe the head of the FBI when he warned him of danger. But Truman had set the tone for the next five years, in which accusations of Communist sympathy would do as much damage to a person as being found guilty of any actual activity.

John Edgar Hoover (1895–1972)
Director of the FBI from 1924 until his death. He trained as a lawyer and worked for Attorney General A. Mitchell Palmer during the 'Red Scare' of 1920. Hoover is credited with developing the FBI into an efficient and effective criminal investigation organisation in the 1920s and 1930s. A fanatical anti-Communist, he used the powers of his office to spy on Martin Luther King Jr and President Kennedy, among others. He is accused of using the information the FBI had to maintain himself in power.

States and cities followed the government's lead and employees had to take loyalty oaths or lose their jobs. In Massachusetts, a person could be imprisoned for even allowing a Communist to use their premises for a meeting. Other states passed their own anti-subversion laws. There were 39 by 1952.

The development of the Cold War, in the period after the Second World War, further increased the growing fear of communism within America. The tension was heightened by a series of events that served to demonstrate the increasing might of the Soviets (see Chapter 5):

● explosion of the first atom bomb by the Soviets in 1949

● fall of China to communism in the same year

● start of the Korean War in 1950

● race between the USA and the Soviet Union to develop the hydrogen bomb.

How important were the House Un-American Activities Committee hearings in the development of McCarthyism?

The House Un-American Activities Committee (HUAC) had been set up in 1938, when there was a very tense situation in Europe. The job of the Committee was to monitor activities of extremist groups of both left and right, which might present a danger to the United States. Even from its early days, it was used more against Communists than against Nazis. To deal with the new supposed threat, the Committee was revived and began to hold hearings to investigate those suspected of subversive activities. These began in 1947.

Witnesses were called before the Committee and asked questions about their beliefs and actions. The question frequently asked was: 'Are you now or have you ever been a member of the Communist Party?' If someone was shown to have Communist connections, even in the past, they could be in trouble. They would also be expected to 'name names' (i.e. give the Committee the names of other Communists).

One of the most famous attacks – and the one that brought HUAC's activities much more to the notice of the general public – was the investigation of Hollywood between 1947 and 1951. According to Hoover, the Communists had been targeting Hollywood since 1935. In 1947, he wrote that 'Communist activity in Hollywood is effective and is furthered by Communists and sympathisers using the prestige of prominent persons to serve, often unwittingly, the Communist cause. The Party is content and highly pleased if it is possible to have inserted a line, a scene, a sequence conveying the Communist lesson.'

Cited for contempt: Found guilty of not respecting the court and its authority. This usually carries a jail sentence.

When the hearings began, those who refused to answer the Committee's questions were **cited for contempt**. The playwright Arthur Miller was interrogated by the Committee about meetings of Communist writers which he attended nine years before. When he refused to name other people present, he was cited for contempt, fined $500 and given a suspended prison sentence. This experience prompted Miller to write *The Crucible*, a play about the witch-hunts in Salem, Massachusetts, in 1692. In all, 12 actors and writers were sent to prison. For others, their careers were finished and they were **blacklisted** by Hollywood, even when they had not been convicted of any offence. Merely being called before the Committee could finish a career. Of course, some people named names; for example, a young actor called Ronald Reagan.

Blacklisted: Put on a government list, which contains the names of people or organisations who they think cannot be trusted or who have done something wrong.

People called before the Committee believed that their rights would be protected by the Constitution. The First Amendment guarantees the right

J. Parnell Thomas, Chairman of HUAC (right), administers witness oath to Robert Taylor (left), Hollywood film star. Taylor testified that a number of his fellow actors were communists and were a 'disrupting' influence in the motion picture industry.

How useful is this 1947 photograph to a historian writing about the impact of the HUAC hearing?

to free speech and free assembly but, in 1948, in the case of 'Dennis versus the United States', the Supreme Court held that First Amendment rights could be cut off by Congress if national security was at stake. In other words, people could be sent to prison for things they said. Some pleaded the Fifth Amendment, which says that no one has to implicate himself or herself in a crime (i.e. the right to silence), but the Committee usually treated 'taking the Fifth' as an admission of guilt. With the support of the three branches of government, HUAC was eating away at the constitutional rights of American citizens. The hearings seemed also to confirm that there were spies operating in the United States.

Alger Hiss was a worker at the State Department. He had been a New Dealer, had been with FDR at Yalta (see page 136) and had been an aide to Secretary of State Dean Acheson. He was suspected of treason when another witness named him as having belonged to a subversive organisation in the 1930s. He was convicted of perjury (lying to a court) and sentenced to five years in prison, in January 1950. The following month, the British arrested Klaus Fuchs for spying. He confessed and named others who worked at the Los Alamos project, where the atomic bomb had been developed; including a man called David Greenglass. He, in turn, named his sister and brother-in-law, Ethel and Julius Rosenberg, who were arrested and convicted of spying and passing secrets to the Russians. Throughout the trial they protested their innocence but, in spite of the fact that they never admitted the crime, and in spite of having young children, the couple were sentenced to death and were executed in 1953.

It now seems from the decoding work done by the Venona Project that both Hiss and the Rosenbergs were working for the Soviets, though many at the time and since have been convinced of their innocence. These high-profile cases convinced Congress that more needed to be done to protect America from the Communist threat.

In 1950, Congress passed the McCarren Internal Security Act. All Communist organisations had to register with the Attorney General; no Communist could be employed in a defence plant. A further Act, in 1952, strengthened its terms so that Communists could be denied passports, foreigners suspected of subversion could be deported and, in a national emergency, the authorities could detain anyone they classed as subversive. Truman felt that the Act was going too far and vetoed it but, when it returned to Congress, only 58 people in either House supported him. The fear and determination to take action was now widespread. Yet Truman must take his share of the blame. He had begun government sanctions against Communists and had played up the threat in order to get support

Joseph Raymond McCarthy (1908–1957)

As a young man he served in the Second World War, before changing his politics to Republicanism and entering the Senate in 1946. In February 1950, McCarthy caused a sensation by claiming to hold a list of 205 Communist Party members working in the US State Department. (This number was reduced to 57, over a number of speeches.) McCarthy continued a public witch-hunting campaign against members of the Truman Administration. When it was shown that he and his aides had been falsifying evidence, President Eisenhower renounced him. However, by this time, many people in public life and the arts had been blacklisted as suspected Communists or Communist sympathisers. McCarthy died of liver disease brought on by excessive intake of alcohol.

for both the Truman Doctrine and the Marshall Plan (see Chapter 5). Both the Republicans and Democrats had emphasised their commitment to root out and remove Communist spies in order to help their election prospects. They had stirred up a process which was moved on by others, notably Joe McCarthy.

Why did Joseph McCarthy have such an impact?

Senator Joseph McCarthy was looking for an issue with which to make his name, and the anti-Communist crusade that America seemed to have embarked on suited his purposes. He did not start the 'Second Red Scare'. It may be that he really did have information about spies in government which the Venona Project has confirmed existed, but McCarthy was also a liar, a drunk and a bully who took the anti-Communist hysteria to new levels. He ruined people's lives, damaged the reputation of his country and gave a new word to the English language – **McCarthyism**.

McCarthyism: Fear of internal subversion, aggravated by genuine fears from the Cold War. This created a 'Red Scare' far larger in scale and far more damaging to society than that of the early 1920s.

The impact of McCarthy was enormous. The Republicans could make the Democrats look bad with accusations of treason, so they encouraged his charges. They had been out of power for 20 years and had now found an issue on which to attack the Democrats. In response, the Democrats had to show that they were just as tough on Communism and subversion by denouncing it just as forcefully. By playing party politics with the issue, both parties gave credibility to McCarthy and must take their share of the blame for his activities.

McCarthy also found support among the public. America was not doing as well in the Cold War as Americans felt they should, especially in Korea, so there had to be an explanation: enemies in government gave them a reason. Certain groups, such as the Catholic Church, gave McCarthy their support not only because he was a Catholic, but also because Communism is atheistic. They supported McCarthy's 'religious' crusade to root it out.

McCarthy found support among ethnic groups, too. Poles, for example, had no love for the Russians, many of them having come to America to escape Russian oppression. McCarthy was a skilled politician and manipulator of the media, but he had a willing audience for his message.

He also had his critics. In 1950, the Tydings Committee looked into his accusations and called him 'a fraud and a hoax'. Studies have shown that for all McCarthy's skill in gaining and maintaining press attention, the majority of the press was critical of him. Yet the HUAC investigations continued and McCarthy's net spread wider. People were afraid to confront him in case they found themselves accused and brought before the Committee.

When the 1952 election brought Eisenhower to the White House, many hoped that he would stop what had now become known as the 'witch hunts'. But Eisenhower refused 'to get down in the gutter with that guy', believing

George Catlett Marshall (1880–1959)
Soldier and diplomat. Served in the Philippines and in Europe during the First World War. As Chief of Staff in the Second World War, he organised the expansion, training and equipping of the army and air force to enable America to fight the Nazis and the Japanese. In 1947, he became Secretary of State under Truman and was responsible for the Marshall Plan to help European recovery. In 1950, he became Secretary of Defense. He was awarded the Nobel Peace Prize in 1953.

What does this extract tell us about McCarthy's views?

that, if he ignored McCarthy, he would fade away. The new President seemed to be a little afraid of McCarthy: in 1953, he dropped a paragraph from a speech he was about to make in which he would have defended McCarthy's latest target, George Marshall. Eisenhower had let down a personal friend, an action he later regretted bitterly. Ike was worried what an out-and-out attack might do to the Republicans in Congress, many of whom supported the Senator. He did not want to divide his Party. In a sense he was right to leave McCarthy alone because, as his accusations grew wider and more extravagant, he began to be taken less seriously.

'... this is not a period of peace. This is the time of the "cold war". This is the time when all the world is split into two vast, increasingly hostile camps ...

The reason why we find ourselves in a position of impotency is not because our only powerful potential enemy has sent men to invade our shores, but rather because of the traitorous actions of those who have been treated so well by this nation. It has not been the less fortunate or members of minority groups who have been selling this nation out, but rather those who have had all the benefits that the wealthiest nation on earth has had to offer – the finest homes, the finest college education, and the finest jobs in Government we can give.

This is glaringly true in the State Department. There the bright young men who are born with silver spoons in their mouths are the ones who have been the worst ... In my opinion the State Department, which is one of the most important government departments, is thoroughly infested with Communists.'

Why did McCarthyism decline by the mid-1950s?

By the mid-1950s the Red Scare was over and McCarthy was finished. He had become an embarrassment at home and abroad. His friends, Roy Cohn and David Schine, toured US embassies in Europe searching out 'leftist' books, which held the United States up to both fear and ridicule even among its allies. Now they were in the White House, the Republicans had no further use for him.

McCarthy was essentially responsible for his own downfall. He attacked the widely respected institutions, such as the Supreme Court and the army, which was too much for many Americans. When he began to accuse decorated soldiers, in 1954, Congress had had enough and went on the attack. The televised hearings showed the public what a bully McCarthy was.

When the Senate finally censured McCarthy, by a vote of 67–22, he was finished. It had taken them four years to pluck up the courage to do so and, even then, it was primarily the Democrats who voted against him.

Although McCarthy was finished by 1954, the HUAC hearings continued for several years and loyalty oaths remained in place in the states for a long time. In the same year as its censure, Congress also passed the Communist Control Act, which banned any Communist from holding any office in any labour organisation. It also banned 'Communist infiltrated' organisations from the National Labor Relations Board (NLRB).

What impact did McCarthyism have on the USA?

The damage done to ordinary people by the anti-Communist hysteria was massive. Hundreds lost their jobs due to the blacklists or for having been called before the Committee; for example, 300 teachers lost their jobs in New York City alone. Firms could be blacklisted as well as people, damaging their ability to conduct business. Between 1950 and 1952, 117 people were cited for contempt of Congress and jailed – more than in the whole of the previous century.

A person did not need to be a Communist to suffer. Anyone who was radical could be accused, a problem which continued in the USA long after the hearings ended. Traditionally left-wing organisations like unions dropped demands for social change and concentrated on being mere pressure groups. Politicians who called for a radical agenda were accused of being 'red'.

It could be argued that within government itself the damage was worse. The State Department which – according to historian Hugh Brogan – contained some of the most talented men in US history at the time, lost hundreds. The loss of these men meant that policies were followed that were not necessarily the best for America. For example, the 'Asia desk' lost most of the people knowledgeable about the area, which was to have devastating consequences for American policy towards Vietnam. The government simply had no one who really knew the country.

Even outside the United States, the effects of McCarthyism were felt. European youth became very anti-American, as their actions seemed to confirm a lot of what the USSR had said about America and Americans.

1. In what ways did the development of the Cold War affect America internally between 1945 and 1953?

2. Why was Joseph McCarthy so successful in his anti-Communist campaign between 1947 and the mid-1950s?

8.4 How far did Eisenhower continue the policies of his Democratic predecessors?

Politicians of both parties admired 'Ike' Eisenhower. In fact, Truman had once offered to help him achieve the presidency, and both parties considered him as a candidate. He chose to go with the Republicans as they more suited his own views, but the fact that he was considered by both gives some indication of the moderate nature of his political views.

During his Administration, 'Ike' was a very popular president. He was well liked by the voters. Part of this popularity was due to his success as a general during the War. This gave him the advantage of fame and meant he was not linked to any particular political faction. On the other hand, it also meant he had unrealistic expectations about what politicians can achieve. Many of the plans and promises he made turned out to be unrealistic once he was in office.

Eisenhower, personally, also had far more interest in foreign affairs than domestic, so he often gave more attention to external issues. He did have major domestic issues to deal with as well, notably:

How useful to historians are badges such as this?

- Joseph McCarthy

- the growing importance of the civil rights issue

- the economy

- whether to continue Truman's social reforms.

Why did Eisenhower win the 1952 Presidential election?

In 1952, Truman decided not to stand again (he was exempt from the provisions of the Twenty-Second Amendment limiting a president to two terms). The Democratic candidate was Adlai Stevenson, a bright but rather shy man. Few believed he would win against Eisenhower, the genial and popular war hero. Eisenhower's popularity was a major part of the

Campaign badge from 1952. Campaign badges or buttons are a popular feature of American elections.

Republican victory, but there were many reasons why the Republicans retook the White House after 20 years.

The choice of Richard Nixon as Republican vice-presidential candidate was astute. He was an experienced politician, where 'Ike' had little experience. So the combination gave the impression of stability. Nixon had made a name for himself in the anti-Communist crusade, so voters felt the Republicans would deal effectively with the Communist threat at home and abroad. In fact, Truman's foreign policy had many major successes but, when the election came, the USA was bogged down in war in Korea which seemed to be going nowhere and achieving nothing. 'Ike' promised to end the Korean War, if necessary by going there himself. His background as a soldier gave people confidence in his ability to handle the Cold War threats. The Republicans cleverly played on these weak areas for the Democrats and on the financial scandals that blew up, with the slogan 'K1C2', signifying Korea, Communism and Corruption.

One aspect of the election which was pointing towards the future was the use of television. The Republicans broadcast several effective advertisements focusing on Eisenhower's honesty and integrity, to contrast with the scandals in which the Democrats were embroiled. In 1960, television was to play a crucial role in the presidential election and its importance would continue to grow alarmingly.

One reason for Republican victory may have been that people were ready for a change. Eisenhower received 33.9 million votes (55 per cent), taking 39 states, including five in the South. Stevenson polled 27.3 million votes, but this gave him a mere nine states. On the back of Eisenhower's popularity, the Republicans also retook Congress with narrow majorities of 48–47 in the Senate and 221–213 in the House of Representatives.

How successful was Eisenhower in dealing with Congress?

Republican control of Congress did not last long and the Republicans did badly in the 1954 mid-terms, mainly because of the recession which had been caused by Eisenhower's cut in defence spending (see below). However, 'Ike' got on reasonably well with the Democrats on **Capitol Hill**, particularly as he interfered little in legislation, certainly far less than Truman had. But faced with a Democratic Congress – 48–47 in the Senate and 232–203 in the House – he was convinced that the Republicans needed to broaden their base of support and be careful not to be seen as extreme.

Capitol Hill: The US Congress, the Senate and the House of Representatives all meet in the Capitol Building on Capitol Hill, Washington DC. The expression 'Capitol Hill' is often used as a nickname for Congress.

In some ways, the 1956 presidential election was a re-run of 1952, and with a similar result: Eisenhower took 35.6 million votes and Stevenson took 26 million. 'Ike' was still very popular and, though he had not achieved a great deal, there had been good relations with Congress, which the public liked. The country was stable and prospering, and many black people voted Republican because of what 'Ike' was doing for civil rights.

In foreign policy, the President also seemed to be successful. He had improved relations with the USSR, while the Democrats seemed confused over whether to applaud or criticise him for this. When two crises broke out, in Hungary and Suez, during the election campaign it worked in Eisenhower's favour, encouraging the desire for the President who had made peace in Korea.

In spite of Eisenhower's victory, Congress remained Democratic (49–47 in the Senate and 234–201 in the House of Representatives). This might indicate how much of Eisenhower's victory was due to his personal popularity.

In the final mid-terms of the Eisenhower years, there were large Republican losses in both houses: 64–34 and 282–154. These were mainly due to the second 'Eisenhower recession', as well as his failure to achieve a meaningful Civil Rights Act. The new Congress contained a lot of young, liberal Democrats and relations between them and 'Ike' were not as good as before. This new generation wanted more action as they went into the new decade – the 1960s.

Throughout his years in office, although Eisenhower did not get everything he wanted, he did get much of his legislative programme passed: 73 of the 83 bills he sent to Congress. This contrasted sharply with the difficulties Truman had had with Congress. While Truman had problems even with his own Party, 'Ike' was able to work equally well with a Republican or a Democratic Congress.

What was 'Eisenhower Republicanism'?

One of the reasons 'Ike' got on so well with people of differing political views was that he was a moderate. He did not hark back to the days of Coolidge and Hoover, but asserted a new brand of Republicanism. He referred to his political beliefs as 'dynamic conservatism' or 'the middle way'. By this, Eisenhower meant that he was a **fiscal conservative** who promised to balance the budget and to lower taxes. He also said that he would end the 'creeping socialism' of the Democratic administrations. Like many Republicans, 'Ike' wanted to reduce the role of federal government. Yet, he did accept that the world had changed. He knew he could not, and did not want to, undo all that the Democrats had done in the previous decades. Eisenhower accepted that business needed to be regulated and that some level of welfare was now a feature of the American system. In his own words, Eisenhower was 'conservative when it comes to money and liberal when it comes to human beings'.

When he appointed his Cabinet, Eisenhower's support for big business was clear. Three members of the Cabinet had been executives at General Motors, and several had been Wall Street lawyers. The Democrats joked that the Cabinet was eight millionaires and a plumber (union leader Martin Durkin was Secretary of Labor, but lasted only a year.)

Eisenhower appointed, to federal commissions and other offices, people who thought the way he did about reducing the role of government; for example, Ezra Benson, the Agriculture Secretary, wanted to cut farm subsidies. However, their aims of reducing federal spending were not as easy to put into practice as they hoped.

Fiscal conservative: Belief in low taxation and low federal spending, and balancing the budget.

Eisenhower's domestic administration (1953–1961): leading posts

Secretary of the Treasury:	George M. Humphrey (1953–57)
	Robert B. Anderson (1957–61)
Attorney General:	Herbert Brownell Jr (1953–57)
	William P. Rogers (1957–61)
Secretary of the Interior:	Douglas J. McKay (1953–56)
	Frederick A. Seaton (1956–61)
Secretary of Agriculture:	Ezra Taft Benson (1953–61)
Secretary of Commerce:	Sinclair Weeks (1953–58)
	Lewis Strauss (1958–59)
	Frederick H. Mueller (1959–60)
Secretary of Labor:	Martin P. Durkin (1953)
	James P. Mitchell (1953–61)
Secretary of Health, Education and Welfare:	Oveta Culp Hobby (1953–55)
	Marion B. Folsom (1955–58)
	Arthur S. Fleming (1958–61)

How successful was Eisenhower in economic affairs?

Gross domestic product (GDP):
This is a measure of a country's
wealth.

Eisenhower was fortunate in being president when the economy was doing extremely well. **Gross domestic product (GDP)** grew from $355 billion in 1950 to $488 billion in 1960, while rising wages and falling hours meant that the average worker had a real income twice that of a worker in the 1920s. Per capita income rose from $1,720 in 1940 to $2,699 in 1960. Why was there such growth?

Spending had risen after the Second World War (e.g. the spending on the GI Bill and savings amassed during the War). By the 1950s, the cumulative effect was being felt in economic growth. Businesses, as well as individuals, had been spending after the War, and investment in plant and equipment had risen to $10 billion a year. The public sector, too, experienced growth (e.g. spending on the military was almost $40 billion a year). Technology advanced, with new goods such as televisions having the kind of impact that the radio had had 30 years before. The continued growth of car ownership and the availability of credit helped to fuel a consumer boom even bigger than that of the 'roaring twenties'.

However, there were massive inequalities in the country, with as much as 22 per cent of the population living below the poverty line. Even those who bought the new consumer goods often went into debt to do so. The very real problem of poverty in America was not tackled until the 1960s.

The economic policies of the Eisenhower Administrations show both his fiscal conservatism and the fact that he had accepted some of the changes the Democrats had brought. As a Republican, 'Ike' wanted to reduce the role of federal government, which the Republicans felt had grown far too much in the previous 20 years. This would, in turn, cut federal spending and allow him to reduce taxes, which were indeed cut by $7 billion.

The Reconstruction Finance Corporation – which was started by the Republican President Herbert Hoover but which had played such an important role in the New Deal – was finally abolished. There was also a desire to abolish that other renowned New Deal agency the Tennessee Valley Authority (TVA), but the TVA was widely supported in the South so abolishing it would be unpopular. However, federal subsidies to the TVA were slashed from $185 million, in 1952, to $12 million in 1960. 'Ike' felt that the production of power was a function of private business and not the role of government. So, as well as reducing aid to the TVA, he sold off atomic power plants to private industry and vetoed a plan for hydro-electric power production in Hell's Canyon.

A more important measure was the Submerged Lands Act 1953. Until this Act, the sale of rights to drill for offshore oil along the US coast, especially in the Mexican Gulf, were controlled federally. This meant that the whole country benefited from the sales. Eisenhower's Administration gave the rights to offshore oil deposits to the states, which meant that the money would only benefit that area. Truman had twice vetoed bills like this. But support for business and a desire to reduce federal power saw it passed now.

Although the Office of Price Administration had effectively finished by the end of 1946, the Korean War had seen inflation rise and more controls introduced. Now the war was over, they were not needed so any remaining price controls were abolished. Yet Eisenhower also vetoed a bill to abolish the Council of Economic Advisors set up by Truman, accepting that the USA had changed and that federal government now had an economic responsibility which it had never had under Hoover.

Eisenhower hoped that this reduction in federal interference in the economy would allow him to cut federal spending. In fact, over the period 1953–61 federal spending rose by 11 per cent. Much of this was spent on arms and the space programme, but spending in some areas could not be cut as easily as the government hoped. Continuing agricultural overproduction meant that subsidies rose from $1 billion, in 1951, to $5.1 billion by 1960. American farmers simply produced too much (e.g. a beef cow cost $179 in 1952 and $90 in 1956), so if prices were allowed to fall to their true market value then millions of farmers would go out of business. The Administration had no choice but to continue the subsidies. The Soil Bank was set up, in 1956, to get farmers to cut production. It paid $750 million to farmers to put land into the 'bank', in other words not to farm it, and $450 million was spent on conservation measures. Farmers, however, tended to put the worst land into the bank, which meant that production barely fell. The Republicans might not like the fact that government was subsidising agriculture, but the 1920s and 1930s had shown that there really was no alternative.

Why did the 'Eisenhower Recessions' take place in 1953 and 1957–1958?

As a Republican, Eisenhower wanted to reduce spending. The ceasefire in Korea and the New Look policy (see Chapter 5) allowed cuts in military spending in 1953, but this put 3.7 million people out of work. In fact, the recession ended quite quickly and 'Ike' did not have to resort to New Deal-style measures. However, it did damage the Republicans in the 1954 mid-term elections.

There was a second recession in 1957–58 with five million unemployed and production falling by 14 per cent, again largely due to cuts in government spending. Unemployment remained high until the election. In fact, there were more people in work in 1960 than in 1952, but the second recession in a decade helped John F. Kennedy to power. It damaged the reputation of the Republican government for managing the economy. Even though 'Ike' had promised to balance the budget, while he was in office there had been a total $20 billion deficit. Eisenhower had wanted to reduce spending but there were not that many areas where money could be found. Foreign policy considerations led to spending on education as well as on the space programme and, though he was a Republican, Eisenhower had social concerns. These led him to continue some of the work of the Democrats and even, in some cases, extend it.

How successful was Eisenhower's social policy?

With regard to social policy, 'Ike' did not go so far as the Democrats. He had criticised the 'creeping socialism' of their policies, yet he accepted that the federal government did have a responsibility to the poor and weak in society. This is shown in the creation of a government Department of Health, Education and Welfare – a Cabinet-level post.

As well as increasing the minimum wage from 75¢ to $1 an hour, 'Ike' helped the poor by extending social security to cover 10.5 million more Americans. There was also $1 billion for low-cost housing. All of these measures built on the work of Roosevelt and Truman. Republicans now largely accepted the responsibility of the federal government towards the poor. As 'Ike' said, 'The banishing of destitution and cushioning the shock of personal disaster on the individual are proper concerns of all levels of government.' In spite of this, Eisenhower was no New Dealer. He also said that 'If all Americans want is security, then they can go to prison.'

Republican transport policy also seemed fairly liberal entailing, as it did, massive government spending. The Republicans cooperated with the Canadians to build the Great Lakes–St Lawrence seaway, and the 1956 Highways Act built 41,000 miles of interstate highways with federal government putting up 90 per cent of the money to the states' 10 per cent at a cost of $30 billion. Although both of these measures were to increase trade and business, their aim was not to create jobs. Even so, the Highways Act was a massive boost to the economy providing thousands of jobs not only in construction but also in related areas such as motels, garages, diners etc.

Providing healthcare had been an aim of the Truman Administration but, while 'Ike' opposed most of the Fair Deal, he did pass measures for health. The Kerr–Mills Bill gave matching federal money to states that set up their own healthcare for the elderly poor. In fact, this was not very effective, as most states did not take up the challenge. More successful was a $30 million polio vaccination programme. Although it was a year before there were sufficient vaccines to meet demand, it was an important step in eradicating the disease.

An important measure passed by the government was the National Defence Education Act (NDEA) 1958, which gave $887 million for science and language teaching, as well as student loans for science-related courses. A similar measure had first gone to Congress in 1955, but had failed to pass because it was opposed by Catholics who wanted help for **parochial schools** and by civil rights activists who tried to add a de-segregation amendment.

Parochial schools: In this case, religious schools.

What got this Act passed was the launch of 'Sputnik' by the Russians on 4 October 1957. The USSR successfully launching a space satellite long before them, shook the Americans' faith in their technological superiority and panicked them into taking action. The NDEA was as much, if not more, about foreign policy than about education, as was the creation of the National Aeronautics and Space Administration (NASA) the same year.

The 'middle way', 'constructive conservatism', 'Eisenhower Republicanism' – whatever one chooses to call it – was clearly different from the Republicanism of the inter-war years. The New Deal and the Second World War had changed America far too fundamentally for it to go back. Eisenhower knew and accepted this. He was an extremely popular President who seemed able to pursue his aims of a basically conservative economic policy while, at the same time, accepting and even extending the social welfare programmes developed by the Democrats. This steering of the 'middle way' initially led historians to see the Eisenhower presidency as somewhat dull and lacking leadership. Later, historians realised that, in fact, 'Ike' had made much progress. He was simply subtler and less confrontational than his predecessor or successors. As the historian Paul Boyer puts it, in *Promises to Keep* (1999):

1. What was 'Eisenhower Republicanism'?

2. Was Eisenhower a successful president in domestic affairs? Explain your answer.

'rarely in our history has a president better fit the national mood than Dwight David Eisenhower. By 1953, Americans had endured a quarter-century of upheaval – first a stock-market crash and crippling depression, and then a world war and a menacing Cold War. Americans craved peace and stability. This is what Eisenhower delivered.'

8.5 How far were the 1950s an 'Age of Affluence'?

The term 'The Affluent Society' was coined by economist J.K. Galbraith as the title for a book about the 1950s. It has since come to be used to describe the decade almost as frequently as 'roaring' has been used to describe the 1920s. Were the 1950s really an age of affluence? Some did not think so. Journalist William Shannon said that the decade was 'one of flabbiness and self-satisfaction and gross materialism … The loudest sound in the land has been the oink and grunt of private hoggishness … It has been the age of the slob.' But American GNP grew from $318 billion, in 1950, to $488 billion by 1960 and average incomes were twice those of the 1920s. The decade was not one of continuous growth and wealth.

There were recessions in 1953 and 1957–58, unemployment reached 7.6 per cent and the national debt rose to $290 million by 1960. Yet, for the majority of Americans, the 1950s were a prosperous decade.

As in the 1920s, higher wages brought material comforts. By 1960, 60 per cent of Americans owned their own homes, 75 per cent owned cars and 87 per cent owned at least one television. The spread of the use of electricity allowed more people to have washing machines, dishwashers, freezers, stereos etc. There were more homes for them to put their goods in. Between 1945 and 1950, five million houses were built. This created demand for furnishings, decorating materials and repairs. People's lives at home became more comfortable.

Real wages: What can be bought with money earned, while taking into account inflation.

At work, too, lives got easier. Wages rose and hours fell; meaning that **real wages** rose 10 per cent over the decade. Labour-saving machinery and automation were also introduced in factories. There was a shift in jobs from the production line to the office. Over the 1950s, the number of industrial workers fell from 39 per cent to 36 per cent of the work force, while the number of clerical workers rose from 40 per cent to 46 per cent. In some industries automation brought fewer jobs but, in others, it meant easier conditions with greater productivity and higher pay. These factories turned out a whole range of new goods, from ballpoint pens to transistor radios. New types of music, notably rock and roll, and the rise of the 'teenager' created a mass market for records and record players. There was also an amazing range of goods made from the new materials, such as plastics. Many of these goods were bought on credit. The first credit card was issued in 1950, but this meant that by 1960 consumer debt was $2 billion.

Pastimes continued to grow. Sport was now televised, increasing its popularity. The massive growth in car ownership meant that people continued to travel and visit new places. With the development of the aeroplane and jet engine in the Second World War, travel took people to far more places. Communications across America became faster and easier.

One medium that began to suffer in the 1950s was the cinema. Competition from television forced the studios to come up with new innovations, such as 3-D and the production of lavish musicals, which television could not reproduce. Films such as 'The Robe' and 'Seven Brides for Seven Brothers' were great box-office successes, but the cinema began a decline which continued well into the 1980s and which only reversed when the coming of video made films widely popular again. The growth of

Is this picture useful in telling us about family life in the 1950s?

A family in the United States watching the television at home in 1955.

Homogenising: Creating a shared set of experiences and values.

Materialism: Valuing goods and possessions more highly than personal virtues such as honesty. Being more concerned with what you have than what you are.

television in the period was massive. In 1949, approximately one million households owned a television set; by 1960, it was 49 million. Between 1945 and 1955, $15 billion was spent on television sets and repairs. To millions of people it opened up the world, giving access to sports, news and entertainment. It was important in **homogenising** the United States. Television and advertising helped to sell goods; they also encouraged a culture of **materialism**. More money was spent in America on advertising than on education and more money was spent on television sets than on school buildings.

Although the spread of car ownership created thousands of jobs in production and related industries, it also brought a rise in accidents and deaths and an increase in pollution. It also encouraged the flight to the suburbs. People could live outside the cities and drive in for work. This meant that the cities were left to those who could not afford to move out, so less was spent on them, thus creating ghettos.

Straight after the War, the GI Bill pumped $20 billion into the American economy. Both Truman and Eisenhower increased expenditure on social security, education, housing and airports. Spending on roads alone had pumped $2.9 billion into the economy by 1960.

Half of all federal spending was on defence. The launch of 'Sputnik', in 1957, led President Eisenhower to introduce the NDEA and to set up NASA. The arms and space programmes put money into the economy and created thousands of jobs, particularly in the South-West. In Texas, Nevada and California, new industries such as computing brought work and people to the areas. They were based around defence plants and became known as the 'sun belt' industries. The space programme also brought new products on to the market, such as Teflon, transistors, electronics and home computers. Along with the jobs, this military spending created a large section of the economy with an interest in maintaining the Cold War. In his final speech before leaving the White House, Eisenhower warned about this development of what he called the 'military industrial complex'.

Oligopoly: Control of an industry by a small group (e.g. the car industry being dominated by the three corporations of Ford, General Motors and Chrysler).

As in the 1920s, the 1950s saw the spread of **oligopoly**. In cars, steel, aluminium, oil, aircraft, chemicals and electrical goods, a few companies controlled the bulk of the industry. In the 1950s, companies who made different things combined into conglomerates or multi-nationals (i.e. they bought up companies all over the world making a variety of goods). This created many new job opportunities, but it also cut down competition and choice. It made some of these corporations very powerful.

The decline in farming continued with more people moving to the towns and cities. Now only 15 per cent of the population lived and worked on the land. As in industry, it was small farms that went out of business with more and more of agriculture becoming 'big business' subsidised by the government.

Disneyland opened in 1955, symbolising much of the affluence of the 1950s. Disney was a corporation that made films, but had now moved into tourism. The theme park at Anaheim was easy to reach by car, and afforded by families with more money and more spare time in which to spend it. The family could marvel at the technology of the rides and spend their money on plastic souvenirs.

In what ways did living standards rise in the 1950s?

How far was federal spending responsible for the economic growth of the 1950s?

Although the majority of Americans did very well out of the 1950s, this was not the case for everyone. Poverty in America was to be a problem tackled by Eisenhower's successors.

8.6 Why did Kennedy achieve so little in domestic reform?

John Fitzgerald Kennedy (1917–1963)
35th President of the USA (1961–63), the first Roman Catholic and the youngest person to be elected US President. He came from a very wealthy Boston Catholic family. His father Joseph had been ambassador to Britain just before the Second World War and 'Jack', as family and friends called him, had an upbringing steeped in politics. Educated at Harvard and briefly at the London School of Economics. After serving in the US Navy during the War, he entered Congress in 1946. In 1952, at only 34 years of age, he became one of the youngest Senators ever. In 1953, he married Jacqueline Lee Bouvier (1929–1995).

'JFK' made his name as a supporter of civil rights' legislation and as a prominent internationalist. During his presidency, Kennedy did not succeed in carrying through any major domestic legislation. However, he did create the Peace Corps (volunteers who give health, agricultural and educational aid overseas). It was in foreign affairs that his presidency was most notable.

On 22 November 1963, during a tour of Texas, JFK was shot while driving through Dallas. He died shortly afterwards. His death caused worldwide grief.

John F. Kennedy's presidency, personality and private life are still the subject of much debate, but did he actually achieve very much?

Deliberately echoing the New Deal, Kennedy talked about how his Administration would bring a 'new frontier'. Kennedy spoke of how the 'torch [had] been passed to a new generation of Americans' and he emphasised how the New Frontier would 'get America moving' again. In foreign policy, it meant taking a strong stand against the Russians and Cubans in the Cold War and, in domestic affairs, it meant reform. Kennedy wanted to do something about civil rights, about poverty, about education, about health and about the economy. To do this, he wanted to harness the enthusiasm of the American people, especially the young. As he so eloquently put it in his inauguration speech, 'ask not what your country can do for you, ask what you can do for your country'.

Why did Kennedy win the 1960 Presidential election?

As a result of the elections, Democratic control of Congress remained strong with 64–36 seats in the Senate and 263–174 in the House of Representatives. However, the 1960 presidential election was one of the closest in American history, with JFK winning 49.9 per cent of the vote to Richard Nixon's 49.6 per cent. Kennedy's youth and energy were popular with younger voters, especially when contrasted with Nixon, the Republican candidate. Richard Nixon had been Eisenhower's Vice-President and, though the two men were not that far apart in age (Nixon was just four years older than Kennedy), they seemed to be of different generations. This was emphasised in the televised debates of September 1960. Nixon came across particularly badly because he was tired, recovering from a knee operation and suffering from flu. Kennedy, on the other hand, was well prepared and fresh having flown in on his private jet. He gave the image of youth and vitality. The four debates attracted an audience of 61–70 million and such debates have since become a feature of American elections.

Kennedy's campaign criticised the Republicans for 'drift' in foreign and domestic policy. The recession seemed to support this charge with regard to the economy. The U-2 incident during the run-up to the election (see Chapter 6) did not help the Republicans either when they were caught out lying. JFK accused them of not standing up to the Communists. He talked of a 'missile gap' that the Republicans had allowed to develop. (Which was not, in fact, the case.) Kennedy also made an issue of civil rights. Although Congress had passed two Civil Rights Acts, it was weak. JFK scored a victory when his brother Robert helped to get Martin Luther King Jr out of jail. The black vote which this gained was crucial to Kennedy's victory.

Robert Francis Kennedy (1925–1968)
Brother of President John F. Kennedy. Lawyer. Served in US Navy during Second World War, then worked on his brother's Senate campaign. He also worked for HUAC. Robert helped to organise JFK's 1960 presidential election campaign, where he earned a reputation for ruthlessness. Appointed Attorney General in 1961, where he fought to convict corrupt union boss Jimmy Hoffa and defended civil rights. Elected Senator in 1964, he spoke out against Vietnam. Robert was assassinated while campaigning for Democratic nomination in 1968, which many believe he would have won.

However, many liberal Democrats were not confident in Kennedy. His voting record in Congress was not especially good and he had friends on the far right. Although his Catholicism worried many voters, notably in the South, the choice of the moderate, Protestant Lyndon Johnson as vice-presidential candidate helped to deliver the votes of the South. Combined with the black vote and the votes delivered by the cities, Kennedy polled enough to become the 35th and youngest US President.

Like FDR, Kennedy surrounded himself with intellectuals and bright young men (but not women). These included his brother Robert, Theodore Sorenson, and Arthur Schlesinger. The White House became known for its culture and glamour, earning the nickname 'Camelot', where people were informal and hard working. Contemporaries talked of the 'buzz', but this has been criticised as creating a sense of crisis about everything and giving the appearance of work as a substitute for real action. Kennedy made a strong inauguration speech, which helped to create a sense of change and optimism. He talked of 'the torch [passing] to a new generation of Americans' and told the people to 'ask not what your country can do for you, ask what you can do for your country.'

Consciously reflecting FDR, Kennedy's Administration was known as the New Frontier. The newspaper columnist Walter Lippman said that Kennedy was:

'a man of the centre ... far removed from the social struggles of the New Deal. Although he had a liberal image his past record and his first two years in office supported this view, disappointing many who had voted for him.'

Kennedy's Administration (1961–1963): leading domestic posts

Secretary of the Treasury:	C. Douglas Dillon
Attorney General:	Robert F. Kennedy
Secretary of the Interior:	Stewart L. Udall
Secretary of Agriculture:	Orville L. Freeman
Secretary of Commerce:	Luther H. Hodges
Secretary of Labor:	Arthur J. Goldberg until 1962, then W. Willard Wirtz
Secretary of Health, Education and Welfare:	Abraham A. Ribicoff until 1962, then Anthony J. Celebrezze

---

Why did economic growth take place during JFK's presidency?

During the presidential campaign, JFK made much of the need to 'get America moving again'. He made economic growth his domestic priority. 'Ike' had inflation running at 3.5 per cent, while unemployment was 6.5 per cent when he left office. To Kennedy, a strong economy was not only essential for the USA itself, but also to strengthen its position in the world. In fact, in spite of the recession, the economy was basically strong, but it had weaknesses which needed addressing.

More in common with Eisenhower than with FDR, Kennedy believed tax cuts would get the economy moving. Although the Democrats had a majority in Congress, Kennedy did not feel he could ask for a tax cut too soon. He had the same problem that Truman had with the conservative coalition, particularly the Southern Democrats. He saw little point in sending legislation to the House which he knew would fail. He felt this would make him look ineffective. It was 1963 before his $10 billion tax cut was put to Congress, but it was to be passed by Johnson.

Kennedy was very concerned about the rise in unemployment and pursued several policies to try and create jobs. The 1962 Trade Expansion Act cut tariffs to encourage trade and, although he didn't cut personal tax, he was able to reduce taxes for business under the Revenue Act, which gave $1 billion in tax credits for new equipment and investment.

Kennedy's increases in defence and space spending were done more for foreign policy reasons than to help the economy. However, the 20 per cent increase in spending on defence and the space programme, which amounted to more than $25 billion, encouraged internal prosperity. They were a major factor in the sustained economic growth which America experienced in the 1960s. By doubling NASA's budget, Kennedy was able to fulfil his promise to put a man on the moon by the end of the decade – a promise fulfilled by Neil Armstrong in July 1969.

Kennedy also used the power of his office to encourage further growth through federal spending. States were encouraged to apply for, and spend, federal grants for housing, school building, highways etc. He was not allocating new money, but encouraging both federal and state authorities to spend what they could as soon as they could to create employment. Whether it was due to Kennedy's spending or not, unemployment did start to fall and was down to 5.3 per cent by 1964.

In his attempts to create jobs while keeping inflation low, Kennedy found himself in conflict with one of America's largest corporations, US Steel. JFK had asked for price rises and wage increases to be in line with increased productivity. The steel industry had 3 per cent productivity and the workers accepted a rise of 2.5 per cent. US Steel then raised its prices, followed by other steel companies. Steel was vital to the automobile industry and to defence. Price rises for steel would have a knock-on effect and worsen inflation.

Kennedy was furious that US Steel was breaking their agreement. He threatened investigations by the FBI and the denial of government contracts. He also put pressure on other steel manufacturers not to follow the price rise. Faced with the threats from the government and the threat from being undercut by their competitors, US Steel backed down and inflation remained below 1.3 per cent.

How successful was Kennedy's social policy?

When he became president in 1961, a great deal was expected of Kennedy because of his rhetoric and because he was a young liberal. The problem was that, in an era of such wealth and growth, many Americans lived in poverty. Kennedy did little about the poor in the first few years of his Administration. However, by 1962, he was starting to act particularly after reading Michael Harrington's *The Other America*, which said that 40 million Americans were living in poverty.

Poverty was defined as a family of four on an income of less than $3,000 per year, and there were millions more living on incomes just above the poverty line. A Senate report, in 1960, estimated that eight million old people had incomes lower than $1,000 per year. The military had also found that a third of draftees (service men and women entering the forces) were medically unfit for service, largely due to poor living conditions having caused poor health. In 1959, it was estimated that the average rural wage was less than 50¢ an hour. The poor were not confined to one area or to one racial group: the rural Deep South, the inner cities, areas of high immigrant populations, Native-American reserves – all suffered deprivation. The causes of poverty were also complex: old age, racism,

Kennedy delivering his inauguration speech, 20 January 1961.

unemployment and poor education all contributed. Kennedy was especially concerned by 'structural unemployment' (i.e. unemployment created not by a recession but by permanent changes in the economy such as automation). Tackling all this was a massive problem.

JFK believed that his improvements in the economy would help the poor, but he also needed to tackle the problem directly. To some extent he continued the work of Truman and Eisenhower, with increases in social security and the minimum wage. The minimum wage (now $1.25 an hour) was also extended to more professions including retail, which was a great help to women. The Manpower Development and Training Act 1962 provided $435 million for school and job-based training, especially for those who had lost their jobs due to automation. Two hundred thousand people went through the schemes. JFK also proposed a $2 billion public works programme, but Congress rejected it.

The Area Redevelopment Act 1961 gave grants and loans for training, development, community facilities as well as help for depressed areas such as Appalachia. The government spent more than $500 million on various schemes and programmes. The Area Redevelopment Act was criticised for not providing sufficient jobs considering the money spent and for some of the schemes it financed. For example, federal money was used to help build two luxury hotels in Oklahoma. The Administration argued that the hotels would create jobs and encourage further development and further jobs in the area.

In practical terms, JFK probably achieved little. The Housing Act, for example, helped property developers more than the poor. However, his speeches raised awareness when he talked about the need to make 'war on poverty', and how there had to be aid, training and education for the poor. His economic advisors, such as the Council of Economic Advisers (CEA), had already begun to formulate programmes that Johnson would adopt.

Although JFK was the first president since Hoover not to have a woman in the Cabinet, he did set up a presidential commission on the status of women, headed by Eleanor Roosevelt. The commission opposed an Equal

Rights Amendment seeing it as a product of middle-class ambition. They argued that practical issues such as poverty, healthcare, education and childcare were much more important. In 1963, an Equal Pay Act was passed. It did not cover all women and had no powers of enforcement, but 171,000 women benefited. The Act passed through Congress without much opposition, but it shows that the Kennedy Administration was moving into new areas of policy.

In the 1960s, the environment also became an issue. Books, such as *The Silent Spring* by Rachel Carson, were having an impact. Kennedy was the first president to start to tackle environmental issues seriously with an advisory committee on pesticides and a Clean Air Act in 1963, which limited pollution from cars and factories. Again, this was an area on which Johnson built.

Two areas where Kennedy proved to be no more successful than Truman were health and education. Like Truman, JFK proposed a health-care scheme funded from a payroll tax, but the idea was rejected for the same reasons as it had been 15 years before. Kennedy's 1961 proposals for education were passed by the Senate but failed to get through the House. The bill proposed to give federal money to states for scholarships and buildings, with the most money going to the poorest states. There had been little spending on schools in 20 years and there was a shortage of teachers, but the Bill failed. It was opposed by those who objected to the cost, by those who objected to federal interference in education and by religious groups. Kennedy would not give aid to parochial schools in case he was accused of favouring the Catholic Church but, when he did not, his own church would not support the bill either. JFK was able to get the Higher Education Facilities Act passed in 1963, which gave $145 million grants for graduate schools in science, language and engineering. This passed through more because it was an extension on NDEA than because of the need for educational reform. Like poverty, Johnson would address health and education more successfully.

Why did JFK achieve so little in domestic affairs?

Firstly, Kennedy was more interested in foreign policy and domestic issues simply did not get as much attention. Secondly, the conservative coalition in Congress blocked many of his measures. They blocked measures on education, healthcare, transport as well as a proposal to set up a department of urban affairs, which would tackle the growing problems of the cities (crime, drugs, decay, housing, transport etc.). His relations with Congress might have been better if JFK had worked at it. Many resented, or at least disliked, his northern liberalism, his ambition and his easy charm – and he did nothing to change this perception.

Yet, although JFK was not a radical president, under him the USA experienced the longest period of continuous economic growth in its history, due largely to military spending and the space race. He did work hard to reduce unemployment. In social reform he was not much more successful than Truman, but who knows what he would have gone on to do had he lived. Kennedy believed that a solid victory in 1964 would give him a mandate for more reform so he would not do too much in his first term to damage his re-election prospects.

It is also important to remember Kennedy's impact in inspiring a generation. He laid much of the groundwork for Johnson's Great Society in terms of bringing social issues to the forefront, starting some policies moving, and in leaving a strong economy so that the Great Society could be paid for.

1. What were the aims of the New Frontier in domestic affairs?

2. How successful was the Kennedy Administration in dealing with these problems?

8.7 Why did Johnson embark on the Great Society?

**Lyndon Baines Johnson
(1908–1973)**
A Southerner, born in Texas. He
trained and worked as a
teacher. Entered Congress in
1937 as a Roosevelt New
Dealer. He was a Congressman
until 1948, when he became a
Senator. He was Senate
Majority Leader (1954–60)
where, according to historian
William Chafe (*The Unfinished
Journey*, 1991), 'he dominated
the Senate as no one had
before'. He was crucial to 'Ike'
in helping to get the 1957 Civil
Rights Act through, and as
President he was far more
involved in the details of
legislation than 'Ike' or JFK had
been. In 1960, JFK chose him
as his running mate because
Johnson would bring the
Southern Democrat vote to
complement Kennedy's
popularity in the North.

Consensus: Agreement, a sharing of
aims and values.

When JFK was assassinated in 1963, Lyndon Baines Johnson (LBJ) found
himself in a similar position to Truman in 1945. He not only had to take
over the White House, he also had to deal with the country's shock and
grief. He inherited a cabinet who, largely, did not like or trust him. He and
Robert Kennedy particularly disliked each other. However, the presidency
was a job he had worked for and wanted. The liberals in Congress were
worried by LBJ's Southern background and voting record (e.g. supporting
HUAC and Taft–Hartley), but they had forgotten his role in civil rights and
the New Deal.

Johnson felt the need to create **consensus** to help the country get over
the assassination. He also believed that it was his job to create consensus
in the country. LBJ was able to present the need for unity to the country
and therefore use the national grief to force through some of JFK's
measures. Ironically, in spite of his desire to create consensus, the Vietnam
War and Johnson's pursuit of it, along with the race struggle, were to
divide the country as it had not been since the Civil War.

To an extent, Johnson wanted to continue the work of the New Frontier.
He supported Kennedy's aims in wanting to tackle poverty, to improve
education and healthcare and to help African-Americans. When Kennedy
was killed, several of these measures were being blocked in Congress and
Johnson was determined to see them through. But he wanted to go much
further than that. Like Kennedy, Johnson also believed that the power of
the federal government could be used to make life better for the American
people. He spoke of creating a 'Great Society', which would do all that the
New Frontier had set out to do, and more besides.

Why did Johnson win a landslide victory in the 1964 Presidential election?

Johnson won by the largest majority in American history up to that point.
The Democrats got 61.1 per cent of the vote; the Senate and House of
Representatives had large Democrat majorities, 68–32 and 295–140
respectively (though they lost 47 House seats in 1966).

Why did Johnson have such a massive victory? Firstly, he had achieved
a lot in 1963 and the mood was, for a while, supportive of more reform.
Secondly, Vietnam had yet to become as divisive as it would over the
following years. Thirdly, and most importantly, the Republican candidate
Barry Goldwater was thought to be too right wing. The Republican Senator
from Arizona was fairly extreme on many issues. He opposed civil rights,
opposed taxation to pay for social reform, and supported the use of nuclear
weapons in Vietnam. Even many Republicans found him too far right. The
Democrats were able to exploit this very effectively. Goldwater's election
slogan 'In your heart you know he's right' was mimicked with 'in your guts
you know he's nuts.'

Johnson felt the victory gave him a mandate for further domestic
reform. However, although Johnson had a large majority, there were many
Southerners and white, working-class Democrats who did not like many of
his policies. He would not be able to get everything he wanted.

Why did the American economy continue to expand?

Federal deficit: The amount of
money the federal government owes.

Under LBJ, the economy continued to thrive. GNP increased by 7 per cent
in 1964, by 8 per cent in 1965 and by 9 per cent in 1966. The **federal
deficit** fell by $1 billion and unemployment dropped below 5 per cent.
Why was this so? For one thing, LBJ pushed through Kennedy's tax reduction bill, cutting taxes by $10 billion. The economy was also helped by

general world economic growth. As with JFK, military spending, especially on Vietnam, helped to boost employment.

The US economy had grown almost constantly since the Second World War, but Michael Harrington's estimate of 40 million Americans living in poverty was what Johnson wanted to address.

Why did LBJ launch a 'war on poverty'?

Blue-collar jobs: Manual work, as opposed to white-collar jobs in offices.

Poverty was worst in the cities. Changes in technology meant fewer **blue-collar jobs** were available and affluence meant those who could, moved to the suburbs. At the same time as this so-called 'white flight', there was large migration of blacks from the South to the northern cities – seven million between 1950 and 1970. The ghettos, with their high crime, drugs and welfare families, were seen as much as a race problem as a poverty problem. In 1965, 43 per cent of black families lived in poverty and fewer than two-fifths of blacks finished high school.

There was also uneven income distribution among whites. Poverty was highest among blacks, female single-parent families, the old, the sick and the poorly educated. In areas like Appalachia the decline of traditional industries was a major cause of poverty.

If LBJ wanted to end poverty in America, he also had to bear in mind the various interest groups like corporations, unions and the professions. These groups had their own interests to protect and were not necessarily going to support welfare reform. Neither were these groups or Congress likely to want to pay for mass welfare programmes. Luckily, the strong economy meant Johnson's plans were easily affordable for the first two years.

Johnson's Administration (1963–1969): leading domestic posts

Secretary of the Treasury:	C. Douglas Dillon (1963–65)
	Henry H. Fowler (1965–69)
Attorney General:	Robert F. Kennedy (1963–65)
	Nicholas Katzenbach (1965–67)
	Ramsey Clark (1967–69)
Secretary of the Interior:	Stewart L. Udall
Secretary of Agriculture:	Orville L Freeman
Secretary of Commerce:	Luther H. Hodges (1963–65)
	John T. Connor (1965–67)
	Alexander B. Trowbridge (1967–68)
	Cyrus R. Smith (1968–69)
Secretary of Labor:	W. Willard Wirtz (1963–69)
Secretary of Health, Education and Welfare:	Anthony J. Celebrezze (1963–65)
	John W. Gardner (1965–68)
	Wilbur J. Cohen (1968–69)
Secretary of Housing and Urban Development:	Robert C. Weaver (1966–69)
	Robert C. Wood (1969)
Secretary of Transportation:	Alan S. Boyd (1967–69)

What were the aims of the Great Society?

In spite of the difficulties, LBJ wanted to do something about poverty but he wanted to go beyond that. He talked about creating a 'Great Society'. In a speech, in March 1964, he explained what that meant:

'The Great Society is where every child can find knowledge to enrich his mind and enlarge his talents. It is a place where leisure is a welcome chance to build and reflect, not a feared cause of boredom and restlessness. It is a place where the city of man serves not only the needs of the body and the demands of commerce but the desire for beauty and the hunger for community. It is a place where man can renew contact with nature. It is a place which honours creation for its own sake and for what it adds to the understanding of the race. It is a place where men are more concerned with the quality of their goals than the quantity of their goods.'

How did the Great Society programmes attempt to deal with America's domestic problems?

Before and after the election, Johnson launched a massive legislative programme. The 89th Congress passed more than 60 pieces of legislation, including 11 conservation bills, four education bills, 10 health measures,

---

Some of the Great Society measures:

1964   Tax Reduction Act – cut taxes by $10 billion to encourage growth.

Manpower Development and Training Act – expanded a 1962 Act with job training for the poor.

Economic Opportunity Act – created a range of poverty programmes under the Office of Economic Opportunity.

National Wilderness Preservation Act – created 45 national parks.

1965   Elementary and Secondary Education Act – first federal money to go directly to help schools.

Higher Education Act – scholarships and loans for college students.

Medical Care Act – healthcare for the poor, the disabled and the elderly paid for from taxes and from federal funds.

Omnibus Housing Act – money to build cheap housing and provide rent aid for the poor.

Appalachian Regional Development Act – $1 billion for highways, health centres and development programmes.

National Endowment for the Arts – federal money to help and support the arts and culture.

1966   Demonstration Cities and Metropolitan Development Act – subsidies for housing, slum clearance and transport in 'model cities'.

Urban Mass Transportation Act – money to help cities develop public transport networks.

Clean Water Restoration Act – $3.5 billion to clean up rivers and prevent pollution.

Highways Beautification Act – limitations on the number of billboards beside the highways.

Endangered Species Protection Act – protection for threatened species, making such protection a national goal.

1967   Air Quality Act – limits on sources of pollution including car exhausts.

1968   Wild and Scenic Rivers Act – protection of sections of eight named rivers from development.

an increase in the minimum wage and an increase in social security to two million more people. He knew he had to act quickly, before the mood for reform evaporated.

Passing JFK's tax cut encouraged continued growth and allowed the Great Society to be paid for without raising taxes. This was important as it maintained support for the President's programmes. Once the Vietnam War started to take the money and taxes were raised, support for the Great Society declined.

By far the most important measure against poverty was the Economic Opportunity Act, which set up the Office of Economic Opportunity, headed by Kennedy's brother-in-law, Sargent Shriver, to coordinate the various schemes. It set up:

● VISTA (Volunteers in Service to America)

● Head Start where children went to pre-school classes

● Job Corps to give skills to inner-city youths

● Community Action Programmes (CAP) which set up clinics, law centres etc.

Head Start had some successes with eight million children benefiting from the programme, but it and CAP especially got caught up in local politics and ethnic conflicts. These limited their effectiveness. The promise of CAP was that there would be 'maximum feasible participation' of local people but, when these people criticised local councils and city authorities, the federal government would always back the authority. What Johnson was not facing up to was that in order to tackle poverty properly there needed to be much more fundamental change in the way society was run. That would mean challenging the political system – something he was not prepared to do.

Job Corps also had problems as much of the training was done in camps, where discipline led to problems. However, some large companies like IBM did get involved in the scheme and eventually it had some success finding 10,000 jobs. Eventually, $10 billion was spent on the 'war on poverty'. However, poverty was not only an urban problem. Some of the poorest parts of America were rural, such as Appalachia in the South-East. The Appalachian Regional Development Act gave $1 billion for highways, health centres and development. But most of the schemes were short term and many contracts went to 'outsiders'. The problem was that the main industry – mining – was in decline and there were few other businesses. What Appalachia needed was jobs.

As a trained teacher, LBJ knew the importance of education in lifting people out of poverty. The Elementary and Secondary Education Act, begun by JFK, was passed giving $1 billion for poor students in public and parochial schools. Local school boards decided where the money went, so it was frequently spent on middle-class children rather than on the poor it was intended for. To get it passed by Congress, Johnson had to respect states' rights. What really mattered was that federal government was now taking a role in education. More successful was the Higher Education Act, which provided $650 million for scholarships, low-interest loans and resources for colleges, benefiting 11 million students.

The 'Great Society' went beyond material wealth. Johnson wanted to improve the environment in which people lived, both in the cities and in the countryside. To improve life in cities both housing and transport reform were supported with the Omnibus Housing Act giving $8 billion to fund three million units of low and middle-income housing as well as rent aid. The Demonstration Cities and Metropolitan Development Act gave

$1.2 billion in subsidies for housing, recreation, slum clearance, transit systems etc. Johnson understood and believed that people were affected by their surroundings and improved living conditions would create a better country. Even transport was supported to make the cities cleaner, through the Urban Mass Transportation Act and the creation of the Department of Transport. Cities like Washington and San Francisco used the Act to develop clean and cheap public transport networks.

Outside the cities, Johnson wanted to create an environment 'where man can renew his contact with nature'. It was in the 1960s that people were starting to realise the dangers of pollution and the threats to the land and animals of economic development. The National Wilderness Preservation Act created 45 national parks, including Redwood in 1968, and protected nine million acres of forest. The Endangered Species Protection Act protected 833 species of plants, animals and birds. The government spent over $35 million cleaning up rivers and extending its power to control various kinds of pollution. The president of the National Geographic Society called LBJ 'our greatest conservation president'. Even America's roads were made to look better through the Highways Beautification Act, sponsored by the President's wife who also wanted to create beauty and green spaces in the ghettos. Claudia 'Ladybird' Johnson was criticised for this, but she, like her husband, believed that people had the right to live in an attractive environment whatever their wealth.

They also believed that not only the rich should have access to culture, so the National Endowment for the Arts gave money to theatres, operas and art galleries. More than 700 companies got money, but there was much criticism, then and since, that the government has no business financing art.

Johnson's commitment to improving the nation meant that the 'Great Society' tackled an immense range of issues, but perhaps the most important was healthcare. The Medical Care Act set up the first federally funded healthcare system: Medicare for the elderly and Medicaid for welfare recipients. Six and a half billion dollars were spent on hospitals, nurses, doctors, nursing care and medical tests. In fact, it was less than Truman had proposed. It did not cover most prescriptions and was to prove very expensive. For many, though, it meant access to healthcare which they had been previously denied. The United States was one of the very few developed countries that had no government healthcare. Johnson's Medical Care Act was, therefore, of major significance.

1. In what ways and for what reasons did Johnson want to introduce major domestic reforms?

2. In which areas do you regard the Great Society as having been most successful:

(a) education

(b) inner-city reform

(c) the environment

(d) healthcare?

Give reasons for your answer.

8.8 How successful was the Great Society?
A CASE STUDY IN HISTORICAL INTERPRETATION

As Johnson expected, public support for liberalism and reform did not last long. By 1966, people were tiring of change and of the liberalism which had dominated politics for the previous five years. They were also disillusioned with policies which were now seen to have weaknesses (largely because they had been rushed). Recipients of welfare resented the federal intrusion, while conservatives resented federal government moving into so many areas of people's lives. The 'Great Society' had raised expectations that could not have been met realistically, especially the 'war on poverty'. The historian William Chafe says, '… when measured against the expectations set forth by Johnson, the war on poverty remained a disappointment'. But was the Great Society a failure?

It is probably true that the government underestimated the size and scale of the problem. LBJ wanted to achieve consensus but, in order to get real change, the existing systems and structures would have had to be challenged, which he was unwilling to do. Political scientist Ira Katznelson argues, in *Major Problems in American History Since 1945* (2001), that the problems went back as far as the 1940s. Basically, the Democratic Party was not prepared to challenge the system. It wanted to work within it and this prevented the Great Society from effecting real change.

Another problem was that, in the rush to get legislation through, much was not thought through properly and money was often spent on the wrong things (e.g. a lack of spending on sufficient teachers under Head Start). William Chafe argues that part of the problem was Johnson himself, who personalised everything and refused to compromise or make sacrifices. However, Johnson felt that if he did not rush legislation through then the national support for the Great Society would have gone. As Johnson's aide Jack Valenti said, 'Of course we made mistakes. We were doing things!'

It was estimated that the Great Society would cost $1.4 billion in 1966, rising to $6.5 billion in 1968 and $10.4 billion in 1970. In fact, they never spent more than $2 billion in a year and 20 times more was spent on the war in Vietnam than on all the Great Society programmes put together. It has been said that it substituted good intentions for cold, hard cash. Yet at the same time, Medicare was set up in a way that would see the costs to the federal government soar from $40 billion in 1965, to $125 billion in 1975 and to $400 billion in 1985.

In spite of the amount spent, many groups were left out. By emphasising opportunity, the Great Society did not help those who could not take up the opportunities (e.g. the old, disabled, single mothers etc.). Many criticised the government for trying to force middle-class values on the poor, wanting them to help themselves out of poverty when they did not have the skills to do so. Katznelson claims that the Great Society 'favoured equality of opportunity rather than equality of results'.

Historian Allen J. Matusow, in *The Great Society: a Twenty-Year Critique* (1986), claims that the 'war on poverty' was lost. The only real solution was to re-distribute wealth through taxation, which the Great Society did not do. Matusov also questions whether health improved as a result of the Medical Care Act. As he points out, the poor did have access to healthcare before the Act through charities. All the Act did was to end up paying doctors for services which they had previously given for free.

For all its shortcomings, there were successes. According to the US Census Bureau, the number of families in poverty dropped from 40 million in 1959 to 28 million in 1968 and to just over 25 million two years later. While it might be argued that the general economic growth could account for this, after Johnson left the White House the number of poor families remained almost the same and, in the 1980s, rose again above 30 million. For black people, there was also improvement with the number earning less than $3,000 a year falling from 41 per cent in 1960 to 23 per cent in 1968. The Administration had shown that poverty mattered and, more importantly, that it could be addressed by federal government. As Johnson's domestic affairs advisor Joe Califano said, 'We simply could not accept poverty, ignorance and hunger as intractable [difficult to remove or deal with], permanent features of American society.'

The Great Society also did the following:

● It protected 7,200 miles of river, 14,000 miles of trail and 83 million acres of wilderness.

● It increased the number of students graduating from high school.

● It introduced consumer protection and safety in cars with seatbelts.

● It saw poverty levels drop and life expectancy rise.

---

1. According to the census, the number of families in poverty dropped from 40 million in 1959, to 28 million in 1968 and to 25 million in 1970. What do these figures tell us about the success of the 'war on poverty'?

2. How far do historians agree on the success of the Great Society?

According to John McCormack, the Speaker of the House, the 89th Congress was 'a Congress of accomplished hopes. It is the Congress of realised dreams.' Historian Paul Boyer says that 'The Great Society made the United States a more caring and just nation.' That seems a judgement most presidents should envy.

Source-based questions: American Anti-Communism

SOURCE A

There shall be a loyalty investigation of every person entering the civilian employment of any department or agency of the executive branch of the federal government …

The standard for the refusal of employment or the removal from employment … shall be that, on all the evidence, reasonable grounds exist for belief that the person involved is disloyal to the government of the United States.

Truman's Executive Order 9835, 1947

SOURCE B

… the decision that would affect our lives was being made at the Waldorf-Astoria Hotel in New York. There, on 27 November 1947, the representatives of the motion picture industry formally decided to fire any accused worker who would not freely answer all the questions asked by the Un-American Activities Committee and could not clear himself of charges that he was or had been a member of the Communist Party.

From *It's a Hell of a Life But Not a Bad Living* by Edward Dmytryk, one of the Hollywood Ten, 1987

SOURCE C

It was the great body of the nation, which, not invariably, but in general, kept open its mind in the Hiss case, waiting for the returns to come in. It was they who suspected what forces disastrous to the nation were at work.

From *Witness* by Whittaker Chambers, 1952

SOURCE D

[1949] had brought nothing but bad news to McCarthy. He had angered prestigious senators in both parties and he had problems at home … in a crisis he would do anything … A poll of Washington correspondents had chosen him as America's worst Senator. In two years … he would be up for re-election.

From *The Glory and the Dream* by William Manchester, 1974

SOURCE E

The censure resolution avoided criticising McCarthy's lies and exaggerations; it concentrated on minor matters – on his refusal to appear before a Senate Subcommittee on Privileges and Elections, and his abuse of an army general at his hearings.

At the very time the Senate was censuring McCarthy, Congress was putting through a whole series of communist bills. Liberal Hubert Humphrey introduced an amendment to one of them to make the Communist Party illegal.

From *A People's History of the United States* by Howard Zinn, 1980

---

1. Study Source A and use your own knowledge.

Why did Truman issue the Loyalty Order?

2. Study Sources A and B and use your own knowledge

How useful are these sources to an historian studying the anti-Communist hysteria of the period?

3. Study Sources C, D and E and use your own knowledge.

Assess the extent to which McCarthy should be blamed for the anti-Communist hysteria in the decade after the Second World War.

8.9 An in-depth study: Who was more effective in domestic reform – JFK or LBJ?

8.9.1 How successful was Kennedy's New Frontier Programme?
8.9.2 How 'great' was Johnson's Great Society Programme?

Framework of Events

1961	JFK sworn in as thirty-fifth president of United States
	Launch of New Frontier Programme
	Council of Economic Advisers created
	Minimum Wage Act
	School Assistance Bill fails to pass Congress
	Health care for elderly fails to pass Congress
	Housing Act
	Area Redevelopment Act
1962	Trade Expansion Act
	Manpower Development and Training Act
1963	Equal Pay Act
	Clean Air Act
	JFK discusses 'war on poverty' with advisers
	Assassination of JFK
	Lyndon Johnson becomes thirty-sixth president of United States
1964	Tax Reduction Act
	Economic Opportunity Act
	National Wilderness Preservation Act
1965	Elementary and Secondary Education Act
	Higher Education Act
	Medicare Act
	Medicaid Act
	Omnibus Housing Act
	Appalachian Regional Development Act
	National Endowment of the Arts Act
	Water Quality Control Act
1966	Demonstration Cities and Metropolitan Development Act
	Urban Mass Transportation Act
	Highways Beautification Act
1967	Air Quality Act
1968	Wild and Scenic Rivers Act
	Housing Act
	Occupational Health and Safety Act

Overview

Valley Forge: the place, during the American War of Independence where George Washington saved the American army from destruction.

BETWEEN 1961 and 1969, the USA was led by two administrations that put domestic reform at the centre of their agenda. From 1961 to 1963, John F. Kennedy proclaimed the New Frontier Programme. The title of this plan conjured up images of America's past and the 'pioneer spirit'. JFK saw a 'new frontier' of challenges. Kennedy stated, in a speech while campaigning for president on 29 October 1960, at **Valley Forge**, Pennsylvania:

'Twenty-four years ago, Franklin Roosevelt told the Nation "I, for one, do not believe that the era of the pioneer is at an end; I only believe that the area for pioneering has changed." The new frontiers of which I speak call out for pioneers from every walk of life.'

Kennedy planned a programme of major domestic reform that included education, health care and helping the poor.

When Kennedy was assassinated, his vice president, Lyndon B. Johnson, entered the White House. From 1963 to 1969, Johnson engaged in a great domestic reform programme, known as the Great Society, with a specific emphasis on a 'war on poverty'.

8.9.1 How successful was Kennedy's New Frontier Programme?

What was the New Frontier Programme?

When JFK was sworn in as president on 20 January 1961, he set out the broad goals of his New Frontier Programme. He stated:

'... we stand today on a new frontier, a frontier that will demand of us all qualities of courage and conviction. For we are moving into the most challenging, the most dynamic, revolutionary period of our existence – the 1960s. The next 10 years will be years of incredible growth and change – years of unprecedented tasks for the next president of the United States.'

The whole tone of JFK's speech suggested major challenges and changes. The 1950s had been a decade where the Republican President Dwight Eisenhower wanted to preserve rather than change American society. Both JFK and LBJ wanted to deal directly with problems at home and wanted to

---

The American Government: a brief introduction

- The United States is a federal state. This means political power is split between a central, or federal, government and 50 state governments. State governments have direct responsibility for social security, education and law and order within their own state. During the 20th century, the **Federal Government** became involved in these areas of policy.

- The USA chooses a president every four years. The president is elected in early November and takes up office on 20 January.

- The president chooses the government. The leading members of the government form the Cabinet. The president also has many personal advisers. These usually work for the Executive Office of the president.

- Unlike Britain, no government member can be a member of the national parliament called Congress. This idea is called the separation of powers. In practice, it means the president can govern only with the cooperation of Congress.

- The Congress comprises the Senate (100 members) and the House of Representatives (435 members).

- The House of Representatives and one third of the Senate are elected every two years. Each state elects two senators. The House comprises of 435 congressmen who are chosen on a basis of state population. Populous states, such as California and New York, have many more congressmen than states such as Montana or Rhode Island.

- The president can propose legislation but Congress passes these proposals into law.

- A president can veto Congressional legislation but, if two thirds of Congress agrees, the presidential veto can be overridden.

- Even if the president and Congress agree, the US Supreme Court can declare a law or action by the president unconstitutional.

Federal Government: the national government.

ensure that the USA confronted communism abroad. They wanted the USA to be seen as the leader of the Free World against the USSR and Communist China and so they could not afford social divisions at home.

On the surface, it might seem that the USA required little social change. The 1960 census showed that the USA's 180 million people were the most affluent in the world. Per capita income had risen from $1,501 in 1950 to $2,219 in 1960. Even though **inflation** had reduced, a 50 per cent growth in personal wealth was still very impressive. However, when Kennedy took office, the US economy was in **recession**. There was 6.5 per cent unemployment and inflation at 3.5 per cent. In addition, there were groups and areas in the country that had not benefited from the affluence of the 1950s. **Appalachia** was one area that suffered economic hardship. Also, the elderly and those on low incomes had missed out on '**the American dream**'. In preparation for office, JFK had set up a number of task forces to investigate different areas of policy. One group, under Senator Paul Douglas of Illinois, reported to Kennedy on depressed areas. Such reports played an important role in shaping JFK's domestic policy.

Some historians believe that the domestic programme was a reaction to the challenges of the Cold War. According to historian James N. Giglio, in *The Presidency of John F. Kennedy* (1991), 'The New Frontier embraced the past as much as it did the present.' In this sense, Kennedy was completing the work begun by the previous Democrat presidents, Frank D. Roosevelt (1933–45) and Harry S. Truman (1945–53). Under Roosevelt, the USA had been transformed by the social policies of the New Deal. These policies were continued with Truman's Fair Deal. After the brief interlude of Eisenhower's administration (1953–61), social reform was back at the centre of the domestic programme. Policies such as federal support for health care for the elderly had been a policy originally put forward by President Truman.

Inflation: an increase in the general level of prices.

Recession: a period of economic stagnation when unemployment rises as production falls.

Appalachia: mountainous area of eastern USA, which covers parts of West Virginia, Virginia, North Carolina, Kentucky, Tennessee and Georgia.

'**The American dream**': the belief that the USA has no discrimination against a person's background, either in wealth or race; the belief that if a person is intelligent enough and works hard they can 'reach the top'.

Opposition to the New Frontier

In *The Unfinished Journey: America Since World War II* (1999), historian William H. Chafe provides a brief assessment of Kennedy's period as president. He believes:

> There was something larger than life about the man, his presidency, his death, and his impact on the American people.

Many contemporaries believed that the youthful Kennedy, his dynamism and style, represented the new generation. They believed that his tragic death cut short a presidential career of great promise. Such views are supported in the works of several of Kennedy's close associates. These works include *Kennedy* (1965), by his presidential counsel, Theodore Sorensen, and *A Thousand Days: John F. Kennedy in the White House* (1965), by Arthur M. Schlesinger. However, some people consider the reality of JFK's period as president to be very different. BBC journalist Henry Fairlie claims, in *The Kennedy Promise* (1973), that JFK's New Frontier was a complete failure.

In many ways, Henry Fairlie's assessment is nearer the truth. American political scientist, Richard E. Neustadt, stated, 'Presidential power is the power to persuade.' For all his personal charm, JFK found it very difficult to persuade Congress to pass his New Frontier Programme.

First, Kennedy lacked a strong political mandate. He had won the presidency by the slimmest of margins. He won by 118,574 votes out of 68 million cast. His Electoral College victory of 303 to Nixon's 219 was due to paper-thin victories in a number of states. JFK then had to deal with many senators and congressmen who had won by large majorities and had years, if not decades, of political experience at national level.

Second, with Lyndon Johnson as his vice president, JFK had lost a Senate majority leader who could have helped him with the passage of his New Frontier Programme. Instead, JFK relied heavily on a close aide, Larry O'Brien, to persuade Congress. O'Brien lacked LBJ's ability and contacts.

Finally, and perhaps most significantly, Kennedy faced a **conservative coalition** in Congress. Such a coalition had been in existence since FDR tried to reform the US Supreme Court in 1937.

To make matters worse, key post holders within Congress were hostile to the New Frontier. Senate minority leader, Republican Charles Halleck of Indiana felt that JFK had 'stolen' the 1960s election. He remained a fierce opponent. Congress was also dominated by committee chairmen who had the power to delay and even 'kill off' presidential proposals for legislation. One of the most powerful positions was chairman of the House Rules Committee. He had the power to assign Bills (proposals for legislation) to specific subject committees such as agriculture, finance, foreign affairs, and so on. In 1961, the chairman was archconservative South Democrat Howard W. Smith of Virginia. He bragged that he would turn JFK into a 'do nothing' president. Fortunately, with the assistance of the speaker of the House of Representatives, Sam Rayburn, JFK was able to oust Smith from his post on 31 January 1961. By enlarging the membership of the House Rules Committee, JFK won the vote 217 to 212. Ominously, 22 Republicans and 64 Southern Democrats voted against JFK.

Reform in five areas

In January 1961, Kennedy wanted to pass legislation in five key areas: federal assistance to schools, medical care for the elderly, housing reform, aid to depressed areas and an increase in the minimum wage.

In education reform, the New Frontier could be judged a failure. In February 1961, JFK submitted a School Assistance Bill to Congress. He asked for $2.3 billion over three years to help construct new schools and to increase teachers' salaries. As a Roman Catholic, he was sensitive to the issue of Catholic Church schools. However, the first amendment of the **US Constitution** stated that the Church was separate from the state and so the Assistance Bill did not cover Catholic schools. The USA's Catholic bishops therefore opposed the Bill and the USA's first Roman Catholic president! The Bill passed the Senate but was defeated in the House.

Health care for the elderly fared no better. JFK wanted to increase social security taxes by 0.25 per cent. The House Ways and Means Committee effectively 'killed off' the proposal. Its chairman, Wilbur Daigh Mills, was a long-time opponent of the health care part of social security.

Fortunately for Kennedy, he did get an increase in the minimum wage. He proposed an increase to $1.25 per hour. Although Congress passed this, important groups of workers were excluded from the minimum wage. South Democrat opposition, led by Carl Vinson of Georgia, made sure that 150,000 laundry workers were excluded. The majority of laundry workers were female African-Americans. In total, 350,000 poorly paid workers were excluded from the Minimum Wage Act.

The Area Redevelopment Act of 1961 was also passed. This provided $394 million over four years to aid areas such as Appalachia. Although around 26,000 new jobs were created under the Act, an attempt to give more money ($455 million), in 1963, failed to pass Congress. The Manpower Development and Training Act of 1962 had greater impact. This provided job training for the poorly educated across 40 states that had applied for funding.

The Housing Act of 1961 was of greater success. Kennedy got Congress

---

Conservative coalition: informal group of senators and congressmen. The group comprised of Republicans and Southern white Democrats. They opposed social reform and improvements in African-American civil rights.

US Constitution: the document that contains the rules and regulations that govern political activity in the USA. It was drawn up in 1787 and finally agreed by all original 13 states in 1791. It has been amended 26 times since 1787. The first 10 amendments were in 1791.

Wilbur Daigh Mills (1909–92)
Mills was a congressman from Arkansas who had received a law degree from Harvard University. He was a member of the House of Representatives from 1939 to 1977 and chairman of the House Ways and Means Committee during Kennedy's and Johnson's presidencies. In 1972, he ran for Democrat nomination for president, but was unsuccessful. His career effectively came to an end in 1974 when he was caught drink-driving in Washington DC with a stripper called Fenne Foxe, known as the Argentinean Firecracker.

to give $4.8 billion to fund housing projects for the poor. However, Congress acted mainly to help the US out of the 1960/1 economic recession rather than to show long-term sympathy for the poor.

Kennedy's legislative record had mixed success by the time of his assassination. Historian James Giglio, in *The Presidency of John F. Kennedy* (1991), claims that JFK's record was impressive. He cites, as evidence, the fact that in 1961, 33 out of 53 major recommendations to Congress became law. In 1962, the figure was 41 out of 54 and in 1963, 35 out of 58. Giglio suggests that this is a good record compared to other presidents since 1935. However, out of JFK's five 'must' Bills of 1961, the three that passed into law were amended in a radical way by a conservative-dominated Congress. In *Decade of Disillusionment: The Kennedy-Johnson Years* (1975), historian Jim F. Heath declares:

> One suspects that considering what he concretely achieved – not proposed or hoped to achieve – Kennedy would rank his own domestic record as disappointing. Although his programmes were designed to aid and advance the welfare state, Kennedy was decidedly not even a committed social reformer. Kennedy moved cautiously in the comfortable ruts worn by Roosevelt, Truman and even Eisenhower.

8.9.2 How 'great' was Johnson's Great Society Programme?

Did Johnson continue the New Frontier Programme when he became president?

Kennedy's presidency was cut short by an assassin's bullet on 22 November 1963. When Lyndon Johnson became president he made sure that he would gain popularity and acceptance by publicly linking himself with the martyred president. In a speech to the joint houses of Congress on 27 November 1963, Johnson made clear his immediate aim as president. He declared:

> 'All I have, I would have given gladly not to be standing here today ... let us continue, let us here highly resolve that John Fitzgerald Kennedy did not live or die in vain ... This is no time for delay. It is a time for action.'

Thus, Johnson used Kennedy's memory to push through important Acts of Kennedy's domestic programme.

The links with the New Frontier also went much deeper. Education, health care, and regional regeneration were all central planks of Johnson's own domestic programme. There was considerable overlap between the New Frontier and Johnson's own domestic programme, which he entitled the Great Society.

In broader context, both the New Frontier and the Great Society were part of a longer-term development in American domestic politics that went back at least as far as Franklin Roosevelt's New Deal of 1933–45. In that development the US Constitution required the Federal Government to 'promote the general welfare' of the US population. From 1933 to the 1960s, the Federal Government took a commanding role in dealing with the USA's domestic problems. The Kennedy-Johnson years saw the highest point of federal attempts to deal with domestic issues such as poverty.

Of the five 'must' bills at the start of Kennedy's presidency, Johnson continued work in a number of areas, most notably education, health care and aid to depressed areas.

Education

Kennedy tried and failed to pass the School Assistance Bill of 1961. When Johnson became president, education was given the top priority in domestic affairs. As a former schoolteacher, Johnson valued education as a way to help the poor to advance in the world. His own personal experience was central to this belief. When he signed the Elementary and Secondary Education Act into law on 11 April 1965, he stated:

'I believe deeply that no law I have signed or will ever sign means more to the future of America.'

1965 proved to be the high point in LBJ's educational policy. The Elementary and Secondary Education Act gave funds to school districts on the basis of the number of low-income families (those earning under $2,000 per year). By 1968, 6.7 million poor children received assistance. This particularly benefited poor states such as Mississippi. The Act gave funds to improve library resources, textbooks and other school resources and it also aimed to encourage student participation in subjects such as art and music. Finally, the Act gave funding to aid children with disabilities. Over 26,000 students benefited. This aspect was a direct continuation of Kennedy's more cautious plans to aid disadvantaged students. Through **Executive Orders**, JFK had increased school lunch and milk programmes for the poor. This enabled 700,000 children to enjoy a daily free school lunch and free fresh milk. Enrolments in elementary schools increased from 39 million in 1962 to 46 million in 1970.

In 1965, Johnson persuaded Congress to pass the Higher Education Act. This granted federal scholarships for undergraduate students. It also gave students loans to pay for university education. By 1968, grants amounted to $131 million with loans of $182 million. Johnson broadened the scope of **Eisenhower's National Defense Education Act of 1958** and these reforms meant that the college-graduate population increased from 17.3 per cent in 1962 to 23.4 per cent in 1976.

Executive Order: a rule or regulation issued by the president to help implement an aspect of the US Constitution or an Act of Congress.

Eisenhower's National Defense Education Act of 1958: this Act was passed in direct response to the USSR's successful launching of the first satellite in space, called *Sputnik*, in 1957. Eisenhower believed the USA was falling behind the USSR in technological education so this Act aimed to promote scientific and technical education.

Health care

Like Kennedy before him, Johnson was keen on providing welfare help for the elderly in health care. Unfortunately for Kennedy, the chairman of the House Ways and Means Committee, Wilbur Mills, obstructed his plan. Johnson, on the other hand, was able to use his influence in Congress to get the Medicare Act passed in 1965. As in JFK's proposal, this Act provided free health care for the elderly paid out of social security taxes.

In 1965, Johnson took his health care reforms further. This provided free health care for certain groups of the poor and people with disabilities below the age of 65.

Aid to depressed areas

Kennedy had had some success in providing help to areas facing economic problems. Like most of his legislative record he had moved cautiously.

In 1963, JFK read a newspaper review of a study entitled *The Other America* (1962), by Michael Harrington. Harrington argued that although most Americans had a high standard of living, 40 to 50 million Americans lived in poverty. Kennedy was so impressed by Harrington's work that he asked his advisers to draw up a plan to deal with the issue of the poor underclass. Unfortunately, JFK's assassination cut short this plan. However, Johnson continued the policy. The big difference came in terms of scale and ambition. According to Paul K. Conkin in his biography of LBJ, *Big Daddy from the Pedernales* (1986):

> Johnson's goal was to perfect every institution, to solve all pressing problems, to eliminate glaring inequalities and injustices, to realise the dream of equality for all.

In his State of the Union address of 8 January 1964, Johnson made clear how ambitious he was on the issue:

> 'This administration today, here and now, declares unconditional war on poverty in America.'

What was Johnson's 'war on poverty'?

Johnson's 'war on poverty' was the central plank of the Great Society Programme. Johnson turned the issue that Kennedy had talked briefly about before his death into a personal crusade. At the University of Michigan, on 22 May 1964, Johnson talked openly for the first time about creating the Great Society. As historian Paul Conkin notes:

> Johnson talked about a perfect America. He seemed to want to solve all its problems and to do it all quickly.

The cornerstone of the 'war on poverty' was the Economic Opportunity Act of 1964. The Act created a new federal agency – the Office of Economic Opportunity (OEO). JFK's brother-in-law, Sargent Shriver, who had run Kennedy's **Peace Corps**, headed it. The OEO had the task of coordinating a large number of schemes. Based on the Peace Corps, VISTA (Volunteers in Service to America) gave middle-class young people opportunities to help the needy within the USA. By 1968, 3,000 middle-class people had volunteered. The Head Start Programme gave poor children classes before they started school. Jobs Corps aimed to offer skills training to inner-city youths. These programmes did have some success. Head Start involved eight million children. Jobs Corps found jobs for 10,000 youths. Its effectiveness was due, in part, to the involvement of firms such as IBM, the computer company.

The most controversial part of the Economic Opportunity Act was the creation of Community Action Programmes (CAPs). In *State and Society in Twentieth-Century America* (1997), historian Robert Harrison notes:

Peace Corps: an organisation created by JFK, which enabled US citizens to volunteer to work abroad, helping in Third World countries.

Johnson proudly holding out the Economic Opportunity Act, which he signed into law on 20 August 1964

> [The CAP] was only part of the whole anti-poverty package, but by its explosive political impact it coloured public reaction to the whole enterprise.

The aim was to encourage new attitudes among the poor by allowing them to play a part in a federal programme. In part, it aimed to empower Southern black people in determining policies that affected them. Unfortunately, many CAPs, particularly in northern cities, were dominated by militants who criticised the Johnson administration for not doing enough. Johnson received criticism from within his own Democrat Party. Mayor Richard Daley of Chicago stated that involving the poor in the CAP was like 'telling the fellow that cleans up [at the newspaper] to be the city editor'. Sociologist Daniel Patrick Moynihan went further by saying:

> The programme [CAP] was carried out in such a way as to produce a minimum of social change its sponsors desired and to bring about a maximum increase in the opposition to such change.

Perhaps the most innovative Act passed to aid inner cities was the Demonstration Cities and Metropolitan Development Act of 1966. According to historian Paul Conkin, in *Big Daddy from the Pedernales: Lyndon Baines Johnson* (1986):

> … the major stated goal of the Act was to improve the quality of urban life 'the most critical domestic problem' facing the USA. Its main weapon was to be comprehensive demonstrative projects in slum or blighted areas, designed to improve the welfare of people who already lived there.

The Federal Government offered local governments 80 per cent grants to deal with issues such as crime prevention, health care, recreation and job creation. In 1966, Congress authorised spending of $412 million that rose to $512 million in 1967. However, like CAPs, it was difficult to evaluate the success of the Demonstration Cities and Metropolitan Development Act. Suffice to say that in 1968 Congress cut off funding for the projects.

Johnson was determined to continue to help inner cities and, in 1968, he proposed the most ambitious federal housing initiative in US history. He proposed the building of 26 million housing units over 10 years. The Housing Act of 1968 authorised a total of $1.7 million for the first three years. The Act led to the building of cheap, rather poorly built homes. Builders and developers reduced their involvement because of limits on profits. When Richard Nixon became president, in 1969, he removed many restrictions on developers and reduced federal funding following scandals about the quality of the housing produced.

Johnson's policies to aid the poor and develop the economies of depressed regions went beyond inner cities. The Appalachian Regional Development Act of 1965 allocated $1.1 billion to programmes aimed to raise the standard of living in the Appalachian mountain area. This was a direct continuation of reform begun by Kennedy. The Omnibus Housing Act of 1965 was also a clear continuation of Kennedy's reform. The Act provided the construction of 240,000 houses and $2.9 million for urban renewal. Johnson achieved where Kennedy had failed.

The future Republican president, Ronald Reagan, claimed that in the 'war on poverty', poverty won! The over-ambitious claims of Johnson to eradicate poverty and the lack of coordination of federal programmes brought a political reaction against direct federal involvement in welfare. From 1969, the Federal Government reduced its role in welfare.

In *Liberalism and Its Challengers: From FDR to Bush* (1992), historian Alonzo L. Hamby declares that LBJ 'in his striving for hyper-accomplishment he simply tried to do too much.' Mark I. Gelfand in 'The War on Poverty', in *The Johnson Years* (1981), claims:

Conservatives are prone to stress the shortcomings, label the whole effort a failure and demand a rollback of federal intervention. Radicals are likely to employ similar characterisations but call for greater federal control.

However, according to the US Census, the number of families in poverty dropped from 40 million in 1959, to 28 million in 1968 and to just over 25 million in 1970. Part of this change can be attributed to a thriving economy. Johnson's 'war on poverty' clearly had a considerable impact on the USA, although not quite to the extent that he had planned.

Environment and consumer protection

By the early 1960s, the US Government was becoming more aware of the environmental effects of an advanced industrial society. An important catalyst for change was the book *Silent Spring* (1962), by Rachel Carson, a former member of the Federal Fish and Wildlife Service. She highlighted the indiscriminate use of chemicals such as DDT and its effects on the food chain. Ultimately the Federal Government would ban DDT in 1972.

During Kennedy's administration, the first steps were made to improve the environment of cities and urban areas with the Clean Air Act of 1963. This limited the pollution emissions from cars and factories. JFK also extended the National Park Service by approving legislation that made Padre Island and Point Reyes National Seashores.

Johnson went much further in the Great Society. He created a new Federal Pollution Control Administration. In his environment legislation, he amended Kennedy's Clean Air Act to make it more effective and supplemented it with the Water Quality Control Act 1965, the Water Resources Planning Act 1965, the Clean Water Restoration Act 1966 and the Air Quality Act 1967. The combined effect of this legislation made Johnson the most effective defender of the environment in US history to that time. Also, like Kennedy, he made direct attempts to extend the National Park Service. The National Wilderness Preservation Act of 1964 added 54 new areas to the National Park Service.

Johnson also became involved in the area of consumer protection in a way not seen since Theodore Roosevelt's presidency of 1901–9. The Fair Packaging and Labelling Act 1966, the Automobile Safety Act 1966, the Meat Inspection Act 1967, the Poultry Inspection Act 1967, the Coal Mine Safety Act 1967 and, most important of all, the Occupational Health and Safety Act 1968 provided US consumers and workers with effective protection.

Why was Johnson more successful than Kennedy in domestic affairs?

In his assessment of the Great Society, historian Paul Conkin, in *Big Daddy from the Pedernales: Lyndon Baines Johnson* (1986), notes:

Johnson loved it. His domestic triumphs alone sustained him during the darkest days of the Vietnam War. What president ever did so much for the American people?

Veteran US diplomat William Averell Harriman observed:

LBJ was great in domestic affairs. Harry Truman had programmes, but none got through. Kennedy had no technique. If it hadn't been for … Vietnam he'd [LBJ] have been the greatest president ever.

This is borne out by looking at Johnson's legislative record. Historian Vaughn Davis Bornet, in *The Presidency of Lyndon B. Johnson* (1983), states:

The percentages of Johnsonian legislative successes are awesome: 1964 – 58[%]; 1965 – 69[%]; 1966 – 56[%]; 1967 – 48[%] and 1968 – 56[%].

During the eighty-ninth Congress, 1965/6, Johnson passed the bulk of his Great Society Programme. In achieving this remarkable success, Johnson had the support of a Senate and House dominated by liberal Democrats. This was a far cry from the conservative coalition that had faced Kennedy. Nevertheless, Johnson himself recognised the debt he owed Kennedy and his legacy. In 1971, in retirement, Johnson wrote:

> I never lost sight of the fact that I was trustee and custodian of the Kennedy administration.

However, whether Johnson realised it or not, his Great Society went far beyond anything that Kennedy had said or proposed. Johnson's administration of 1963–9 proved to be the most reforming administration in the 20th century.

Who was more effective in domestic reform: JFK or LBJ?

1. Read the following extract and answer the question.

Without the interest of Kennedy and, to a much greater degree Johnson, the "war on poverty" would never have been declared. It was Johnson's eagerness to seize on the sketchy pilot programmes that had been [made] under the Kennedy administration and convert them into a much larger, more comprehensive and more ambitious programme.

R. Harrison, *State and Society in Twentieth-Century America* (Longman, 1997, p 297.

Using the information in the extract, and from this section, explain whether Johnson's Great Society Programme was merely a continuation of Kennedy's New Frontier Programme.

2. What do you regard as the most successful domestic reform policy of the Kennedy-Johnson years? Explain your answer using information from this section.

Further Reading

Texts designed for AS students

JFK & LBJ by Derrick Murphy (Collins Historymakers, 2004)
Promises to Keep by Paul Boyer (Houghton Mifflin, 1999) – easy to read and well-illustrated narrative.
Politics as Usual: the age of Truman and Eisenhower by Gary W. Reichard (Harlan Davidson, 1988) – an easy-to-read but detailed narrative that emphasises the continuation in policy.

Texts for A2 and advanced study

The Unfinished Journey by William H. Chafe (Oxford University Press, 1991) – critical narrative with a good section on Johnson.
The Truman Years 1945–53 by Mark S. Byrnes (Longman, Seminar Studies series, 2000) – has a strong narrative but also has useful sections containing primary and secondary documents, a timeline and glossary.
Promises Kept by Irving Bernstein (Oxford University Press, 1991) – dense and quite hard to read, but useful in that it argues Kennedy did a lot more than he is given credit for.
Lyndon B. Johnson and American Liberalism by Bruce J. Schulman (St Martin's Press, Bedford Series in History and Culture, 1995) – a brief biography with a very useful document section.

Websites

Most presidents have their own libraries, which are on the internet.
www.trumanlibrary.org – on the Truman Years.
WWW.EISENHOWER.UTEXAS.EDU – on Eisenhower.
WWW.LBJLIB.UTEXAS.EDU – on Lyndon Johnson.
WWW.JFKLIBRARY.ORG – on John F. Kennedy.
CSTL.SEMO.EDU/MODERNPRESIDENCY/LINKS – a site full of links to other sites so it's a
 good starting point.
WWW.PBS.ORG/WGBH/AMEX/PRESIDENTS/INDEX – a site from the American Public
 Broadcasting Corporation and has pages for all American presidents.

Television and videos

'LBJ' – four-part documentary on Johnson for PBS (1997).
'Truman' – a video written and produced by David Grubin for 'The American
 Experience' series (1994). It is divided into three one-hour episodes: the first
 covers Truman's political rise and the dropping of the atom bomb on Japan in
 1945; the second episode covers Truman's Administration in domestic and
 foreign affairs up to 1949; the third episode concentrates on the Korean War.

9 From Nixon to George W. Bush, 1969–2008

Key Issues

- To what extent did domestic policy become more conservative between 1969 and 1992?

- In what ways did the US economy change between 1969 and 1992?

- Did the power of the President change in the years 1969–1992?

9.1 How far did domestic policy change under Nixon, 1969–1974?

9.2 Historical interpretation: The Watergate scandal

9.3 What impact did Ford's presidency have on domestic policy?

9.4 How successful was Jimmy Carter in domestic policy, 1977–1981?

9.5 To what extent was the presidency of Ronald Reagan a turning point in domestic affairs?

9.6 In what ways was George Bush Senior's domestic policy different from that of Ronald Reagan?

9.7 How far did Bill Clinton change US domestic policy between 1993 and 2001?

9.8 Was George W. Bush's presidency a complete failure?

Framework of Events

1968	Nixon wins presidential election
1970	Nixon proposes Huston Plan
	Environmental Protection Agency established
1971	Nixon introduces wage and price freeze
1972	Watergate break-in
	Equal Rights Amendment passed by Congress
	Nixon wins landslide in presidential election
1973	Trial of Watergate burglars
	Senate creates Special Committee to investigate Watergate
	Vice-President Agnew resigns; replaced by Gerald Ford
	'Roe v Wade' Supreme Court case
	OPEC quadruples world oil price during Yom Kippur War
1974	Supreme Court orders Nixon to release Watergate tapes
	Whip Inflation Now (WIN) program
	Indian Self-Determination Act
	House Judiciary Committee votes to impeach Nixon
	Nixon resigns; Ford becomes President
1975	Ford pardons Nixon
1976	Carter defeats Ford to become 39th President
1978	Double-digit inflation and rising interest rates
1979	OPEC doubles price of oil following Iranian Revolution
	(March) Three Mile Island Nuclear Accident
1980	Reagan is elected President
1981	Reagan survives an assassination attempt
	Major cuts in taxes and domestic spending
	Severe economic recession begins
1982	Equal Rights Amendment fails to be ratified by states
1984	Reagan defeats Mondale in landslide election victory
1986	Immigration Reform and Control Act
	Federal budget deficit rises to $221 billion

1987	Iran-Contra Scandal
	October: Stock Market Crash
	Trade deficit with other countries reaches $170 billion
1988	Bush defeats Dukakis to become President
1989	'Exxon Valdez' oil spill in Alaska
	Supreme Court limits abortion and restricts civil rights laws
1990	Federal Clean Air Act is passed
	Bush and Congress agree five-year budget deficit reduction plan
	New recession begins
1991	Controversy over appointment of Clarence Thomas to Supreme Court
1992	Supreme Court upholds 'Roe v Wade' decision on abortion
	Arkansas Governor Bill Clinton defeats Bush in presidential election.
1993	Oslo Accords and Washington Agreement on Israel/Palestine
1994	Republicans gain control of both houses of Congress
	Republican 'Contract with America'
1996	Clinton defeats Bob Dole to win a second term
1997	Whitewater investigation
1998	Attempted impeachment of Bill Clinton
	US forces engaged in former Yugoslavia
2000	Contested presidential election sees George W. Bush win by the narrowest of margins
2001	9/11 attacks on US
	Taliban government in Afghanistan overthrown
2003	Iraq War
2004	Bush wins second term in office by narrowly defeating John Kerry
2005	Hurricane Katrina
2006	Democrats gain control of both houses of Congress
2007	US signs up to international plans to combat global warming
2008	End of the Bush administration. New race for the White House.

Overview

THE period 1969–2008 was one of considerable social, economic and political change within the United States. In 1968, Nixon won a narrow victory over his Democratic Party opponent, Hubert Humphrey. His victory was aided in no small way by the split within the Democratic Party, which produced George Wallace's American Independent Party.

Nixon inherited a country riven with social and political strife. The anti-Vietnam War movement had helped to topple Johnson's Administration. The riots at the Democratic Party Convention in August 1968 were the culmination of anti-war demonstrations across the country. In addition, the country was affected by racial conflict. The assassination of Martin Luther King led to race riots in almost every major city. Social conflict continued for much of Nixon's first term.

The year 1969 was also a turning point in politics. The New Deal coalition began to fall apart. From 1932 to 1969 the Democrats had been the dominant national party because they were able to win support from blue-collar workers, Catholics, Jews, blacks, southern whites and northern liberals. The social turmoil of the 1960s had led to the fragmentation of this coalition. From 1969 to 1992, the Republicans emerged as the dominant party in presidential politics. They also greatly increased their power in Congress and in state governments.

In national government, major changes occurred in the Supreme Court. The liberal court of Earl Warren came to an end in 1969 when he was retired. He was replaced by Warren E Burger (1969–1986) who took a more conservative view of the Supreme Court's role. In 1986 William Rehnquist replaced Burger and continued his predecessor's move to the right. In 2007 Rehnquist died and was replaced by John Roberts, the first Roman Catholic to hold the post. As a result, by 2008 seven of the nine Supreme Court Justices were appointed by Republican presidents, hence the Supreme Court was expected to take a more conservative view on moral issues such as gay rights and abortion.

The period after 1969 saw major changes in the power and authority of the President. Nixon's first term was the high point of 'imperial presidency'. However, the Watergate scandal of 1973–74 temporarily destroyed presidential power. It was only with the first term of Ronald Reagan's presidency (1981–85) that presidential power regained much of its prestige. Even that was temporary. The Iran-Contra Scandal of 1987 was another blow to presidential authority.

There were also major changes in the relationship between the federal and state governments. Lyndon Johnson's 'Great Society' was the high point in federal involvement in social and welfare matters. From 1969, financial decision making in these areas was gradually handed back to the states. It began with Nixon's 'revenue sharing' with the states. It accelerated under Reagan. From 1969, both major parties came to oppose 'big government' from Washington DC.

In economic terms, the United States had experienced two decades of crisis and adjustment. The Vietnam War had placed great strain on the US economy, leading to inflation. In 1973, the OPEC decision to quadruple the price of oil plunged the world into economic recession. The Iranian Revolution of 1979 created another major oil price increase. Combined with Reagan's economic policy, the USA experienced the worst economic recession, 1981–83, since the Depression of the 1930s.

Economic crisis helped to fuel major changes in the US economy. Many old manufacturing industries, such as car manufacture and steel, shed thousands of jobs. New industries associated with information communication technology grew. Many industries relocated to the 'sun belt' of the South, leaving behind a 'rust belt' in northern states such as Michigan.

The civil rights years had brought gains for African-Americans (see Chapter 7). However, major social problems remained. Inner-city ghettos, the rise of violence and drug abuse, together with poor education, remained important social issues. These were not confined to African-Americans. Hispanic Americans also faced similar problems.

In the period 1969–2008 civil rights embraced issues such as women's rights and gay rights. Such developments resulted in a right-wing backlash. From the 1970s the evangelical religious right gained influence in US politics. From the 1980s the religious right played a major role in the politics of the Republican Party. In the 2008 presidential election, Mike Huckabee, former Governor of Arkansas and evangelical minister became a serious candidate for the Republican nomination as president in the 2008 elections.

By 1992, the Republicans had dominated national government for over 20 years. Bill Clinton's victory over George Bush Senior started almost a decade of Democratic Party rule. During Clinton's second term, he became only the second president in US history to be impeached, over the Monica Lewinsky affair. The other was Andrew Johnson in 1868. Clinton survived the process but his reputation was damaged in many people's opinions.

From 1989 US presidential politics was dominated by two political families, the Bushs and the Clintons. George H. Bush was president from 1989–1993. His eldest son George W. was president from 2001 to 2009 and younger son Jeb became Governor of Florida. On the Democrat's side Bill Clinton was president for two terms from 1993 to 2001. In 2008 his wife, Hillary, a US Senator for the state of New York, became a leading contender for the Democrat nomination for president in 2008.

1. Write a brief account of the issues identified next to each president in the mind map.

2. Identify other issues and policies that you regard as successful which you could put next to each of these presidents.

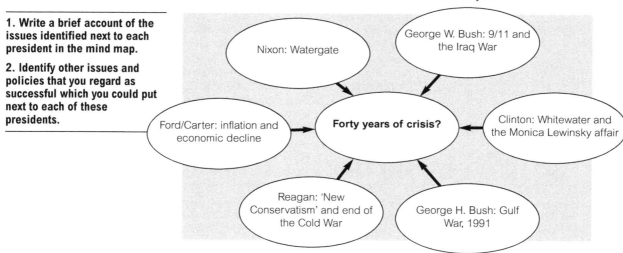

- Nixon: Watergate
- George W. Bush: 9/11 and the Iraq War
- Clinton: Whitewater and the Monica Lewinsky affair
- **Forty years of crisis?**
- Ford/Carter: inflation and economic decline
- Reagan: 'New Conservatism' and end of the Cold War
- George H. Bush: Gulf War, 1991

9.1 How far did domestic policy change under Nixon, 1969–1974?

Richard Nixon narrowly won the 1968 presidential election over Democrat Hubert Humphrey by 31.7 million votes to 31.3 million. The electoral college made the gap wider (301 to 191) because Nixon won in 32 states. Nixon claimed he represented 'Middle America' – a group he later described as the 'silent majority'.

However, Nixon had to deal with a Congress dominated by the Democrat Party. In the 91st Congress (1969–71), the Democrats controlled 58 seats in the Senate and 243 out of 435 in the House. In the 92nd Congress (1971–73), they still controlled 54 Senate seats but increased their hold on the House with 255 seats. As a result, Nixon's attempts to follow a conservative domestic policy were severely limited. Congress could, and did, introduce legislation that Nixon disliked. For instance, Congress passed the Twenty-Sixth Amendment in 1970, which lowered

Richard Milhous Nixon (1913–1994)
37th President of the USA (1969–74), a Republican. Born in Yorba Linda, South California, and brought up as a Quaker. Attended Whittier University, before serving in US Navy in Pacific in Second World War. Nixon was elected to House of Representatives (1946) and Senate (1950). Member of Joseph McCarthy's campaign against communists in USA. Vice-President to Eisenhower (1953–61). Lost to John F. Kennedy in 1960 elections. Lost Governor's election in California in 1962. As President, he was responsible for US withdrawal from Vietnam, and the improvement of relations with Communist China. Nixon was the only president ever to resign from office – on 9 August 1974, over his involvement in the Watergate scandal. He was threatened with impeachment (trial for serious offences whilst in office) on three counts:

- obstruction of the administration of justice in the Watergate investigations;
- violation of the rights of citizens (e.g. attempting to use the Internal Revenue Service, FBI and CIA as weapons against political opponents);
- and failure to produce 'paper and things'. President Ford granted him a pardon in 1974.

the age of voting in elections from 21 to 18. This was ratified by the states in 1971. Congress also passed the Federal Election Campaign Act in 1972.

Nevertheless, Nixon attempted to change radically the role of the federal government. He also planned to develop a new base of support for the Republican Party.

Nixon's southern strategy

Nixon's victory in 1968 had seen the end of the Democrat's control of the 'Solid South'. Nixon won southern states such as Tennessee, North and South Carolina, Virginia and Florida. The Democrats also lost states such as Mississippi and Alabama to George Wallace's American Independent Party.

In developing a strategy, Nixon was helped by a Republican aide, Kevin Phillips, who produced 'The Emergence of a Republican Majority' in 1969. This suggested the Republicans could capture votes from the middle class, southern whites, Catholics and westerners.

During his first term in office, Nixon deliberately adopted policies that were aimed to win over the South. He opposed an extension of the 1965 Voting Rights Act. He also wanted to modify the Fair Housing Act of 1968, which would have had an adverse effect on African-Americans.

Nixon also wanted to prevent any further desegregation of schools in Mississippi. However, the Supreme Court thwarted him. In 1969, in 'Alexander versus Holmes County', the Court demanded school integration with all possible speed. In 1971, in 'Swann versus Charlotte Mecklenburg Board of Education', the Court attacked de facto segregation. The Court advocated bussing children between black and white neighbourhoods in order to achieve racially-integrated schools. However, in 1974, in 'Milliken versus Bradley', the Court limited the amount of bussing.

These developments were slightly surprising because Nixon had nominated a conservative Chief Justice, Warren Burger, when Earl Warren retired in 1969. To make matters worse, when liberal Justice Abe Fortas retired, Nixon's attempt to appoint a conservative Southerner backfired on two occasions. In 1969, the Senate rejected his nomination of South Carolina's Clement Haynsworth. In the following year, the choice of G. Harrold Carswell of Florida was also rejected. However, by the time he resigned from office, Nixon had been successful in appointing three conservative justices: Harry Blackmun of Minnesota, Lewis Powell of Virginia and William Rehnquist of Arizona.

Nixon's southern strategy did show results. In 1972, he won every southern state. Also, since 1969, the South has no longer been a solid Democrat area.

The Nixon Administration, 1969–1974: leading members

President:	Richard Nixon
Vice-President:	Spiro Agnew (1969–73)
	Gerald Ford (1973–74)
Treasury:	David Kennedy (1969–70)
	John Connelly (1970–72)
	George Schultz (1972–74)
	William Simon (1974)
Justice:	John Mitchell (1969–72)
	Richard Kleindienst (1972–73)
	Elliott Richardson (1973)
	William Saxbe (1973–74)
Chief White House Aides (1969–73):	H.R. 'Bob' Haldeman and J. Ehrlichman

How reliable is this source as evidence of the Kent State University shootings of May 1970?

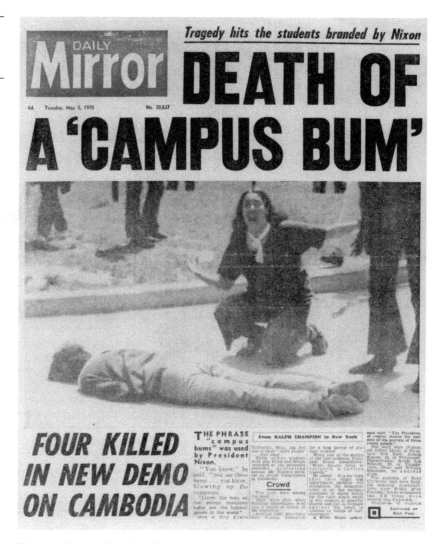

Front page of 'Daily Mirror' in the UK, 1 May 1970.

The problem of radicalism

During the 1968 presidential campaign, the nation seemed to be overrun with radical groups. At the Democratic National Convention, radical groups such as Students for a Democratic Society (SDS) and the Youth International Party (Yippies) did battle with the Chicago police. In addition, the Black Panther Party and other radical black groups demanded fundamental social change. Across America, a variety of radical groups opposed the USA's continued involvement in South East Asia.

By the early 1970s, the feminist movement was demanding equality for women. Similarly, the gay liberation movement was demanding equality for gays.

Student protest against the Vietnam War reached its height in May 1970 when it was announced publicly that US troops had invaded Cambodia. The shooting of four students at Kent State University by Ohio National Guardsmen caused national outrage. Nixon did not help matters by referring to the college students as 'campus bums' at an informal briefing at the **Pentagon**!

Fortunately for Nixon the student protest movement split asunder of its own accord. The SDS fell apart at its national convention in 1970. A group

Campus: Area of land which contains the main buildings of a university, such as the lecture rooms, administration offices, sports facilities, and some living accommodation for students.

Pentagon: Building in Washington DC which is the headquarters of the US Department of Defense.

Cartoon by Mike Peters, 1982, 'Look guys, why don't we just say that all men are created equal … and let the little ladies look out for themselves?' published in 'Dayton Daily News', 1982.

---

1. What point is this cartoon making about the campaign for equal rights for women?

2. How useful do you regard this cartoon as evidence of US opinion on the campaign for women's rights?

---

known as the Revolutionary Youth Movement demanded violent revolution and lost support accordingly.

Beginning in 1967, the CIA (see panel on page 318) launched 'Operation Chaos' against left-wing groups. This was supported by the FBI's 'Cointelpro' programme. Both organisations amassed information on left-wing groups. In particular, the Black Panther Party was targeted for special attention. In 1969, 28 party members were killed by police. Many more were imprisoned.

By the time of the 1970 mid-term elections, Nixon had campaigned against what he called 'the rock throwers and the obscenity shouters in America'. He appealed to the great 'silent majority' of America. By that stage, the student protest movement had dissolved into attempts to find alternative lifestyles.

Sexual equality: The idea that men and women have the same civil, political and social rights.

Of greater significance was the rise of a militant feminist movement associated with the National Organisation of Women (NOW). Founded in 1966 by Betty Friedan, the author of *Feminist Mystique*, NOW supported the campaign for **sexual equality**. This reached its height in the Nixon era. In 1972, the Educational Standards Act laid down that colleges had to set up affirmative action programmes to ensure equality of opportunity for women. In the same year, Congress passed the Equal Rights Amendment which, if ratified by the states, would have guaranteed sexual equality in the Constitution. Finally, in 1973, the US Supreme Court, in 'Roe versus Wade', legalised **abortion**.

Abortion: When a woman ends her pregnancy and loses her baby, usually deliberately.

In 1970, following police raids on gay clubs in New York City, the Gay Liberation Front was created. Almost 800 gay organisations had been established across the country by 1973.

Nixon and the environment

Superficially, Nixon's presidency seemed to be successful in environmental matters. During his first term as President, Congress passed the Water Quality Improvement Act. This attempted to control pollution caused by industry and power companies. Congress also passed the Clean Air Act, which attempted to control **pollution emissions** from cars. The Resource Recovery Act promoted the recycling of waste. At government level, the National Environmental Policy Act 1970 created the Environmental Protection Agency, which enforced federal law on the environment.

Pollution emissions: The amount of air pollution produced by industry and private car use.

In developing these environmental laws, Nixon played an insignificant and reluctant part. Several environmental laws were passed over Nixon's veto. When forced to appoint a head of the Environmental Protection Agency, Nixon chose William Rogers who proved to be ineffectual.

Nixon's social policy

Sociologist: Someone who studies or teaches sociology – the study of human societies and relationships between groups in these societies.

In 1969, Nixon appointed a leading **sociologist** and Democrat, Daniel Patrick Moynihan, as his urban affairs adviser. The result of this development was the Family Assistance Plan. This proposed to end handouts to the poor, with a minimum annual income of $3,000 for a family of four. It was criticised by conservatives for being too radical and by liberals for its low payments. As a result, it was defeated in the Senate and dropped.

In the area of affirmative action (see page 213), Nixon introduced the Philadelphia Plan which required trade unions working on federal projects to accept quotas for African-American workers. This greatly extended affirmative action to include almost 300,000 firms by 1974. To assist this attempt to win African-American support, Nixon appointed James Farmer, the founder of CORE, as an assistant secretary in the Department of Housing, Education and Welfare (HEW).

However, the Democratic-controlled Congress passed legislation less to Nixon's liking, such as the Occupational Health and Safety Act of 1970. Congress increased social security benefits by linking increases to the rate of inflation. It also increased **food stamp funding**.

Food stamp funding: Food stamps are given to the unemployed instead of money. They can only be used to buy food.

Nixon and the economy

Stagflation: Rising inflation and rising unemployment at the same time.

Economic problems plagued the Nixon presidency. By the early 1970s, the US economy was suffering the effects of what became known as **stagflation**. Inflation stood at 3 per cent per year in 1967. By 1973, it had increased threefold to 9 per cent; by 1974, it had gone up another 3 per cent. The unemployment rate was 3.3 per cent in early 1969. By 1972, it had risen to 5.6 per cent. This had been caused by a variety of factors.

Firstly, the joint costs of the 'Great Society' and the war in Vietnam had resulted in a large government **budget deficit**. In addition, the USA was facing stiff competition in world markets from Japan and West Germany.

Budget deficit: Where government expenditure is greater than government income from taxation.

Secondly, as the world's greatest consumer of oil the USA was vulnerable to oil-price increases. During the Yom Kippur War of 1973 between the Arabs and the Israelis, the Arab-dominated, oil-producing group OPEC (Organisation of Petroleum Exporting Countries) increased the world price of oil by 400 per cent. This was particularly damaging to the US car industry which had a tradition of producing 'gas guzzling' cars which had a fuel consumption of 9 to 12 miles per gallon.

These factors helped to cause the 'Nixon recession' in 1971–74. In response, Nixon tried to reduce inflation. The US central bank, the Federal Reserve Board, raised interest rates. This made borrowing money more expensive. Then in August 1971, Nixon announced his 'New Economic Policy'. A freeze was made on all wages and price increases for 90 days (3 months). Later, in 1973, restraint on pay and price increases was made voluntary.

Also in August 1971, the United States abandoned the fixed exchange rate system established at the end of the Second World War. This aimed to create stability in international trading. The backbone of the system was the US dollar. However, with its economic difficulties, the USA could no longer underpin the system. The Smithsonian Agreement of 1972 saw the formal end to fixed exchange rates across the western world. As a result, the US dollar was devalued. This made exports cheaper and imports dearer. To protect the US car industry, Nixon also placed a tariff on imported Japanese cars.

These measures, along with a tax cut, did lead to some improvement in the economy. This allowed Nixon to win re-election in 1972. However, the combined effect of increased economic competition, oil price rises and a flexible exchange rate system all led to major restructuring in the US economy during the 1970s.

Summary

When Nixon came to office, in 1969, he faced social discord, a faltering economy and a Democratic-controlled Congress. He did make some important changes. Congress finally agreed to his revenue-sharing plan with the states in 1972. The liberal Supreme Court of Earl Warren was altered with the appointment of more conservative justices. However, Nixon's domestic policy and, with it, his reputation as President, was overshadowed by the Watergate scandal of 1973–74. This became the greatest political scandal in 20th-century American history.

1. What difficulties did Nixon face in domestic affairs between 1969 and 1974?

2. How successful was Nixon in dealing with America's domestic problems 1969–1974?

9.2 The Watergate scandal
A CASE STUDY IN HISTORICAL INTERPRETATION

The Watergate scandal dominated American politics from 1973 to 1974. It destroyed the Nixon presidency. It also severely damaged the power and prestige of the office of President. The reasons for the scandal go far beyond the investigation into a burglary at the Democratic Party headquarters in Washington DC during the 1972 presidential election campaign. Following the break-in and the trial of the burglars, Nixon was accused of obstructing investigations into the affair. He claimed executive privilege for not cooperating with a Senate investigation. He also lied about the involvement of the White House in the affair. The result was a temporary collapse of presidential power. By August 1974, he realised he would be impeached. The impact of the Watergate scandal on the American political system is still open to debate. So, Nixon became the first President to resign whilst in office.

What were the causes of the Watergate scandal?

(a) Nixon's personality
A long-term cause of the scandal was the personality and psychological make-up of the President. Nixon has been subject to several psychoanalytical studies. In *Richard Nixon, A Pyschobiography* (1997), Volkan, Itzkowitz and Dod point out that Nixon was an introvert with a strong

---

CIA (Central Intelligence Agency): Created by the National Security Act 1947. Originally a counter-intelligence agency for use outside the USA. The CIA was involved in the overthrow of the Arbenz regime in Guatemala in 1954 and the Allende regime in Chile in 1973. Under President Nixon, the CIA was also used to 'spy' on Nixon's political opponents.

FBI (Federal Bureau of Investigation): An agency of the US Justice Department

created in 1908. Its main role is to deal with federal crimes. The longest-serving director was J. Edgar Hoover (1924–72). He was a noted anti-communist and opponent of the civil rights movement. The FBI was used for surveillance of US citizens during Hoover's period in control.

NSA (National Security Agency): Created by presidential executive order in 1952. Involved in intelligence gathering. Operates surveillance installation at

Menwith Hill, Yorkshire. This was used to monitor all telephone calls out of the UK during the Cold War.

DIA (Defense Intelligence Agency): Created by a Department of Defense Directive in 1961 during John F. Kennedy's Administration by Robert McNamara, Secretary of Defense. The DIA coordinated the intelligence-gathering operations of the three branches of the armed forces, such as U-2 spy flights by the US air force, naval intelligence-gathering ships,

such as the 'Pueblo', which was captured by the North Koreans in 1968, and the 'Liberty', which was attacked by the Israelis during the Six-Day War with the Arabs in 1967. Army intelligence, known as G-2, was involved in domestic surveillance. In the 1970s, the DIA was reported to have 25 million dossiers (files) on civilian radicals, students and politicians (according to Marian Irish and Elke Frank in *US Foreign Policy*, published in 1975).

sense of inferiority. His humble Quaker background in California helps to explain this. He suffered physical abuse from a strict father. He was in awe of his mother, whom he adored. He constantly referred to her throughout his life as a 'saint'. As a result of this background, Richard Nixon resented those with more privileged backgrounds, such as the East Coast liberal elite. Nixon was also suspicious of others and feared 'enemies everywhere'.

To Nixon this problem was made clear, in 1971, when a State Department official, Dr Daniel Ellsberg, released to the press 'The Pentagon Papers'. These secret documents on US involvement in Vietnam showed that the government had lied to the American people about why it had become involved. From that incident on, Nixon was determined to prevent any other leaks about the government reaching the press.

Given his psychological make-up, Nixon was almost bound to engage in actions which spied on his political opponents or anybody else he felt might threaten his position as President. He engaged in surveillance of opponents and actively plotted to discredit them. This led to a break-in of the Democratic National Headquarters during the presidential campaign of 1972. It involved bugging the offices of Democrat National Chairman, Larry O'Brien.

Watergate also involved other illegal activities. Successful attempts were made to discredit leading Democrats who could have been formidable opponents to Nixon in the 1972 election. A malicious rumour was spread that the wife of Edmund Muskie of Maine, who was a Catholic, had had an abortion. Senator Scoop Jackson of Washington was accused of having had an affair with a younger woman. The overall aim was to secure the nomination of liberal George McGovern of South Dakota as his opponent.

(b) Nixon's hopes of a landslide victory

In 1960, Nixon suffered a narrow defeat in a presidential election. He believed John F. Kennedy 'stole' the election because political supporters in Chicago had tampered with the votes, thereby securing Illinois and the election. In 1968, Nixon narrowly defeated Hubert Humphrey in a three-way contest that included George Wallace of the American Independent Party. Nixon planned to 'win big' in 1972 and ensure a second term. This would mean that he would be President during the bicentennial celebration of 1976, the 200th Anniversary of the Declaration of Independence.

To achieve this end, Nixon used any means at his disposal to ensure a victory. Like other Presidents before him, such as Lyndon Johnson, Nixon bugged the opposition to find out their campaign strategy. Nixon stated, in 1977, that Watergate emerged 'exactly how the other side would have played it'. It was 'all politics pure and simple'. As Maurice Stans, former chairman of CREEP (The Committee to Re-Elect the President) stated, 'to him [Nixon], on the political battlefield "the end justified the means"'.

(c) The Imperial Presidency

Nixon's presidency can been seen as a longer-term process, which Arthur Schlesinger identified as the rise of the 'Imperial Presidency'. By the early 1970s, the office of President had amassed enormous power. The President had the awesome power to launch an all-out nuclear war. However, within the United States, he was limited by the terms of the Constitution. This was made clear in Nixon's first term as President when he had to work with a Democrat-controlled Congress. With his power over the intelligence agencies such as the FBI, CIA, NSA and DIA (see panel on previous page), the President had, at his disposal, the power and authority to spy on others.

The White House from 1970 coordinated the work of the intelligence agencies as part of a plan to end the social disorder caused by radical and

Timechart of the Watergate scandal

1972

28 May: First break-in by Watergate burglars at Democratic National Headquarters in Washington DC.

17 June: Second break-in which leads to arrest of James McCord and Cuban-exile burglars at Watergate Building.

15 September: Grand Jury **indicts for trial** Gordon Liddy, Howard Hunt and Watergate burglars.

Indicts for trial: When either a law official or a grand jury makes a decision which suggests there is sufficient evidence to try a person for a crime.

1973

8–30 January: Trial and conviction of James McCord and Gordon Liddy for Watergate break-in.

7 February: Senate establishes Select Committee on Presidential Campaign Activities under chairmanship of Sam Ervin.

19 March: James McCord gives a letter to federal judge John Sirica alleging that high-ranking White House officials were involved in cover-up of burglary.

27 April: FBI Director Patrick Grey resigns after it is revealed that he destroyed evidence given to him by Nixon's legal adviser John Dean.

30 April: Resignations of Nixon's closest White House advisers, Haldeman and Ehrlichman, and Attorney General Kleindienst. John Dean fired by Nixon.

27–28 June: John Dean testifies to Senate Committee linking White House with Watergate break-in.

13 July: White House junior official Butterfield reveals existence of tapes of all conversations made at Nixon White House.

10 October: Vice-President Spiro Agnew forced to resign over income tax evasion.

20 October: 'Saturday Night Massacre' – Nixon asks Attorney General to fire Special Prosecutor into Watergate scandal, Archibald Cox. When he refuses, he is sacked by Nixon. He also sacks Assistant Attorney General, William Ruckelhaus, when he refuses to sack Cox. Eventually, acting Attorney General, Robert Bork, sacks Cox.

1 November: Leon Jaworski becomes Special Prosecutor into Watergate scandal.

6 December: Gerald Ford becomes Vice-President.

1974

1 March: Grand Jury indicts for trial former Attorney General John Mitchell, Haldeman, Ehrlichman and other White House aides for conspiring to hinder Watergate investigation.

24 July: Supreme Court demands that Nixon release tapes on Watergate.

27 July: House Judiciary Committee begins impeachment proceedings against Nixon.

8 August: House Judiciary Committee agrees to impeach Nixon for lying and obstructing investigation into Watergate scandal.

9 August: Nixon resigns as President.

left-wing groups. Once established, this network was then used against Nixon's political opponents, the Democrats.

(d) The CIA Trap theory

This theory comes from the belief that the CIA attempted to stop the agency falling under the control of the Nixon White House. According to supporters of this view, former CIA agents, such as James McCord, deliberately botched the bugging of the Democrat Headquarters in order to create political problems for Nixon.

At the Senate Committee hearings into Watergate, McCord, a former CIA agent and one of the burglars, wrote a memorandum which stated:

> 'It appeared to me that the White House had for some time been trying to get political control over [the] CIA. When linked with what I saw happening to the FBI – political control by the White House – it appeared then that the two agencies were no longer able [to conduct their own business].'

(e) The work of Nixon subordinates

Subordinates: Those individuals under a person's management control.

Throughout the Watergate scandal and since, Nixon has claimed that the burglary and other supposedly illegal activities were the work of overzealous **subordinates**. Individuals, such as Gordon Liddy, were regarded as having acted on their own initiative. If the White House was involved, it was associated with Nixon aides H.R. 'Bob' Haldeman and John D. Ehrlichman, rather than Nixon himself. As the President he was forced, eventually, to accept responsibility for the acts of others.

According to Maurice Stans, chairman of CREEP:

> '[Nixon's] tragic downfall through Watergate was the result of excesses of loyalty, first by his campaign staff who wanted him to win an overwhelming [victory] in the 1972 election through a petty burglary unknown to him, and second, by his endorsement of a cover-up to protect his staff and through them his re-election.'

Why was Nixon forced to resign over the Watergate scandal?

Nixon was on the verge of impeachment, in August 1974, because he was accused of using agencies such as the FBI and CIA for political purposes in order to discredit opponents. He was also accused of lying about his involvement in the scandal and of using his position as President to obstruct justice.

Throughout the scandal, Nixon consistently refused to cooperate with the Senate Investigating Committee, the Special Prosecutor into the affair and even the Supreme Court. He claimed 'executive privilege'. This meant he used the issue of national security to refuse to give evidence. It formed the basis of his refusal to hand over tapes of conversations in the White House on the affair. In ascertaining why Nixon was forced to resign, a number of issues arise.

(a) The role of two 'Washington Post' reporters

According to their book *All the President's Men* (published in 1994), Bob Woodward and Carl Bernstein, two investigative reporters working for the 'Washington Post', played a major role in linking Nixon with the Watergate break-in. On 19 June 1972, an article by the two reporters linked the burglars with Howard Hunt, a White House aide. They uncovered an illegal 'slush fund' of hundreds of thousands of dollars which had been used by CREEP for illegal activities during the 1972 presidential campaign. Later investigations highlighted the roles of Maurice Stans and other senior Republican Party officials, including Attorney General John Mitchell.

During their investigations, Woodward and Bernstein were aided by an anonymous White House official, whom they nicknamed 'Deep Throat'. In their study of the Watergate Case, called *Silent Coup: The Removal of a President* (1991), Len Coldny and Robert Gettlin believe 'Deep Throat' to be the name given to several anonymous sources used by the reporters.

At the time, and in the subsequent Hollywood Film 'All the President's Men', Woodward and Bernstein were portrayed as the driving force behind the investigations which finally led to Nixon's resignation.

(Top) Syndicated cartoon by Jules Feiffer, 15 July 1973; (bottom left) cartoon by Paul Conrad, published in 'New York Times', 11 September 1972; (bottom right) 'Nixon in Tape Web' by Robert Pryor, 1975.

1. **Explain how each cartoon tries to explain the Watergate scandal.**

2. **Which cartoon do you regard as the most effective in getting its message across? Explain your answer.**

3. **How useful do you regard these cartoons in explaining the Watergate scandal?**

(b) The Congressional investigations

Although Woodward and Bernstein may have highlighted many of the links between the burglars and the White House, it was the Senate Investigating Committee that acted as the main driving force leading to impeachment. It was in front of the Committee that John Dean, the President's legal adviser, linked Haldeman, Ehrlichman and Nixon to the burglary and other illegal acts. It was also in front of the Committee that Alexander Butterfield announced that Nixon had installed a tape system which recorded all his conversations in the White House.

With extensive national television coverage, the Senate investigating hearings helped to build up opposition to Nixon. In the House of Representatives, the House Judiciary Committee amassed sufficient evidence to recommend the impeachment of Nixon. This decision forced the President's resignation.

(c) The role of the Supreme Court

On 24 July 1974, the Supreme Court ruled unanimously that Nixon should hand over to the House Judiciary Committee tapes of 54 conversations made during 1972. When these were published in written form they linked Nixon to the cover-up. They also revealed that the President made racist comments about other politicians, and that he swore constantly. Swear words were replaced by the phrase 'expletive deleted'. This decision brought the whole affair to a head. Within three weeks, Nixon was on the verge of impeachment by the Judiciary Committee, which forced him to resign on 9 August.

(d) Nixon's personality

In her study *Richard Nixon: The Shaping of His Character* (1991), Fawn Brodie declares:

> 'Nixon lied to gain love, to store up his grandiose fantasies, to bolster his ever-wavering sense of identity. He lied in attacks, hoping to win. And always he lied, and this most aggressively, to deny that he lied. Finally, he enjoyed lying.'

As Nixon once explained, he was not the first President to use the FBI or CIA to watch and report on political opponents. However, his compulsive habit of covering up and lying eventually undermined his position.
'Bob' Haldeman, one of Nixon's senior aides, stated:

> 'it really doesn't matter why or who ordered the Watergate break-in. What really matters is how we dealt with it after it happened, and that's where we made our fatal mistakes. I agree with Nixon's statement to David Frost [television interviewer] that, "I gave them a sword and they stuck it in me".'

What impact did the Watergate scandal have on American politics?

(a) The increase in Congressional control of the Executive and its agencies

The Watergate scandal led to major attempts by Congress to hold the President, federal government and intelligence agencies more accountable. It resulted in the passage of several laws on campaign finance, freedom of information and more openness in government.

Building on the Federal Election Campaign Act of 1971, Congress established limits on fundraising in elections. The law of 1974 limited individual campaign contributions to $5,000. These helped the growth of Political Action Committees (PACs), which circumvented the law.

The Privacy Act was also passed in 1974. This permitted individuals to see information kept on them in federal files. In 1975, the Hughes–Ryan

Undercover operations: Attempts to find out information in secret.

Amendment required the President to report to Congress on all **undercover operations**. In 1977, Senate and House committees were created to monitor the intelligence community.

In 1978, Congress passed the Ethics in Government Act which required all senior government officials to disclose their finances. It also established the Office of Government Ethics to monitor the process. In October of the same year, the Foreign Intelligence Surveillance Act required the CIA to obtain a court order before it could place a wiretap. In 1980, the Intelligence Oversight Act provided new requirements on the CIA to report its activities to Congress.

(b) The high-water mark of the Imperial Presidency
According to historian Stanley Kutler, in *Wars of Watergate: The Last Crisis of Richard Nixon* (1990):

> 'Watergate altered public perception of the presidency. Watergate transformed American attitudes towards government, and especially the presidency.

> Watergate bestowed a new vulnerability on the presidency. Once peerless and invincible, presidential majesty seemed diminished.'

1. Why are there differing interpretations about what caused the Watergate scandal?

2. Explain why you think Nixon was forced to resign the presidency by 1974?

3. 'Watergate marked a turning point in American politics.'

Assess the validity of this statement.

The changes in American public opinion aided the election of Jimmy Carter in 1976. It took until the 1980s, under Ronald Reagan, for the prestige of the presidency to recover – albeit for a short time. Following the Iran-Contra Affair of 1986–87, the presidency was again tainted with scandal.

(c) The Democrat and Republican Parties
The Watergate scandal greatly aided the Democrat Party in the short run. It helped them to increase their control of the Senate and House in the mid-term elections of 1974. However, in the longer term, it led to a revitalised Republican Party, which was more conservative. In many ways, Watergate helped to lay the foundations for the Reagan Revolution of the 1980s.

Source-based questions: Richard Nixon

Source A

What were Richard Nixon's main strengths and weaknesses? I'd say his strengths lay in his intellect primarily. He has a brilliant mind in the areas in which he is interested. He is like a racehorse specifically trained to run a particular race. He's running for the race to be President and that's what he lived for.

I would say his major weakness was in interpersonal relationships. He was a fellow who at the time I knew him was very weak in family relationships and in friendships. He had no strong friendships. Some of the worst times I ever spent with him were when he tried to fire somebody. He knew he had to do it, but he couldn't do it. It was a little bit like killing the Thanksgiving turkey with a dull axe, hack away and back off and ask somebody else to do it. He

was terrible at that kind of thing.

From an interview with John Ehrlichman in 1987. John Ehrlichman was a senior White House aide under Nixon and was jailed for his part in the Watergate scandal.

Source B

My appraisal of him today is as objective as I can phrase it:
– Richard Nixon was a man from a modest, near-poverty background endowed with extraordinary ambition, and energy and drive.
– He was an inherently timid man, uncomfortable in social settings yet dominant in political gatherings, and one of the most eloquent speakers of our time.
– He was a person of broad vision, seeking to innovate in major national events rather than merely respond to them.
– He was a man with a brilliant mind; a keen

Source-based questions: Richard Nixon

student in evaluating the pros and cons of a problem; decisive when he was satisfied with the facts before him; working at his job all the waking hours; probably the most hardworking President of this century.

– He was extraordinarily sensitive to criticism; impatient with opposition; often bitter in defeat; and he was frantic over leaks.

A recollection of Richard Nixon by Maurice Stans in 1987. Stans had been Chairman of CREEP (Committee to Re-Elect the President) in 1972. He became Secretary for Commerce in Nixon's Administration, 1973–74.

Source C

He was accustomed to rely entirely on his own perceptions; his decisions were mostly taken alone. Morally he was a shallow man; the only [views] he ever mentioned were those he learned from his Quaker mother and his football coach. The rich and honourable traditions of American Republicanism meant nothing to him by comparison. He had been poor, so he would never cease to be preoccupied with the rich, envying them, fearing them, craving to be one of them. He lost the Presidency to John Kennedy, so the latter's good looks, wit and charm became another painful obsession. He had lost the gubernatorial

[governorship] election in California in 1962, and blamed his defeat on a hostile press. 'Congratulations gentlemen,' he said ungraciously to reporters, 'you won't have Richard Nixon to kick around any more.' Within him was a darkness that he mistook for the light. Eventually it would destroy him.

From *The Longman History of the United States of America* by Hugh Brogan, 1999 – assessing Nixon's character.

---

1. Study Sources A, B and C.

How far do these sources agree about Nixon's character and personality?

2. Study Source B.

How reliable is this source as evidence of Nixon's character and personality?

3. Study Sources A, B and C and use information from this chapter.

'Nixon's fall from office was due mainly to defects in his character and personality.'

Assess the validity of this statement.

9.3 What impact did Ford's presidency have on domestic policy?

Gerald Ford (1913–2006)
38th President of the USA (1974–77), a Republican from Grand Rapids, Michigan. He was elected to the House of Representatives in 1949; was nominated to the vice-presidency by Nixon (1973) following the resignation of Spiro Agnew. Became President when Nixon was forced to resign following the Watergate scandal. Ford granted Nixon a full pardon (September 1974). His visit to Vladivostock in 1974 resulted in agreement with the USSR on strategic arms limitation. Defeated by Carter in 1976 election by a narrow margin.

Gerald Ford entered the White House, in August 1974, at one of the most difficult times in US history. The Watergate scandal had severely damaged the political system and, in particular, the office of President. In economic affairs, the country faced rising inflation and unemployment. In foreign affairs, the Portuguese empire collapsed in 1974–75 resulting in the formation of extreme left-wing governments in Portugal's former African colonies such as Angola. In 1975, Ford faced the humiliation of the fall of South Vietnam, Laos and Cambodia to communism (see Chapter 6).

When he entered the White House, Ford became the only person in history never to have been elected to the post of either President or Vice-President and yet attained both offices. Yet he had some advantages. According to the historian Hugh Brogan, in *The Longman History of the United States of America* (1999):

'Ford was a good-humoured, honest, straightforward man, who did not pretend to genius. The new President's family was attractive and reassuring: they began to exorcise the cloud of sulky secrecy which had lain over the White House for so long.'

The Nixon pardon

Within weeks of taking office, Ford faced controversy. On 8 September 1974, he gave a full pardon to Nixon for 'any and all crimes' committed during his presidency. Without such a pardon, Nixon would have faced trial and likely imprisonment for his role in the Watergate scandal. Ford argued that he wanted to end the crisis faced by the USA as a result of the Watergate scandal, which had taken place over 18 months.

The Ford Administration, 1974–1977: leading members	
President:	Gerald Ford
Vice-President:	Nelson Rockefeller
Treasury:	William Simon
Justice:	William Saxbe (1974–75); then Edward Levi (1975–77)

Economic policy

In October 1974, Ford introduced his plan to end the economic problems facing America. In the WIN (Whip Inflation Now) programme he called for voluntary restraint on pay rises. However, this had little effect on rising prices. Ford cut federal spending. He also supported the Federal Reserve Board (the US central bank) when it raised interest rates.

Ford's failure to bring about major economic change resulted in a severe economic recession in 1974–75. The major cause of this recession was the world economic slowdown, which was accelerated by the 400 per cent increase in oil prices made by OPEC in October 1973.

By election year, 1976, unemployment had risen to 8 per cent. Areas such as Detroit were badly hit as the US car industry faced competition from more fuel-efficient Japanese cars.

The 1976 elections

The Democratic Party couldn't wait for the 1976 elections. With the fall of Indo-China to communism, a severe economic recession and the fallout from Watergate, the Democrats were in a very strong position. After the 1974 mid-term election, they held 61 Senate seats and 291 out of 435 House seats.

The Democrats chose a former Governor of Georgia, Jimmy Carter. He had a reputation of being an outsider untainted by Washington politics. He was also honest – a major advantage in 1976.

For all Ford's problems, he only narrowly lost the election. Carter polled 49.9 per cent of the vote, compared with Ford's 47.9 per cent, winning 297 against 240 electoral college votes. In Congress, the Democrats kept 61 seats in the Senate and increased their House representation by one.

1. What problems faced Ford during his presidency?

2. Given his short period in office do you regard Ford as having been a successful president?

Explain your answer.

9.4 How successful was Jimmy Carter in domestic policy, 1977–1981?

Jimmy Carter planned to offer a new style of presidency. After his inauguration, he broke with tradition and walked with his wife down Pennsylvania Avenue to the White House. He had won the presidency partly because he was an outsider from a southern state. However, his inexperience in dealing with a Democrat-dominated Congress created major problems. One commentator stated that 'Carter couldn't get the Pledge of Allegiance through Congress!'

Macroeconomic policy: Economic policy that affects the whole economy, such as the national employment figures or inflation.

James Earl Carter (1924–)
39th President of the USA (1977–81), a Democrat from Plains, Georgia. Jimmy Carter served as a physicist in the navy, before taking over the family peanut business. Entered the Georgia State Senate in 1962 and was elected governor eight years later. In 1976 he defeated Gerald Ford in the presidential election, becoming the first southern president since the American Civil War. During his presidency, control of the Panama Canal Zone was returned to Panama, an amnesty programme for deserters and draft dodgers of the Vietnam War was introduced, and the Camp David Agreements for peace in the Middle East were drawn up. Defeated by Ronald Reagan in 1980.

Carter's lack of a clear policy and his lack of optimism compounded his own problems in the future. Hugh Brogan states, in *The Longman History of the United States of America* (1999), that 'The new president was inclined to view the present as one big emergency and the future as marked by a sharp diminution of promise of American life.'

Carter's economic policy

When he entered office, Carter used 'demand side' policies to stimulate the economy. These had been the basis of US **macroeconomic policy** since the Second World War. However, very high fuel prices and foreign competition had caused the severe recession facing the USA from the early 1970s. These two developments led to a rise in inflation and in unemployment at the same time, known as stagflation. Stimulating demand through increased consumer spending only helped to increase inflation as well as the purchase of imports such as foreign cars.

In the first year of Carter's term in office, unemployment dropped slightly from 8 per cent to 7 per cent. However, inflation kept rising, reaching 10 per cent by the end of 1978. By 1980, inflation rose again to 13 per cent, with interest rates at 20 per cent.

The inflation rate was boosted in 1979 because of the Iranian revolution which led to the fall of the Shah of Iran. It also resulted in the OPEC decision to double the price of oil. On 23 October 1979, Carter was given power by Congress to introduce petrol rationing.

To make matters worse, there was a nationwide reaction against a

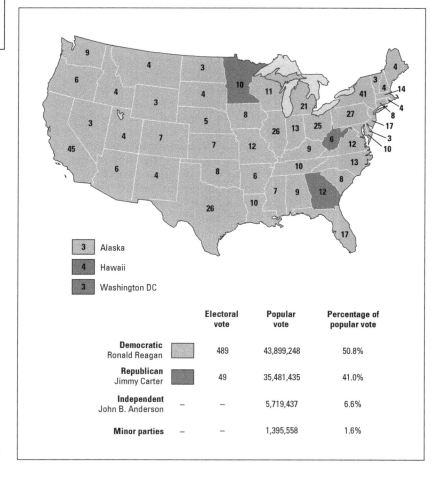

	Electoral vote	Popular vote	Percentage of popular vote
Democratic Ronald Reagan	489	43,899,248	50.8%
Republican Jimmy Carter	49	35,481,435	41.0%
Independent John B. Anderson	–	5,719,437	6.6%
Minor parties	–	1,395,558	1.6%

The presidential election of 1980

big-spending government. In 1978, in California, a statewide referendum accepted Proposition 13, which drastically cut state taxes. This action was followed by other states.

Changes in government

Carter did have some successes. He greatly increased the number of ethnic minorities in government. The highest-profile appointment was that of SCLC's Andrew Young to the US ambassador's post at the United Nations.

Carter also created a new government department, Energy. In 1979, he divided the Department of Health, Education and Welfare (HEW) into the separate departments of Education, Health and Human Services.

Carter's Administration, 1977–1981: leading members	
President:	Jimmy (James Earl) Carter
Vice-President:	Walter Mondale
Treasury:	Michael Blumenthal (1977–79); then William Miller (1979–81)
Justice:	Griffin Bell (1977–79); then Benjamin Civiletti (1979–81)

The 1980 elections

Carter became the first one-term president in the USA since the Second World War. He lost the 1980 election for a variety of reasons. In foreign affairs, he faced the humiliation of US embassy staff in Iran being held hostage. They were only released in January 1981. Carter took responsibility for a failed military mission to release the hostages. He also faced humiliation when the USSR occupied Afghanistan in 1979. Carter's decision to boycott the 1980 Moscow Olympics only added to his problems.

At home, the economy was in a recession with high inflation, high interest rates and unemployment.

Opposing Carter in the 1980 election was conservative Republican Ronald Reagan, former governor of California. Reagan supported a new approach to the economy, known as 'supply side' economics. He also had support from fundamentalist religious groups which had grown in influence during the 1970s. The most influential was the 'moral majority' pressure group run by Reverend Jerry Falwell.

Reagan also had the backing of women's groups opposed to feminism. These were led by Phyllis Schafly and the National Right to Life Committee. The latter had 11 million members by 1980.

In *The Limits to Liberty* (1995), historian Maldwyn Jones notes:

'The election was the most devastating rejection of an incumbent president since Hoover's defeat in 1932. For the first time since 1954 the Republicans won control of the Senate. They also gained 33 seats in the House. The main reason for the Republican landslide was the discontent produced by unemployment, inflation and the faltering economy. But the voters also seem to have been demanding a stronger foreign policy and more decisive leadership.'

As a result, the 1980 election – like in 1932 – brought about fundamental change in US domestic history. The two-term presidency of Ronald Reagan was aptly termed 'The Reagan Revolution'.

1. What problems faced Carter in domestic affairs?

2. Why did he last only one term as President?

9.5 To what extent was the presidency of Ronald Reagan a turning point in domestic affairs?

Ronald Wilson Reagan (1911–2004)
40th President of the USA (1981–89), originally a Democrat but left to become a major anti-communist Republican. He was a Hollywood actor (head of Screen Actors' Guild after Second World War) before becoming Governor of California. Defeated Carter in the 1980 presidential election. During the 1980s, he launched the biggest peacetime military build-up in US history. Supporter of the 'Star Wars' initiative. However, from 1985 he negotiated with Soviet leader Gorbachev towards reducing nuclear weapons in START (strategic arms reduction talks). He was wounded in an assassination attempt in 1981. Re-elected in 1984, in a landslide victory.

Reagan was 69 on Inauguration Day 1981 – the oldest person to become President. A former Hollywood actor, Reagan was charming and good-natured. He acquired the title 'The Great Communicator' for his ability to speak well on television.

Unlike his predecessor, Reagan had a clear view of what he wanted to achieve. He wanted to restore prestige to the office of President. He also wanted to restore the USA's standing as the world's greatest power. At home, he wanted to bring about fundamental social and economic change. In doing so, he planned to dismantle the New Deal welfare state which had existed since the mid-1930s.

'Reaganomics'

Ronald Reagan had inherited an economy that had been in difficulties for almost the whole of the 1970s. Unemployment had averaged 6.2 per cent over the decade, compared with 4.1 per cent in the 1960s. Inflation had reached double-digit levels.

In response, Reagan produced the 'Program for Economic Recovery'. The basis of this plan was a rejection of 'demand management' macroeconomic policy. This had attempted to create low inflation and unemployment through the manipulation of the rate of direct taxation and of government spending. Instead, Reagan supported 'supply side' economics. This aimed to create economic growth through improvements in productivity and output. It was to be achieved by major tax cuts as an incentive to work and a reduction in government spending.

The first part of this economic policy passed Congress in two Acts in 1981: the Omnibus Reconciliation Act and the Economic Recovery Tax Act. To prevent a major budget deficit, the first Act aimed to cut federal government spending in over 300 programmes. The Office of Management and Budget, part of the Executive Office of the President, calculated that spending would be cut by $963 billion between 1981 and 1987. The Congressional Budget Office calculated the cut to be $1,041 billion. In the second Act, personal income tax was cut to 25 per cent. These changes were more remarkable because the Democrats still controlled the House of Representatives.

What message is this cartoon trying to make about Ronald Reagan's economic policy?

Cartoon by Ben Sargent in 'Texas Monthly', 1983, showing Reagan as the proud rooster.

These measures helped to bring about economic recovery. Real GNP grew by 11 per cent by the end of 1984 – one of the fastest economic recoveries since the Second World War. Unemployment declined to 7 per cent by 1984 and inflation dropped to 3.8 per cent over the same period. Such developments helped to ensure a landslide victory for Reagan in 1984.

However, although Reagan had cut federal programmes, such as welfare payments, he launched the biggest peacetime build-up of the US armed forces in history. This had the effect of creating a huge federal budget deficit by the mid-1980s. The trade deficit alone was $170 billion by 1986. This led to the Balanced Budget and Emergency Deficit Control Act of 1985 (also known as the Gramm–Rudman Act). The aim of the Act was to reduce the federal budget deficit gradually until it disappeared (supposedly) by 1991. However, by the time Reagan left office, it was far from its goal.

Overall, economic recovery did create thousands of new jobs in the USA, the rate of inflation fell and economic growth occurred. According to Joseph J. Hogan, in *Reaganomics and Economic Policy* (1990):

> 'The overall economic performance of the United States during the Reagan era was little more than average for OECD (Organisation of Economic Cooperation and Development) countries, while the claim that this performance was the product of [Reagan's policies] is untenable.
>
> The great federal budget deficits, the large trade deficits and their impact on converting the US into the world's leading debtor nation are the [main] legacies of the Reagan era.'

Social policy

The attitude of the Reagan Administration to social policy was affected by a number of factors. Firstly, Republicans were concerned by the growth of what they saw as a dependent underclass in US society. Martin Anderson, Reagan's first Domestic Policy Adviser, identified those on welfare programmes as having a disincentive to work. Secondly, the Reagan Administration wished to cut federal programmes as part of their new approach to economic management. Finally, Reagan wanted to develop a new relationship with the states – New Federalism – where the states would take more responsibility for their welfare.

The welfare programmes identified by the Administration included healthcare for the elderly (Medicare), healthcare for the poor (Medicaid), means-tested aid to Families with Dependent Children (AFDC) and food stamps. In 1981, around 3.7 million families received AFDC; about 20 million people received food stamps and 21.6 million received Medicaid. Approximately 20 per cent of the African-American population participated in these programmes.

Reagan's main reform was the Omnibus Reconciliation Act of 1981. This Act cut AFDC and food stamps by around 13 per cent between 1982–85; child nutrition programmes were cut by 28 per cent; and Medicaid was cut by 5 per cent. As a result, the number officially defined as 'poor' increased from 11.7 per cent of the population in 1979 to 15 per cent by 1982 and 13.5 per cent thereafter.

Another important feature of the Omnibus Reconciliation Act was the attempt to reduce the dependency underclass known as 'workfare'. To receive AFDC payments, people had to do community service. By January 1987, 42 states had followed the federal government's lead and had established programmes where welfare payments were linked to some form of work. The workfare provisions in the 1988 Family Support Act reinforced this development.

In aiding the unemployed, the Reagan Administration began to work in partnership with the private sector. An example was the Job Training and Partnership Act of 1982. In *The Limits of Social Policy* (1988), Nathan Glazer notes that the Reagan Administration 'believed people could manage by themselves and had no need of federal government interventions'.

Dilys Hill, in *Domestic Policy in the Era of 'Negative' Government* (1990), states that:

> 'Where the Reagan Administration did not succeed was in cutting middle-class entitlement programmes of social security, Medicare and military and civil service pensions. The less well-defended bore the brunt of domestic cutbacks.'

New Federalism?

Linked to cuts in welfare was the plan to reduce the size of the federal government. Beginning with Nixon's revenue-sharing plans of the early 1970s, successive Republican governments had attempted to give more responsibility to state and local governments. In April 1981, Reagan set up two committees on the issue: the Presidential Advisory Committee on Federalism and the Coordinating Task Force on Federalism. Both were dominated by conservative Republicans.

In his 1982 'State of the Union Message' to Congress, Reagan announced his plan to reduce federal spending. It was to be part of his plan to bring government 'closer to the people'. Money would be given to the states by the federal government in block grants. The states had the discretion to use the money as they saw fit.

However, these plans were not passed by Congress. They also received a lukewarm response from many states. The National Governors' Association saw New Federalism as a way of simply cutting government programmes.

The federal judicial system

One of the most significant changes to occur in Reagan's presidency was in the federal judicial system. In his two terms of office, Reagan appointed 290 district and appeal court judges – about 40 per cent of the total.

Of equal significance was Reagan's impact on the US Supreme Court. Following the retirement of Earl Warren in 1969, Presidents Nixon and Ford had appointed more conservative judges to the Court. Reagan completed the process. In 1986, when Warren Burger retired as Chief Justice, Reagan nominated the conservative William Rehnquist of Arizona as his replacement. He also successfully nominated two other conservative justices, Antonin Scalia and Sandra Day O'Connor – the first woman justice.

However, in 1987, Reagan faced embarrassment following the retirement of Justice Lewis Powell. On two occasions, Reagan failed to get his

---

Reagan's Administrations, 1981–1989: leading members

President:	Ronald Reagan
Vice-President:	George Bush Senior
Treasury:	Donald Regan (1981–85)
	James Baker (1985–88)
	Nicholas Brady (1988–89)
Justice:	William Smith (1981–85)
	Edwin Meese (1985–88)

nominee accepted by the Senate. Firstly, Robert Bork and then Douglas Ginsburg were rejected. The latter revealed during the Senate hearings that he had smoked cannabis at university. Eventually, a more moderate conservative, Anthony Kennedy, was accepted.

The Reagan Court produced judgements that reflected its new conservative majority. In 'Wards Cove versus Atonio' in 1987, it provided restrictions on affirmative action. However, the Court did not go far enough to the right for Reagan's liking. For instance, it continued to uphold the 'Roe versus Wade' decision of 1973 which allowed abortions.

The decline of the Reagan Presidency in 1987

The Iran-Contra Scandal of 1986–1987

Reagan's popularity took a major blow in 1986–87 with the uncovering of the Iran-Contra Scandal. In Lebanon, in the early 1980s, several westerners had been held hostage by militant Islamic groups – many linked to Iran. Among the hostages were American and British citizens. The latter included Terry Waite and John McCarthy. The Reagan Administration had stated consistently that it would not do deals with terrorist organisations over the keeping of US hostages. On 3 November 1986, a Beirut newspaper claimed that the USA had shipped 500 anti-tank missiles to Iran, which was at war with Iraq. In return, US hostages were released in Lebanon. The money received from the arms sales was used to help the Contra rebel forces fighting the left-wing government of Nicaragua.

In a joint Senate–House investigation of the affair in 1987, top White House aides were implicated. These included Chief of Staff Donald Regan and National Security Advisers Robert McFarlane and Admiral Poindexter. The key witness was Lieutenant-Colonel Oliver North who admitted taking part. He implicated the others.

Although no evidence was produced to link President Reagan directly with the affair, he suffered badly as a result. Later, in July 1988, Attorney General Edwin Meese was accused of corruption and forced to resign.

Black Monday, 19 October 1987

The buoyant stock market, which reflected the economic recovery from 1983, came to an abrupt halt on 19 October 1987. The **Dow Jones stock index** fell 508 points. Almost $500 billion in the paper value of American companies was wiped out. This was around 20 per cent of the stock value of the USA.

When combined with the increase of the national debt, which had risen to $1.4 trillion, the final Reagan years were a period of considerable economic uncertainty.

Dow Jones stock index: The listing of shares on the New York (Wall Street) Stock Market.

Reaganomics: The economic policy of President Ronald Reagan. It was based on 'supply side' rather than 'demand management' economics. It involved big cuts in direct taxation and the reduction of the federal budget.

1. In what ways did Reagan's Administration change social and economic policy between 1981 and 1989?

2. To what extent did Reagan bring about fundamental change in domestic policy?

Summary

According to Dilys Hill and Phil Williams, in *The Reagan Legacy* (1990):

'The restoration of American pride and the regeneration of American power were major achievements of the Reagan Administration.'

Yet, at home, Ronald Reagan left a nation where the gap between rich and poor had increased. '**Reaganomics**' had limited success in bringing economic recovery. The reduction in taxes and huge military expenditure merely created a vast federal debt.

However, Reagan did restore much of the prestige to the presidency, which had been lost in the 1970s. His almost monarchic style had made him popular. It had also prevented him from being implicated in policy failures of his subordinates or even directly in the Iran-Contra Scandal.

9.6 In what ways was George Bush Senior's domestic policy different from that of Ronald Reagan?

George Herbert Bush (1924–)
41st President of the USA (1989–93), a Republican. From rich New England family, attended Yale University. Fought as fighter pilot in Pacific in Second World War. Became rich oilman in Texas. Director of the CIA (1976–81) and Vice-President (1981–89). As President, sending US troops to depose General Noriega of Panama was popular at home. Success in the 1991 Gulf War against Iraq further raised his standing. However, despite signing START I (July 1991) and reducing US nuclear weapons, Bush's popularity at home began to wane. Defeated by Democrat Bill Clinton in the 1992 presidential elections.

George Bush Senior became the first Vice-President since Martin Van Buren in 1837 to win a subsequent presidential election. In 1988, he defeated a lacklustre Democrat, former Governor of Massachusetts, Michael Dukakis. He also won because he had been associated with Ronald Reagan's presidency. Was Bush's presidency a continuation of Reagan's?

Economic policy

Bush had inherited a very large federal budget deficit. During the election he had committed himself to not raising taxes by making the statement: 'read my lips – no new taxes'.

In addition, a Democrat-controlled Congress was opposed to any further cuts in welfare. In 1991, Bush faced major expenditure when the Gulf War took place. Also, between 1990 and 1992, an economic recession reduced tax revenues. By 1992, the federal budget deficit had risen to $400 billion. This created problems because the Gramm–Rudman Act of 1986 had required the President to balance the budget by 1993.

In 1990, Bush was forced to raise taxes and to make cuts in military and domestic expenditure of $492 billion. However, these measures failed to make any impact on the recession. Interest rate cuts by the Federal Reserve Board, down to the lowest level for 18 years (3.5 per cent), made little difference.

Bush also faced major problems with America's savings and loans companies, the equivalent of British building societies. Even before Bush became President, these companies had been facing severe financial difficulties. When he came to office, Bush produced a federal rescue plan to save these companies. The plan involved the expenditure of $50 billion. However, by April 1990, the rescue figure had risen to $325 billion. Matters were made worse when one of Bush's sons, George W. Bush, was involved in one of the savings and loans companies in difficulty.

Unfortunately for George Bush Senior, his Administration found it difficult to work out an aid package with the Democrat-controlled Congress. A Senate committee reported that George Bush Senior was the only president since Herbert Hoover who had seen the average standard of living decline while he was in office.

In spite of his triumph in the Gulf War of 1991, Bush was seen as a failure in economic matters.

Social policy

Bush Senior tried to carry on Reagan's policy but in a more conciliatory way. In education, he put forward his goals in 'America 2000' in September 1989. The aim was to raise the high school graduation rate to 90 per cent, to improve maths education, to increase adult literacy and to improve anti-drugs education. Bush also proposed a New American Schools Development Corporation, which would be a partnership with private business to raise educational standards. However, to achieve 'America 2000' Bush had to work closely with the states and with Congress. Congressional opposition brought the proposal to an end.

On environmental issues, Bush got Congress to pass the Clean Air Act of 1990 to cut pollution. In October 1992, shortly before the election, Bush signed the Energy Policy Act. This was a major attempt to limit dependence on imported oil through energy conservation and the promotion of renewable energy.

Civil rights

A major crisis began for the Bush Administration in 1991 with the Rodney King affair. King was an African-American who was brutally attacked by members of the Los Angeles Police Department, in March 1991. A passer-by videoed the event. When the police were acquitted in the spring of 1992, serious racial rioting occurred in South Central Los Angeles – an area of great social deprivation.

The Bush Administration failed to show decisive leadership in the affair. Bush and his Vice-President, Dan Quayle, blamed the riots on a failure to keep law and order and a fall in family values. Only in early May did Bush suggest that an emergency programme for the poor should be implemented. By 22 June, Bush signed the Urban Aid Supplemental Bill into law, which provided $1.1 billion aid for inner cities – a figure well below what Congress had wanted.

A minor success was the Americans with Disabilities Act, passed in July 1990, which barred discrimination against people with physical or mental disabilities. However, in October 1990, Bush vetoed the Civil Rights Act on the grounds that it established quotas for ethnic minorities. Then, in 1991, he accepted a slighted amended version of the 1990 Act.

In nominations to the Supreme Court, Bush continued the conservative policy of his predecessor. In 1990, he nominated David Souter to replace William Brennan. What proved a major embarrassment for Bush was his nomination of African-American Clarence Thomas to replace the former NAACP lawyer Thurgood Marshall in 1991.

Not only was Thomas inexperienced, but a former colleague also accused him of sexual harassment. In the Senate judiciary committee hearings on the Thomas nomination, Oklahoma University law professor and conservative Republican African-American, Anita Hill, claimed that Thomas had a poor record on civil rights as well as sexual harassment. On 15 October 1991, the Senate approved Thomas by 52 votes to 48 – the narrowest for a successful candidate in the 20th century.

1. In what ways did the USA experience radical political, economic and social change between 1969 and 1992?

2. What do you regard as the greatest change in US domestic history in the period 1969–1992? Explain your answer.

9.7 How far did Bill Clinton change US domestic policy between 1993 and 2001?

The 1992 presidential election

By 1992 the Republican Party had won five of the six previous presidential elections. In 1991, it seemed that the Republican incumbent, George H. Bush would win a second term as President. In that year President George H. Bush led a coalition of forces, with UN backing, which removed the Iraqi army from Kuwait. He seemed unbeatable. However, within 18 months he had lost the presidential election to his Democratic opponent, Bill Clinton.

Part of the problem was the downturn in the economy. To cope with the problems caused by the recession many companies began to cut costs by downsizing – reducing the size of their workforce and/or making more workers part-time. By the end of 1991, 25 million workers – approximately 20 per cent of the workforce – were unemployed at some point. In addition, the US balance of trade with the rest of the world was declining, and by 1991 was $150 billion in deficit. Going into an election year the economy remained depressed.

George H. Bush was also a victim of his own actions. In the 1988 presidential campaign he had used the slogan 'read my lips, no new taxes'. But when he was faced with a growing budget deficit – partly fuelled by the

Bill Clinton and running mate Al Gore celebrate victory in 1992.

costs of Operation Desert Storm – he advocated raising federal income tax from 28 per cent to 31 per cent, which caused a revolt among Republican congressmen in the House of Representatives.

In 1992 George H. Bush faced a very accomplished campaigner in Bill Clinton. In 1979 Clinton had become the youngest governor in Arkansas history. He was young, energetic and charismatic, and he reminded many Americans of John F. Kennedy. He ran on a ticket of change, promising to

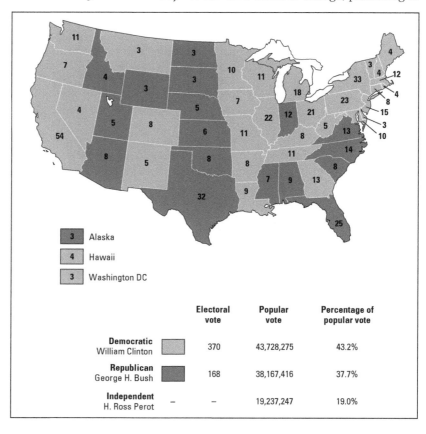

The US presidential election of 1992

		Electoral vote	Popular vote	Percentage of popular vote
Democratic William Clinton		370	43,728,275	43.2%
Republican George H. Bush		168	38,167,416	37.7%
Independent H. Ross Perot		–	19,237,247	19.0%

cut the defence budget following the end of the Cold War and to increase tax relief, which pleased middle-class voters.

The presidential election of 1992 was a three-horse race, the third candidate being an independent, Texan billionaire Ross Perot, who attacked the failures of the federal government. As a result, Bush lost potential support to Perot, who took 19 per cent of the popular vote. This allowed the Democratic candidate to win the race to the White House.

Clinton's first term in office, 1993–97

Economic reform

During Clinton's first term as president, the US economy came out of recession. This was partly the result of the growth of IT and what was termed the 'dot.com revolution', which helped fuel the US and world economies.

Clinton's economic policy involved increasing taxes on large corporations and the rich. He hoped this would help reduce the federal budget deficit. Clinton's proposals only narrowly passed Congress, by 218 votes to 216 in the House of Representatives and by 51 to 50 in the Senate. In fact, the vote was a tie, 50/50, in the Senate. The Vice President – who is Chair of the Senate – voted for Clinton, to break the tie.

Clinton also faced a revolt from his own Democrat Party in Congress when he proposed that the US joined the North American Free Trade Area (NAFTA). This was negotiated by George H. Bush and aimed to create a free trade area comprising the USA, Canada and Mexico. Many Democrats feared it would cost US jobs, and the proposal only passed through Congress with Republican support.

Health care reform

Clinton's major proposal for change in his first term was health care reform. The US lacked a national health care system, and by the early 1990s nearly 40 million Americans lacked health care insurance. Clinton planned to give every US citizen (and all legal immigrants) health care insurance. Clinton's wife, Hillary Rodham Clinton, played a major part in leading this reform. The proposal, however, met with massive opposition from health insurance companies and the health drug industry. By 1994 it was clear that this reform would not be accepted by Congress, and it was dropped.

The mid-term elections, 1994

1994 was the year of the mid-term elections, when the whole of the House of Representatives and one-third of the Senate faced re-election. Mid-term elections are always a useful guide to the popularity of the president, and in these the Democrats were humiliated. In the Senate, the Republicans won a majority of 52 to 48. In the House, they won a clear majority of 234 to 204. This was the first time since 1952 that the Republican Party had controlled both houses of Congress. Under the leadership of the new Speaker of the House of Representatives, Newt Gingrich, the Republicans planned a 'contract with America'. Gingrich planned to dismantle what he called the 'corrupt liberal welfare state'. It was a radical programme involving welfare reform, less environmental legislation and a demand for a balanced budget.

However, by 1995 this 'Republican revolution' had fizzled out. Gingrich proved to be an unpopular leader, and Clinton was able to portray the Republican Party as too right-wing.

The 1996 presidential election

By 1996 Clinton had recovered much of the ground he had lost in 1994. The economy was performing well. In foreign policy the US seemed to be the dominant force in world politics, following the collapse of the USSR in 1991.

In 1996 Clinton won Congressional support for increasing the minimum wage and broadening access to health care insurance. The most important piece of legislation in 1996 was the Personal Responsibility and Work Opportunity Act. This gave state governments responsibility for many federal welfare programmes. However, Republicans in the Senate helped pass a law reducing funding to other welfare programmes by $56 billion. Clinton was aware that many American voters supported these cuts and, although it alienated support from some Democrats, Clinton entered the election year portraying himself as a middle-of-the-road moderate.

The 1996 election added support to the view that Clinton was 'the comeback kid' and 'Slick Willy' when it came to winning elections. He defeated his Republican opponent, Bob Dole, by 379 electoral college votes to 159, taking 49 per cent of the popular vote. Ross Perot ran again, gaining just 8 per cent of the vote this time. Dole received 41 per cent of the vote. The Republicans, however, maintained control of the House of Representatives, and even increased their hold on the Senate.

Clinton's second term, 1997–2001

For most of his second term Clinton faced allegations of scandal. The two major scandals were the Whitewater property scandal, which dated back to the time when he had been Governor of Arkansas, and the Monica Lewinsky scandal. Clinton became only the second president in history to be tried for impeachment. The other was Andrew Johnson, in 1868. (Richard Nixon had avoided impeachment in 1974 by resigning.)

The Whitewater affair

In 1979 Clinton and his wife had invested in a property development at an Arkansas resort called Whitewater. The property investment failed, amid allegations of fraud and corruption. In 1994 a Republican, Kenneth Starr, was appointed to investigate the Whitewater case on behalf of Congress. The investigation did not prove that the Clintons themselves were guilty of any wrongdoing, but several of their close associates on the project were found guilty.

During the course of the investigation, however, Starr had uncovered sexual harassment allegations against Bill Clinton, by Paula Jones. All these allegations and rumours surrounding the Clintons received considerable publicity. As Starr was a Republican, the Democrats accused him of partisanship.

The Monica Lewinsky affair

The Whitewater investigation led directly to the Monica Lewinsky affair. Monica Lewinsky had been a junior employee at the White House. It was alleged that Clinton had got her to lie under oath that they had not had a sexual affair. Clinton himself denied the affair on national television. However, in 1998, Starr persisted in his investigation, and in August of that year Clinton was forced to testify before a **Grand Jury**, the first president ever to do so. On 17 August a turning-point occurred when Clinton reversed his position and admitted to the affair. This was a major public humiliation and confirmed that Clinton had previously lied.

Starr's Report was submitted to Congress on 9 September 1998 and the House Judiciary Committee, which was controlled by the Republicans, voted to impeach the President. This view was confirmed by the whole House of Representatives on 8 October. Clinton was accused of lying under oath to a federal Grand Jury and obstructing justice. Under the **impeachment** procedure the president was tried by the US Senate. The

Grand Jury: A judicial process by judge and jury to determine, based on evidence, whether or not a person should face a legal trial by judge and jury.

Impeachment: Legal process set up by the US constitution whereby public officials such as the President can be removed from office if they have been found guilty of committing crimes and misdemeanours.

impeachment process lasted from 1 January to 12 February 1999. The Senate rejected the charge of lying under oath but split 50/50 on the issue of obstructing justice. However, for Clinton to be impeached and removed from office a two-thirds majority was required on both charges, so Clinton was acquitted.

The Monica Lewinsky affair completely undermined the Clinton presidency. He was publicly humiliated and shown to lack honour or integrity.

Foreign policy

Bill Clinton had the benefit of being president when the USA had unrivalled power across the globe. In 1991 the USSR collapsed and the Cold War had come to an end. Also in 1991 US forces had been the principal participant in the expulsion of Iraqi forces from Kuwait.

Somalia

In early 1991 the government in the East African state of Somalia collapsed. In 1992 George H. Bush received UN backing to send in US troops to restore law and order, and when Clinton became president he continued this policy. Unfortunately, US troops faced major problems restoring law and order, as portrayed in the Hollywood film *Black Hawk Down*.

The Middle East

A far more serious long-term international issue was the search for peace in the Middle East. Again, Clinton continued the policy of his predecessor through leading negotiations between Israel and the Palestinians. A breakthrough occurred in 1993 with the Oslo Accords, when Israel's Prime Minister, Yitzhak Rabin, agreed to allow Palestinian self-government in the Gaza Strip and in Jericho on the West Bank. The agreement was formally signed at the White House on 13 September 1993. However, violence returned to the Middle East with the assassination of Rabin in 1995 by an Israeli opposed to the agreement. In 1998 Clinton again helped negotiate an agreement. This time it was between Israeli Prime Minister Benjamin Netanyahu and the Palestinian leader, Yasser Arafat. Under the Wye River Accord, Israel agreed to hand over more land to the Palestinians on the West Bank in return for security guarantees from Arafat.

Former Yugoslavia

In 1991 Yugoslavia began to disintegrate. Before 1991 it had comprised six republics, based on ethnic lines, but several of these republics now desired complete independence. War broke out between the republics and the Yugoslav government, dominated by Serbia and Croatia. The worst fighting occurred in the state of Bosnia and Herzegovina. Here the population contained several ethnic groups – Croats, Serbs and Bosnian Muslims. A civil war occurred within Bosnia. Massacres of ethnic groups occurred, mainly by the Serbs. This 'ethnic cleansing' forced the US to act. In 1995 the US negotiated a ceasefire and a peace plan for former Yugoslavia. To enforce the peace, NATO sent 60,000 troops.

A far greater problem in former Yugoslavia was Kosovo. This was part of Serbia but contained an Albanian majority. Fighting occurred in Kosovo between the Yugoslav army, under Serbian control, and the Kosovo Liberation Army. Thousands of Albanian Kosovans were forced from their homes as the Yugoslav army engaged in 'ethnic cleansing'. To restore order, NATO intervened. Air forces, under US leadership, engaged in a 72-day bombing of Serbia to force them to the conference table. On 3 June 1999 an agreement was reached: Kosovo was given self-government within Serbia and the Yugoslav army was forced to leave

Clinton: an assessment

When Clinton gave his final 'State of the Union' message to Congress in 2000, he was able to state that the US economy was booming and US power seemed unchallenged across the globe. However, Clinton left a mixed legacy. He had planned major reforms of health care and the welfare and tax systems but, because of a hostile Congress from 1994, many of his reforms never became law.

In addition, Clinton's second term was dominated by scandal. Clinton had damaged his own reputation and the office of the presidency through his lying about the Monica Lewinsky affair.

Yet Clinton won two presidential elections by sizeable majorities. Faced with a hostile Republican Congress from 1994, Clinton was able to portray himself as a moderate – an occupier of the centre ground of US politics. One of Clinton's legacies was his ability to change policy to meet the demands and desires of the US electorate. He clearly deserved the title 'The Comeback Kid'.

1. How far did Clinton continue policies he inherited from George H. Bush?

2. How successful was Clinton as president?

9.8 Was George W. Bush's presidency a complete failure?

A mandate to govern?

George W. Bush won two presidential elections by the narrowest of margins. His victory in 2000 was surrounded by controversy. Bush won 50,456,062 popular votes, but his Democratic opponent, Al Gore, Clinton's Vice President, won 50,996,582 votes. Yet Bush still won the election. This was due to the US system of electing presidents. If a candidate wins a majority within a State, even if that majority is by only one vote, the entire electoral college votes of that state go to that candidate. Each state has electoral college votes comprising the combined number of Senators and Congressmen that state possesses. The minimum is 3 electoral college votes for states such as Delaware. California now has 55 electoral college votes (54 in 2000).

When the votes were counted, the whole result hinged on who won the state of Florida, which was not clear, and in dispute. Considerable controversy surrounded the electronic voting system used by Florida to count votes. In the end, the election was decided by the US Supreme Court on 12 December 2000. In the case Bush v Gore the Supreme Court awarded the

Supporters for Gore and Bush face off outside the US Supreme Court.

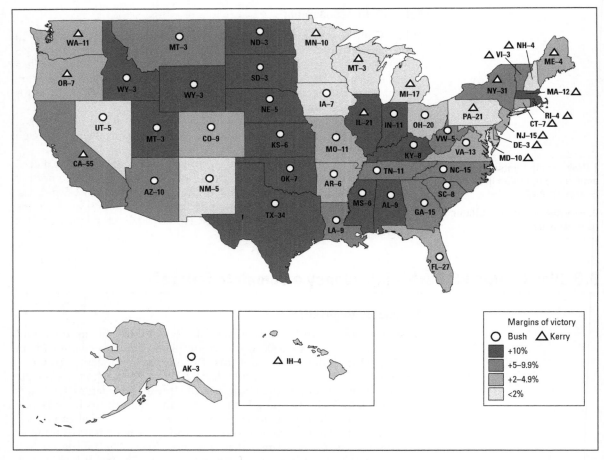

2004 presidential election results by state, including electoral votes.

Florida election to Bush, in a 5 to 4 decision. As a result, Bush won Florida's 25 electoral college votes (now 27) making a total of 271 electoral college votes to Gore's 266. Thus Bush won the presidency.

The former Green Party candidate, Ralph Nader received 97,421 votes in Florida (nearly 3 million nationwide). Many analysts argue that Nader pulled votes from Gore, thus tilting the election in Bush's favour.

The 2004 presidential election was also incredibly close. Facing opposition from Democrat candidate John Kerry, the election was eventually decided by voting in the state of Ohio. In the end, Bush won 50.73 per cent of the popular vote to Kerry's 48.27 per cent. In electoral college votes Bush won 286 to 251.

The margin of victory won in elections determines the President's mandate (authority) to govern. Bush's mandate was in doubt in 2000, and by the narrowest of margins in 2004.

Thematic questions

Study these two cartoons by Guardian cartoonist
Steve Bell and answer the questions that follow.

SOURCE A

SOURCE B

**1. How do these cartoons portray the two presidential
candidates in the 2004 Presidential Election?**

**2. How useful are cartoons such as these as historical
evidence of the Election.**

Give reasons for your answer.

The terrorist attack of 9/11

One of the most defining moments in modern US history was the terrorist attacks on the World Trade Center in New York and the Pentagon in Washington DC, on 11 September 2001. The attack caught the US completely by surprise. Within days of the attack, however, the main culprits had been identified – the Islamic terrorist organisation al-Qaeda, led by a Saudi millionaire, Osama bin Laden. Bin Laden had been supported by the USA when he fought the Soviet occupation of Afghanistan in the 1980s. He was also held responsible for a previous attempt to blow up the World Trade Center in 1998.

9/11 inaugurated GWAT (the Global War against Terror). The US put together a worldwide coalition to combat Islamic terrorism. The first part of GWAT was to deny al-Qaeda a training base in Afghanistan. On 7 October 2001 the Taliban-led government of Afghanistan refused to hand over Bin Laden to US authorities. This resulted in the US-led removal of the Taliban government. The US used air strikes and dissident Afghan forces known as the Northern Alliance to oust the Taliban. By 9 December 2001 the Taliban government had been overthrown, and from 2001 to 2008 there was a new Afghan government, under Hamid Karzai. But a guerrilla war now existed in Afghanistan, as the Taliban and its supporters continued to fight the US and allied troops that were stationed there to support the Karzai government.

Another aspect of GWAT was 'extraordinary rendition'. Terrorist suspects were arrested around the world and transported to CIA-controlled prisons in countries such as Romania. Eventually the majority of the suspects were imprisoned at the US military base at Guantanamo, on the island of Cuba. This Guantanamo prison has created considerable international indignation because the inmates had not been tried or convicted.

Within the USA, 9/11 led to increased security. A new government department was created to deal with the terror threat, known as the Office of Homeland Security. In addition, Congress passed the Patriot Act, giving government agencies the right to tap telephones and read emails and text messages. It also set up military courts to hear terror-related cases.

The invasion of Iraq

9/11 and the Iraq War of 2003 were the two most significant events during George W. Bush's presidency. In the wake of the 9/11 attack, Bush made a speech to Congress. He explained that the USA faced 'an axis of evil' of rogue states that had the potential to destabilise the world. These included North Korea, Iran and Iraq, and Bush suggested that the US had to act against these states before they became real threats to the world order.

The state singled out by Bush in 2002–03 was Iraq. Although Iraq had lost the Gulf War of 1991, its dictator – Saddam Hussein – was still in power. Bush claimed that Saddam possessed 'weapons of mass destruction' which, if used, would destabilise the entire Middle East and cause widespread war.

Since the Gulf War of 1991 UN weapons inspectors had been allowed to enter Iraq to assess its ability to manufacture nuclear weapons and whether or not it possessed biological and chemical weapons. From time to time Saddam would expel these inspectors.

Bush used the UN to put pressure on Saddam, and on 8 November 2002 the UN Security Council passed Resolution 1441, which ordered Iraq to disarm immediately or face 'serious consequences'. Under UN pressure, Iraq allowed UN weapons inspectors back into Iraq. During early 2003 the USA, Britain and Spain attempted to get another UN Resolution passed, sanctioning the use of force against Saddam. By early March, however, the French President, Jacques Chirac, stated that he would veto any UN resolution in support of armed force.

On 17 March the USA withdrew their UN Resolution, and two days later – on 19 March 2003 – launched Operation Iraqi Freedom, an all-out attack on Iraq. It involved 250,000 US troops, supported by Allied troops from Britain, Spain, Poland and Australia, and within three weeks Saddam had been overthrown. A jubilant President Bush flew to the Middle East and announced on 1 May 2003 that the war was over. As he spoke, a banner behind him proudly claimed 'Mission accomplished'.

But the US and its Allies then became bogged down in a vicious guerrilla war. Opponents of the US-led occupation attacked on a daily basis, on many occasions using suicide bombers. The US-led occupation also stirred up sectarian conflict between Sunni and Shi'ite Muslims and the Kurdish minority in northern Iraq.

The conflict in Iraq has proved to be very controversial. The US attacked Iraq without the backing of the UN. In fact, UN Secretary General Kofi Annan described the war as 'illegal'. Also the US did not have a clear plan of how to rule Iraq once Saddam had been defeated. (The US Secretary of Defense made the fateful statement that the US armed forces 'do not do state building'.) As a result, law and order and administration collapsed in 2003 and 2004.

The occupation of Iraq caused widespread opposition to the USA throughout the Arab and Islamic world. In addition, the US received international criticism when photographs were released of the maltreatment of Iraqi prisoners in Abu Ghraib prison in Baghdad.

Finally, in January 2004, US officials announced that Iraq did not, after all, possess weapons of mass destruction – supposedly the reason why the USA and Britain had attacked Iraq in the first place. Hans Blix, the Chief UN Weapons Inspector in Iraq told the US Congress that US intelligence reports about Saddam and his weapons programme were 'almost all wrong'.

Compassionate conservatism at home?

As Governor of Texas, George W. Bush had developed his view of compassionate conservatism. The main aspect of this approach when he was President was his policy 'No Child Left Behind'. This was a comprehensive reform of the education system and was signed into federal law in 2001. Under 'No Child Left Behind', Bush set new learning standards for the states. It aimed to ensure that all schoolchildren would be 'proficient' in maths and English by 2014. Also Bush aimed to increase the quality of teachers, with all of them 'highly qualified' by 2005. If states fell short of the standards set in 'No Child Left Behind' they would lose part of their federal funding. However, by 2008 the programme had had very little impact, especially in inner city areas, where education standards were very low.

Although Clinton had the benefit of a growing economy during his presidency, Bush faced a downturn in economic activity in 2001–02. The dot.com boom of the 1990s came rapidly to an end, and stock market share values dropped dramatically in late 2001. In a bid to improve economic activity and reward his supporters, Bush proposed a $1.6 trillion cut in taxes. This was reduced to $1.3 trillion by the Senate.

One of the most controversial acts of the Bush presidency was concerned with environmental matters. Faced with global warming, an international agreement – the Kyoto Protocol – had been signed in Japan in 2001. This set clear targets for the signatories to reduce CO-2 emissions.

But Bush refused to sign up to the Protocol, claiming that it would damage the US economy, which was entering a recession. Eventually, however, in December 2007, in Bali, the US agreed to join international attempts to combat global warming.

Yet within the USA Bush did make some attempt to reduce pollution. The Federal Environment Protection Agency, for example, ordered General Electric to spend millions of dollars removing toxic chemicals from New York's Hudson River.

The US Supreme Court

One of the most influential aspects of the federal government is the US Supreme Court. It has the authority to interpret the US Constitution and is the final court of appeal for federal and state law. The nine justices of the US Supreme Court are nominated by the President and confirmed by the US Senate. George W. Bush had the opportunity to nominate several justices. In October 2005, following someone's resignation as a justice, Bush nominated his long-time friend Harriet Miers for the post. But in the Senate this choice was opposed – even by Republicans – because Miers was seen as a legal lightweight, and she withdrew her nomination. However, the Senate supported Bush's nomination for Chief Justice, John Roberts, when the incumbent retired. Finally, in 2006, Bush's nominee, Samuel Alito, was confirmed by the Senate as a Supreme Court justice. These changes to the Supreme Court meant that its political balance moved to the right, now comprising four conservative justices and four liberal justices, with one 'swing' voter in the form of J.R. Stevens (who had been nominated by President Ford). As a result, the Bush Supreme Court would take a much more conservative view of issues such as **affirmative action** or the 'Roe v Wade' decision of 1973, which legalised abortion in the USA.

Affirmative action: Policy by the federal government which set aside a certain proportion of jobs for members of minorities, such as African-Americans.

Hurricane Katrina

In August 2005 the southern USA was hit by a severe hurricane, Hurricane Katrina. It devastated many Gulf towns, such as Biloxi, Mississippi, but the City of New Orleans, Louisiana, faced the worst problems, when the Mississippi River burst its banks and flooded the city. Nearly half a million citizens of New Orleans were made homeless. The Bush administration received severe criticism for its failure to maintain adequate flood defences in Louisiana and for its inept handling of the aftermath of the hurricane. Its main disaster agency, FEMA (Federal Emergency Management Agency) was itself seen as a disaster of ineptitude and poor leadership.

The mid-term elections, 2006

In the Congressional elections of 2006 the American electorate had the opportunity to pass a verdict on Bush's presidency. In both the House of Representatives and the Senate the Republicans lost their majorities. From January 2007, therefore, Bush became a '**lame duck**' president with little authority over Congress and declining support in the country. According to the British magazine *The Economist*, Bush had become the most unpopular president since Richard Nixon during the Watergate scandal.

Lame duck: Someone who is ineffectual because they have lost their power and support.

A failed presidency?

In the 2008 presidential election race the Republican candidates distanced themselves from the Bush presidency. The candidates who seemed to do well were those who advocated change. Across the USA Bush had become 'yesterday's man'. His presidency was dominated by the twin events of 9/11 and the war in Iraq. By 2008 the war on terror had stalled. US forces and their NATO allies were bogged down in a guerrilla war in Afghanistan against the Taliban and al-Qaeda. In Iraq, the US troops were still dying in the never-ending insurgency (see table).

President George W. Bush departs from his news conference in the White House following the congressional mid-term results.

At home, Bush had achieved little. He began his presidency in the economic recession of 2001, and he ended his presidency in the recession of 2008.

1. In what ways was George W. Bush a victim of circumstance? Explain your answer.

2. Do you regard George W. Bush a complete failure as president? Give reasons for your answer.

US casualties in Iraq, by calendar year

	Deaths	Wounded
2003	486	2,413
2004	849	8,001
2005	846	5,949
2006	822	6,298
2007	901	6,075
2008 (–Feb)	56	34
Total	**3960**	**28770**

Source: www.iCasualties.org

Note: According to CNN in 2008, Iraqi deaths since 2003 stood at 655,000.

Further Reading

Texts designed for AS students

The Enduring Vision, Volume 2, from 1865 by P. Boyer and others (D.C. Heath & Co., 1995)

The American Pageant, A History of the Republic by T. Bailey and D. Kennedy (D.C. Heath & Co., 1979)

America: A Narrative History by George Tindall and David Shi, Seventh Edition (Norton, 2007)

Texts for A2 and advanced study

The Limits of Liberty by Maldwyn Jones (Oxford University Press, 1995)

The Unfinished Journey by William Chafe (Oxford University Press, 1995)

The Longman History of the United States of America by Hugh Brogan (Longman, 1999)

Nixon Volumes 1 and 2 by Stephen Ambrose (Simon & Schuster, 1989)

Watergate and the Myth of American Democracy by L. Evans and A. Myers (Pathfinder, 1974)

Wars of Watergate: The Last Crisis of Richard Nixon by Stanley Kutler (W.W. Norton & Co., 1990)

The Reagan Presidency, An Incomplete Revolution? edited by Dilys Hill (Macmillan, 1990)

The Bush Presidency edited by Dilys Hill and Phil Williams (Macmillan, 1994)

Colossus: The Rise and Fall of the American Empire by Niall Ferguson (Allen Lane, 2004)

The Clinton Legacy edited by Colin Campbell (Chatham House, 2000)

Dead Certain: The Presidency of George W. Bush by Robert Draper (Free Press, 2007)

Films

'All the President's Men' directed by Alan J. Pakula and starring Robert Redford and Dustin Hoffman (1976).

'Nixon' directed by Oliver Stone and starring Anthony Hopkins (1996).

Glossary terms

Profiles

MAIN INDEX